War Experiences Recalled In Shoring Our Society

Americans Remember The Home Front
by Roy Hoopes
Hawthorn, $12.95

Reviewed by Steven Anderson

War, in the experience of the current generation, brought political turmoil and cultural craziness — the 1960s "greening" that irrevocably changed our view of ourselves and our institutions.

But World War II, the great global conflict that preceded us, tended to shore up, rather than break down, the structure of society. Because it was a boon to the economy, and because it provided a national goal about which there was little disagreement, the Second World War unified this diverse nation in a manner that was unprecedented.

It was total war, quite unlike the guns-and-butter-too policy of the Vietnam era. Volunteers who wrapped bandages, school children who bought defense stamps, women employed in heavy industry — all worked toward victory.

They recall their experiences

for us in Roy Hoopes' *Americans Remember The Home Front,* a 400-page volume from Hawthorn, based on interviews and divided into anecdotes.

Beginning with Pearl Harbor and ending with V-J Day, Americans great and small recall their hopes, fears, contributions and disappointments.

To Melville Grosvenor, then assistant editor of *National Geographic,* news of the Japanese attack came at Griffith Stadium near Washington. "I thought it was just talk," he says. "Then more reports came, and you began to see important people get up and go out."

Clifford Eunice heard about it when news came over a radio on a city bus. "The reaction of the people on the bus was a form of paralysis," he says.

As people started going off to war there was sadness. Says Ev-

AMERICANS REMEMBER THE HOME FRONT

AMERICANS REMEMBER THE HOME FRONT

An Oral Narrative

ROY HOOPES

HAWTHORN BOOKS, INC.
Publishers/NEW YORK

To the 132 million Americans
who made this book possible

Grateful acknowledgment is made to the following for permission to reprint previously published material:

Harcourt Brace Janovich, Inc.: For excerpts from *Navigating the Rapids 1918–1971: From the Papers of Adolf A. Berle*, edited by Beatrice Bishop Berle and Travis Beal Jacobs. Copyright ©1973 by Beatrice Bishop Berle. Reprinted by permission of Harcourt Brace Janovich, Inc.

Harper & Row Publishers, Inc.: For excerpts from *Roosevelt and Hopkins: An Intimate History*, by Robert Sherwood. Copyright ©1948 by Robert Sherwood. Reprinted by permission of Harper & Row Publishers, Inc.

AMERICANS REMEMBER THE HOME FRONT

Library of Congress Catalog Card Number: 75-40584

ISBN: 0–8015–0211–X

1 2 3 4 5 6 7 8 9 10

You're damned right I remember Pearl Harbor. . . . What the hell, your country doesn't get attacked every day in the week!

Frank Waldrop, retired managing editor of the *Washington Times Herald*

I told them my name was Johnson . . . and I said: "I just came down to help you win the war." He went back and talked with the boss, and they came out, and we had a talk. And would you believe it, twenty minutes later I was on the payroll.

Smith Johnson, describing how he went to work for the War Production Board in Washington, D.C., in January 1942

You hear a lot about the miracle of production. It was America. It was unbelievable to me.

R. W. Danischefsky, with the Reconstruction Finance Corporation in Detroit

I spent a great deal of time in bathing suits for pinups. That even was part of the war effort. We had to get the leg out because the boys out there needed more pictures. It's funny when you think of it, because our careers were built on the war-camp walls.

Evelyn Keyes, who was Scarlett O'Hara's sister in the movie *Gone with the Wind.*

So, I was canning until midnight, and later, night after night, and I frequently said, "I wish I had Hitler in that pressure cooker."

Martha Wood

All the girls, including my wife, were in the Red Cross because, they said, "You got to be trained; the submarines are coming into Portsmouth." And they were all taught how to give baths. The whole thing was great. Crazy. Everyone was frantic.

Newton Tolman

I remember when there was a false air-raid alarm in New England and we were listening to the radio. My mother was in tears; my aunt, shivering under the dining room table, said: "I hope if it hits, it hits us direct."

Paul Kneeland

I was out raking the yard, and the man that came and brought the telegram went next door to my neighbor, and he asked her if she would come over with him, because it was the third one he had delivered that day in our town. At the time he handed me the telegram, I looked at it, and he said: "It's bad news."

Betty Bryce

A young serviceman on the bus popped and kissed Rosemary, saying, "I always swore I would kiss the first pretty girl I saw when the war was over."

Lois Raymond

Well, I wouldn't want to put the whole country at war just to train someone, but I must say it was an unbelievable experience.

Stephen Ailes, who worked for the Office of Price Administration

I think it was a great thing for America. I think it made a country out of us.

Melville Grosvenor

CONTENTS

Contents

ACKNOWLEDGMENTS

This was a huge undertaking, and I must stress that it would not have been possible without considerable assistance from a lot of people; first and foremost, my editor Carolyn Trager, whose original idea it was, and the nearly two hundred Americans who were kind enough to grant me the time for an interview and permission to publish the results of their conversation in this book. And special thanks should go to Leo and Mary Emma Hershfield, of Bradenton, Florida, who were extremely helpful to me in the early stages of the book; to my brother David Hoopes, who conducted several of the interviews for me; and, of course, to my agent Charles Neighbors. Along the way, many, many friends and acquaintances were most helpful in suggesting and contacting interviewees and providing counsel and often a place to stay overnight for a weary, traveling interviewer. These include: Jack Altshul, Rheidun Atkinson, Donald Baldwin, Mary Betz, Dick Bothwell, Barry Broadfoot, Kent Chetlain, Paul Christensen, Herbert Collins, Mary Jo Deering, Clayton Fritchey, Jim Gallery, A. E. Hoehling, Kay Hoopes, Lydia Hoopes, Grace Powers Hudson, Vernon Jarrett, Tom Kell, Howard Merriman, Amy Bess and Lawrence Miller, Margo Miller, Johnny Moore, Jean and Thomas Page, Tina and Richard Powers, Margaret Rafner, Phil Robbins, Patricia and Thomas Schroth, Hugh Sidey, Carl Spitzer, William Tague, Studs Terkel, Linda and Robert Tracy, James Wright, and Alice and Robert Yoakum.

In preparing the artwork for the collages at the beginning of each chapter, I wish to thank Leo Hershfield for making available to me his extensive collection of World War II drawings, which he did for *PM* and the Office of War Information. I am also indebted to the National Archives and the Department of Defense for permitting me to use photographs from their World War II photographic collections. I wish to

Acknowledgments

acknowledge the cooperation of the Smithsonian Institution and Assistant Curator Herbert Collins for making available to me the Smithsonian's collection of World War II memorabilia. George Asman and his custom photo lab were very helpful in counseling on the reproduction of old photographs, and my son, Spencer, provided valuable assistance in the photographic work. Finally, I wish to thank the many contributors to this book who searched through old scrapbooks in search of 1940s-vintage photographs. These searches almost invariably cost them a good day's work, since it was impossible for most not to linger, lost in recollections of those stirring years.

Of course, the production, under the pressure of a deadline, of such a formidable manuscript could not have been achieved without the help, over and above the call of duty, from transcribers Rhoda Durkan, Pat Faucett, Sallie Hoopes, Margaret and Maxwell Merriman, Linda Texiera, and Beverly Unsworth.

And, finally, the project could never have been completed, especially within the prescribed deadline, without its managing editor—my wife Cora.

INTRODUCTION

On December 6, 1941, the United States was a nation of approximately 132 million people. It had an armed force totaling 1.4 million men, primarily the result of the Selective Service Act, which had been signed on September 16, 1940. A major war had been under way in Europe since September of 1939, and to those Americans who followed events outside their daily lives it seemed more and more inevitable that America would eventually be drawn into the war on the side of England, France, and Russia—against Germany and Italy.

Then, on December 7, the Japanese delivered a surprise attack on the American military base in Honolulu known as Pearl Harbor—and as one American, Marquis Childs, remembers saying to friends at the time: "Nothing will ever be the same again." Today he says, "And it never was the same. It never will be." The truth of this statement is reaffirmed every day.

The Japanese brought America out of its isolation and settled conclusively the debate as to whether or not America should enter the fighting. On December 8, President Franklin D. Roosevelt declared war on Japan, and a few days later Germany and Italy declared war on the United States.

Thus, abruptly, America was involved in a world at war, and in the dark days of 1942 it became more and more apparent that the outcome would probably be determined by whether or not the American people had the strength and endurance to stay to the finish.

One man who was determined that America would see it through was President Roosevelt. Periodically he spoke to the nation over a national radio network in his "fireside chats," inspiring Americans to keep behind the war effort until victory was achieved. Thirty-five years later,

President Jimmy Carter, in a televised fireside chat to the nation, reminded us that, "During World War II we faced a terrible crisis, but the challenge of fighting against fascism drew us together." For most Americans who lived through that period there was never any doubt about the outcome. In four tumultuous years, from 1942 through 1945, Americans put more than 16 million men and women in uniform, and the other 116 million rolled up their sleeves to become, in the phrase that is now a cliché for America during the war, the arsenal of democracy.

They were motivated, of course, by the determination to stop Hitler, avenge the Japanese attack on Pearl Harbor, and get the whole thing over with as soon as possible so they could bring the boys back home. The overwhelming majority of Americans agreed it was a war that had to be fought—and the relatively few who disagreed usually kept it to themselves. It was a time when, as Bill Gold puts it, "You just felt that the stranger sitting next to you in a restaurant, or someplace, felt the same way you did about the basic issues."

Economically, it was the time when the United States finally pulled out of the Great Depression, which, in 1940, was still lingering in many parts of the country. And, if the depression has come to be known as "hard times," it would be fair to describe the war years as "boom times." Anyone who wanted to work and was not in the armed forces could find a job, and the pay was good. There were not too many things to spend your money on, but that was not important, because ostentatious living was "out" anyway, at least "for the duration," as the saying went.

As a result, the booming war years were exhilarating, and many people I talked to look back on them as the most exciting years in their lives. This presents an odd contrast to the hard, grim times of the depression years. During the depression there was genuine human suffering in the country but little tragedy. Few people actually died from starvation or exposure. On the other hand, despite the fact that there were plenty of jobs and good money for everyone at home during the war—and no suffering from enemy military action, as there was in England, France, and Russia—there was the continuing concern for loved ones overseas. Americans were always putting a son or a husband or a father or a brother or a lover or a friend on a train, with the realization that possibly they would never see him again—at least not in one piece or in good health. Thousands of men never did return; over 400,000 Americans were killed during the war and nearly 700,000 were wounded. Although this is a relatively small figure for a nation of 132 million people, if you were the one who received that dreaded telegram, the statistics were meaningless. Many Americans never recovered from the loss of a loved one during the war and to this day find it difficult to talk about the experience—as I found out on more than one occasion in developing this book.

The purpose of this project has been to record, on the printed page, conversations with Americans who were living in this country during the years 1941 to 1945. I have tried to talk with as many people as I could to hear a variety of viewpoints and recollections of personal experiences. In fact, I talked with far more than I have been able to include here; and I wish to thank those I have had to exclude for their time and patience in talking with me.

In planning the book, the first problem was to determine who would be included. The home front, at one time or another, of course, included every American. Some were in uniform, most were not; some were civilians for awhile and in uniform for awhile. Others who were in uniform spent all of their time on the home front, and some spent part of their time on the home front before going overseas. I finally decided to exclude anyone who was in uniform during the war. They will be interviewed for another book, which I am working on now. In some cases, I did interview people about their home front experience before they eventually went into the service, but they were very few.

Many people I interviewed were reluctant at first, but finally consented after some persuasion. Others were eager to talk about their war years, which they remembered vividly. Most people seemed to enjoy the interviews, which usually took place in their homes—but not always. I also interviewed people on a boat in Sarasota Bay, in a corporation office in Pittsburgh, a union office in Chicago, a congressman's office on Capitol Hill, on a fishing pier in the Gulf of Mexico, a veranda overlooking the boardwalk in Ocean City, Maryland, the lawn of the Shaker Village in Hancock, Massachusetts, in a variety of restaurants and bars, (including Studs Terkel's favorite in Chicago), at the poolside of a resort condominium in Florida, in the rehearsal room at Tanglewood, and the editor's office of a large southern newspaper. I even conducted one interview en route from Florida to Washington in my MGB. In all cases, and with the interviewees' permission, the interview was taped, usually on my Sony TC-55.

The new compact, portable tape recorders are incredible instruments. They have revolutionized journalism and added a new dimension to the recording and documenting of history and the editing and publishing of books. The two best-known pioneers in the field of tape recording are Alan Nevins, who launched the Columbia University oral history program in the late 1940s, and Studs Terkel, author of four books based on taped interviews. I am particularly indebted to Terkel for his *Hard Times,* "an oral history of the depression," for blazing trails that started me on my way.

Such projects as this have come to be known as oral histories. But I prefer, in this case, the descriptive title, *oral narrative,* primarily because (1) it is not a history in the academic sense, and (2) once portions of the conversations were extracted for certain chapters and the rest woven together in the way I have done here, they do tell a story with a beginning, a middle, and an end—a narrative. And although it is perhaps unreal to suggest that the nearly 200 Americans I talked to can tell the story of 116 million people who served on the home front during World War II, it is also unreal to contemplate talking to all 116 million of them. If you want to hear individual people talk about a national experience, you have to start somewhere. And maybe, with a little poetic license, a hundred people can speak for a hundred million. I know that, as I neared the end of an intensive period of editing this book, I would wake up in the night sure I heard America speaking—and remembering.

To help them remember, I began the interview with a series of prepared questions, the first one of which was, "Do you remember where you were and what you were doing when you first heard the news of Pearl Harbor?" (Those of you who were alive on December 7, 1941, how would you answer that question? I suspect you remember precisely where you were and what you were doing.) Soon the best interviews would become conversational, with people recalling long-forgotten incidents, as one thing reminded them of another. The interviews usually lasted an hour—in fact, Barry Broadfoot, who did interview books on both the depression and the war years in Canada, uses a sixty-minute tape and says that when it runs out the interview is over, period. He maintains that people exhaust their best memories in an hour. In most cases I would agree. But I had several conversations that lasted for at least two hours, and I could have talked with someone like Carey McWilliams about the war years indefinitely.

The tape recorder, of course, was faithfully taking everything in, which means that when I had completed my interviewing and had the tapes transcribed, I was faced with a mountain of transcripts totaling an estimated 700,000 words. From this staggering Everest of words, I cut and edited to produce what I considered a manageable manuscript, which had to be cut again by my editor because it was felt that it was still too long.

To achieve a narrative form, which I felt would be the most interesting way to tell the story, I extracted each interviewee's account of his or her reaction to the news of Pearl Harbor and selected what I felt were the most interesting and unusual reactions for chapter 1. I also extracted each interviewee's comments on Presidents Roosevelt and Truman, the atomic bomb, and V-E and V-J Days and used what I considered the most significant of these in chapter 10. My final questions in most interviews concerned the interviewee's impression of how the war years affected his or her community, or institution, or the nation, and finally, what impact the war had on his or her life. These comments were extracted to produce chapter 11. This left the bulk of the interview, which consisted primarily of the interviewee's essential experience during the war—i.e., working in the government, in industry, in some war-related effort, or perhaps in a business that was only indirectly affected by the war. These were put together in appropriate groupings to form chapters 2 through 7.

Chapter 8 was put together with a mixture of extracts and full interviews. A similar approach was used in chapter 9—"The Ultimate Cost of Victory"—which was, of course, the most difficult chapter in the book to develop. In both my conversations with participants and in editing the transcripts, I found the discussions about lost or missing loved ones extremely difficult. In some cases the loss of, or concern for, a loved one overseas did not dominate that person's wartime experiences. In other cases it did. But in all cases the experience proved to be a difficult one for them to talk about and for me to inquire about. After much thought I decided to include all conversations devoted to a concern for loved ones overseas in one chapter, as a way of keeping an emotionally charged subject under control. And I think this is most people's method of handling the loss of a loved one: they lock it up somewhere inside them in a special place and do not let it out very often, or they would not be able to function.

Nothing was changed in the substance or content of an interview in editing the manuscript—although in some cases, people called or wrote to me to correct something that had been dredged up inaccurately in conversation after thirty-five years. In some cases, statements that were not 100 percent accurate were left in, even when other interviewees made contradictory statements. This, as I said, is not a history, but a book of recollections—a "memory book," as Studs Terkel described *Hard Times*—and the memory is fallible.

Every effort was made to preserve the language and style of an interviewee, although excess "uhs" and "ahs" and "you knows," repetitions, and false starts were eliminated. The one substantive change I made in editing was rearrangement. In a conversation, a person will talk about one subject, shift to another, then another, and then return to the first subject. To make an interview read smoothly and proceed from one thought to another, I did a lot of cutting, rearranging, and pasting. I also eliminated all of my questions and comments during a conversation, so now the interviews read as if they were one—sometimes long, uninterrupted—dialogue, which of course, they were not.

Altogether, it was a rich and rewarding experience. I have never done a book or undertaken a project such as this, and it could not have been done without a tape recorder. I find it impossible to carry on a conversation while taking notes, and even the best journalists and writers cannot capture the pace and flavor of a conversation with another person as faithfully as a tape recorder does. Most people soon forgot the recorder was present, with the result that I was able to have uninterrupted conversations with approximately 200 Americans about a period in their lives, thirty-five years ago, that is still very vivid in their memories. Winston Churchill called this period the British people's "finest hour," and I would have to say that for Americans as a whole that is not a bad description of World War II. I doubt if the nation has ever been as united in spirit or purpose before or since.

AMERICANS
REMEMBER
THE HOME FRONT

1

"A DATE WHICH WILL LIVE IN INFAMY . . ."

On December 7, 1941, Americans were divided as to whether the United States should enter the fighting in Europe. Germany and Italy were at war with England, France, and Russia, and things were not going well for the Allies. Many Americans—including President Franklin D. Roosevelt—wanted the country to enter the war against Adolf Hitler, who most Americans had by then conceded was an enemy of civilization. But many others were reluctant to get involved. Japan was active in the Pacific and Indochina, but most Americans did not take the Japanese threat seriously. Hitler was the enemy.

By the end of November 1941 it was becoming apparent that the Japanese were getting ready to make a move in the Pacific, most likely to attack British or Dutch possessions—or both. The Japanese had sent to Washington, D.C., two men, whose last names have since become immortalized in American history—Nomura and Kurusu—ostensibly to negotiate a peace in the Pacific. In that this book is an attempt to tell the story of the war years in America in the words of the people involved, I will continue the narrative in the written words of two men who have since died but who were members of the Roosevelt administration at that time.

First, A. A. Berle, who was assistant secretary of state at the time of Pearl Harbor (the secretary was Cordell Hull; Sumner Welles was under-secretary). Two entries in Berle's diary read:

"Saturday, December 6, 1941:

"I am not clear whether Saturday will go down in history as the day when [daughters] Alice and Beatrice went to see *The Student Prince* or the day when, in practice, the war really started. At all events, we were working on the proposed message which the secretary was getting up for the president to send to the Congress. It anticipated that the Japanese would break off conversations. The state of the record was that on November 26 we had handed to the Japanese a rather general plan for peace in the Pacific, that thereafter we had inquired of the Japanese what in the devil they were doing moving their troops around in Indochina, and that the delay in that reply had made it pretty clear that the demarche on November 26 would not be successful. At half past one, or thereabouts, we left the secretary's office; we then thought that we could get in some intensive work on Monday. I went to join the children at the Hay Adams House, where Freddy Lyon [assistant chief, International Conferences] (acting in my name, place, and stead) was feeding them eight dollars' worth of lunch; after which we went to the matinee of *The Student Prince*. At quarter of five we came back to the State Department. . . .

"I took the children home and had a snack, returning to the department about seven. Around seven-thirty, the Army Intelligence reported that they had intercepted the text of the reply which Japan was to make. It was not only a flat turndown, but a coarse and gratuitous and insulting message as well. Bad as this was, the accompanying message, likewise intercepted, was worse. The Japanese envoys were to keep this message locked up in their safe and present it only on the receipt of a signal; and during this time the final dispositions were to be completed. In other words, they were to hold up delivering the answer until certain military dispositions were completed.

"We worked up the text of a message; and I turned in to bed about 1:00 A.M., feeling very uneasy. The waltzes of *The Student Prince* seemed like a dirge of something that may have existed once, but certainly had very little relation to anything one knew today."

"Sunday, December 7:
"Sunday morning, and to the department. The secretary was closeted with Stimson and Knox. We fussed a little more with the message and took a few simple precautions; and when the three cabinet ministers adjourned, we went into the secretary's office. We were discussing the lines of the presentation of affairs to Congress, when the Japanese ambassador requested an immediate appointment with the secretary. He asked for it at 1:00—which happens to be 8:00 A.M. Honolulu time. The secretary fixed the time for 1:45. Sumner Welles and I stayed with the

secretary until 1:45 and then left, just as the Japanese were coming in. We had lunch at the Mayflower and came back about quarter of three. The Japanese had already gone. The news had come in that the Japanese fleet and air force had attacked Pearl Harbor, Manila (this appears to be wrong . . .). A little later it seemed that one of the Japanese expeditions was headed for a British base in northern Burma. . . . At Pearl Harbor it seems that there had been a great deal of damage. The attempt was made to bomb the army airfield, and I gather they got two hangars and perhaps 350 men (this is not yet confirmed), and did a very considerable amount of damage to the shipping. The *Oklahoma* seems to have been hit and put out of action. We have as yet no knowledge of the Philippines.

"It was a bad day all around; and if there is anyone I would not like to be, it is chief of Naval Intelligence."

Before he went to bed on the night of December 7, Harry Hopkins, President Roosevelt's closest advisor, wrote down the events of that day, as recorded by his biographer, Robert Sherwood:

"I lunched with the President today at his desk in the Oval Room. We were talking about things far removed from war when at about 1:40 Secretary Knox called and said that they had picked up a radio from Honolulu from the Commander-in-Chief of our forces there advising all our stations that an air raid attack was on and that it was 'No drill.'

"I expressed the belief that there must be some mistake and that surely Japan would not attack in Honolulu.

"The President discussed at some length his efforts to keep the country out of war and his earnest desire to complete his administration without war, but that if this action of Japan's were true it would take the matter entirely out of his own hands, because the Japanese had made the decision for him.

"The President thought the report was probably true and thought it was just the kind of unexpected thing the Japanese would do, and that at the very time they were discussing peace in the Pacific they were plotting to overthrow it.

"At five minutes after two he called Hull and told Hull of the report and advised Hull to receive Nomura and Kurusu, who had an appointment with him, and not to mention that he, Hull, had the news but to receive their reply formally and coolly and bow them out.

"I heard Hull later report to the President about the interview and I gather he used some pretty strong Tennessee mountain language to the two Japanese emissaries. The burden of his remarks being that he didn't believe a word in the reply to his note and that it was false from beginning to end.

"At 2:28 Admiral Stark called the President and confirmed the attack, stating that it was a very severe attack and that some damage had already been done to the fleet and that there was some loss of life. He discussed with the President briefly the next step and the President wanted him to execute the agreed orders to the Army and Navy in event of an outbreak of hostilities in the Pacific.

"At 2:30 the President called Steve Early and dictated a news release which Steve was to release at once to the press. Steve came in half an hour later and the President dictated a further statement which the President promptly ordered Steve to release."

The press release confirmed what the wire services had already carried. The word rapidly spreading out like prairie fire through the government and Washington and across the nation. The first Americans to get the word were in Honolulu, the government, Washington, and the newspaper and radio businesses. Thousands of Americans are still alive who vividly recall that day, their reaction, and the impact the war had on their lives.

Cornelia MacEwen Hurd, from West Farmington, Ohio, had lived in Honolulu eight years. She was a teacher at the Punahou School, a missionary school that was founded in 1840 for the sons and daughters of Hawaiian chiefs and the children of missionaries. She was an exchange teacher from a New Jersey school who liked Honolulu so much that she decided to stay. Cornelia Hurd describes the scene on that Sunday morning, December 7, 1941, from her patio:

It was 7:55 A.M. I was sitting on the veranda overlooking the ocean and Pearl Harbor, drinking morning coffee. When I heard the blasting going on, I assumed it was the Army Air Force out on the usual Sunday-morning maneuvers, and I paid no attention. Then the radio came on, and the alert started, and I heard them say over the radio, "Hawaii is under attack. The Japanese are attacking Hawaii. Take cover. Do not go

6

into the streets. Pour as much water as you can into big pots and bath-tubs. Do not go into the streets. Hawaii is under attack. Japanese are at-tacking Hawaii." That was repeated over and over.

I had a shelter that we had built earlier, but I would not go into the shelter. The attack came as a total surprise to me and my friends. Six months earlier, we had been taking courses in first aid. We also had sta-tions where we could go to shower and where supplies were stashed, and certain members of the area were given responsibilities in case of attack. But very few people really expected it. I won't say anything about the navy, being a navy wife.

I was sitting on the veranda of our house, about eight hundred feet above the ocean, and it commanded a view all the way from Diamond Head to Pearl Harbor. I saw the attack, I saw the bombs that were dropped in the ocean very, very vividly. In fact, as I first saw them, before I knew about the actual attack, I still thought that it must be the Army Air Force. Then I saw that they almost hit the Royal Hawaiian Hotel, and I said to myself, that was awfully close! The splashes were like plumes, going way up into the air, going splash, splash, one after the other. Then, when I heard over the radio that Hawaii was under at-tack, I ran up the side of my property that had a slight elevation, and there I saw the most dreadful thing I ever saw in my life. The fire, the blasting of the ships, just one after the other, in flames! I had a good view, and I knew it so well, having been there so many years, the almost enclosed lagoon harbor. And the fire and the blaze and the noise was absolutely something I'll never forget. A Japanese plane passed right in front of my yard, not more than forty feet from where I was sitting on the veranda. It was so vivid I could see the face, the profile, and the ris-ing sun on the plane. By noon, we got our breath, the worst was over. But there was a rumor that they would come back, and they did come back. But by that time, our battleships were out in the harbor and ready, and the attack was nothing like the first one. But we underestimated the Japanese; they could have landed, they could have taken Hawaii that day. I don't think there is any question about that.

After the attack on Pearl Harbor, Ms. MacEwen cabled her family three words: "WELL, SAFE, UNAFRAID." She decided to stay in Honolulu during the war and teach school. She met and married her husband there, a sub-marine captain, Adm. Kenneth C. Hurd (ret.).

Americans Remember the Home Front

Sen. George Aiken of Vermont:

I was in Washington. That was Sunday afternoon, and I had gone over to the office for some reason or other. On the ticker, I saw that the Japanese had attacked Pearl Harbor, no extent of the damage done. The next day, I recall, Senator Toby of New Hampshire said to me, "The report is that they've destroyed a good share of our fleet over there." That was the first we knew of it. Of course, Pearl Harbor made our part of the war inevitable. I remember [Sen.] Bill LaFollette, who had opposed our entry into the war and aid to England. The day after the bombing, he came into my office with his uniform on, ready to go.

Congressman Wright Patman (D-Tex.), now deceased, had been in the Congress since 1929.

I was living in the Cavalier Hotel on Fourteenth Street in Washington. It was about two o'clock in the afternoon, and my son, my oldest son, was taking a nap. He was awakened by the radio, and I was too. We were all just kind of waiting to see what was going to happen. We expected something, because our son was here, expected to enlist if we were going to have war, and I had another son in Houston, Texas, and they both enlisted right after that. Then the third one enlisted in the marines right after that, so we were kind of war conscious. Well, everybody was wondering what was going to happen. Nobody knew how extensive it was. It looked terribly bad, and everybody with children were wondering should the children go back to school, college, what'll happen to them, what'll happen to us, should we stay on here in Congress, or go on back home? Things like that. It was an uncertain period for everybody, but especially for people away from home.

In later years, to hear people tell it, it seemed as if half of Washington was out at the Redskins football game on December 7, 1941, in a stadium that would only hold twenty-five thousand people.

Melville Grosvenor, then assistant editor of the National Georgraphic *magazine, distinctly remembers being there.*

I was out at Griffith Stadium watching Washington get trounced. I think it was by the Giants. Anyway, it was an awful day. I was watching this game sorrowfully, and a whisper came around the stands. Everybody was shocked. It got to me, and they said: "Pearl Harbor has been attacked!" I couldn't believe it. The Japanese! I thought it was just talk. Then more reports came, and you began to see important people get up and go out. Then the public-address system sounded: "So and so, secretary of the navy, will you please come to the telephone?" and "So-so, would you please come to the manager's office immediately?" All the bigwigs went. And, of course, everybody was there at the football game, so you knew something hot was going on. And it was an awful feeling. You'd sort of known something like that was coming. And when it did, you said, "I hope they're ready, I hope they're ready!"

On the Friday before, I had had lunch with one of our editors, Ted Vosburgh. He was a violent isolationist. For lunch, we went down to the National Press Club, walking down Sixteenth Street, and he said, "Well, they just captured Singapore, or Malaya, and Japs are coming down there attacking the British, China. If we go to war, it will be the most terrible thing to pull old England's chestnuts out of the fire, we're always doing that," he says. "It would be a terrible thing. I certainly hope they won't do it." He was the most peace-minded person I think I've ever known. Well, Sunday came, and Monday came, and do you know, Ted was rabid that morning. He told me, "That was the most despicable thing, to attack like that." And he went right down and signed up in the air force. The last person you'd ever think. And he became an intelligence officer with the air force, and was assigned to Patton.

I lost a very close friend at Pearl Harbor, Tommy Evans, of my Annapolis class. He was on the *Yorktown,* communications officer. It was torpedoed in the bow, and he and his dad were trapped down there in the communications office and couldn't get out. Yet, they could talk to him from the flight deck. She was heeling more and more, and they knew there wasn't any way they could get them off. And the fellows just played poker down there. They knew what was happening, they knew it, they just couldn't get out. And they went on playing poker till the last man said good-bye, and then they went down with the ship.

Nelson Poynter, editor of the St. Petersburg (Fla.) Times *was on leave, working in Washington for the coordinator of information, Wild Bill Donovan, who was later to become head of the OSS (Office of Strategic Services).*

We had offices in both New York and Washington and were operating twenty-four-hours a day, seven-days a week, and we were in operation that afternoon, when we first learned about Pearl Harbor. I was at home, they called me, and I went right over to the office, and it was in full swing. It's amazing to me, to this day, that so many people were surprised at Pearl Harbor. Of course, it was learned afterward that our navy had broken the Japanese code. They knew, and we knew. It was not such a secret that the Japanese fleet had left its home base and was somewhere in the Pacific. I thought it would hit Manila or Hong Kong, and I think that's part of the reason why our own navy personnel was surprised. It was almost incomprehensible to them that they would strike for Pearl Harbor. I was surprised that they had picked Pearl Harbor, but I was not stunned. My associates in that office, some of the best newsmen you could find, felt the same way. They took it in their stride.

That Sunday afternoon Bill Donovan was at a football game in New York, and they had to page him, and he flew back to Washington. I was with him all evening. Meanwhile, Robert Sherwood had flown down from New York and was over at the White House with Judge Rosenman working on the president's speech to Congress. We knew how badly we had been hurt at Pearl Harbor, and Sherwood called and asked me for any suggestions on the speech. I said this is the time to tell the American people the very worst. This should be the blood, sweat, and tears speech for Roosevelt, so that from here on all the news will be better. It's not going to be better immediately, but it will be somewhat better. It was my judgment then that the American people would have responded to that. On the other hand, perhaps they wouldn't. Actually, the government knew more than they were willing to tell the people of how badly we had been hurt, and Roosevelt's speech was less alarming than it might have been.

One man, Ed Stanley, who was working for our office had been a key man in the Associated Press. He had helped put the AP into the wirephoto business in the early thirties. I said to him, "Pearl Harbor is in the Western hemisphere. Could you urge the Associated Press in sending out a wirephoto picture to get that fact into the picture?" I thought it was terribly important, as far as the American people's public opinion was concerned, that we had been hit in our own Western hemisphere. I thought this would help in regard to Latin American relationships because, since the Monroe Doctrine, the Western hemisphere was supposed to be inviolate. I remember Donovan philosophizing on this. We were grabbing bulletins, all the information we could from Honolulu and the Philippines, and Donovan leaned back to appraise our situation, and he said, "Nelson, we've been hit awfully hard. We're going to have to fight guerilla warfare until we can rebuild our strength." Considering that he had gotten the news only a few hours before, I thought that it was a very shrewd, long viewpoint that he took there, realizing that it was going to be a long war and that we had to keep making a nuisance of ourselves in every way possible while rebuilding our strength from an armaments standpoint.

Bryson Rash was working for the NBC Washington office in the old Trans-Lux office building at Fourteenth and New York Avenue, two blocks from the White House.

I just happened to be at work that afternoon because I did a program on Sunday. After the program I was doing some other chores, when I heard running down the hallway. It was the news editor, who had a piece of teletype copy paper in his hand. I said: "What's the matter?" He said: "The Japs just bombed Pearl Harbor."

I ran into the newsroom, and he ran into the studio to get the bulletin on the air. All the printers in the place were going crazy. In those days there was a bell system, where five bells rang if it was a bulletin and ten bells if it was a flash, and the bells were ringing constantly. While I was in the newsroom, the phone rang, and I picked it up. It was the White House. The voice said, "Mr. [Steve] Early will have a statement." It just happened that I was the only person in the building at the moment who had a White House pass, so I ran over to get the Early statement. There was no statement. Early wasn't there, in the West Wing. This was minutes after the news broke.

Actually, at that time, Japanese envoys Nomura and Kurusu were meeting with Secretary of State Cordell Hull in his office across the street in what is now the Executive Office Building. So most of the people were interested in that story and were at the State Department, and there was nobody in sight at the White House except a policeman. I asked the policeman where Mr. Early was, and he said, "Mr. Early doesn't come in on Sunday usually." I said, "Where is the statement?" He said, "What statement?" So I said, "Don't you know what happened? Pearl Harbor has been bombed!" At that he nearly fainted.

One of the most poignant things I can remember about Pearl Harbor

Day was the crowd that gathered in Lafayette Park, across the street from the White House. In those days you didn't have security like you have now, so some of the crowd walked down the street between the White House and the present Executive Office Building, and they stood on the steps of the old State Department. They watched the comings and goings of the officials in the big limousines at the White House, and the lights were up because of film cameras. In those days, there was no television. The most poignant thing was the quiet interest, just absolute quiet of this huge crowd. It seemed that the realization of what Pearl Harbor meant had settled over the people.

Frank Waldrop was the managing editor of the Washington Times Herald. *He says: "You're damned right I remember Pearl Harbor."*

I was at my office attending to business. I had gone down there, as I customarily did, about ten o'clock on Sunday morning. By noon, or a little after, I had finished going through my stuff, and I went back in the wire room just to look at what the hell was going on, and I saw a dispatch from Reuters that said that two Japanese battleships had been sighted going south in the Gulf of Siam, so I thought, "What the hell. Things are right at the flash point. I believe I'll stick around a while." So I went back to work.

A fellow named Tom Stephens was on the city desk doing the dog watch, and I guess about two o'clock he came belting into my office, his face ashen, and said, "The police radio says that the Japanese have bombed Pearl Harbor!" So I said: "Call the White House and see if you can get a confirmation." I began to put the telephone operators to work finding out where everybody was. Fortunately all of our circulation people were out at the Redskins football game. They had some junket that the kids had wanted to attend, so there was a big crowd of them out there. I called the Redskins office and told them to put on their loudspeaker "All *Times Herald* people report to their office on the double," and about the same time, the navy was calling and the army was calling, and so I didn't have any problem. They didn't say that Pearl Harbor had been bombed, but they did say: "All military personnel report to your commanding officers" or your "posts of duty." The *Times Herald* actually was announced, and a great many printers were out there, by good chance. I also got hold of the head of the composing room, and the people who heard it on the radio didn't have to be told.

They got the hell down there. So by the time the people made it to the office, I had a story and I had gotten a full description of the attack officially, including the losses and all, quite detailed. We didn't publish the details, but we got them.

I wrote the lead couple of paragraphs and then after that I was too damned busy to fool with it. But people just filled in as it came along and built the story. I went to the composing room with the foreman of the typographical end of the paper, Irving Belt, and the *Times Herald* was on the street four hours ahead of any newspaper, I think, in the country. We were sure as hell the first newspaper in Washington. We were off and balling right smack out with it, and what I love, as I look back on it, was when those guys came in there, you didn't have to tell them anything. They knew right where they belonged, and they hit this damn thing, and the circulation department was up, and when the pressman pressed that button, those damned papers went out of there like scared dogs. I think there's a copy of it on the wall over at the Press Club: "Pearl Harbor Bombed." I had a double line on it; we just set type as big as we could get it. What the hell! Your country doesn't get attacked every day in the week.

Merlo Pusey was chief editorial writer for the Washington Post.

I was on duty and running the editorial page that day. The first word we heard came when a copyboy, who was a rather obstreperous youngster, dashed into the office screaming that the Japanese had attacked Pearl Harbor. We didn't believe him, because he was kind of a practical joker, and we thought he was pulling one on us. I didn't believe him because it seemed to me that the Japanese would be insane to attack Pearl Harbor. It was such a crazy thing, because there was nothing in the world they could do that would arouse this sleeping giant more effectively than an attack on Pearl Harbor. Once they launched that, their doom was sealed, and I had that feeling about it at the moment. But of course we checked immediately and found it was true and began frantic operations to prepare for it the next day. I didn't write the editorial. Herbert Elliston [editor], who was then writing most of our foreign-affairs editorials, dashed into the office and wrote it.

Dean Elmer Louis Kayser, George Washington University, in Washington, D.C.:

I had gotten up very late and was shaving when the news came in on the radio. I was then doing foreign-news commentary for radio station WWDC, and I called my wife and told her to call the station and tell them I'd stop shaving and dress and come in immediately and go on the air. I had to go past the Japanese Embassy, of course, so I stopped to see what I could see. They hadn't thrown a military guard around the place yet, just local police, but they were keeping people out of the embassy's compound. Here were the Japanese, working like bees, bringing out files, and they built quite a bonfire in the side yard. Then I went down and went on the air almost immediately, giving a picture of what I had seen at the embassy.

Fortunately, we didn't know as much about Pearl Harbor then as we do now—the stupidity of Washington. Of course, I knew Joseph Grew, and I talked with him very fully after he finally came back to Washington—about the accuracy and the fullness of the reports he had been sending to Washington all along. And, of course, Adm. J. O. Richardson, who was at Pearl Harbor earlier, came all the way to Washington and said to Roosevelt: "Mr. President, I've got to tell you that there is not a single flag officer in the Pacific who can follow the behavior of Washington in this regard, who is not opposed."

The next day, Monday morning, Cloyd Heck Marvin, president of George Washington University, called the whole faculty together. He had called me earlier and said, "I want you, dean, to address this meeting, dedicating the faculty and the university to the cause of the nation in this war which is about to be declared." And so, in no time at all, I was stuck up on the platform to deliver a speech to rally the university. I wish I had a tape of it, because I have been told that it was good.

To set the temperature, I took that magnificent occasion where, at the time of the Nika revolt in Constantinople, when the forces opposed to Justinian could have swept him off the throne in the sudden cataclysm of violence which he couldn't meet, when the Empress Theodora said, "As for me, the purple is the only burial shroud of a princess." She would not run. That's what I took to cite the passion of resistance which would have to be aroused. Curious I'd still remember that.

Edward Stuntz worked for the Associated Press in Washington.

I was sitting there, drinking beer and getting ready for my afternoon nap. Connie [his wife] was making lunch, and this news came on the radio. The thing that brought me out of my daze was somebody on the radio who said something like: "Whatever may be said about this treacherous attack on Pearl Harbor"—I guess I was thinking it must be an Orson Welles type of thing—"the fact remains that the Japanese will have committed national suicide."

That brought me up, and I turned the radio up louder and yelled at Connie to come in, and we listened to what details they had. I ran up the stairs to get some office clothes on and yelled on my way up, "It's war, Connie. It's going to be war." My daughter, Ann, burst into tears. Connie drove me to the office—I was covering the Latin American diplomatic run—and I stayed there practically twenty-four hours. I called up all the various embassies and was getting some reaction stories, and before I got through that night, we got a message from our AP man in Costa Rica that Costa Rica had declared war and rounded up all the Japanese farmers—Costa Rica was full of them, you know. I was still making my calls when my dear old friend Alvareo Concheso, the Cuban ambassador, who was working then for Batista, called me up and said, "Mr. Stuntz, why is it that the Associated Press lets Costa Rica declare war before we do, the Cubans?"

And I said to him, "But, Mr. Ambassador, AP didn't have anything to do with it. We just got a story, which you have read, that the president of Costa Rica announced that a state of war with Japan existed so that he could go out and arrest all these Japanese who might be subversives."

The exact chronology of this escapes me, but after Concheso learned that Costa Rica had declared war and the United States had not, he was boiling and furious at the AP and at me for putting the story out. He thought I had done it. He said, "What am I going to tell Colonel Batista?"

I said, "Tell him that Mr. Roosevelt is said to be preparing a message to Congress for tomorrow." And he said, "But you let Costa Rica declare war. Don't you know that Cuba is always the first to declare war after the United States?"

They took great pride in that. Right after World War I, Mario Menolal, the Cuban president, had his message to his Congress all prepared before President Wilson went to our Congress, but he waited until Wilson made his declaration.

Anyhow, I worked that night around the clock, and from then on, it was grind, grind, grind.

Twenty-year-old Mercedes Fritzching, a Venezuelan citizen born of German parents, was working at the German Embassy in Washington: She says Pearl Harbor meant that her world was "coming to an end"—and it did.

It was a Sunday afternoon, and I was on my way to Constitution Hall for a concert. I was just backing out of the driveway, when my father opened the window and called down and told me that Pearl Harbor had been attacked. I picked up several friends on the way to the concert and told them the news, and we simply couldn't believe it. The concert started, and it didn't seem like anything was unusual until intermission, and then we noticed that people were being called up, and after intermission the hall was only half full—important people had been called up. Then we began to feel the significance of the event.

At that time I was working at the German Embassy as a social secretary to the naval attaché, so going to work on Monday was, of course, quite dramatic, too, because we felt sure it was only a matter of days before war would be declared between Germany and the United States. So that meant that all the files had to be burned—everything, even such ridiculous things as table settings. As social secretary, I just had guest lists and invitations, but we burned everything. And then, of course, the war between the United States and Germany came the following Thursday. I was living at home with my parents. My father was a German diplomat, and we were told that we were just supposed to keep a low profile and stay in our homes, and the time would come when we would be exchanged for the American diplomats in Germany. So we started packing, thinking we would have an indefinite period to do this because they would have to find some ship to take us back to Germany. The State Department said, "Take it easy and just stay home." But apparently the secret service made other arrangements. By the sixteenth of December, we were given the order: All of the German officials had to spend that night in the German Embassy, and the families had to report in front of the embassy the next morning, so we really just had that one night to get our hand luggage packed and walk out of our homes as they were and report to the embassy. We were interned at White Sulphur Springs, in the Greenbriar Hotel, leaving everything behind. We stayed there for five months.

I had been in this country fifteen years, from my childhood. I was aware of the war building up for some years. The attack on Pearl Harbor was totally unexpected. After all, the Japanese ambassador was at that very moment at the State Department and, as it turned out, knew nothing about it. Just like in Germany, you had the conflict between the Nazis and the Germans; in Japan you had the military versus the civilians. So it seemed absolutely incredible. In 1940 there had been so much provocation by the Americans against the Germans stationed in the United States—all of the consulates were closed, and the German consular people were returned to Germany. And I know for a fact, having worked at the embassy during that period, that President Roosevelt tried to provoke the Germans, and the Germans just bent over backward not to declare war. The flags were ripped down from the consulate's house in San Francisco and in L.A. and New Orleans, and all kinds of little incidents which, under normal circumstances, certainly would have gotten Germany to declare war against the United States. But the Germans didn't want that. The thrust of the policy was to maintain neutrality, absolutely, and so for us the idea that the Japanese would take the initiative was simply mind boggling. I think it had the same effect on the Germans. I don't have any knowledge that the German [Army] High Command had any idea that the Japanese were up to this. So once it happened, they had no other recourse.

I thought Pearl Harbor was horrible, horrible! It felt like our world was coming to an end. In a sense, it did.

My sister and I had been in Germany, but as tourists, so we felt completely tied to the United States. And we did all through the war; although we were in Germany, our loyalties were completely here. As a matter of fact, we could have stayed here, but we hadn't been working, except for the little job I had at the Germany Embassy; we didn't know how to earn our living, we were too young, and it seemed perfectly logical in that final horrible moment to go with our parents back to Germany.

Leverett Saltonstall, a Republican, was governor of Massachusetts at the time of Pearl Harbor, having served in the State House since 1940.

I heard about Pearl Harbor over the car radio when we were riding from our farm to our home in Chestnut Hill. When I reached home, I called the adjutant general, and we agreed to call out the whole State Guard that night to guard the various railroad and highway crossings until we knew what the story was.

The first problems we had concerned the railroads and the various utilities—not to have those services broken down. There were no actual attempts to sabotage, or rumors, at that time; that came somewhat later. When Pearl Harbor broke, the army had the responsibility up to the high water, the Coast Guard took over from the high water to a certain depth, and then the navy took over. There was also the problem of how the state fitted in with them. Gradually, that was worked out, so that one phone call would do everything. Remember, we had submarines off our coast.

Kay Halle was working in Cleveland, where she was on assignment for radio station WGAR. A few months earlier, she had interviewed Barbara Ward as part of a series on what the roles of women might be if the United States were drawn into the war.

It was a very dramatic and memorable moment. I was attending the annual meeting of the Institute of Pacific Relations, being held that year at the Country Club in Cleveland, Ohio. Naturally, the subject of the conference was the crisis in the Far East. I was sitting at the end of one long conference table next to my friend Count Carlo Sforza. I had also interviewed him on his passionate opposition to Mussolini. Next to him was Ohio Congresswoman Frances Bolton. That December 7 conference had drawn together a remarkably gifted group of Far East experts, writers, and other dignitaries. The group's director, Edward Carter, had divided the delegates into two groups, who were to go into conference and reassemble after lunch with their assessments of whether and when the Japanese might take some military action against the United States. The two groups returned at around two o'clock, each with the same "educated" conclusion that the Japanese would not take any action for a year or more. While the conference proceeded to analyze their conclusions, I felt a tug at my elbow. It was Clayton Fritchey of the *Cleveland Press*. He handed me a slip of paper which he asked me to take up to the institute's director. It was the announcement just released by Steve Early, President Roosevelt's press secretary, that the Japanese had bombed Pearl Harbor. After Mr. Carter had read the news, my first thought was, where could I be most useful? I went to Washington, and at a cocktail party I met Sam Scrivener, who was an executive at the newly formed Office of Strategic Services—the OSS. He was on the alert for recruits, and, fortunately, I became one.

Jack Altshul was working on the Long Beach Life, *a Long Island weekly newspaper. He was covering a pro football game.*

I was up in the press box, and one of the other newspapermen said something was coming up over the radio that he just "couldn't understand." We listened very carefully, and what we got out of it was that the Japanese were attacking Pearl Harbor. None of us knew where Pearl Harbor was. We didn't even know it was in the Hawaiian Islands. The game was about to start, when somebody made the announcement on the public-address system, and we could see a little stirring, but it didn't seem to sink in. People stayed right through the football game, but by the time the game was over, everybody was talking about it.

I got a sense of it that night. Everybody seemed to feel: Well, this is it, this is the war. And, of course, the next morning, Roosevelt declared war.

In '41 I was twenty-four years old and had been classified 1-B, which was limited military duty, because I only had sight in one eye. I was really not getting anywhere in the newspaper business, and my feeling was that I wouldn't have minded getting into the service. And as a Jew, if this was also going to bring America into the war against the Nazis, I welcomed it. We were all pretty jingoistic at that time—much more so than the future generations. I didn't feel like I was going to go right out and volunteer, but I figured I would be taken, and I was looking forward to it.

In Hopewell, Virginia, Gus Robbins, editor of the local paper, recalls, "It was a beautiful December day."

We got home maybe five-thirty, six o'clock, and I turned the radio on and heard it, and of course I was dumbfounded. Nobody had expected that. I belonged to a public-affairs club that had a dinner meeting once a month, and in early November, just a month before Pearl Harbor, we had Captain Lovett, the head navy PR man down to speak to us. He talked for an hour about how wonderful the U.S. Navy was and if there was a war, we'd wipe the Japanese navy out in five days. The next week he was transferred to Pearl Harbor in command of a flotilla of six destroyers. Three of his destroyers were in dry dock, and all three were destroyed. He survived because it was Sunday and he was at home. But that is an indication of what was wrong with the United States government.

I had been a corporal in World War I, and my first thought was to hunt for a commission in World War II. But it was impossible to find anybody to run the newspaper. We had three small children, and there was no way in the world I could get away. I was losing my editor, losing half of my shop force within less than a year, so I had to do the front office and half the back shop.

Bill Gold was the news director for radio station WCPO in Cincinnati, Ohio.

We were incredulous when the news came over the ticker. It was beyond immediate comprehension. It dawned on us, as the day wore on and as additional information became available, that it really had happened.

I couldn't forget that Cordell Hull announced ten days or two weeks before Pearl Harbor that his talks with the Japanese emissaries were proceeding in a normal fashion but that there would be some kind of delay. The Japanese were to get new instructions from their government and would meet again after a certain date. My male intuition told me there was something rotten in Denmark, but certainly there was no thought in my mind that there would be an outbreak of hostilities, a sneak attack or anything of that kind. It was just a reporter's normal suspicion.

One of the revealing little episodes was that one of the isolationist senators, I can't remember his name, was scheduled to make his standard speech that Sunday afternoon, and the reporters reached him just before he went on with the news of this attack. He said, "Poppycock! Just newspaper stuff," and went out and made his same speech—that there's no danger from Japan; what are we so concerned about?

My first reaction was that I ought to go down and enlist right away. But at that point I had been married a dozen years, had a young child, and, you know, your immediate reaction and what you think after you've talked to your wife about it are two different things.

Ann Hoskins and her husband, Stewart, were running the Lakeville Journal, *a weekly newspaper in Lakeville, Connecticut.*

My parents were up for the weekend, and we'd been listening to a symphony concert. It was interrupted in the middle with the words that Pearl Harbor had been bombed. At first, we didn't understand exactly what it meant, and then suddenly we thought, "My God, we're in it!"

Our first reaction was, "Well, that's settled; at least now we know what we are going to do." It was a terrific feeling of relief that at last there was a solution. We had a very strong America First group here who were pamphletizing and talking against going in. Stewart, in his editorial, said: "Let's wait until we are armed. We can't go in with wooden muskets, for goodness' sake. Let's do it when we're ready, but not now." There was great tension and feelings between people not to intervene. But the minute Pearl Harbor happened, there was utter unity, absolutely. I remember that Monday morning after Pearl Harbor, I went down to the bank, and a woman standing outside said, "Do you suppose they will bomb us right away?" She was sure it would come.

Don Baldwin was on a picnic in Idaho. He was working for an Idaho Falls newspaper, circulation 5,000.

We heard it on a little car radio, so I dropped my wife and small son where we were staying and dashed fifty-five miles to Idaho Falls, and we put out an extra telling about the Japanese attack. I thought I was probably going to go. I was rather exhilarated by the thought. A great many of my friends had been going into the service voluntarily. I had a small son and I thought, well, this was an opportunity. But I didn't, for several reasons—mainly because I got involved in newspaper work, and the draft board kept turning me down for that.

Marquis Childs was a correspondent in the Washington Bureau of the St. Louis Post-Dispatch.

I wasn't at a football game as almost everybody else was. I remember hearing it first over the radio. And then driving out to some friends' house in Virginia, people I had known very well, and all of us saying, "Nothing will ever be the same again." And it never was the same. It never will be.

Robert Bender, a young man just out of college, was working for NBC in

New York. Although not at the office that day, he had a special reason for remembering Pearl Harbor.

I was in Chatham, New Jersey, living with my folks, and I was stunned. But what is interesting is that a year before, perhaps to that exact date, I was studying journalism at Rutgers University, and I faked an Associated Press story saying that the Japs had attacked Pearl Harbor. I had been in Hawaii and in Australia with my dad, so I knew the area and the names of the fields. I described the Japanese coming over and the damage they did. All hell broke loose at the college! Then they realized it was a fake, and I almost got thrown out. Of course, I apologized profusely, and I remained in Rutgers. And at the time of the actual bombing I immediately thought of my story, and I thought if only there had been some way of showing people that this could happen so we should be better prepared.

John W. McCormack was the majority leader in the House of Representatives. On Sunday, December 7, 1941, he was back in Boston, and he got the news from a very reliable source.

The telephone rang. I answered it, and it was the White House calling me. FDR came on the phone, and he told me about Pearl Harbor. I hadn't heard about it. He also said he wanted me to be back in Washington by the next day. I told him that I came home to address a luncheon meeting of the Boston Chamber of Commerce on Monday, and he told me he needed me in Washington. I said: "That's all, Mr. President, I'll be there." So Mrs. McCormack and I went back.

I took it bitterly! The very attack on Pearl Harbor was war itself. The formal declaration was a mere formality, and I introduced a resolution declaring war the next day. There's a picture over there of Roosevelt signing the resolution. The country was intensely isolationist for several years prior to Pearl Harbor, and when I say intensely isolationist, I mean it. Three months before Pearl Harbor we had a very important bill up in the House to extend the Selective Service Act one year. We couldn't get it extended for two years; [Speaker Sam] Rayburn and I knew it. So we decided to extend it for one year, let the next year take care of itself. The isolation feeling was so strong, that bill passed the House by one vote, 203 to 202. There is no question in my mind that at least 90 of those members that voted against were for it. They recognized the absolute necessity for it, but they were thinking about the next election.

We couldn't get a declaration of war through Congress. If Pearl Harbor hadn't happened, in my opinion the intense isolationism was so strong, we never would have entered the war.

We were back in Washington the day after Pearl Harbor for the meeting of the Congress.

YAMAMOTO

Because in 3 hours
he taught America
a lesson it had been
unable to learn in
5 years —
This monument was
erected by A
UNITED PEOPLE

By Leo Hershfield, PM

The News-Gazette
CHAMPAIGN-URBANA—THE HOME OF THE UNIVERSITY OF ILLINOIS

CONGRESS DECLARES WAR

BRITAIN RUSHES
DECLARATION OF
WAR ON JAPS

Roosevelt Cites The Infamy
Of Jap Attack On Hawaii

WASHINGTON, Dec. 8—(AP)—The United States, through its Congress, declared war today on Japan.

Text Of Message

BATES
BARBERSHOP

The president began his speech:

"Yesterday, December 7, 1941, a date which will live in infamy, the United States of America was suddenly and deliberately attacked by naval and air forces of the Empire of Japan. . . ." The news hit Americans with varying degrees of shock and dismay, depending on their age, temperament, and awareness of what was going on in the world. Some were too young to know what was really happening; just that something sickening and frightening had taken place. Others, who felt American involvement in the fighting in Europe was inevitable, were relieved that finally the anxiety and tension of a threatening war would be gone. And most Americans, many of whom had never heard of Pearl Harbor, could not believe any nation would attack a United States military base.

On the eve of the attack, the mood of America was essentially isolationist. Among those few who supported intervention in the war, the focus was on Europe, where American sympathies were overwhelmingly for the Allies—Great Britain, France, and Russia. But very few Americans thought we would actually get into the war, despite Roosevelt's efforts to enlist the country on the side of the Allies. Virtually no one suspected we would be fighting the Japanese. But on a beautiful Sunday morning, with American soldiers and seamen enjoying a day of leisure in Honolulu, and 100 million Americans doing what Americans do on Sundays, the Japanese achieved what Mussolini, Hitler, Churchill, and Roosevelt had been unable to do for two years. In a four-hour attack on the U.S. fleet, with planes from carriers far out at sea, they stunned America on a day still seared in the memories of all Americans who were old enough at the time to know what was happening.

In interviewing people for this book, the first question I usually asked was: "Do you remember where you were, what you were doing, and your reaction when you first heard the news of the attack on Pearl Harbor?" Ninety-five percent of the people said something like, "I certainly do!" It was a traumatic experience for the nation, and it is reflected in the responses individual Americans gave thirty-five years later to that question. Here is a sampling of that response, which reveals the depth of the impact the attack had on America and the extent to which it united the country, perhaps as never before—or since.

Studs Terkel in Chicago:

I was lying on the divan when I heard the news, and I thought: "What's going to happen tomorrow?" The next day was Monday. I was a gangster in a soap opera, it may have been "Ma Perkins." But it was canceled. A bunch of us actors all went to a big room where the engineers were, and we heard Roosevelt on the radio with his "Day of Infamy" speech. And that was it. My reaction? Not surprise. There was shock, of course, at the event itself. But I was not surprised that the U.S. entered the war, because the indications were there.

Carey McWilliams had just been married and was living in Hollywood. He had the radio on.

I was shocked beyond measure. Of course, you could sense the preceding six months' tension and trouble. But I never thought they would do such a crazy thing. But in an odd way I had a certain feeling of relief. Some of the worst years in my life, in many respects, were 1939 and '40 and into '41, because the domestic tensions were getting very ugly. The Christian-front stuff was coming along, America First, all this isolationist business, and I was of two minds about all this. I was quite skeptical, by 1939, that France and England, with or without the United States, would ever do anything to stop the kind of aggressions that were going on. At the same time, I thought we should certainly do anything we could to help anybody that was resisting. But nobody was resisting! So this was terrible. And then in August of 1939, when the Nazi–Soviet pact was made, as you know, the reaction in this country was poison-ous, because this was regarded as a tremendous betrayal by the Soviets, immoral, which it was, in a manner of speaking. But I felt at the time that I could understand the Soviet attitude. For God's sake, they'd been trying for ten years to get France and England and Italy to do something. And then when they saw France and England give away twenty-six Czech divisions! Well, what do you expect them to do? Anyway, they created a very ugly mood in this country, particularly on the West Coast and particularly in left-of-center circles. Friend against friend.

I can see something more clearly in retrospect than I could see at the time: On the day that the Nazis moved into the Soviet Union my wife and I were driving down the coast from San Francisco to Los Angeles. We stopped at Pismo Beach, where we always stopped for the won-derful clams, and who should come in but Robert Oppenheimer and his then great friend Haakon Chevallier. They were driving north. We sat down to dinner together. Both of them, incidentally, were several degrees to the left of me at that time, politically. They had long, long faces because this was the end of the world. The Soviets were weak and couldn't stand up to this, it was a question of months maybe. I said, "I think you guys are out of your mind; this is the end of Hitler. He has made the key mistake." What I didn't appreciate at the time, but do now, is that the Japanese probably would not have struck at Pearl Harbor in December if the Nazis had not moved into the Soviet Union in June. The Russians had their hands full. They would not do much about anything Japan might do. But I also think, in a perverse way, and ironically maybe, we owe Japan a debt of thanks. Pearl Harbor ended this goddamn domestic bickering, got the whole nation together, and enabled the nation to do what Roosevelt really wanted to do, in a way, but didn't have political support for.

Celeste Kavanaugh was a senior at the Florida State College for Women in Tallahassee.

I was on a house party with a group of friends, and we had gone to a movie that Sunday afternoon and returned to my friend's home, where we were met with the news. One of my best friends, Admiral Angus's daughter, was with me that day, and I remember she burst into tears. I think she realized the impact a little more than the rest of us, but we were all thoroughly shocked.

Heli Swyter in Houston, Texas:

I was in the hospital with my son, who was born two weeks before Pearl Harbor. Since I had some complications, I had to stay in the hospital longer than usual. Of course, the news of Pearl Harbor shocked me, because it was such an unexpected attack. That meant we were going to be in the war, I was sure. My husband left in April that year, and I did not see him for four years. I was interviewed by a newspaper reporter because I was in the hospital having a son when Pearl Harbor was attacked and my husband was overseas. I felt all right, but everybody made such a fuss over me that pretty soon I began to feel sorry for myself.

ViCurtis Hinton was a student at Howard University in Washington, D.C.

I'll never forget. I was at Camp Lee, below Richmond, visiting some friends. We were getting ready to come back to Washington when we heard about Pearl Harbor. All I could think about was getting home, as if something might happen at home. I was in school in Howard University. I was just scared to death of the war, I didn't know what it meant and didn't know what would happen about my brother. He was not in the service at that time, but he was old enough to be drafted. My father had been in World War I. I didn't know what was going to happen. I didn't know whether they were going to bomb Washington. It was a really funny feeling.

Coralee Redmond, her husband, and her boys, had gone up into the hills around Beach, North Dakota, to cut a Christmas tree.

When I came home and we drove back into the yard, the girls came running out—my girls were high school students at that time—and they said, "Mom, where's Uncle Ben?" And I said "He's in Pearl Harbor," and they said "Pearl Harbor has just been bombed!" So it really was quite a shock.

A promising young actress named Evelyn Keyes was in Hollywood, where she had just signed a contract with Columbia Pictures.

It was a Sunday. I was at Charles Vidor's house. He was later my husband; he wasn't then. It was quiet. I remember the sunshine, of all things, because it seemed incongruous that the sun was shining when we heard this news. Someone telephoned. They said: "Did you hear? The Japanese have attacked Pearl Harbor!" We immediately turned on the radio—that was before television—and we didn't ever stop listening. Of course, I thought it was the end of the world. Shock! Horror! We were on the West Coast, and we thought surely they would be along here.

Charles was already in his forties, and I remember thinking it was a relief that he wouldn't have to go. But people started going off to war— my own brother went—and they showed up in sailor's uniforms, and they seemed almost soft, childish.

Joseph Clement was married, had a baby boy, and was living in Milwaukee, Wisconsin, working for the Nesco Company, which made pots and pans.

That's one of those times when you remember everything. It was a Sunday morning, and we were at home having breakfast. We got the news over the radio that Pearl Harbor had been bombed, and like everybody else, we didn't know what the score was. I went back to the plant the next day, and it took a little time for everybody to get their bearings. But it wasn't long before they realized that they would have to shut our department down because we were making consumer goods. So I started making plans to get another job. I had a kind of interest in aviation. I had built my own glider, so I thought I might be useful in that area. I went home to see my folks and stopped at Curtiss–Wright Company in Saint Louis, and they definitely were interested. They were starting up a department, employing people like mad, trying to get ready for some of these programs that they were developing. Everything was in a mess, but they definitely had some programs jelling.

Newton Tolman had a farm going in Nelson, New Hampshire, where he was living with his wife, Janet, and a young son.

I was down in the cornfield, and when I came up, Janet told me. I don't remember whether she had heard it on the radio or somebody had called her up. It could have been both, because everybody was calling everybody. I was never too happy about the war. In the Civil War, my grandfather, at eighteen, was hired by his brother, who was twenty-four and much richer, to go into the service. It ruined his health, and the old farm fell down. I had to eventually rebuild it. War was not for me. I didn't really believe in it much. On the other hand, I was young, and my wife was the founder of the Young Republicans Club in New York, with Tom Dewey and all those flag-wavers. But now we were attacked. The Japs bombed Honolulu, where my aunt had taught at the Punahou Academy, since the 1930s, and we had various relatives out there and Hawaiian friends. So, by God, they might as well have been knocking at our doorstep. I think I must have been bombed in my mind. I went off then and signed up with the navy.

But I got out of it; God was on my side. I never knew why I got out of it, except that when I was interviewed for the navy, they said: "What have you done for more than six months to make a living?" And I had twenty-eight sheets of paper to honestly answer the question, and I think the psychiatrist thought he was dealing with a lunatic. I didn't dare tell my wife until twenty-five years afterward that I was pretty relieved that I didn't get into that.

Clifford Eunice, a construction engineer, was about to take a job building an ordnance factory.

Yes, sir, I was on a Greyhound bus. It was almost within the city limits of Little Rock, Arkansas. I was working for Dupont and on my way to Pryor, Oklahoma, where we built the Oklahoma Ordnance Works. Dupont had already constructed the powder works on the Mississippi River north of Memphis, known as the Tennessee Powder Works. It was constructed for the British government. We hadn't declared war yet, so the U.S. built a powder works for the British. The bus was loaded. A gentleman on the bus had a small radio, and it was playing real low; then, all at once, he turned it up loud, and the announcer said: "I repeat, we have just received word that the Japs have bombed Pearl Harbor!" You could have heard, sir, a pin hit the floor. Nobody breathed hardly, so they could be sure to hear this newsman. He said: "The damage is not known yet, but we have just received this message that we have definitely been heavily bombed, and we won't have any report on damages until later." The reaction of the people on the bus was a form of paralysis.

Alice Newcomer [Baker] was a student at George Washington University in Washington, D.C.

A very good friend who lived across the hall in the dormitory rushed over, and said, "They've bombed Pearl Harbor! I just heard it on the radio." I said, "Is it bad?" And she said, "It couldn't be worse." So I said, "What do you mean?" She said, "It's going to ruin my senior thesis on our neutrality in Latin America!"

W. P. Laws owned a grocery store in Ocean City, Maryland.

I was in here listening to the radio and they came on the air about two o'clock in the afternoon on Sunday. Dr. Townsend was sitting across the street out front about half asleep and the flies were kind of buzzing around him. But I went over there and woke him up and told him what had happened. I said, "I believe we're in war." Dr. Townsend came over here and he listened and he said, "Yeah, that's Roosevelt for you," or something like that. He was a Republican and he never liked Roosevelt, or made out he didn't.

John Rettaliata and André Hubbard were helping to open a new plant for the Grumman Corporation in Bethpage, Long Island. Grumman builds fighter planes.

RETTALIATA: Plant 2 was then by far the largest plant that we had ever built. It was specifically built to produce the TBF-Avenger, which was the navy's front-line torpedo bomber. We had an open house to show the plant to all our employees and their families, on the actual day— December 7, Sunday. We were there when the announcement came over the loudspeakers. I guess shock was the best way you could express my reaction. I don't think the word was passed on, but I think they got rid of most of the people. I can remember that.

HUBBARD: They thought they had better clear the plant immediately. There could have been sabotage. I remember them taking away the food. We gave orders to remove that. People started to take the hint.

A young boy, Tony Taylor, was doing what most people in Washington were doing.

I was listening to the Redskins football game. I was twelve or thirteen years old. I didn't pay too much mind. I was into the football game. But every time the news came on about it, I knew it was something kind of mean. Even a twelve-year-old kid knew it had to be pretty bad.

I was a youngster, and it didn't hit me like it would somebody a lot older. I felt this through my father and my mother. They were pretty upset, and naturally I was upset because they were concerned. If I was, say, eighteen or nineteen, I would have been thinking about going to school or college or a job. At that age, man, I was a youngster; I could only react through my folks about something like that. I remember them talking about tightening their belts. There was a lot to fear about who was going into the service and what that meant and who would be coming back. I had some cousins who were in the service along with my uncle—the reason I mention my uncle was because he lived with us— and my brother. I don't think my brother was old enough then to go in. He went in later on, but he was still faced with it.

Mabel Wiggins was in Saint Paul, Minnesota, where her husband was managing editor of the St. Paul Pioneer Press and Dispatch.

I was sitting in the living room listening to opera. Russ was upstairs, and I called, and he instantly went to the office. I thought: Here we go, everybody is going to go to war. And I'll stay home. My older son had just graduated from high school, and I knew he'd go. I thought the younger one probably wouldn't. I thought: There they go.

Charles Keller was a professor of history at Williams College in Williamstown, Massachusetts.

I was sitting at my desk, here in this house, reading the proof of a book that was about to appear. We didn't have the radio on. At four o'clock, two young men rang the bell. They were coming for tea. They were both students, seniors at Williams College. One was named Fred Rudolph, and one was named Bob Griggs. And they told us what had happened. At that point we turned on the radio, and that was it. Fred Rudolph is now a professor at Williams College, and he served in the war in the medical corps. Bob Griggs went in the air force and was killed over Berlin. About 1943, it was.

I have to admit, I was one of those who said, though I didn't teach that way, "This is our war, and we should have been in it before." And I had approved everything that Roosevelt had done. I remember the evening of December 6; we were at the faculty club, and the history department's Arthur Buffington, who died shortly after, said, "Don't be surprised if the Japanese attack." So we weren't surprised. I suspect my original reaction was, "It's about time."

Dr. Benjamin Spock:

I was at home working in New York City, where I had been practicing pediatrics since 1933. I remember my wife and my oldest son went to see *Dumbo,* the Disney film. They urged me to come, but I said I had too much desk work to do, so off they went. I had the music station playing, which soothes me when I have to do desk work. The music was interrupted to tell this horrible news, and I had difficulty continuing my work after that. After a while Jane and my son came back from the movies, and my wife said, "Oh, you should have gone, it was wonderful." And I said, "Do you know what has happened? Since you've been away the Japanese have bombed Pearl Harbor." And she said, "You really should have come."

Hezekiah Goodwin was running a dairy farm in Falls Village, Connecticut, in the Canaan Valley, just south of the Massachusetts border.

I lived a mile off the road then, Dudway Road, and we had this farm there. It didn't belong to us, it belonged to my aunt, yah. And we were getting up there with this wood, and we heard it on the radio. Well, we were stunned, of course. And we kept wondering what we were going to do. I had registered for the draft in 1940, but I was deferred and continued to be deferred for occupational reasons. I was running the farm. We milked about sixty cows.

John Holton, at that time the director of quality control for the Carrier Corporation plant in Syracuse, New York, heard the news while he was driving his car.

First, there was disbelief. Then I recognized that something of great importance had happened, I guess is the best way to put it. I began to try to figure what effect it might have on us. The Carrier Corporation had been manufacturing primarily air conditioners and refrigeration and some heating equipment. We knew, of course, from the activities prior to the war, that we were very apt to get into it and were concerned about the future of air conditioning. We'd felt that while it had a lot of industrial uses, it was primarily a luxury rather than a necessity and began to wonder what effect the war would have on the business. As it turned out, it was more of a necessity than we realized.

Democratic Congressman Norman Mineta was ten years old, a Japanese Nisei living in San Jose, California.

We were at home when the news came in. I think we had just come back from church. It was sort of a very quiet situation around the house and then a lot of phone calls coming to the house and people wondering. My dad was a leader in the Japanese community in San Jose, and people would seek him out for advice and for a number of reasons. So when the initial reports started coming in, people would call in, wondering what this means to us.

I've only seen him cry three times, and one was on Pearl Harbor Day. He could not understand why they had attacked Pearl Harbor. He was sitting in his office, which was in the house, wondering why they had done that, crying.

Also, on that day, the FBI started picking up a number of Japanese as suspects. My father was trying to prevent the FBI from arresting a lot of these people. They had done nothing; the only thing that they had done was to be born of Japanese ancestry.

The building next door belonged to the Japanese Association; it was a sort of a community building. The executive director of the association lived in the back of that building with his family, and the FBI came and arrested him on the spot and took him away. Their daughter, who was about my age, came running over, climbing under the hedge, coming into our yard yelling that they were taking her father away and crying as she ran. So my dad went next door to see what was going on, but by that time, in less than fifteen minutes, they had picked him up, and boom! he was taken away.

I really didn't know what was going on. But I remember my dad saying at mealtime that night: "They may take me, they may take Mom, but remember you are American citizens. They can't do these things to you, and whatever happens to any of us, this is our family home."

Thomas Page, in his last year at Harvard Law School, was at the Aga-wam Hunt Club in Providence, Rhode Island, with a friend who was skeet shooting.

I was sitting in a car listening to the New York Symphony when I heard it. For some odd reason, it did not really surprise me. The fact of Pearl Harbor, I think, surprised me, but I had decided about two weeks before, there was a very strong likelihood of war. There was an English couple, a guy named Tom Harris and his wife, who did a thing called mass observation. They would observe what people were eating, reading, and the way of advertisements to determine what people really were doing. His theory was that it isn't what people told you they were doing, but what they really were doing. And I looked at the *New York Times Sunday Magazine*, maybe a week or two before Pearl Harbor. It was filled with semiwarlike copy and ads. And I thought, my God, this is really an illustration of this guy Harris's theory of mass observation—the country has almost accepted the inevitability of some kind of military action and is all geared up for it mentally. And they were bellicose. I remember very clearly saying to myself: If that guy is right, we're on the verge of war.

Ten-year-old Ray Hartman in Chicago remembers that day vividly.

I was at the Bears' professional football game in Chicago, Illinois, that Sunday, and they stopped the game and announced that Pearl Harbor had been attacked by the Japs. There was complete silence really—shock, I think, at first—and then there was a great disbelief. People really couldn't understand the impact of it at the moment. At my age it seemed a little glamorous, because I had an older brother that was anxious to enlist and I just idolized him for thinking that way and wanted to do the same thing he did.

At Leon Sylvester's gas station near Sedgwick, Maine, a gathering of Down Easters remember Pearl Harbor—Sylvester, Forrest Eaton, James Saunders, and later they were joined by Ronald Gray.

EATON: I was lobstering. I got the news when I got home. I don't remember how I heard it, but I heard it. I thought it was an awful thing, was what I thought.

SAUNDERS: I was working on a dairy farm in North Blue Hill. Yep. The first I got the news was from the *Bangor Daily News*. It must have been the next day. I don't remember my reaction. But that was 1941, and in 1942 I went to work for the South Portland Shipyard. All my friends were going to work there at the same time. I thought it would help out quite a lot more than it would to stay on the farm. And it commanded better wages—much better.

SYLVESTER: I was in Stonington, Maine. I just been to a wedding, and the fellow that was married was called out at midnight; they had to get him out of the camp; he had to go back into the service. My reaction to Pearl Harbor and the war was that there was nothing I could do—just pay attention and mind my own business.

GRAY: Pearl Harbor didn't change my life much. I kept right on lobstering.

Peggy Blassingame was eleven years old and lived on an island in the Gulf of Mexico, off Bradenton, Florida.

I was sitting in the living room at home in Anna Maria, Florida, and my mother was very, very pregnant. She was listening to the news; I am sure I was not—I would have had no interest in the news—and she started to cry, "Oh, my God! Oh, my God! The Japanese have bombed us. It's war! It's war!" I had my girl friend with me, Polly Moore. My father was down on the beach shooting shells with a friend with a BB gun, and at that time there were no other people on the beach. Polly and I just took off out of the house; war sounded pretty terrifying. We ran down to the beach, and when I saw my father, I started yelling that the Japanese had bombed Pearl Harbor. They didn't believe me, and we kept yelling, and finally they started running as fast as they could. The rest of the day is very blurred, but I do remember my initial reaction to my mother's reaction to the news, and I was scared.

I guess I had heard about the First World War. I knew that war meant people got killed, but I hadn't been raised with a war. My father is a writer, and I did not think about how the war might affect him. I was just scared that they were all going to come and kill us. At the time I never even realized that he would be going into the war. Soldiers were soldiers and they fought, and I guess writers were writers and they stayed home and wrote.

Mary Moore Lacey was married to her first husband, a naval aviator assigned to a torpedo squadron on the U.S.S. Yorktown. She was in Norfolk, Virginia.

The *Yorktown* had been out in Pearl, and in the fall of '41 it came around to the East Coast, and we wives had met the ship up in Portland, Maine. They were in the northern Atlantic for a while, and then in November we went to Norfolk and lived in a hotel down on Virginia Beach. There was a whole crowd of wives down there in temporary quarters.

Pearl Harbor kind of stunned us. But, at the same time, we weren't really awfully surprised, because there had been a lot of rumors around Hawaii when we had been there the summer before. People in Hawaii in those days talked about moving up into the hills and finding a cave and putting food away in the hills, to get ready for the Japanese attacks. It was something that was going to come. It was a strange atmosphere. Still, there was immediate traumatic reaction. I felt as though I had been hit in the solar plexus. Then, if you tried to think about it for a minute, you'd rationalize that they were naval officers and military flyers; that was their profession. As navy wives, we had a role to play too. So we all had a stiff upper lip, and that's what we had to do. The news was devastating! We kept saying, where is the fleet, where is everybody? There was an immediate reaction of indecision, because the *Yorktown* was scheduled for dry dock, and we all breathed sort of a sigh of temporary relief. We knew the boys were going to be around for a while. And then the word came that the *Yorktown* had come back to the air station and they were loading all the planes aboard. She was supposed to be sea ready—almost immediately. One day it was on, one day it was off. When it really did leave, it was almost as though we were relieved from the terrible tension.

Peter Scaglione was working in the front bar at the Columbia Restaurant in Tampa, Florida.

Everybody was so excited—and later they heard the president say that the war was on. Everybody was so mad. Some boys who were friends of mine said, "I'm going to the war right now. I'm going against those Japs." They joined up right away.

37

Young Hugh Sidey in Greenfield, Iowa:

I had just gotten back from attending Sunday School and church, which we always did every Sunday and then had Sunday dinner. I can't remember whether we had had dinner or were preparing to have dinner, but I was up in my bedroom changing clothes. You always changed into your play clothes after church; and we always had the radio on during Sunday dinner—the Longine Symphonette, which we played as a kind of background music for our Sunday dinner. Suddenly I heard my mother exclaim and then call up the stairs: "The Japanese have attacked us."

Necei Degen in Massachusetts:

I was in Malden, a Sunday afternoon. Cold. Sunny. About noontime. I was walking to a friend's home. Arriving. A hushed household. Radio on. And there it was.

My initial reaction was one of great somberness, because I realized this was going to change my life.

I must have been twelve years old. But I had a great sense of history. I had been into the Civil War at that point, and I was into the romantic novels of that period. I felt it in my bones, I really did, very keenly.

Anna Mae Lindberg was living in a suburb of Pittsburgh, where her husband worked in a U.S. Steel mill.

I remember like it was yesterday. I was sitting at the sewing machine making something, and I had the radio on. My husband was working in the mill. We were in a two-family house; and I remember running down the stairs and telling the people downstairs to turn on their radio, that something big had happened. I don't know whether I was naïve, but it was just a complete shock to me, and I remember not being able to absorb it. My husband and I were just the age. We had brothers and sisters who were all going to be involved. We thought, this is not the radioman's war; this is our war. My first instinct was for survival—how to keep my people out of it. There wasn't any great thing: "This is my country, we are going to have to make do and go save everybody!" That's not true. I wouldn't have said this before Vietnam.

Dorothy Currier was working for the Massachusetts Farm Bureau in Waltham.

I was going to the movies in my car when the news came over my car radio. I kept on, not realizing the impact at the moment, and went to the movies, but when I got in, they had stopped the show. A man came out in front of the curtain and said, "Pearl Harbor has been attacked." I had no brothers, and my father was way too old to be involved. I wasn't married, so I had no personal contact with the war. I was completely and utterly shocked and unbelieving. I just didn't believe it. Nobody would attack the United States! I had been to Pearl Harbor in 1930. I took what I thought was a halfway-around-the-world-trip in 1930, and I ended up in Scofield Barracks. It was nothing but a play army. They gave parties, and we went to dances and Chinese restaurants. All I could think of immediately was Scofield Barracks, up there in those beautiful mountains of Hawaii, and the planes coming zooming in. It hit me awfully hard in that respect, because I had visited this peaceful, calm island that hadn't been discovered except by the U.S. Army.

Judson Phillips, a free-lance writer—mostly of detective novels:

I was sitting in the kitchen in a farmhouse in Vermont listening to the New York Giants football team play somebody or other; and I guess eight million other people were, too, because it happened on a Sunday afternoon during pro football time. I didn't know where Pearl Harbor was. But every ten minutes after that, there was more on it. So it wasn't very long before we realized it wasn't just a little bombing somewhere. I was thirty-eight years old, married, and I thought, "Jesus, I might have to go to war at this late date." I had missed World War I by being slightly too young. I would have been drafted then in another year, and as it finally turned out, while I registered for the draft in this war, I was too old—by a slight shade, unless it had gotten worse.

R. W. Danichefsky was working in Detroit for the Reconstruction Finance Corporation, concerned with financing such war industries as the Packard Motor Company, which was making engines for the British, and Continental Motors, which was making tank engines.

I had just come in from a golf game and stopped to see a cousin of mine I hadn't seen for some time. We were sitting listening to the radio when the news came in. My reaction was one of complete surprise and some bewilderment as to what we would be doing. I had been assigned to Detroit, and we had five projects going in the area. We would soon have forty-two. I don't think most of us thought much at that time about what the effect on our own personal lives was going to be. I think it was more a feeling of we had a job to do and let's get it done.

John R. Shepley, an eighty-one-year-old Saint Louis banker, has lived through more than one war.

I was driving home on the Ladue Road in Saint Louis County, and I was actually crossing the terminal railroad tracks, and I had my radio on, and the news of Pearl Harbor came over the radio—and I said: "Here we go again."

Mary Speir was married and living in Westminster, Maryland, with her husband and only son.

When I heard the news, I was worried about my son, who was in college at Western Maryland. I naturally hoped the war would be over before he would ever get into it; I was scared all the time and worried all the time about it. He never was drafted. He enlisted in the air force, and then they shifted those boys from the air force when they needed infantrymen. He went right through England into Belgium. My husband caught up with him and saw him and had a five-day leave with him two weeks before he was killed.

Mary Devereux Crist's husband was in the marines, stationed at the navy yard in Philadelphia.

I had come from Philadelphia down to my mother's house in Chevy Chase, Maryland, bringing my six-week-old baby on the day coach. My mother was just cutting her seventieth birthday cake when we got a telephone call from a friend saying that the Japanese—I'll say *Japanese*, I usually say *Japs*; I can't get over how I feel about them; anyway—that the Japanese had bombed Pearl Harbor; and there was a great to-do about how I'd get back to Philadelphia, where my husband and two boys were. I didn't believe it was the whole Japanese Empire. I thought some isolated group of dissidents under the Japanese admirals had strayed away from orders that had been given them.

We were told not to go to the railroad stations, so I had to figure out some kind of formula to give my baby. And the next day my husband was immediately ordered to put on his uniform and stand by in his quarters for further orders.

One ten-year-old boy living in Corpusville, Indiana, never quite got over the excitement of Pearl Harbor and the war. Twenty-nine years later Richard Lingeman published a best-selling book, Don't You Know There's a War On? The American Home Front—1941–1945.

I have a fairly clear memory that I was listening to the radio, I guess to a football game. I don't remember exactly hearing the words announcing it but just that I had heard the words. But I remember going out, seeking a friend who lived next door who was my age, as if I had a need to see somebody. Something that was kind of vast and beyond comprehension had happened. It was certainly exciting, though not exactly fear, but a kind of vague anxiety too. I can remember the next day at school the teachers talking about it and a lot of rumors going around. I remember one of the teachers said, "They've got Wake. . . ."

Alice Marriott in Washington, D.C.:

We were sitting in our library at home on Garfield Street and we heard over the radio that Pearl Harbor had been attacked. We were very upset about the whole thing, especially since our friend Capt. Merlin S. Benyon had been called to the Pacific on duty and was on the *West Virginia,* and they didn't say right off whether it had been sunk or not. They said so many of the ships had gone down, and then, of course, it came out in the paper that he stayed on the bridge and commanded his ship and was shot in the stomach. He was one of the heroes of the battle. He commanded the ship while he was dying.

In Mount Pleasant, Michigan, Betty Bryce was having company.

We just finished dinner when the news came over the radio. I was stunned, because we knew things were going on but never expected anything like that. My son, at that time, was about fifteen, and, of course, I thought the war would be over before he ever gets there. I had two sons. The other was two years younger. I thought both of them would escape. Even up till he was a senior in high school, I kept thinking he wouldn't have to go, because it was getting near the end of the war. He was killed just six weeks before the war ended.

Richard Spitzer and his wife were living in Shortsville, New York, thirty miles south of Rochester.

That's a date my wife and I remember very easily because our first child was born on December 9, and my wife went to the hospital in Rochester for that birth, and the hospital was blacked out under emergency conditions.

Pauline Christensen, a widow with two young sons in Evansville, Illinois:

It was Sunday, and we were sitting at home, and the housekeeper came tearing in to tell us what she had just heard on the radio; I thought it was catastrophic! It just seemed unbelievable. I was in the education publishing business, and I had two sons—one in grammar school and one in junior high school. They were too young for the service, and this was one reason, I think, I felt that I had to get involved and make a contribution to the war effort. So I joined the Red Cross Motor Corps as a driver.

Patricia Pavlic was a navy wife, living in Annapolis, Maryland.

My husband was on duty at the Naval Academy. We were having a cocktail with friends—and, of course, nobody believed it. It was a shock! But immediately the men called in and were ordered back to the academy. There was no waiting. They reported back to see what was to be done. Very shortly after that, on the seventeenth of December, my second child was born, early by a month or so, I'm sure because of the shock.

Francis Martin, the president of the First National Bank and Trust Company in Ridgefield, Connecticut, was listening to the radio.

We were naturally upset, because it was a terrible thing. To think that our people fell asleep and weren't aware of what was going to happen. We had one Ridgefield man who was one of the head ones in the navy, and he never should have been in at all. I won't mention his name, but he was one of the ones asleep. It was too bad.

David Soergal was an engineering student at the University of Wisconsin in Madison.

I was in my room doing some homework, and I remember the news coming over a small radio that my roommate and I had. I turned back to my studies and continued. No comment from my roommate. We were nearing the period of final exams for the first semester, and people were more concerned about getting good grades than about a war starting. It was almost a subconscious awareness that the engineering people and the scientific people were not going to get involved.

Helen Wilson, in Mount Pleasant, Michigan:

I was a high school student. It was one of those traumatic times when you felt something important was going on. I had an older brother, and the thought immediately was that he would have to go. There was no women's lib then, and you thought in terms of: "This will affect my brother." I didn't particularly like him, but nevertheless he was my brother. He was two and a half years older and ripe for the draft. He went off from Mount Pleasant someplace to be examined physically, and he was not really a strong boy, and you sort of hoped he'd get through it. We really thought he would be disappointed if he didn't make it. I think at that time teen-agers—I hope others besides myself— were so wrapped up in themselves. We didn't read a lot, we didn't have television. We were concerned more with our day-to-day life, and my brother was off someplace. I hoped he'd be all right, but it wasn't any real concern.

Sally Lucke was a little girl living in Columbus, Ohio, where her father worked for the Galena Shale and Tile Company.

It was a really beautiful day, and my Dad was out working in the yard right next to the window, and I was in the living room playing the piano. The radio was on in the background, and they came in with the news of the bombing of Pearl Harbor. I had no sense of fear, it was just like total amazement at first, and then I ran out into the yard and told my father what had happened. His reaction was anger!

I was not very aware at that age of people going off to war. I was just mainly afraid that my father would be going off to war, and I can remember being afraid we'd be bombed.

Eleanor Kuhne was working for the Washington Gas and Light Company in Georgetown. She doesn't remember why she happened to be at work, but she heard it on a radio at the office.

I was shocked. Nobody was expecting that. At least nobody that I knew. I felt that they had a heck of a nerve attacking us, like a mosquito attacking a rhinoceros. But I didn't feel that we would lose the war. I thought people would be hurt and killed. I felt the horror of that at the bombing of Pearl Harbor.

Kent Chetlain was in his first year of high school in Winnetka, Illinois.

My father, who is still practicing law in Chicago and almost eighty years old, had foreseen the approach of World War II and felt that we should buy a farm so that we would be assured plenty of food in case of scarcities, which ultimately developed. So we were in the process of looking at farms. It was a cold, wintry day, and we had blankets on our legs because our heater didn't work in our car. We were en route from Glencoe to Woodstock, Illinois.

Like everybody else, we were astounded. I guess our reaction was no different than millions of other people.

Mary Dandouveris lived in Racine, Wisconsin. She was in high school at the time, the oldest of six children.

We were all sitting around home listening to one of our favorite radio programs when they interrupted to tell us, and we couldn't believe it. As teen-agers we tended to romanticize. I was a great buff of the Civil and Revolutionary wars and I remember thinking: "Oh, what a thrilling experience this is going to be to live through a war!" It took a couple of years before maturation set in so that I began to fully appreciate the horrors of the war. But I'll never forget that first instant of thinking what a glamorous, romantic period this was going to be.

Smith Johnson owned a small rubber plant in Middlefield, Ohio.

We had just driven back from Warren, Ohio, and when we got to Middlefield about five-thirty, we turned the radio on, and that's where we got the news. Of course, I was shocked like everyone else, and I knew we were in the war, and it flashed through my mind, "What's going to happen to me? What's going to happen to the family? What's going to happen to the business?" We had a business there with five hundred people, and I was president of it.

We were manufacturing rubber products for civilian use. We didn't have a single job for the government. I realized immediately that the rubber business was probably going to be affected, and, boy, was it ever! The next week I laid off three hundred of our employees and kept more or less of a skeleton crew.

2

WASHINGTON AT WAR

The impact of the attack on Pearl Harbor was almost as dramatic on Washington as it was on Honolulu. As Bryson Rash says of the nation's capital: On December 6, "you seldom, if ever, saw a uniform on the street. By the evening of December 7, there were uniforms all over the place." A. E. Dolph Hoehling, a young Naval Reserve ensign on duty in the old Navy Department on Constitution Avenue, who later wrote a book, *Homefront USA*, recalls his impression of that night, watching the soldiers "in their World War I tin hats and Enfield rifles," roll in over the bridges. "I remember the trucks coming in all night long. They had a dimout and finally there was a yellow glow on all the Washington streets. I would say it was about 10 P.M. before we had a full complement. I stayed until about three in the morning. The city was buzzing all night long."

President Franklin D. Roosevelt, the man who had put the nation on the road to economic recovery in 1939, quickly became the nation's wartime leader, our commander-in-chief. And with FDR providing the words and inspiration, almost overnight Washington was transformed from a sleepy little southern town, as more than one person I talked to described it, into the capital of a free world. With Paris burning, London under siege, and Moscow threatened with a Nazi invasion, the people of the Allied nations instinctively looked to Washington—invulnerable from land, sea, and air attacks—as the center of Allied resistance.

For Americans, Washington became the focal point of everything that went on in the nation. Washington regulated prices; allocated scarce commodities; rationed gasoline, tires, sugar, shoes, meat; organized a nationwide system of civil defense and blackouts; awarded defense contracts; told the farmers what they could and could not plant and industry what it could and could not produce. And the War Department, soon to be housed in its huge pentagon-shaped headquarters across the Potomac in Virginia, recruited the nation's young men and women, and drafted as many additional men as it needed to build an army, navy and air force that would turn back the enemy in Europe and the Pacific. At the same time, Washington became the communications center of the nation. The Office of War Information, assisted by the nation's newspapers, magazines, and radio networks, kept the nation informed of the latest war news as well as of the stream of regulations and orders pouring out of Washington.

To arouse this great sleeping giant of America, and transform it into the most devastating war machine in the world, Washington needed people— and they came to town by the thousands. One of them, Smith Johnson, who had to close his small rubber plant in Ohio immediately after Pearl Harbor, tells how he decided to come to Washington: "I went out to lunch with a fellow in Cleveland—this was about December 20th—and he said, 'Let's have our tea leaves read.' I said I never thought that tea leaves were anything to go by but that I would. The lady came over and looked in the cup and said to me, 'Well, you're going to make a big change.' I said, 'What's that?' and she said, 'You're going away and work at another job. You're going to work in Washington.' I said, 'Who, me? In Washington? When's all this going to happen?' She said, 'On the 13th of January.'

"I didn't really think of going to Washington, but after awhile I began to think, well, why not? So on the twelfth day of January—which was no preconceived plan, I didn't even think about it until quite awhile afterwards—I packed my grip, got on the train, and went to Washington, knowing nothing about it at all. I had heard there was a rubber office there, so I went up there that morning and told them my name was Johnson and that I was president of Johnson Rubber Company in Middlefield, Ohio. This fellow said, 'What do you want?' 'Well, nothing,' I said. 'I just came down to help you win the war.' He said, 'Who sent for you?' I said, 'Nobody. I just came down. I know you're going to need help.' He said, 'Wait a minute.' He went back and talked with the boss and they came out and we had a talk and, would you believe it, twenty minutes later I was on the payroll."

In different ways, thousands of Americans shared Mr. Johnson's experience, and in the following pages a few of them recall what it was like to work in Washington during World War II.

Stephen Ailes came up from Martinsburg, West Virginia, to work for the Office of Price Administration. He still lives in Washington today—as president of the American Railroad Association.

The city then was full of a lot of people running around not sure what they were doing. Although a lifelong Democrat, I had been quite disillusioned with FDR's ability to run anything, and I was terribly concerned about how the government was going to get organized to fight the war. However, when I went to work in OPA, I was overcome by the enthusiasm, the dedication, of everybody in that place. Working in a war agency was a hell of an experience. You just routinely worked till midnight; you worked Saturdays. You always had in mind the fact that all these guys were in foxholes someplace or sitting out on some cold deck somewhere. All of us had relatives and pals doing that, and the result was that the amount of effort you put out to do a good job in these war agencies was incredible. I was in OPA for four and a half years, and I remember thinking, I'll never again work in a situation quite like this where there's so damn much enthusiasm and so much cooperation, so little rivalry. Everybody just had to get the job done.

I suppose I was as well educated as most people around, but the word *inflation* was literally not in my vocabulary. The idea that you could have a spiral up and a spiral down was something that was lost on me. But early on, you began to understand what the hell was going on there and that OPA did a hell of a job. I worked with Mike LaSalle and the people in OPS later, and I watched this last price control effort, and we talked about double-digit inflation without doing anything about it. But you know, at OPA we were trying to hold the line, and we thought a point-one increase in prices was a disaster. You take a look at the four or five years that OPA control remained in effect: I bet the total increase in the cost-of-living index isn't over 2 or 3 percent. A remarkable job. It had a lot of concomitant bad results, you understand.

Funny thing, most of the people who worked in that area did not believe in price controls as a way of coping with that kind of problem, because what you do is to create great distortions in the economy, and you don't get at the cause of the trouble.

I was in the end of the business where we were writing the regulations. OPA was also in the rationing business, and then we had an enforcement department. We had industry people working with us, and they fell into two categories. There were people who understood what the hell this was all about and believed very strongly that it would be bad if the price level went way up in the country; there were a lot of guys overseas whose families are going to be in great hardship because of the nature of the allotment. Don't forget, that soldier, in '42, made something like thirty-one dollars a month. A lot of people understood that. But you still had a lot of boneheads who said: "I've got a right to raise my price. One of the rights of the private enterprise system is to set the prices on your product. The government shouldn't be interfering with that." You just have to tell people like that that they just don't get the point.

You also ran into some chislers but not a great many. Interestingly enough, if you have an enforcement department which will go after the chislers, the remaining 95 percent of the people will comply. The one thing that loses compliance altogether is the notion that you're making a sucker out of a guy, that he's complying but the guy down the street is not. But if you say, "You have an obligation to comply, and we're enforcing that obligation," then the guy will do it, and you get damn good compliance.

There were all kinds of people right through American industry who were absolutely determined that they were going to live up to the requirements the government put on them.

But it was a war situation. We had nine or ten million people in the service, the casualty lists were coming in, the future of the country was at stake, and it was the patriotic thing to do. Subsequent efforts at price control have been a different situation.

I remember Washington as being not too bad a place to live during the war. It did cost you a little bit more money, but not a hell of a lot. I remember I was paying $45 a month for the house we rented in Martinsburg, a big old farmhouse, and I'm quite sure that the house I rented down here, down by Fort Belvoir, a beautiful country place, small, probably cost me something like $50 a month. Nothing was all that expensive in 1942. Scotch was about $2.98 a bottle; later, you couldn't get it. I remember a standard you would get when you went to somebody's house was rum old-fashioneds, just awful! Booze, good whisky, was just terribly scarce.

I'd say that one of the startling things for me was that it was the first time I'd ever worked with blacks. When you came here in '42, there were black secretaries. And I'll never forget, a fellow called me up—a lawyer—and asked me if I'd come up and explain to him some part of one of our regulations. I went up, opened the door, and walked in his office, and I'm sure I must have looked just as startled as I could be to find a black sitting behind the table. I never even thought about there being a black lawyer. This fellow was a professor at Howard, extremely able. This was just a totally new experience.

Al Sweeney was from Cleveland, Ohio. He served in the navy three months in 1941, until he contracted pneumonia and was discharged because of a spot on his lung.

I had graduated from Wilberforce University in Ohio—they call it Central State University now—before I went into the service. Right after I got discharged, I was given a TR, or whatever they called it, for a Pullman back to Cleveland, on the old C&O Railroad. When I got down there, they wouldn't give me a Pullman. So I got angry, tore that TR up, and caught a Greyhound bus to Washington. In those days, you know, there was discrimination. I always wanted to come to the nation's capital, so I came to Washington.

I got a room at the Twelfth Street YMCA in Washington, where I stayed for several years. And the first job I had was as a building guard at the Department of Commerce. Then, after about two or three weeks, I got a job with the General Accounting Office as a clerk. In those days they called a civil service grade CAF; I guess I was CAF-2, made about $1,440 a year. I stayed there about a year and went over to the Office of Price Administration, first as a clerk, and then got involved with several of the black employees who felt they were being underutilized. They were college graduates too. At that time, the OPA, under Leon Henderson, was a pretty progressive agency, probably way ahead of its time, as far as equal or fair employment practices were concerned. Finally they hired me as a junior economist. In those days they called it P-1 grade.

As I recall, it was the first time blacks in government got really top jobs. The head of sugar rationing was a fellow by the name of Charles Quick, a lawyer. Robert Ming became the interstate-commerce commissioner. He was a big attorney in the Office of Price Administration. It was probably the most liberal agency that came along to this day. Outside my experience with the Office of Transportation, it was probably the most interesting government job I ever had. After Henderson left, a fellow by the name of Chester Bowles came in. He introduced visual aids in the presentation of the budget, and used a lot of the advertising techniques in getting the job done. He was very creative.

And there was a very good spirit in the agency at the time. OPA got a lot of criticism because of price control, but it was a good agency.

Several of us blacks made a breakthrough because of OPA. We got professional experience there. I remember a fellow named Louis Welters, in personnel, who later became personnel officer in one of the large agencies. But he would not have gotten that experience without the opportunities at OPA. Right after the war they sent me over to the International Monetary Fund. That was about the only place we could go, but they wouldn't hire me. They had a lot of excuses. But I had an ace in the hole. While I was in college, I used to work on the college newspaper. So when I left OPA, I began working for newspapers.

For Tom Page, a young man in his mid twenties, working in Washington during the war was a heady experience.

I went to work shortly after I was married, which was on December 8, 1942, for an agency called the Board of Economic Warfare—partly because I liked the guy I was going to work for, W. Park Armstrong. Then I discovered the guy I liked so much had gone somewhere else! A typical government story. So for a couple of years I was engaged in a lot of things, like collecting information about enemy countries to be used as target information. For example, where in the German aircraft production line do you bomb to achieve a certain effect? Would you bomb airframe factories or would you bomb the people who made the motors or would you bomb the aluminum plants? At that time, we were mainly after things like aluminum plants. In later years we turned to things like ball bearings. I remember seeing a document of our British counterpart in our files. It laid out basically the whole bombing programs of the British government for the next year and a half. I was amazed that you could find this while wandering around in somebody's files. Almost anyone could see the damned thing; we all had security clearance, but it didn't mean much.

During the war years our interests were identical with those of the Soviet Union. And our agency had a whole apartment building at 2501 Q Street loaded with refugees, interesting people—a Babel of languages, a wealth of information, and a lot of them had come out of very liberal backgrounds. When the war in Europe was drawing to its close, the interests of the Soviet Union started to go in different directions. I had an idea that the industrialization of Japan had been done by three nations, the U.S., England, and Germany, which had built most of the major factories in Japan. This information was very useful for the purpose of bombing targets, and my idea was to get hold of what had been done in Germany to round out our picture. So we put together a whole team of people, and we ran around the United States and England asking everybody who had worked in Japan where to go in Germany to find what we wanted to know about Japan. We would go to people and say, "Who are your German counterparts? Who represented German engineering firms in Japan? Who represented Krupp for gun manufacture, steel companies? All of the companies, where were they? Who were the people?"

We built a whole file. We had a bunch of women who did this. The job was called the Page Project, as they had to put a name on it for security reasons.

By this time the divergence between the policies of the Soviet Union and the United States was quite apparent, and some of the people I worked with didn't agree with the postwar policies of the government of the United States. So one day I was sitting in my office when a guy showed up and said he's Lt. Cmdr. So-and-So, and he understands I'm an expert on Germany. Well, I didn't want to deny this, so I said, "Yeah, sure." "Well," he said, "the question I would like to ask you" (mind you, he had just walked in the room, no call ahead or anything else) "is where would you go in Germany to find out about Russia?" God, I thought this guy was a fool to come in and ask what was a very sensitive question. So I said, "Let's go out; I want to get some fresh air."

I told him I didn't think he should go around our building asking this question. Well, he said he didn't really want to ask anybody but me. So I went down to his office and told him where I thought you'd go in Germany to find out about Russia—what government agency would have all the files. What I told him was elementary. But I thought it was terribly delicate, because the Russians could set you up, catch you trying to do it, and then have a big diplomatic uproar. Actually, the U.S. did go in and grab that section of German intelligence that dealt with the Soviet Union, including some of the key personnel. We grabbed all their records, and we grabbed a German general who was an expert on the Soviet Union. We grabbed the Foreign Office files, we grabbed everything we could get our hands on. As I remember, the Russians did complain.

The Board of Economic Warfare was a lead-time agency. It dealt with bombing targets—where you were trying to strike at the industrial capacity of a nation—and blockades. But by 1944 the war had moved into occupational phases—they were landing and driving tanks through the valleys—and economic warfare faded out in significance.

I was going to go back to California, but a friend who lived here said, "Oh, don't do that. I know a guy who would love to have you. He worked for a thing called Office of War Mobilization and Reconversion for a general named Lucius Clay, and Justice James Byrnes." I asked someone who Clay was, and he came back a day later and said he was probably the most powerful man in Washington. So I said: "How come the general has so much clout?" And this guy said to me, "One of the Clays of Georgia, his grandfather, was in the Senate, and as a young boy General Clay was a page boy in the Senate. He's kind of got relations with the Senate." And I said, "What about the House?" He said, "Well, as a young engineer officer he built a dam called the Red River Dam. Biggest thing that ever happened in the congressional district." And I said, "Whose congressional district?" He said, "A congressman called Sam Rayburn. Sam's always thought that was the finest thing that could have happened in his district and that's one of the finest men he ever met." I said, "You don't have to tell me a helluva lot more."

Planning for blackouts was a fascinating exercise. I think General Clay or somebody felt that the United States was sitting up singing and dancing all night. Goddamn it, they ought to get next to the war effort. No more of this fancy civilian living. So we would have blackouts. This would curb the Sodom and Gomorrah aspects while everybody was being frozen to death in Europe. Everything was supposed to close— places of entertainment and public assembly—at midnight, every night, effective almost immediately! The general just issued this order, as I remember, but it really was illegal. It never got published in the *Federal Register*, where you publish legal documents, because everybody said it wasn't legal. One of the reasons given for the blackout was that it would save coal needed for the war effort. Actually, all the electrical plants that operate on coal have an immense excess capacity after ten o'clock at night. So there's no energy saving of any kind; but this was the alleged reason, so you couldn't let it get into the form of an Executive order, because it would get litigated and upset.

You had to get people to agree without ever litigating. The thing was comic. There were two old ladies who had chili parlors in Washington with an all-night trade, and they refused to close. Byrnes wrote them a letter on White House stationery saying that the national war effort required that they comply with the law and close. And the old ladies wrote back in their scribble that they didn't use much power and they made very good chili and they weren't going to close. It all got in the paper, but we never could get it to the lawyers. There was also a fag joint that wouldn't close. So somebody said, "Can't we get to the Washington police and get them to bust it on the grounds that it's a homosexual hangout?" As I remember now, the commissioner of police thought it was a damn-fool order and wouldn't have anything to do with it. So the order ended up in our office, with everybody complaining all over the United States.

The whole country started questioning the point of this blackout. Arbitrary bureaucracy! It became a helluva hot potato.

And then suddenly Mayor LaGuardia, under pressure from New York night-life industry, announced that night life was a special part of the economic life of New York, and they were going to stay open until three o'clock, or whatever. He just announced that despite the federal restrictions and regardless of the rest of the country, they were going to stay open until three.

Overnight this stream of fire hoses that the press had played on us just swung and played on New York. The rest of the United States then said: "New York may be unpatriotic, but we're not. We're going to do our part for the boys overseas. It's disgraceful that New York cannot see its way to do the same."

Meanwhile, we all were trying to figure out how the hell to get out of the blackout mess. This took the heat off for the moment, and then spring may have come, or something happened in a matter of weeks, and we said, "The coal shortage is now ended, and we are happy to announce we can eliminate the blackout."

We got into almost anything that came along. For example, we got into planning for V-E Day. Germany was in shambles; nobody knew whether they'd won or lost, because there was no one to announce they'd lost. As I remember, we sat around for a month and planned exactly what we'd do on V-E Day, then we decided when it would come, which it inevitably would, and what was the best time to have it. What do you do? Do you close the government? Do you close war-production plants—you still have a war going in the Far East? What kind of holiday do you have? Who makes speeches on the radio? You plan it like you would a great event. Sunday is a dead day, so, I think, everyone agreed that if you have an option when to announce, you wouldn't do it Sunday. And then you assign some day during the week and you don't do it at midnight in the United States, because everybody's in bed. So you do it in a manner designed to have everybody celebrate Victory 1 with a minimum dislocation in terms of moving on toward Victory Number 2, which still lay ahead and was going to be a messy problem.

I remember going to a meeting about it at the Commerce Department. Representatives of all the agencies of the government were there except the Office of War Information. You'd think they would have been the ones to plan it, but they weren't even there. I was sent at the last minute. And suddenly, after they went through what they're going to shut down, whether the day off would be with or without pay, what the unions will do, somebody said, "There is no one here from the War Shipping Administration. Are they going to close the shipyards that day?" Someone else said, "Mr. Page is here from the Department of War Mobilization. He can decide for them." Here I am, twenty-five or twenty-six years old. Chrissake, shipyards all over, millions of people working in them. And I thought, I just can't say I'll go home and find out. I got to make the decision. So I said, "Yes."

After the meeting I ran back to my office and said, "For better or worse I've closed the shipyards on V-E Day!"

Life in Washington was kind of interesting during the war. Generals were big out in the country. One star—a brigadier general—was a big man. But in Washington I remember riding in a bus, hanging on a strap, right next to a guy with one star. They were nothing much. You needed at least two or three stars to make an impression. Lot of brass.

I think you always felt sort of guilty being out of uniform. I had a theory that everybody overseas really would like to be back in the United States living it up. And everybody in the United States felt guilty about being in the United States and thought they ought to be overseas. So nobody, in that sense, was happy.

There were only a couple of restaurants that were any good. One was opposite the Mayflower. I remember that well because it was a fairly good French restaurant. I was eating there one time when the president of Haiti came here on a state visit. He was black, and he wanted to go eat in a restaurant. The problem was, Washington was segregated. How do you do it?

Well, they had an orchestra in this restaurant. Somebody came up with a marvelous solution. The president of Haiti arrived with his party. The orchestra stood up and played the Haitian national anthem, or maybe it was "The Star-Spangled Banner." Somebody in a loud voice announced, "Ladies and gentlemen, the president of Haiti," to which he marched down to his table and sat down. Otherwise, they wouldn't have served him.

It was an exciting, exhilarating time, particularly as the enemy started to collapse. People would come back with bottles of champagne; they'd cross French and German flags, and we'd sit around drinking champagne to celebrate the end of the fall of France. And people wandered in and out arranging missions, capitulations. It was interesting.

Alice Newcomer Baker found herself immersed in the war effort immediately after graduating from George Washington University.

I graduated in 1943 and went to work for the Lend-Lease Program as an economic analyst. It was a very small organization, only four or five hundred employees, and yet they handled billions of dollars worth of war materials. It really was the agency which established the orderly economic way of supplying war materials to our allies. The atmosphere at Lend Lease was great because you felt you were doing something that was worth doing. It was pretty heady for someone who was twenty-one years old.

I worked in a section called Reverse Lend Lease. We were responsible for encouraging assistance to the United States from our allies to the extent that this could be given without involving foreign currency. The problem was not what they could do; the problem, especially for the British, was how many dollars they had. For example, if bases were built for the Americans in Britain, and British workmen were used to construct the base, the British paid the workmen and the cost was entered as reverse lend lease, a war contribution from Britain to the United States. Obviously, it couldn't even out financially, but that was not the idea. It was to even out with "equality of sacrifice." And the criterion always was: Is it an essential war material? And the next question was: If it is nonessential war material, can the ally afford it?

There was never any question of our supplying planes, ammunition, all those materials. That obviously was sent as lend lease. But when we got into things we called "essential civilian supplies"—food stuffs and related materials—to what extent should we supply these to the British population on lend lease, and where do we draw the line? I remember there were endless memoranda about toilet paper, whether it was an essential civilian supply which the government should finance or whether the British should pay for the toilet paper that we sent. I don't remember how that one came out. But those things just went on endlessly.

I remember only one other woman in the Lend-Lease Administration who was in a professional position, and that was a woman who was perhaps thirty, thirty-five. She was a lawyer. In day-to-day doing things it was quite a handicap to me to be a woman. I was very conscious of that. I don't think I ever have been good on the telephone, but I did have this dread of the telephone because of the number of times that I was treated rudely. The assumption was that I was the secretary and that it was not appropriate that I had been asked to call an important man and ask him a question. It was a kind of unconscious sexist attitude. Finally, I had to leave the job because I married Ed [Baker] and they didn't want both of us working in the same office.

Sherman Briscoe was working in the Department of Agriculture as the only black out of more than 490 information specialists.

When I went to work for the Department of Agriculture in 1941, they brought in five or six of us at that time. In the civil service regulations then there were very strict requirements for coming in. For example, in the newspaper field, one who came in as an information specialist would have to have written in a specialized field for at least a year. This doesn't mean sports or society or something; this means writing in the field of agricultural production or economic affairs or some specialized field like financing or finances. Well, you don't have this on black newspapers. So no one would ever have qualified to come in under this rule. They relaxed the rule for about a year, and then they were going to go back to the old system and make it very difficult for anyone to come in without these qualifications. The Roosevelt administration had been convinced that it ought to bring in some blacks, so all of us came in at the same time, in June 1941, because the law would be changed on July 1.

I was hired specifically to serve black newspapers, to get them the kind of information they could use about the programs and activities of the Department of Agriculture. I worked there twenty-seven years. I could have been promoted out of this job and into programs serving everybody, working across the board, as they called it. But I refused to do that because there was something like 490 working in information in the department, and there was just one serving the black press. And I didn't want to move out of there.

The black press deals in personalities rather than subject matter. It deals with a black person in relation to the subject matter. In order to bring the program of the Department of Agriculture to life, I would visit farm families all across the South and Michigan and Ohio, and I would interview these farmers to find out what help they had been able to get from the Department of Agriculture and how they had utilized this help. We'd take pictures of the people, prepare a story, and send it out to the black press. They were very widely used. They had never had anything like this before.

Everybody fully supported the war. There was a feeling about segregation in the armed services, but I don't think any blacks tried to duck the military because of this. I think the blacks felt it was their war as much as anybody else's because of Hitler and also the feeling that Pearl Harbor was an underhanded sort of thing. So as far as I know, the blacks gave full support to the war effort.

Ray Madden (D.-Ind.) came to Washington in 1943 and served in the Congress for thirty-three years.

When I came to Washington, there was far more activity than there was in Gary or Indianapolis or any other Indiana town, although we had three major steel plants in Gary and they were humming to provide steel for the war effort. I was on the Naval Affairs Committee. Carl Vinson was the chairman; Lyndon Johnson was a hillbilly rookie from Texas and nobody paid much attention to him. Carl Vinson put me on a subcommittee to go to Honolulu to hold hearings on defense housing in March of 1945. He said there were thousands of mechanics, engineers and electricians, and brick layers, carpenters, over at Pearl Harbor preparing those ships and they couldn't get any place to live. So we went over and held hearings for about two weeks, and found out that the Chamber of Commerce, the fruit people, the pineapple people, and the army and the navy were all feuding with one another about where they were going to build defense housing and that was what was holding it up. So we went out and designated the land and wired back that we had gotten a location and everything was all set to go. And two months after we got back around 250 defense houses were built for families to move into.

It was unfortunate that we got into the war. It was the same type of international mess we were in before World War I. It was the battles over their war machines. Hell, they had the war machines; it was easy for them to go to war.

In 1941, "the media" usually meant radio. One of NBC's, and later ABC's, men in Washington was Bryson Rash.

We were the information media and we had a tremendous impact on the people in this nation. Electronics always has had since the early days, so we felt we were contributing greatly, not only in putting out information on the war but also supplying the government resources needed to accomplish some of the things they had to do. For example, at one point I think somebody said, "Well, in order to get metal, we had better start collecting tin cans." The air was flooded with information on how to contribute tin cans. The media was also used on rationing. One of the interesting things about World War II was that there was very little patriotic flag-waving. There were no big parades, no rabble-rousing speeches in the sense of big public displays. There were no marching bands all over the place. That was different from World War I.

There was only voluntary censorship, and immediately after Pearl Harbor we became very conscious of what we were doing—too much so, perhaps, because we had no firm guidelines yet. But they were quickly set up for voluntary censorship, and there were few breaches of this procedure—only two or three incidents throughout the entire war when the media breached the voluntary censorship. Of course, the biggest one was the report of the breaking of the Japanese code after the Battle of Midway. After guidelines were set up, it was a simple operation. We felt little constraint—we didn't report troop movements or ship movements and we didn't do weather forecasts on the air, which was interesting. Had there been an enemy attack planned or executed, one of the vital things would be the weather.

There was an enormous influx of people to Washington. On December 6 you seldom, if ever, saw a uniform on the street, although there were a great number of military people in the area. By evening of December 7 there were uniforms all over the place, and in subsequent days, months, and years you saw uniforms everywhere.

After Pearl Harbor, by nightfall, you had army personnel around the White House grounds with armored cars. The second thing they did was put antiaircraft guns and army personnel on the railroad bridge across the Potomac, at Fourteenth Street, and started laying a pontoon bridge. It seemed incredible, but that bridge was the only railroad link between the North and the South east of Harper's Ferry, West Virginia. If saboteurs wanted to really bother you, they could have blown up that railroad bridge. They had a pontoon bridge completed as fast as they could.

What I did, and others in the other networks did, was to help act as liaison between the networks and the government. The government could go to an individual in a network and say, "We need this"—things like recruiting, information on food rationing, scrap metal, and all the other programs that existed during wartime.

I did the broadcasts out of the White House when the president went on the air, or when the secretary of state went on the air, which was rare. Most of the traveling I did was under government auspices with the president. We always left here in secret with the president. We'd be told by the White House, say in the morning, that the president would leave that evening. Frequently, you wouldn't be told where he was going, and you didn't know how to pack, whether for cold or warm. Usually it was someplace like Hyde Park or Warm Springs. They'd tell you you were going to leave town at six o'clock and to be at home at five, packed. The phone would ring, and they'd say, "We'll meet you at such and such a place." Sometimes it was the White House garage on M Street; sometimes it was the Bureau of Printing and Engraving; odd, obscure kinds of places, not necessarily the White House. Then the army would come along with the secret service and take all your luggage, and you'd get into automobiles or a bus and go to a railroad train. It would be parked out on the line somewhere, not necessarily a station. All the shades were drawn, of course, and you'd start moving. Then you'd get someplace else, and you'd stop, and the president's car, with him aboard, would be put on, and you would take off.

On trips to Hyde Park, I don't know what the routing was, but it was a circuitous one so you wouldn't get too near a coastline. You also had an engine running ahead of you and an engine behind you so that, if you had a problem, the engine and maybe a car running ahead of the president would take the flak, if there was any. That was also true in peacetime.

As a sidelight, we never had White House passes until the visit of the king and queen of England in 1939, I think it was. Prior to the outbreak of World War II you just went in. Secretaries from other office buildings downtown used to sit on the White House lawn and eat lunch. It was wide open. If you wanted to get from, say, Pennsylvania and West Executive Avenue to down around Pennsylvania and Fifteenth, you'd cut through the White House grounds. I think the formal White House credentials were at the insistence of Scotland Yard for the king and queen of England rather than for the president.

I don't recall that we suffered many hardships during the war. You had limitations, but they were not severe. You were inconvenienced, let's put it that way. For example, sometimes you had difficulty getting meat if you didn't have enough ration stamps, or butter, but that didn't really bother you a great deal.

Usually everybody worked long and hard, and there wasn't too much socializing. There was some, of course, but you had the problem of what the heck are you going to feed people? I suppose you could get stuff on the black market; I know it existed, but anybody in a public position or anybody who was closely involved with the war just wouldn't touch black market.

Many times we took our vacation at home. Traveling was crowded and hard to get. Air travel was not very easy in those days. Practically all the aircraft manufacturing facilities were devoted to the war effort. You didn't have an airlines transportation system like you have now, and the military had priority. As a matter of fact, where the Pentagon is now was the airport for Washington before the war. The old Hoover Airport was the darndest thing you've ever seen, because it had a major highway running through the middle of it. They had a big traffic light, and when a plane was going to take off or land, they'd turn on the red lights to stop the traffic.

Hilda O'Brien, just out of Columbia University Graduate School, came down to work in the war effort.

I was first hired by the Justice Department in a section that really had to do with foreign agents who were registered in the States, as they are today. I didn't stay there too long, because that operation was phased out, for one reason or another. Right after that I received a call from the Office of Censorship and went there to be interviewed by Colonel Shaw, who was head of the special section they were just setting up. He sold me on the glamor of this work and how they really felt that my background was just what they wanted. So I went to work there. I felt very much involved in the war, because our little section was really a counterespionage section. We did basic research on any suspected espionage that might show up through the watch on the mail. This mail was picked up in offices all over the country, and anything suspicious would come into Washington for further analysis. There were some cases that developed out of finding a microdot on a piece of mail. It was a tiny little bit of film, no bigger than a period on an envelope or on a letter. And stuck onto the period would be this tiny little dot of film, which, when blown up, would reveal some code or something of that sort.

Another very interesting thing was the use of open code, which is extremely hard to find and requires people who have a keen knowledge of the idiom in a language. For instance, in our section we had people who knew French very well and Spanish and other foreign languages and would be able to recognize in the letter where the language was strained. It would be recognized that "Aunt Louise had pneumonia last week" would mean something else. The language would be forced a little bit to get across the message. Open code is difficult to detect because it's not like a cryptogram, which is mathematically set up and can be analyzed much more easily.

I lived in Georgetown and shared a very arty sort of basement apartment with a Brazilian girl who worked for a purchasing agency. We had the usual dates and parties at our apartment, mostly people in the service.

One of the things I did in Washington was to volunteer in a service center near Union Station. I worked every Sunday morning from eight to twelve. There, of course, we were right in the heart of the problem of servicemen going in and out, and their wives and children—particularly the wounded men coming out of Walter Reed or Bethesda who had been very badly injured, amputees. Many times this would be their first weekend out or first night or day out from the hospital. That brought us very close to the war. We got to know them well. There were several who became regulars and would be there every weekend. They were lonely, but I would say there was not a feeling of depression. There was more of a feeling of exhilaration. Of course, there was a lot of cynicism, and it's true, there were some I know who would say they were sorry they had been saved—that sort of thing—people who had lost both arms or both legs. But on the whole, there was quite a cheerful spirit.

Frank Waldrop was managing editor of the Washington Times Herald, *owned by Cissie Patterson, daughter of Robert McCormack, who owned the* Chicago Tribune *and was a bitter opponent of Franklin Roosevelt and the New Deal. The* Times Herald *and Cissie Patterson also opposed Roosevelt, and, as Frank Waldrop, now retired and living in Washington puts it, "I was Cissie Patterson's hired gun."*

   I don't think I actually expected an attack on the city of Washington by a military force, but in those days, anybody who didn't expect the Germans to do anything they could to make life difficult for us was an idiot. During the First World War, they did sabotage to the extent they could, so it wasn't a matter of their not being willing to do it; it was only a matter of their being able to do it. There was always this edge of possibility. There used to be a great deal of sardonic wit about which city was the more important target. Birmingham was pretty sure that Hitler had it number one on the list because it was a steel-making town, and since steel is the base of war, naturally Birmingham was more important than any other city in the country, and it was going to be bombed first. Atlanta's position was, "What the hell are you hicks talking about? Atlanta is a great rail transportation crossroads of the Southeast, and if you take out Atlanta, no trains can run." So obviously they were going to take out Atlanta.
   But when you'd look out the window, you'd see that the only rail link on the East Coast crosses the Potomac River from Alexandria right into southeast Washington. Now, where in the hell are you going to run a train from all the troop-training stations—all through Southeast? The army was all stationed south of the Potomac, and there's that damned one bridge to come over. Alexandria figured it was going to get it first, but the troops were hung on that bridge, just like blackbirds. It was under twenty-four-hour guard. Not only did they have that under guard, but they had a standby—an engineer's pontoon bridge downstream. So Washington was quite visibly prepared for the possibility of genuine military assault of some kind. Don't forget, Tokyo was further from the war than Washington was, and it got bombed. People who thought the war was sort of a game anyhow maybe didn't think anything about it. But anybody who was the least bit serious minded about the war knew it.
   It was difficult getting out the paper. And we had an extra problem. We had to maintain protection from the sabotage of patriots. There were guys who were certain that Hitler was running the paper and that

Tojo was downstairs setting type. If you criticized Roosevelt, you might as well have been . . . well, let's put it this way, we weren't supporting the war, we were supporting the country. We didn't believe that the United States should have been put in the position we were in—of being confronted with a war on two fronts—and we never hesitated to say so. But that's a far cry from attacking the troops, you see, and attacking the whole war effort, whatever that means. We had to win the war. We never had any difficulty on that front.

We had the same problems as everyone else as far as the loss of people to the military. But we also had the problems of people on the paper who had been uncomfortable—even before the war started—because our policy was not sympathetic to Roosevelt and his program. There were people who had scruples of all kinds about the war, and they were perfectly legitimate, and it was natural that there would be such things. They took it very hard that we were not properly worshipful toward the administration, even in peacetime. It would reach a point from time to time that they couldn't stand it any longer, and they'd leave. On top of that, we had people in the city who were outraged by our scandalous attitudes, and they were always organizing boycotts of circulation, boycotts of advertising, and general denunciation. Thank God we didn't have TV in those days! They would have all been parading around out front and carrying on the way they did when they struck against Kay Graham.

I don't remember the war years as exhilarating. I used to go around and do my stretch at the Stage Door Canteen when I had time. It was heartbreaking, really. I don't think it was quite the same fear it might have been at someplace where you had large blocks of troops gathered together, sort of keeping up their courage, you know. The war was not a fun-and-games thing around Washington. Too many people here knew better. My recollections of it are not at all in the sense of excited adventure.

Cornelius Pitts was an eighteen-year-old boy, from a family of eleven children, living in New Orleans when the war began. He came to Washington to work in the government during the war and still lives there as the proprietor of a motor inn.

I don't recall registering for the draft after Pearl Harbor, but I do recall receiving a telegram from the War Department, asking if I would

be willing to accept what they called at that time a war service appoint-
ment for the duration of the emergency, as a clerk-typist in Washington,
D.C. I had taken an exam a year or two before that time and was al-
ready on the Civil Service register in New Orleans. So the first week in
March 1942 I reported to Washington for work. I didn't want to come to
Washington, but my father really urged me to leave.

My first job was as clerk-typist in the quartermaster general's office
out at the Army War College. I was there roughly about a year and then
transferred to the Pentagon in 1943, to the Ordnance Department.

I felt I was making a contribution to the war effort and was very glad
to be a civilian. I didn't have any philosophical reason for not wanting
to go in the army, but I felt it was rather risky and dangerous. I also
wanted to be around to help my parents. I had two brothers in the navy
and one in the army, so I felt that three out of my immediate family was
sufficient. They didn't have to take the whole family.

I made quite a name for myself in the Mail and Records Section of the
Ordnance Department. I was considered a speed demon on the typewriter—over 100 words a minute—so they decided they'd give me a little better job. I was soon transferred to Charts Section, doing statistical
typing.

At the Pentagon most of the blacks were assigned to the mail and
records sections. Seemed like in almost all the agencies the blacks were
concentrated in those sections, and they had low-paid black supervisors
who would really drive the workers all day long. That's why I enjoyed
the transfer to the Charts Section, because I moved into a white section,
and of course it was entirely different. Nobody pushed you, nobody
rushed you. You just did your work. I knew I was a good worker, and I
think they really respected me for my ability. I stayed there through the
war. My highest pay was $1,620 a year.

When I became twenty-one, I purchased a cab and drove it at night
after work. I did very well, even though there was gas rationing. Cab
drivers always had ways of getting gas. I think cabs were allowed eight
gallons a day, but we were able to double that by using the black
market.

There were many drunk servicemen, but I don't recall any problem. I
used to hack around the big hotels and had a lot of high-ranking
military personnel. They weren't big tippers, but they were consistant
tippers, a dime, fifteen cents.

I was so anxious to avoid going into service that I talked to some fellows in New Orleans while I was classified 1-A here. I was getting

ready to be called for my examination, and the fellows told me that in New Orleans they were turning down blacks for the least of things. So I went back home for a little while, just so I could get called by the New Orleans draft board. The examination officer asked me if I had any physical defects that I knew of. I said, "Well, my feet are always giving me trouble, these fallen arches I have, I just can't stand on them." He just took my word; he looked at my feet and rejected me on the basis of what I told him. In the South, in New Orleans, the whites thought it was a big honor to serve the country, all that sort of thing. They didn't feel that the blacks really had a stake in it. So if they had any reason to turn you down, they'd turn you down.

R. W. Danischefsky spent the first year and a half of the war working in Detroit for the Reconstruction Finance Corporation, then was transferred back to wartime Washington, which was an exhausting, but exhilarating experience. He is an industrial engineer.

I moved into Washington as regional engineer, and then after about another year I became what they called the principal engineer, in charge of all field operations. You see, just before the war and immediately after the outbreak of the war Detroit had the bulk of the defense-plant program. A lot of the procedures and methods that we started in Detroit later became standard, and so my being transferred to Washington was primarily an effort to unify the operations all over the country.

There were so many people moving in here that rental places were extremely hard to find. I lived with a cousin of mine over in Georgetown and spent two complete weekends looking for a place to rent before I finally found this place over in northeast Washington. I got up at six o'clock on Sunday morning—the house was to be open that afternoon. I borrowed my cousin's car, went over, and the house was open. I looked around, and it was satisfactory. There was a real estate Open sign standing inside the door. I left that there and locked the door. So the next morning I went over to the real estate office and asked them if this house was still available. They said it was, and I told them I'd take it. He said, "When do you want to look at it?" I said, "I've seen it." He said, "How did you get in?" I told him the door was open. He said, "We had our salesman go out there in the afternoon, and the place was locked." I said, "He was a little late. I got there about seven-thirty Sunday morning." So I got the house. There was a terrific shortage of housing.

At that time Washington was very interesting. There seemed to be a universal feeling of doing something for the government—much different from what we ran into in the Vietnam situation. It was amazing to me the spirit and the willingness of everybody to do something—work odd hours, work nights, change their schedules, or work overtime. From the day that the hostilities broke out until Labor Day of 1945 I didn't take a day off, including weekends. It wasn't unusual—seven-day weeks. We had to; we were so far behind in purchase orders. The rest of it was in travel, and no one bothered about overtime. I think the shortest day I put in in all that time was probably twelve hours. Everybody was willing to do it. Of course, we didn't have much time for social life. By the time you got home from the office, you were ready to go to bed and start the next day.

Mostly what I did in Washington was apply some of the Detroit know-how that we had developed out there into the other outlying regions. I worked principally on what we called property records. The only records we had at that time were purchase orders, and it became necessary to set up some sort of property records. In the Ford setup, which probably had more subcontractors than anybody, a machine tool would be bought and delivered to, say, the River Rouge plant in Detroit. It would be there for a couple of months, and then that machine tool might be sent to a plant in Tulsa, Oklahoma. A machine tool of a special nature might move around four or five times. It was extremely difficult to maintain records of both the location and condition of that tool, so it became necessary to set up what we called asset property records for these leased tools.

Ultimately we realized that this equipment would become surplus, and we'd have to sell it or store it or do something with it, so we had to know what we had and where it was. It was amazing to me how many of the industries after the war adopted the program that we had established for maintaining records of the machine tools.

Kay Halle, a young radio broadcaster from Cleveland, worked for General Wild Bill Donovan at the Office of Strategic Services.

One's training period at OSS was like the best telescoped college education. General Donovan had assembled so many top experts in so many fields and he was smart enough first to learn the rudiments of intelligence gathering from the British. I was assigned to a branch called Morale Operatons—MO—whose chief concern was to destroy the enemy's will to fight.

Most of the operations still remain secret. I did exact a note from General Donovan before I left the agency, as we called it, which he signed, giving me the authority to refuse for publication any interviews revealing specific MO wartime activities.

Everyone I saw and worked with at headquarters felt a strong sense of misson—a fire in the belly—and enjoyed working at concert pitch.

There was fun, too. I became known in our branch of Morale Operations as Mata Halle, after one of our graphic artists surreptitiously transposed the letters of my name on my wooden desk marker. For days I was puzzled at the smiles it inspired because I had not faced that side of my desk. Then one day a grinning Douglas Fairbanks, Jr., who had come in for a briefing, picked up the marker and turned it around for me to see.

Washington was then a quiet southern town. It was within human proportions then and, thank God, still is, which makes us the envy of other cities. But the war was a transition period for Washington. In the bringing together of our allies during the war, whose leaders worked here and came to know our city better, Washington seemed to grow from a bureaucratic conglomerate to the powerful world capital it is today.

Connie and Ed Stuntz, now retired and living in Florida, were living in Wellington Villa, a "suburban commune," as Stuntz calls it, halfway between Washington and Mount Vernon, Virginia. Connie worked for the Red Cross and the United Nations Information Office. He had been a reporter for the Associated Press, and although he was not in good physical shape, he knew he had to get in the war effort somehow.

Ed: I had come back from Europe in 1937, and at that time the AP was having correspondents back from Europe interviewed by a local man. They asked me what I thought about the possibilities of world war. My colleagues and I all felt that it was inevitable. But my answer was that it wouldn't be a war like World War I—entrenched troops facing each other over four or five years. Forget about the Maginot line and the Hindenburg line; they'll flank those, and then the war will be extended out into the Far East. In other words, there'll be war all over the world. That interview was never used. The general manager sent word that this was warmongering.

Our general manager had made a remark that it was economically impossible for Hitler to declare war. My answer to that was that everybody knows that but Hitler. Hitler's idea of economy was that what he hasn't got, he was going to go take.

I had tried to enlist before Pearl Harbor. As I told a friend of mine on AP, "We're either going to become the biggest military force in the world or we're not going to survive. I want to get in and get a commission. I don't want to have to be a foot soldier or anything." I was too old, even then, to be drafted, and this was just before the draft.

Admiral Pettingill, I think it was, down at the navy yard in Washington had okayed me, but then the Bureau of Medicine washed me out. I had been injured when I was a kid riding a horse—crushed my right leg and twisted up my back. Then shortly before I came back from Italy, I had gotten into a row with Mussolini's Blackshirts, and they beat the hell out of me: My car had been laid up for several days with a weak battery, and I'd asked them to charge the battery in this garage behind the American Express. I went in there kind of nervous and grumpy and probably arrogant, because I was young then, and these Blackshirts didn't impress me worth a damn—I didn't even know that the garage-man was a Blackshirt until later. I said, "Why can't you take care of this automobile? I've paid you." He said, "Because we don't want to serve you. We're not serving Englishmen and Jewish Americans." That made me sore, and I said, "Okay, I'll send around and get this car." He said, "You take it now." I started to walk away, and he swung me around. I was carrying a stick because I was limping, and I broke it over his head, but he was too much for me. I kept lashing out, but they knocked me down, and I vaguely recall their stomping on me—there were a couple of guys. Then the American Express boys and several of the correspondents got over there and pulled these people off me. I've never had a decent back since. Also, I did have hypertension.

But I had already bought the uniforms, had a desk down in the Navy Department, and had gone on this trip with the admirals all over the country, and they bilged me out. It's an awful thing to be told that you're not man enough to fight for your country. I went pretty much to pieces over it. Here I had been telling everybody we were going to have this war and we might as well get ready for it, and I had been covering wars and been shot at more than a lot of people who went through World War II. I knew that I could face up to fire, and to be told that I wasn't fit for combat shook me up.

In June 1942, I went into the State Department—in [Nelson] Rockefeller's Office of Inter-American Affairs, the forerunner of the Office of War Information. Among other things, we put out a radio news report to Latin American radio stations.

I was put on as the day news editor, to sort of tailor the report that went out and check with the Spanish translators. I had a policy laid down for me not to cover up our losses, to let them know the truth. We had a lot of eager beavers in there, and I had to watch several people very carefully for fear they might minimize the Russian losses and overplay the German atrocities. I knew perfectly well that if we started talking about the German atrocities, we wouldn't get anywhere with the Latin Americans, because they knew damned well that we were committing just as many atrocities as the Germans. I mean, you can't put men in war out there without there being atrocities.

They wanted to minimize our losses in the Pacific, but my theory was that you'd never get any sympathy from Latin America by claiming victory all the time, or supremacy, because they didn't like our supremacy anyhow.

In Washington they ran the gamut from complete lethargy to what you might call a silly acceptance of the necessity of war. Then you had the flag-wavers and the chest thumpers, who said, "We'll go over there with a division or two, we'll clean them up like we did in World War I," which we didn't.

We shipped our children off to Cuba because it had gotten to be impossible to find a place to live in Washington with four children. They had two sets of grandparents in Cuba, and we figured they'd be just as safe there as in Washington and a lot more comfortable. Washington was getting to the point where you had to queue up maybe a block or two before you got to the drugstore to buy a pack of cigarettes.

CONNIE: We were able to get along very nicely with our rations, but there was a lot of black market. I remember the wife of one of the AP correspondents who was very proud of herself because she had what she considered prominent friends. When he came home, she gave a big dinner for his return. Everybody at the table had a beautiful Delmonico steak—there were about twelve of us—and he said to his wife over the table, "Good heavens! You must have given up all the ration points we have for a month of Sundays." She said, "I got it on the black market," and he said, "If you got it on the black market, I am not going to eat it." And he picked up and left. Several of the guests got up and left too. Well, they were divorced shortly thereafter. She'd been having a lovely time in Washington while he was batting around in the war zone.

In April of 1942 I walked into the Red Cross and told them that translation was my forte, Spanish, Italian, and French—and I went to work right away on the search for lost people.

I remember once having a call from a senator's secretary who said that the senator wanted to get in touch with somebody they thought was in Saint Thomas, the big concentration camp in the Philippines. I said that we had no lists. And she said, "Well, what are you doing over there? Why don't you have any lists?" I said, "Lady, we are losing this war, or don't you know that? They have two hundred thousand of our people, and we don't have eighteen of theirs." The attitude in Washington was they just couldn't believe we were losing the war.

I had been with the Red Cross for ten days when they put twenty-five thousand messages from all over Europe on my desk and said to sort them out according to languages. I told them that I spoke Spanish, Italian, and French, and none of those messages were in those languages. They said, "Well, make a try at it." So I sat down and called every legation and consular service in town and said, "What is the outstanding characteristic of your langauge?" I remember the Bulgarians said that if it looked like French and wasn't, it's ours. The Hungarians said that if every third word ends in *unk*, it's Hungarian. I distributed those messages by the rules they had given me.

I worked in the Red Cross until August 1944, then I went to work for the United Nations Information Office. Our mission was to gather information from all the sources we could and send it to the various legations of the British Commonwealth, the State Department, and the free governments of France, Poland, and so forth. It was fascinating work.

ED: The spirit in Washington after 1943 was beginning to be, "Well, all we have to do is to just keep in there." One of the great sayings of the time was "Don't forget there's a war on." If you went out to dinner with some friends, someone would say, "Well, I can't stay long, you know, there's a war on"—that sort of thing. Nobody challenged that; those who weren't doing much and didn't feel very close to it were seeking ways to get involved.

During the war I was very restive about being kept in Washington, what I called the Battle of the Potomac. In our office whenever one of our younger people would go and sign up in the marines or the infantry or the Air Corps, we'd say, "Coward. You can't take it here." Because we were working fourteen, sixteen, eighteen hours a day and on call most of the time, never knowing when everything might collapse around us, and these guys went off and had good company command —we envied them very much.

Then there was the flak you would get for not being in uniform—not from the servicemen but from civilians, girls. "There goes a 4-F. Look at him, he's young enough to be in uniform." The servicemen did not do that. I think there were some occasions when they would see a civilian living it up and say, "Well, buddy, you're having a hell of a good war, aren't you?" and that sort of thing. But not too much in Washington, because the servicemen either came back from duty or were about to go out on duty and were all scared to death anyhow, and they realized that if you weren't in the war, you probably had a pretty good reason.

Merlo Pusey was an editorial writer for the Washington Post, *later a biographer of Charles Evans Hughes and* Post *publisher Eugene Meyer, as well as author of, appropriately,* The Way We Go to War.

You know, we backed into the war without really facing up to the issue. We kept edging into it a little bit at a time, largely because Congress had passed a Neutrality Act and had also forbidden convoying. In spite of that, FDR started convoying by sending our navy ships to support the lend-lease operation that was then going. This worried me a great deal, this edging toward the war when we were pretending to be entirely neutral, particularly to have the president taking so much responsibility. Do you remember the *Greer* incident in the Atlantic? It was a destroyer and it was going to Iceland and it encountered a German submarine, and Roosevelt told the country that the submarine had deliberately attacked the *Greer* without provocation when the Greer was on a legitimate mission. He said it was a dastardly attack upon our naval vessel, and as a result of this, he ordered stepped-up American operations and told our navy to shoot first at German and Italian ships of war in the Atlantic. Within ten days, I think, the Naval Affairs Committee of the Senate began looking into this, and they found that a British plane had spotted the German submarine and had told our destroyer where it was, and the destroyer had followed it until it got in contact with the submarine, and then it broadcast its position to the

British so the British could drop depth charges on it. An act of war—and Roosevelt didn't say a word about this. This kind of deception, I felt, was outrageous, and I spent a lot of time exposing things of that sort and then delving into what the government was doing, and I followed mostly not the war itself, which was handled by [Herbert] Elliston and other members of the staff, but the activity of our government in connection with the war. That was sort of my general field.

I thought there were a lot of brilliant strokes in Roosevelt's conduct of the war. I thought his decision to attack in Europe first and to deal with the Hitler situation was entirely right. What troubled me was his sort of devious way of going about things and the power that he seized here and there to conduct the domestic operations without bothering to go to Congress. His use of his commander-in-chief powers—that disturbed me a great deal.

I thought getting into the war was inevitable, because I don't think we could rationally have stayed out of it. But the thing that troubled me about it was that they all pretended to be protecting our neutrality when actually they were moving closer and closer toward the war. I think Hitler, with all his scandalous inhumanity, had sense enough to try to prevent provoking the United States. He knew what had happened in World War I—that the United States had been provoked to the point where it couldn't possibly stay out. He tried to avoid that sort of thing this time and at the same time accomplish his purpose by destroying shipping in the Atlantic.

So, I think, we inevitably had to get into it. I don't think we could possibly have escaped it and retained our moral stature and self-respect, because civilization was under attack. I just wish we had done it honestly and openly in our constitutional way of doing things instead of backing in by the back door. I think Roosevelt had a moral responsibility for leadership. If he had been less of a politician and more of a statesman, he would have taken a stand instead of trying to do it covertly. He could have done it openly and tried to persuade Congress to go with him, and I think that in the end there would have been a better feeling about it if he had done it that way.

The *Post* was in the forefront of the campaign to get us quickly into the war mood. And the four years during the war was the most interesting period since I've been in journalism. My recollection is that we worked a six-day week; in those days, I usually worked on Sundays and had a day off during the week—when I usually went home and worked on my book.

Herbert Elliston was the editor, and Alexander Casey Jones was the managing editor, a very dynamic character. We supported Roosevelt most of the time during the war. The most interesting interview I attended during this period was immediately after Pearl Harbor. Within a day or two after Pearl Harbor, Churchill popped over here by air and suddenly turned up. Not a word was said about it, but it was whispered about that Churchill was in town, and surmising that he would probably be at the press conference, I made a special point of being at the White House press conference the next day. Sure enough, he was there, and after a few preliminary questions to FDR, he turned the forum over to Churchill for questions. Everybody wanted to know everything that Churchill could tell us about the war and how it was going. He was a short man, and as soon as he started to speak, the people in the back cried out, "We can't see him. We can't see him." So he got up on a chair and answered questions from there, and he was a marvelous character. I've never met a man who had quite the sparkle and vigor, and the profound flow of information that came out of that man was amazing. It was just a marvelous experience to listen to him.

Eugene Meyer, who was the publisher of the *Post* in those days, knew most of the military people, and he used to invite them in to lunch, and we got a chance to talk to them and to hear firsthand about what they were doing in North Africa or Italy or wherever the chief operation happened to be at the time. Members of the cabinet would also come in from time to time and a lot of the military, General Marshall, and Sumner Welles was a fairly frequent visitor. He was under secretary of state at the time and a very knowledgeable, professional diplomat, who seemed to know everything that was going on in the world.

Meyer was a great admirer of Henry Kaiser, who had turned to mass production of ships as soon as we got into war, realizing that the war was likely going to be won or lost by shipping. So when Meyer heard Kaiser was coming to Washington, he invited him over to the *Post* for lunch. Kaiser came in, and after the pleasantries were exchanged, Meyer said, "Well, what brings you to Washington, Mr. Kaiser?" He said, "Well, I have an idea. I'm trying to sell the government on the construction of some baby aircraft carriers because it takes two or three years to build a big carrier, and these things can be produced in a matter of months. While they don't have big armor and all that, they're small ships, and we can turn them out in relatively fast order, and the ship I have in mind would carry fifty planes, and it could ferry planes to any part of the world where they're needed, very fast, and I think it would be a great aid in continuing the war and winning it."

Meyer asked him what he'd done about it, and he said he had an appointment that afternoon with a navy committee. But he called Meyer within an hour after lunch and said he'd already been over to the Navy Department and they'd given him eighteen minutes and turned him down. Meyer was distressed, and Kaiser was terribly upset. Meyer said, "Well, stick around for a couple of days." Kaiser had said, "I'm licked. I'm going home. I'm catching the afternoon train to California." Meyer said, "Oh, stick around for a couple of days, and let's see what can be done." So Meyer got a hold of Wayne Coy, who was a White House aide at the time, told Coy about it and then he pulled some other strings, and Kaiser got busy and pulled some strings and got an appointment at the White House. He laid the idea before the president, and before Kaiser left, he had an order for building fifty of these carriers, and then he began turning them out about one a week.

Somebody mentioned the incident to Meyer, and, as I recall, his response was, "Yes, there are many opportunities in journalism to put in a plug at the right time."

He did a lot of things at that time of that sort, in which we all were involved in a way. He put on a show called "Back the Attack," which was a tremendous display of armament on the Monument Grounds. He got the army to put this on—it was in connection with one of the bond drives. His idea was to let the country know what the country is turning out to support our boys abroad, and they put on a magnificent show, which got a big press. They covered the Monument Grounds with this equipment, and it gave a big boost to local morale. It was Meyer's basic idea, and he had a hard time selling it to the army. As a matter of fact, he didn't get it sold to the army until he convinced [Henry] Morgenthau [secretary of the treasury] that it would be a great thing to support the bond drive by showing the people what the country was doing with their bond money.

I always felt that I knew we were going to win the war, but, of course, our spirits all went up on D day. There was a tremendous anxiety that prevailed in the country after the invasion of North Africa; things seemed to be moving so slowly in North Africa and then through Italy. There was a great deal of impatience, and the *Post* was calling for a second front rather vehemently—I think somewhat to Meyer's distress and rather to my distress, because I had the feeling that we'd better leave those things to the military. But we all had a feeling of tremendous relief when D day occurred and we had our troops in Europe and they began moving fast and it looked as if the end was only a relatively short period away.

There was one very important contribution that the *Post* made, and I was only incidentally involved in it. Near the end of the war the government had developed this unconditional-surrender formula, and they were going to smash the enemy governments completely, as they did with the government in Germany. But after the collapse in Germany, unconditional surrender became an awfully big hurdle to get over in Japan, because the Japanese interpreted this as meaning that they'd sweep out the emperor and he'd never be permitted to come back again. And since the emperor was tied in with their religion and national feeling and Shintoism, they were not willing to surrender. There were a good many estimates that it was going to take so many hundred thousand lives to force unconditional surrender on the Japanese and that we would have to invade the islands directly at a tremendous cost in American lives. This bothered us, and we spent a lot of time worrying about it over at the *Post* and thinking about it and what could be done and began to write a series of editorials questioning the unconditional formula. We thought the government ought to spell out precisely what Japan would have to do, and if we spelled it out precisely, not necessarily sacrificing their emperor, we'd make much more progress and end the war that much sooner with less loss of life. There were a lot of editorials to that effect, largely written by Elliston. At the same time, Admiral Zacharias was quietly working in the navy to the same end, trying to convince the Japanese that unconditional surrender didn't mean what it seemed to mean. We didn't think that that was enough; we thought the government ought to spell out what they had to do precisely. Truman finally did that at Potsdam, and we were delighted to have him do that, and then the Japanese did come along and surrender. No invasion of the mainland was necessary, and obviously a tremendous saving of life resulted. Of course, the bomb played a big part. But after the war the navy gave us credit for helping to convince the Japanese that they could get by without giving up their emperor system and finally inducing the president to do the spelling out he did at Potsdam.

Americans Remember the Home Front

Marquis Childs, syndicated columnist:

I was a Washington correspondent for the *St. Louis Post-Dispatch*. There were three of us in the bureau.

The change in wartime Washington occurred so rapidly. It was a change of pace and mood, above everything else—an acceleration. As usual, Roosevelt was right at the center of it.

Roosevelt got more assertive. There was the famous time when he presented the Iron Cross to *New York Daily News* correspondent John O'Donnell—I don't remember the date, but it was after the war had begun, I think—for his continuing isolationist, anti-Roosevelt activity. I don't know whether you could go so far as to say pro-Nazi, because he probably was not, but he was very isolationist and anti-Roosevelt and faulted our military people for having allowed Pearl Harbor to happen. That group had a powerful appeal to a helluva lot of Americans, who believed that Roosevelt was bent on an intrigue to get us into the war. On the other side, there was the Committee to Aid the Nation by Helping the Allies. They didn't have anything like as violent an approach. Lindbergh came back from that trip to Germany and talked about how the German air force was invincible. You remember the outcry, and perhaps the thing that fed this very feeling was Roosevelt's statement that we could produce fifty thousand airplanes a year. And, of course, soon after Pearl Harbor we started out to do just that.

I wouldn't say Washington was exhilarating. It was a time, in the first place, when most newspapermen wanted to get overseas. The ones who were really smart got into the liaison field—got into China, into Chungking. But a lot of us were in Europe, in and out. I was in South America for a while, but that was not in the heart of it. When my draft number came up, I was too old. I suppose I could have had a commission, but I didn't have any great urge. I guess I felt I was contributing to the war effort. I don't know that it was true. It was sort of a rationale.

Air travel was difficult. You had to have priorities, especially for overseas. I remember I went with a group of five or six journalists who were invited by the Swedish government to visit Sweden, quite early during the war. We were on one of those old Pan American clipper ships made of basketwork, and we got as far as Bermuda. It happened to be beautiful spring weather, and we were bumped by some top brass for three or four days. It was great. Not too much complaining, except that we wondered if we would ever get out of Bermuda.

Most of my experience during the war was overseas, and when you came back, you felt things were still so normal here, that we hadn't been touched by the war. I was in Cologne the day after it was taken. I remember the feeling, God, it is going to take the Germans twenty-five years ever to come back in any form. Then to come back to the United States—without a touch of the war. For most people it existed only in the radio and newspaper reports—unless, of course, you had a member of your own family immediately in it.

Smith Johnson, a rubber manufacturer from Ohio, could not wait to get involved in the war effort, and by January 13, 1942, he was in Washington working for the Rubber Division of the War Production Board. He will never forget the experience.

In a very few days I discovered that there were seventy people in the Rubber Division and not one rubber man. There were nickel, steel, leather men, and no wonder they were glad to see me. I was first put on an allocation board with five fellows, and none of them knew anything about rubber—their job was to decide who could use reclaimed rubber for articles—so they more or less left it up to me to decide whether the thing was necessary or not. We had everything you could think of. I remember one request for rubber pads for rams out in Wyoming, so they wouldn't kill each other when they were fighting.

Later I was put in charge of rehabilitation, the conversion of the industry to war. I was coordinator. They moved me into another office; I was in fifteen different offices before I got through the year and a half. You never knew what was going to happen in the confusion.

Every concern had its own representative in Washington; it was the most iniquitous thing you ever saw. For instance, there was a firm that wanted to build a plant. At this time I was in charge of the allocation of materials—when anybody wanted anything in the rubber industry, I had to sign the thing, or my assistant did. If a person had a broken-down machine and needed to buy one, he had to come down and make a request. So one day my assistant brought in a pile of requests. I leafed through them, knowing the rubber business. Here was a rubber factory requested by a man whose company was owned by the deputy director of the WPB. He was the guy who was supposed to be enforcing the law, and he was breaking it completely, because on a factory you had to put in a facilities request, and he was putting through machinery requests to build a whole factory. My assistant said, "What'll we do about this?" And I said we shouldn't sign it because that's absolutely illegal, and he said, "But the deputy director is asking you. If I don't sign it, what am I going to do? I've got a wife and two children." He said he was going to lose his job if he didn't sign it. Finally I said, "Oh, I'll sign it. Give them the plant." So he got the plant, but it was completely illegal.

There was also one company that wanted to get rubber for tire patches, and, boy, they wined and dined me. They sent me a case of champagne and took us to Atlantic City—we spent a weekend there, and they footed all the expenses. But I didn't give them any extra rubber. There were so many times that people would give us cocktail parties, and we went and didn't even know why we were invited. I don't drink much of anything, but there was a lot of this going on. Nobody offered a cash bribe—just gifts, like a dozen pair of silk stockings when nobody could get them.

Most people were patriotic, except for these big companies. It appeared in Washington as though every company in the country was saying, "How much can we make out of this war and how little do we have to give for it?" The rubber companies, the steel companies—all of them—they were so selfish, it seemed to me.

Crazy things went on in the government. One time we got word that we were going to be moved to the Municipal Building, so I went down there, and they showed me this nice big room. I had twenty-six people to allocate here and there, and I got the desks all arranged. We finished up at five o'clock at night. I went home feeling good, and in the morning I went to work, opened the door to Room 3140, and to my consternation, there wasn't a single thing in there—not even a wastebasket! Then I met my assistant and asked him what goes. He told me the furniture was all piled up down in another room—they had come in at one o'clock in the morning and moved me out. They wanted this for a guy who had more authority than I had.

A while after that, Mr. Johnson received a letter saying that his services were no longer required in Washington for the war effort. He spent the rest of the war in Ohio, making rubber for the war effort, which was also an interesting experience, recounted in chapter 3.

3

INDUSTRY AT WAR

Outside of Washington, the war had the greatest impact on the nation's industries. And they performed what has since been described as a "miracle of production." Some of the statistics of this performance suggest that the accolades are well deserved. In 1942, American industry, for example, built 48,000 military aircraft; in 1943, 86,000, and more than 96,000 in 1944. During the war it also built 5,200 ships, and by the end of the war it was able to build a Liberty ship from stem to stern in forty-two days. In 1944 it produced 50 percent more munitions than the enemy nations and 45 percent of all the munitions produced by all the nations at war. Industry also increased its labor force 36 percent between 1940 and 1944 and the average work week from 37.7 to 46.6 hours. This miracle of production was achieved by men and women such as these:

After Pearl Harbor, Smith Johnson had gone immediately to work for the War Production Board in Washington. His small rubber company in Middlefield, Ohio, had made washing-machine and refrigerator gaskets, and he was ordered to cease all civilian production work. While working in Washington, he was lucky enough to land a war contract for his plant back in Ohio:

I didn't go to Washington to attempt to get business or anything like that. I was honestly going to help them win the war. But it just happened that I met a fellow one day at a cocktail party—his name was Burns. He was an engineer, a very nice elderly fellow. I told him about being in the rubber business and making certain things and thought no more of it. A month later I got a call from him asking me to come over to his office.

He said, "I talked with you at that party, and you interested me because of your rubber experience and what you were doing in your plant. I'm putting ten ammunition companies in business making boxes for holding ammunition—.30 and .60 caliber. Every one of them is going to need a gasket. Can your company make it?" I told him I didn't know. But I phoned my uncle, who was looking after the business, and asked him if he could make this gasket. He said, "Well, sure. Try anything. We're not doing anything here." I told him to come down to Washington and we'd work it out. In about a month we were in production, and the business continued through the entire war. We made sixteen hundred dollars' worth of gaskets every day, which was pretty good for a little company. In fact it saved our existence, I guess, because it took time to get into these other things. We also had a molding company, and we got to making gaskets for B-29 bombers and shell gaskets and all sorts of things. Our employment went from nothing up to 850 in about a year and a half. But it got going from the fact that I was in Washington—no other reason. If I hadn't gone down there, I would never have got the business.

While I was in Washington, we had a fire in the plant, and I came home.

The fire didn't destroy the part that made the ammunition-box gaskets, but the other part was gone, the part making gaskets for B-29s. We decided to build a building because we wanted to continue to make these gaskets for the B-29s. We were one of three suppliers to the government.

So I made up plans for this facility and had to send it to Cleveland for the War Production Board and from there it went to Washington. Remember, this was a 100-percent war plant—very essential. So one day the manager of the WPB in Cleveland came up, and I talked our plans over with him, and I thought we got along fine. Two days later I got a call from a friend of mine in Washington who said, "You know your plans for that building got turned down by the facility board in Cleveland." He said that I had better get the hell down there.

So I got on the train and went to see him. He said, "I don't know where your request is, but it's probably over at the Facility Bureau. Why don't you go over there and see?" So I walked in cold turkey, not thinking I knew anybody at all, but who was sitting at that desk but one of my former receptionists. She said, "Boy, have I got something for you." I said, "Did they turn it down?"

"Well," she said, "it might be turned down. We got a letter from Cleveland yesterday, and it was denied; but look here." On her desk was the Johnson Rubber Company request for my gaskets. I asked her what happens now. She said, "You know, mail gets lost down in Washington, you never know when a letter is going to get anywhere. I'm about to take this in and have it signed right now." She took it in, and the fellow, not knowing it was denied, signed it and sent it out to Johnson Rubber Company. I never heard one word from the guy in Cleveland. We built the building in about six months and continued the rest of the war making gaskets for the B-29s.

The company now is quite prosperous. I sold out about ten years ago to Johnson Rubber, but I was out there last summer, and they now have eight hundred employees. They do something like $34 million a year. I started it in 1928 with five people. And it covers five acres now.

R. W. Danischefsky, an industrial engineer with the Reconstruction Finance Corporation in Detroit:

At the time of Pearl Harbor we had five projects in Michigan. By the end of December we had forty-two projects. Our plants included the Packard Motor Corporation, making engines for the British, and Continental Motors, making tank engines. All of this was under what was then called the Lend-Lease Program—the Reconstruction Finance Corporation was a lending agency. The purpose of having the RFC in these operations was to avoid the necessity of the military services going through the routine of getting appropriations through Congress to finance these things. The total program ran to almost $10 billion, and this was to provide machinery and equipment in existing plants, the building of entirely new facilities such as the Willow Run Bomber Plant, magnesium plants, aluminum plants, and all sorts of industrial facilities to provide materiel for war. The plants were owned by the government and subsequently were declared excess. They all became surplus at the close of the war.

I was a supervising engineer. The operator of a plant became an agent of the government, and the plant was completely supervised by supervising engineers. We approved all purchase orders, appropriations, payments, and had complete control of the project. Suppose Ordnance wanted to establish a gun plant—they would come in and work with what we called the lessee to prepare preliminary estimates and make up a schedule. It was up to the supervising engineer to maintain control of expenditures, approve payments, and, in the case of construction, to supervise construction, approve contracts.

Here's an example of the way it worked. Chrysler Corporation became a subcontractor for building the nose and the center section of the Martin-bomber fuselage. They arranged to utilize the old Graham Page automobile plant in Detroit, which took money to pay the rent and equip the plant. They provided an estimate of their requirements, a complete, itemized list of all the machine tools and equipment they would need. They submitted that to the air force. Most of the contracts at that time were fixed-fee contracts. Assume that, for the sake of simplification, you could make x item for a million dollars. It was determined that probably a normal profit on a million-dollar contract should be, say, 10 percent, so the government would provide you with all the machine tools and everything that you needed, taking into consideration your cost figures, and when the contract was finished, you would get $100,000 profit, the government paying all the expenses of manufacturing, with certain controls. The air force would come to RFC and say, "We've got a contractor in Detroit that needs $90 million to equip a plant to build something that the services need." They would approve it, and it would go ahead. It wasn't a direct negotiation with defense plants. It was all what we called sponsorship by one of the services.

I would get a telegram simultaneously with the lessee, which in the case I mentioned was Chrysler, stating that x number of dollars had been appropriated for what we called a plant corp.—defense plants corporation. It might say: PLANT CORP. 119; $89 MILLION HAS BEEN APPROVED FOR THE CONTRACT ON MARTIN BOMBER. CONTACT CHRYSLER. Chrysler at the same time would get a note on their telegram to contact me, and we'd be writing purchase orders the next day. We'd get together immediately, day or night.

Where the lessee had his own plant, you could get into production almost immediately on certain phases. But on a bigger program, where you might have to build a plant and everything, it might be a matter of a year. But there was very little lost time.

You hear a lot about the miracle of production. It was America! It was unbelievable to me. One of my first experiences was with Chrysler, where we were faced with the question of clearing their plant and moving a bunch of machine tools. We sat and discussed this for maybe an hour, then one of the men, sitting over there with a pencil and pad, said, "Now this is what it's going to cost to clear this equipment out and bring in the new equipment." I said, "What did you do, just reach up in a hat someplace and get a number?" He said, "No, this number will stand up." I subsequently found out that these people had knowledge of that type of thing because of their model changes every year. They just take the number of machine tools, and regardless of whether it's a small tool or a big tool, they have an average figure of so much, and that covers it. I finally got to where I'd go out to these outlying places and become a genius, simply because I'd figured out that the average machine tool cost roughly one dollar a pound to move out. You could apply it across the board. That's what it cost to bring it in, set it down, move it out, process it for storage.

Capt. Fred Kirkham today lives in Bradenton, Florida, where he is a licensed pilot for ships up to 100,000 tons. At the time of Pearl Harbor he was on the destroyer Lang, *up in Reykjavík, Iceland. Before too long, he would be working in the shipbuilding industry.*

Just before the war I was working for the Public Loan Corporation in Hartford, and I was chasing a fellow on the draft board. He was a little delinquent on his payments. He told me that he was going to get me, so rather than be a doggie, I joined the navy in Hartford. They told me, "Oh, you won't get out of town. You'll just patrol up and down the river and do that type of work." Well, no sooner had I signed up, I was down in Newport, and with my experience on boats, I was in charge of a netlayer, that's the one with the Y on the front of it. We put the nets down across Charleston Harbor and Newport. Then I was transferred from there to the destroyer *Lang.*

After Pearl Harbor I was transferred to a troop carrier. We picked up a bunch of supplies and troops from the British and took them in to Malta. On our way back, when we got outside of Gibraltar, the vessel I was on was sunk. I was a radio operator, and I was heading up to the radio shack. Believe it or not, at that time there were (I can tell it now, of course) over 596 German subs that we had charted. It was our duty, every time we picked up a sub on our sonar and radar, to send that information back to whatever command ship we happened to be with at that time. I was going up to the radio shack when we were torpedoed, and that was one reason I was able to get off the boat. Several hundred men were lost. There were nine of us on this large wooden raft. We drifted south and got caught in the doldrums. A peculiar thing, when you're on a raft like that, after a few days your normal body functions cease, and that of course affected my stomach. They finally picked us up on the Sargasso Sea. We were on there thirty-four days and were picked up by a British vessel and taken in to Bermuda. Then they transferred the whole group of us back to the naval hospital in Portsmouth, Virginia.

While I was missing, my folks had received a telegram from the secretary of war stating that I was missing in action. Then I wrote to them from Bermuda, and were they really surprised to hear from me. They had given me up for lost. In fact, my obituary had appeared in the local paper, the *Guardian,* and they had saved it.

I was discharged from the hospital because of the ulcer I developed on the raft. I was unfit to go back to duty. This would be early 1943. At that time I was living in Quincy, Massachusetts. So I went back to Quincy, and on the way up there, a fellow sat down beside me. I was reading, and of course I was in uniform at that time, and he started asking me a lot of questions. He asked me where I was going. He wanted to know what vessels I had been on, what I knew about the submarines that had been sinking some of the vessels off the coast. I said it was none of his business. Well, to make a long story short, he thanked me and said I gave all the right answers. Then he identified himself as an FBI man. He wanted to know what I was going to do. I told him at this point I hadn't made up my mind. He said: "Do you still feel that you want to do something?" And I said, "Why not?" He said, "All right, we've got a job for you down at Hingham. We built a shipyard down there, making LCIs, DEs, and LSTs. We're hiring men, and we want you to go down there to be in charge of the installation of the radios." But he said I was strictly on my own. "I'll check with you every once in a while, or someone will," he said, and they did all the time I was there.

They wanted me to make sure every man did his job. In other words they were afraid of sabotage, and I think not without reason, because some of our cables were sabotaged. But it was never found who did it.

I turned in two different fellows who were sort of drifters. They had hooked up some of the wires in the electronic equipment wrong. I asked them why, and they answered: "Oh, golly, I don't know." Once, you could understand, but when it happened two or three times, then you checked them out. I just couldn't take a chance that they might have been saboteurs. After you help pick up fellows at sea, you just don't take a chance. Also if they hook it up wrong, I'd want them out of there anyway, because I couldn't get paid for the job until it was accepted by the navy inspectors. After I turned them in, I asked the FBI fellows about it, and they said not to worry, that they were in the army now—drafted.

We had a bit of bribery. In fact, I got a lot of that myself because I was the one that promoted the men. First I had gas coupons offered to me and then meat coupons. I would lie if I didn't say I had a little piece of meat once in a while. You got so damned little meat.

We also had "Rosie the Riveter." A lot of gals did welding work. As a whole, I'd say they did a pretty good job. Of course, some of the Rosies were conducting a little business on the side. The oldest profession. Some were doing it for promotion and some for actual dollars. But they didn't cause any problems. My men didn't come in contact with them too much. A vessel would have to be fairly well along before we could start on it. They were working in another part of the shop. And, of course, the yard was so darned big, there'd be thirty or forty boats working at the same time. My particular division had about one hundred men. But I had a couple of women—tack welders for putting up the U-shaped hangar that you ran your cables through. They were good, and they liked it because they didn't have to kill themselves on the job.

I did have some uncomfortable experiences being in civilian clothes. But then, of course, I wore my "ruptured duck"—remember the ruptured ducks? There was a mistake and they had rated me a 4-F when I was supposed to have been a 2-B—anybody that came out of the service. When I got the ruptured duck, I always wore it, and everybody knew what it was and that helped a lot.

There was a tremendous black market in Hingham, no question about that—gasoline, tires, food stamps, et cetera. I think the Godfather and his people were involved and, of course, there were a lot of phony stamps around. The shipyard was the biggest industry—the only industry in Hingham. It was running three shifts with about ten thousand people to each shift, and lots of people seemed to be chiseling for more. They were all fighting for that dollar. They all wanted to get into the shipyard because the shipyard was paying more than anyplace else, and then, it gave the young people a draft status they wanted. Having been in the service—and shipwrecked at sea on a raft—some of the things that happened in those days still bother me. I used to get real provoked at some of these fellows in the yard and some of the civilians when I saw them chiseling and trying to get theirs. That bothered me, especially when I found fellows that wouldn't work properly. I transferred some of them the hell out.

Patricia Megargee was just out of high school when the war began, and her parents wanted her to go on to college. But she felt the times were out of joint, and she wanted to get involved.

Gradually everyone started going off. All the boys who had been going to Lawrenceville and Choate and the various schools were graduating and instead of going on to college were taken into the army. I had a brother, two years younger; later on, he was in the navy. He was on a ship that went to Anzio; he was very uncommunicative, like kids are today. He didn't finish high school, ran off and joined the navy before the proper age. My parents were very upset about that. They were also upset about the fact that I didn't go on to college.

It was a strange time; there didn't seem to be any point in going to college. Everything was out of kilter. We went to visit a very good friend of my mother's up in Connecticut. Her husband was an officer in the navy, and she had gone to stay on a farm. She had just decided to leave her apartment in New York and sort of hole up there for a couple of years. It was strange. People were going into things like that. I went up to stay with her. I wasn't getting along too well with my stepfather. He wanted me to go to Finch and be finished. I thought that was a complete waste of time, so I stayed with this friend of Mom's and heard that they were looking for help at Pratt & Whitney, in East Hartford. We were in a little town called Winsted, Connecticut. I drove in one day with some neighbors and was interviewed. I was either just eighteen or not quite eighteen. Anyway, they said, "Fine."

They were desperate for people to work. They put me into a training program for about two months, every day, eight hours or whatever. Oh, I was so pleased with myself. Mother was furious. I just kept telling her it was for the war effort. I got this certified machinist certificate, and I remember I was so proud. They put you through this thing about how to run these machines, how to read calipers and micrometers and various testing devices. We were in a separate building for the training. Then we went into this big factory; it covered miles. You'd check in, and then you'd walk and walk and walk and walk until you got to your own little niche. It was very exciting. As a matter of fact, I really wouldn't mind doing it again.

I ran a Norton OD grinder, OD being "outside diameter." We would put parts under this thing and then grind various portions of the flanges and what have you. These were parts that would go into the Pratt & Whitney engines. Pratt & Whitney made the engine, and I think

Republic made the airplane itself. I was in the engine section, and Hamilton Propeller was right adjacent to it.

It was nifty! Great fun—if you were eighteen, anything was fun. In my particular area there were mostly men working, but it was so vast, it's hard to explain. There were trucks that drove right down the aisles where people would walk. Small, sort of Jeeplike things. Or if there was a fire, a sort of mini-firetruck would come. It was so vast that you couldn't see from one end to the other. It was like a small town all under this one roof.

I was very unsophisticated at the time, but I was very zealous, probably overzealous. I remember some of the older guys who had been there for years used to say, "Hey, kid, don't be in such a hurry!"

But I'd get into the thing and geared up for it and I'd just keep plugging away, measuring and grinding, measuring and grinding, and they'd say. "Hey, kid, take it easy." They'd been doing it for fifteen or twenty years, and they didn't want me approaching what they had done at the end of the day because then they didn't look good, and of course they could do it with one hand tied behind their backs.

I got into the night shift because it paid more money and it worked out better as far as my getting a ride in the car pool. We had maybe a forty-minute drive into East Hartford, and it got a little complicated with the driving business. I didn't have a car and so I was in a car pool, and you paid so much a week to drive with these guys, nice country-type of guys, who had been doing this kind of thing all their lives and were either too old or for some reason or another didn't go in the service. The ones I rode with were kind of paternalistic about the whole thing. They thought it was funny that I would want to do that rather than go into the hairdressing business or something. We'd work from midnight to seven, only seven hours instead of eight hours. You got the benefit of the extra hour because you were on the night shift.

It was always an exciting thing to drive up there at eleven-thirty at night. From a distance you could see the plant, all the antiaircraft lights on the roof, and you just felt like you were involved in it, so that when you got letters from your friends overseas, you weren't as cut off as you would have been if you weren't doing anything.

I didn't have a car, so gas rationing didn't bother me. Shoes were a problem. If you were working and you needed shoes for work—and you needed really rugged shoes in that kind of work—it didn't leave you anything left over for dancing shoes, although there was no partying up there, because it was farm country.

Finally enough pressure was brought to bear that I said, "All right, I'll come back home." At that point Mother was in Bay Head, New Jersey. So I went down there for a couple of weeks for a vacation and then went to New York to look for a job, because I still wasn't going back to school. Because of the training I had had in Pratt & Whitney, I applied for a job at the Navy Department, at the Office of Inspector of Navy Materiel, and got a job as inspector of materiels the navy had ordered to be shipped to various places out of the New York area. I'd go to a different factory every day and inspect different types of gauges that go into aircraft. I even went to a nut and bolt factory in Purchase, New York, to inspect the bolts and nuts. It wasn't that involved. All you did was measure the bolts, take test samples, and make stress tests, mechanical tests. If you were conscientious and did all these things, the margin for error was almost nonexistent—unless they went out of their way to slip something over on you, which some of them did, I would guess, from what I've read.

I lived in Westchester and commuted to New York or to wherever it was I was going that day. Social life was practically nonexistent, except when someone you knew would come home on leave or something; then it would be a mad whirl for about a week, come home at two or three in the morning, still have to get up at seven and catch the 7:55 to New York. But when you're that age, you can do almost anything. Then you'd collapse and did nothing for about two or three months.

There were certainly opportunities to form all sorts of relationships with people you were working with if you were so inclined. But theirs was a different kind of background, and there was no point in pursuing anything along those lines.

Later, I started working for a modeling agency, and they told us very definitely that they would prefer that we go one or two afternoons or evenings a week to this Stage Door Canteen. The atmosphere there was sheer desperation. I mean, people coming in, and it wasn't just our own servicemen, people from Australia, Canada, anyone who happened to be passing through. They wanted someone to talk to, and there was a desperate kind of quality about the thing—like here you are, now sit down and be charming, sparkle—a very unnatural situation. I didn't like it at all; I wasn't good at it. I met some very nice Norwegian sailors, but we were not supposed to go out with them, which was great, because I didn't want to. Some of the girls did violate the club rules and go out with them. Why not, if they felt like it?

We were an awful lot squarer in those days than eighteen-, nineteen-, twenty-year-old kids are now. When I was going out with my husband, who had been married previously, divorced, and was seven years older than I, I can remember my mother telling me that under no circumstances was I to get near Al's apartment. Now, I was twenty-one, I had been working for three years, supporting myself. He had some records, and I wanted to hear them. We were going to Cavanaugh's, down on twenty-something street for dinner one night, and his apartment was nearby. So he said let's go have a drink and listen to some records, because it's too early to go to dinner, which we did. It was perfectly fine—no passes, no nothing, and if there had been, I could have handled it. Mom was absolutely horrified! I was twenty-one years old! She said, "Patty, you went to a man's apartment? And there was no one else there?" Oh, my heavens, it was really something. When I think of the changes! And I felt guilty, I was afraid to tell her I had been in a man's apartment!

If you ask me what are my most vivid impressions of the war years, I'd have to go back to the factory, driving down and seeing the antiaircraft guns on the roof and the lights and the feeling of just being involved. There was something about the smell of the airplane factory, the noise and the excitement and the lights and the machines going and that oily smell you get from machines!

James Majors, from Nashville, Tennessee, came up to Chicago in 1939, job hunting. "There was just no place you could get your hand on money at that particular time—especially the blacks. The way things were in the South, I said this is not for me, and as soon as I got big enough, I was going to cut out. So I dropped out of school. Everybody was crisscrossing the country, riding the rails, thumbing, hoboing, getting where they could, checking to see if they could find a job and moving on to someplace else if they couldn't." He ended up in Chicago because, he says: "I had noticed on packages, most everyone I picked up said Made in Chicago. I figured I couldn't help but find a job there."

At the time of Pearl Harbor I was working as an elevator operator for VL & A, a sporting goods firm down on Wabash Street, one of those high-class places. I had no idea we would be involved in the war, because of the snow job we had had that we were going to stay out of this thing. Then they started taking guys, and guys were volunteering. First they took the unmarried guys; then married guys; then married guys with kids; then married guys up to age forty-four. I was working with the WPA when the draft was going. I had quit the job at the sporting goods company. As an elevator operator a guy had to pay half of his salary to stay groomed, so to speak. They demanded too much for the salary. This was a place where all the movie stars came. Wallace Beery—I met him there on the elevator—and Cary Grant, because we sold all that big safari-type sporting goods. So I just quit and went to work as a supervisor of a play lot for the Urban League. It was a pretty good job. I worked nine to five, and the kids got out of school at three o'clock, and by the time they got on the play lot, I only had about an hour's work.

But still, this was not what I wanted to do. So I got a job in a plant at 147 South Market Street. The Select Novelty Manufacturing Company. They were making boutonnieres out of walnuts and peanuts. And then they went into making boutonnieres out of war stamps. I became supervisor of a bunch of women there, and it was my job to go down and buy these war stamps in big sheets: fifteen hundred, two thousand, five thousand to a sheet. I remember I used to go up and down La Salle Street. They had booths out in front of the banks, and it used to be a real thrill to me, because I would walk up and say: "I want to buy some stamps." They would ask me how many I wanted, and I would say: "Oh, about two hundred." And they would say, "Two hundred stamps?" and I would say: "No, two hundred dollars' worth." They'd look at me as if to say, "What in the hell is this dude doing?" They didn't know whether I was a damned fool or patriotic or what. I never told them what I was buying the stamps for. After I found out that they were in competition for their own private charities, I used to split it up. I could have gone right in the bank and buy them. But I gave all of them a play.

After the boutonnieres were made, they would be delivered to five-and-ten-cent stores and other shops; we used to take them in big soup boxes. There would be dollar boutonnieres and fifty-cent ones, and the stamps were made in the shape of a flower. They were very beautiful things and very popular. They used to give them away as prizes. That company pioneered this thing.

At that time I had gotten married and had one kid. I wanted to get in a defense factory because I would hear of guys making forty-five dollars a week, and I said this is good money, plus a defense job. My goal was always to do as well as I possibly could. So I went to International Harvester and applied for a job. At that time, if a guy worked for the stockyards or McCormack or as a Pullman porter, he was considered upper middle class. Those were the best jobs for blacks at the time. I had a second child on the way, and on the seventeenth of February, 1943, I was hired at International Harvester.

They had a lot of black guys at Harvester, but they were in the foundry. They must have had about forty-five hundred to five thousand workers, but in the production work, where the machine work was done, they had approximately fifty blacks.

I started out pushing a broom. They put me on third shift—six nights, at forty dollars a week. I thought that was something, because I was working five and a half days and a supervisor for thirty dollars at Select Novelty. Here I was pushing a broom for about the same time at forty dollars a week. Then I went from broom pushing to a single-spindle drill. This was in one of the highly classified departments—Department 11. I thought, well, here I am on my way up, and I went from a single-spindle drill to a drilling machine. On the drill I was working on all sorts of things—drilling roller shafts for the tank treads to roll on and then the shaft that supports the roller. Then I moved up to a milling machine, and from that to a lathe operator. I would take the raw material, fit it into the lathe, trim it down, and measure it with a snap gauge with a ten-thousandths-of-an-inch tolerance in diameter. Then I went from the lathe to a grinder—on the finished product.

By that time, I was making seventy-five to eighty dollars a week. And I held this job until they were taking guys up to forty-four years of age in the draft—fathers, everything they could get their hands on. This was in June of '44. I was making just about as much money as any production worker could, other than a skilled tradesman. The good part about it was that I was the only black, except for one other, who was a machinist and could serve all around, from the drill press all the way up to the grinder.

They had given me these six-month deferments—three of them—because I was a father and worked in a defense plant, that sort of thing. So when they finally decided they were going to reach back and grab everything walking, I went down and took my physical. They grade you based on your ability, and I qualified for the marines all the way down to zip. While I was there, here come three guys into this room. And the marine standing up there was some kind of sharp, believe you me, in his marine blues, his white cap, the salad on his chest, and a little braid on his shoulder. I looked at him and said, "Now, there's a guy." So I went into the Marine Corps.

Today, Jerome Thirion is a tall, tanned man of sixty who is vice-president of a large resort condominium on the west coast of Florida. During the war he lived in Buffalo, where he worked for a company that manufactured windshield wipers and related automobile equipment.

The conversion from peacetime to wartime activities at the plant went pretty smoothly because most of our equipment was basically usable. We had a very large machine department, a large die-casting department, and it was just a matter of changing the dies and setting up for government specifications.

I was directly responsible for procurement of the war materials which were necessary to keep the machinery moving. My job was to keep the materials flowing into the plant so that the equipment was constantly in operation, day and night.

As the war progressed, they were, of course, increasing the manpower demand. I had a draft number, like everybody else, and my superior was continually in contact with my draft board. Because of the type of work I was doing, he was able to keep me out of the war, although it was getting to the point I didn't have any friends left—everybody was in the war. Several of my friends had even come back. My boss's letters to the draft board kept me out of the service; and then the ironic thing was, as powerful as he was, the head of this corporation and everything else, he was drafted himself.

It was a very depressing time, because you lived day to day; you never knew when we were going to be bombed. If they could bomb Pearl Harbor, they could bomb over here. It was depressing to pick up the paper and read the casualties.

Having a young family, I was involved quite a bit in neighborhood activities. I think we were all involved in the home-front kind of thing—newspaper drives, scrap-metal drives, rallies, war-bond drives in the plant. Eventually I did take the physical examination. I appeared to be somewhat on top of the ladder, because they were really combing everybody at that point—some of these fellows couldn't hear, couldn't see too well, were badly knock-kneed. When I got up there, the guy just took one look at me and said, "You're okay." I was twenty-six on V-J Day, and that night when the Japs quit, they said over the radio that nobody over twenty-six was going to be called. I was on the way and had said good-bye to everybody, but they relieved me of going.

David Soergal, just out of the University of Wisconsin, went to work for General Electric, in Schenectady, New York.

I went to GE headquarters with no sense of wartime emergency, working in test-engineering programs that were being carried out during the thirties, so nothing was different there. Then they had engineering-advancement programs that you had to qualify for, and I got wrapped up in them. The initial job I had was a war-related effort, but it was hard to distinguish. It was working on big electrical-system equipment that would process bauxite into aluminum. And, of course, the aluminum would go for airplanes, but the connection was pretty remote. GE made the processing equipment; we never handled the aluminum. There were a lot of navy, army people around, coming in and out of GE, but when you're a test engineer, you're not involved with them. The bosses handle them.

I guess I spent about six months, nine months, on that test job, and, incidentally, when you're a new employee, you work third shift, from midnight till eight o'clock in the morning. Actually, we worked longer hours, worked overtime too. So really it was just a lot of hard work; we were just doing a job. I was married during those days, married in 1944—and I don't think war was too good for marriages. The intensity of the work—sixty-hour weeks weren't unusual. You didn't have much time at home, and I was taking an advanced engineering course, which was fantastic but took so damn much time in addition to the work. So it was a very heavy load. We really didn't have much family life, and weekends were gone, and we didn't have a car, couldn't go anyplace.

The first indication that there was a war on, about 1944, was my transfer to electronics engineering. I immediately got assigned to the Cape Cod–New London submarine area. GE had a contract, competitive with RCA, to test underwater sound devices, and that was quite interesting. I got linked into the war effort right there. The vehicle we used to test underwater sound was a captured German cruiser. Actually, it was a luxury boat, not a cruiser. It was beautiful; must have been eighty feet long. It was outfitted with electronic gear in the hull, and of course the navy operated it. They had a crew of about forty, and another fellow and I were the engineers working on the system. There were three of us, actually, and another ship on the receiving end. They talked to us and we talked to them by transmission underwater. And that's where I used another captured German device—a wire recorder. It probably came along with the luxury boat. It was a bad design, because the wire would snare up, like a fishing line. Half the time we sat there winding the wire.

We'd spend these wonderful days going out to sea on the German ship, one-day trips. When there was clear sailing weather, we'd go down to the docks about seven o'clock in the morning, go up there and get breakfast, beautiful silverware, the whole thing. I guess that came along with the capture, too.

We paid fifty cents for a meal and, man, ate like a king. They had navy chefs, black fellows, coming out and serving and waiting on you. Conversation was great, lots of wine at lunch. For them, it was a boring assignment. All they'd do was cart us GE guys out in the ocean and bring us back.

I think I should tell you, not being in the service finally got me. My sister was a navy WAVE, a two-striper, and my best friends were coming through Boston, where I was located, and I heard a lot of "You know, you ought to get in the service," and all of that. So I thought, "Well, I'll try it," and went down to the navy recruiting office in New York. I went through all the tests and filled out all the forms. Finally the guy in charge said, "Well, everything's checked out fine, but we notice from your college records that you had hay fever and asthma, and you didn't report that on the form." I asked him what to do and he said, "Well, you've got to go to a doctor and get a release on it." I didn't know any doctors, so I called some guy in Boston, some specialist in allergies, and went to see him. He could see I wanted to get in the war, so he took a lot of scratchings and stuff like this and wrote a nice letter saying I'm totally cured. I paid fifty dollars for that. This guy was a real specialist, you know. That's hard money. I went back to New York, presented my papers, and the guy says, "You know bureaucracy, now you have to get an industrial release. Your employer, General Electric Company, has to release you." I said, "You could have told me that to begin with." So I went to the man who had hired me and said, "I want to leave. I've got all my papers and am all set." He said, "I'm sorry, but I won't release you." And that was the end of that.

Frank Platt was working for an elevator company in Louisville, Kentucky, when the war started. It immediately went out of business, so he went to work for the American Air Filter Company, which was building carburetor filters for aircraft.

Building carburetor filters suddenly became a booming business, particularly after we got involved in desert areas, where aircraft just didn't last any time because of the sand and the grit. There was a big demand for filters. The major problem in our plant was the manpower—or lack of manpower. As a result, in my plant we converted about 90 percent to women. That did create some problems, because the plant wasn't designed to cope with it facility-wise, and certainly the men working there were not used to working with women. We ran a twenty-four-hour, seven-day-a-week operation, and as superintendent, I would try to cover at least a part of all three shifts and would spend a good many Saturday nights bailing somebody out of jail. We took a lot of young fellows in there who were just below the draft age, and a lot of them came out of the hills of Kentucky, had never been in a big city before. As a result, they kind of went wild. They made money that they had never had, and they were on the loose. From time to time we had some troubles in the plant, too, with the girls, but nothing of a real serious nature.

It was a completely new experience for me; I had never been involved in anything like that, and it was interesting. The reason, I guess, I avoided being in the war was that, one, I had two youngsters when the war started, and a third one came along; plus, two, I was plant superintendent for a vital defense industry.

Morale was high in Louisville, particularly due to the nearness of Fort Knox. People became involved in entertaining the soldiers. Louisville did have a number of industries that were directly involved in the war. The Jeffersonville Boat Works built LST landing craft, for which my company was a subcontractor. There were a number of other companies—Reynolds Aluminum did a tremendous business in aluminum processing; the big Charleston Powder Plant; and the Jeffersonville Quartermaster Depot. So there was a great deal of involvement by the citizens of the city. It was active; I was not involved in volunteer work, because I was working seven days a week, and my wife, Louise, had three small youngsters, and it was pretty hard for her to do anything extra.

It was not a pleasant period. I certainly wouldn't want to go through it again or see anybody else go through it, even though we didn't suffer directly by deaths or being injured ourselves.

Joseph Skelly was working for Dupont in New Jersey at the time of Pearl Harbor but shortly thereafter went to work for another company, "for several reasons."

I was given to understand that in all probability I would be transferred to a Dupont plant located in Barksdale, Wisconsin—an ammunition plant. That prospect in itself didn't appeal to me. I was a confirmed New Yorker, and I didn't care to go out and live in the woods, and I didn't like the idea of working in an explosives factory, which I considered to be inherently dangerous. I knew my wife wouldn't enjoy life in that part of the country, and there wouldn't be any professional opportunities for her. And then, I was anxious to get into work which was of a direct engineering-design nature; I had been moved more and more toward work connected with production management, and I didn't care for that. I wanted to be more of a technical person, and this would be a good time to find a job with a more technical organization.

Early in February 1942 I shifted from Dupont to a company called the M. W. Kellogg Company, a big construction-engineering firm that had many war-construction projects.

I was connected with a project concerned with designing plants to make oxygen in the field. In the beginning of the war there was considerable question as to whether or not gas warfare would be used, and if gas warfare did take place, then people who were afflicted by gas would need to have all sorts of oxygen supplies available for resuscitation. It's a pretty hard thing to get oxygen available under battlefield conditions or in devastated areas. Traditionally oxygen was carried in compressed gas cylinders—big, heavy steel things—and there's an awful lot of dead weight carrying those soldiers around. Then when it is empty, in a wartime situation, it's probably thrown away, so there's a loss of a lot of steel. So the NDRC organized what they called the Oxygen Project, which was concerned with trying to develop small, portable units that would extract oxygen from the air under any circumstances, but air that didn't contain poison gas. A half a dozen different types of units for different services were contemplated. One was to be mobile and mounted in a trailer truck, another was to be flown in an airplane, another to be used on board a ship, another one in a submarine. Then there were two basic ways of making oxygen. One was the method that's traditional, which is to cool down air until it turns into liquid and then distill the air into its constituents, nitrogen and oxygen, to get oxygen. The problem for that approach was to try to make very small, portable machines for distilling liquid air, a glorified refrigeration process really.

The other attempt was to use a catalyst which would have the ability to extract oxygen from the air and give it up again in a controlled manner. The catalyst selected was a chemical which is related to hemoglobin. I was assigned to do the basic chemical design for a unit that used this catalyst when mounted on a trailer truck. It wasn't a howling success, however, and finally the attempt was abandoned for two reasons. First, it turned out that the catalyst was extremely toxic, and some people got hurt by breathing the dust that was spilled on the floor. I don't know why this wasn't examined in the early laboratory work, but it wasn't. It was only after some people began to work with the experimental plants in the field that they discovered this. This was far down the road, but wartime research was done under a lot of pressure in a helter-skelter sort of way.

The other reason, perhaps even more serious, was that after maybe fifty cycles in use, its ability to absorb oxygen decreased very rapidly. It underwent some kind of primitive decay. So it was decided, I think rightly, that it wasn't a practical proposition, and they stopped that effort. In one sense, I was disappointed; of course, I would like to be connected with something that turned out to be useful, but in research and development work you have to try a lot of things, and they don't all turn out to be winners.

After that Oxygen Project was finished, I was transferred to a large-scale activity which had to do with plants for manufacturing high-octane gasoline. Kellogg had a program for constructing a number of these plants. They came generally into operation late in 1943 and early in 1944. There was a national total of maybe thirty or so of these plants built by various companies, and Kellogg had about a dozen of them, I think. Well, these plants utilized a new process—the process of catalytic cracking of gasoline. Gasoline previously had been made by cracking oil, through the use of high temperature, and this new process used a catalyst instead of high temperature, and so it gave a better quality of gasoline, and you got a bigger yield of good gasoline from each barrel of oil.

My analysis showed that you had to take into account the specific properties of the individual particles of catalyst, and I reported this to a meeting of engineers who were assembled to discuss operating problems in these plants. Gradually the idea came to be accepted in the trade that the particular formulas that I set out for predicting the effect of the change in the size of the grains of catalyst were sound. I felt pleased that that was a small but positive thing I'd been able to do. That occupied most of my time until the war was drawing to a close.

We worked long hours—six days a week; and Monday, Wednesday, and Friday we worked until, I think, it was nine-thirty in the evening. We quit at five o'clock on the other three days of the week. There were a lot of ups and downs. During the times when our people were taking a beating, it was kind of discouraging, and then as our people began to win, it was more encouraging.

I was given an occupational deferment, and then, rather late in the war, maybe about 1944, I was put into 1-A and called up for a physical. At the examination, because of my asthmatic difficulty, I was considered not suitable for military service. I felt I was doing work that was productive in the war, but nevertheless I felt emotionally uncomfortable about not being in the uniformed services, and I found myself embarrassed in the presence of men in uniform. I tended to avoid them and social situations where there would be a lot of soldiers around.

During summer vacations at the University of Wisconsin, Mary Dandouveris worked in a war plant.

I was able to get a job during the summertime in the J. I. Case Company in Racine, Wisconsin. They had a contract for building whatever was the biggest troop-transport airplane there was—a huge, enormous thing. I worked on the swing shift as a riveter, and I didn't like the shift—3:00 P.M. to 11:00 P.M.—it was cutting into my social life too much, so I asked to be transferred to a later shift, and then I did filing. It was on the graveyard shift, eleven to seven. We were filing the metal for the leading and the trailing edge, which is the outside edge of the plane. You only had one-one-thousandth-of-an-inch error, and there were gauges and inspectors who came around to make sure that you didn't go beyond that. Women were particularly careful, you see, and light fingered enough so that, working the files, you didn't make heavy dents or go beyond this minimum tolerance. It was intricate work that women are particularly good for.

It was interesting how fast these plants converted to an almost all-female crew, except for the older men and the 4-F types who were still around and a few of the older supervisors. These were our school teachers in high school and young college people and women that they had recruited from all over town, and they were manning the factory. That first summer of 1943 that I worked at the plant it was almost like a picnic. People were working both on the graveyard and the swing shift. People knew each other; there was a lot of conversation and lots of camaraderie. Most people had relatives and boyfriends in the service, and the discussion was where and what they'd heard and exchanging news and trying to dope out what was going on. They were pretty nice to us college kids. I never encountered any kind of problem. The second summer I did a different kind of work. By that time, the full-time people had taken over working on the plane parts. Then I was trucking—I was the supply girl on those little trucks that you move parts around on. I would supply the riveters with their parts, and there were some marvelous old men; I can remember that we'd have good conversations, philosophical conversations. There were a couple of rough types.

We were forced to join the union. This was always something that aggravated me—and I used to be a pro-union type. They knew we were students and were there only for the summer, yet we had to pay the heavy initiation fee to belong to the union. The second summer there was a wildcat strike. The plants had gotten awards—you remember the "E" awards for excellence if you met certain production schedules? We were proud of this in the plant, and we were concerned about the negotiations that were going on. I remember the union steward walking in and saying, "I don't know about you people, but I'm walking out." A lot of people did walk out, but I refused to. It was unofficial. The union never called the strike, because it was continuing the talks. I didn't, because I didn't think it was right; we were in a war period, we had a production record we had to maintain, and, I believe, we were running behind that summer, too. So we had a lot of catching up to do. Well, as a result of my not going out, I was asked by the management to work in the office, to keep tabs on the time, because I could handle that kind of job. It meant more money, so I did. I was told by the steward and some of the other people that they would ostracize me. I said, "That's up to you. I don't care." And sure enough, when they did all come back, they wouldn't talk to us. I didn't let it bother me, because I figured that I had a point. So I had my books, and I'd just sit and read at my lunch hour, and it didn't last very long. It wore off when they found out I didn't care. I don't know how the others handled it; there weren't too many others that were in this kind of a position—the types that weren't just working for money. I needed money for school.

Luther Cashdollar was a metallurgist and department head with the Union Electric Company in Pittsburgh.

The first thing that happened after Pearl Harbor was the army ordnance personnel visited our plant to view our operations and to place us in some war production. They quickly decided we were ideally situated to produce fairly large cannon, and we got into production reasonably soon.

I was married and had one child at the time. My age, however, fitted the 4-F category. I did make a visit downtown to the U.S. Navy Recruiting Office and passed the tests—this was sometime during the middle of the week, Wednesday or Thursday. I recall with apprehension getting a red-letter telegram on Sunday morning advising me that under no circumstances was I to allow the draft board to make any moves without contacting the Office of Skilled and Scientific Personnel in Washington, and that locked me into my job here. I suppose that my performance here was more productive than I would have been as a foot soldier or as a technician somewhere.

The morale in the plant was great. The attitude was totally cooperative and all-out. I can't recall a major problem between union and management during that time. Everyone worked a little bit harder, expanded their efforts somewhat, both on the workers' side and the management's side.

We had women workers there but not in production. We had women on the lathes who would cut and test pieces, because a lot of testing had to be done on the cannon from both the breech and the muzzle end. I had two women in the metallurgical machine shop, and all the personnel in the laboratory that worked on the testing machines were girls. In two cases, I think, they were wives of servicemen. We also had a photographer who was a girl. This girl was top-notch, really skillful. But in the cranes and the machine shop they were all men. I shouldn't say this, but it could be that some of these people coming out of the fields just couldn't have passed the service test. I'm not sure about that. But we had no problem manning the plant with males.

From management's side, we would do what had been our normal work at our desks, and then some of us would go into the shop and function as foremen. I remember being a foreman in the melt shop, a chemist in the laboratory, and doing metallurgical work, all at one time, that is, in the same eight hours, or, I should say, in the same twelve hours. There were times, rare, when we were here as long as thirty-six hours. It didn't affect my family life adversely, because my wife was understanding.

I also spent some time in Tulsa during the war. Dr. Michael Yatsevitch, who was the principal metallurgical engineer of U.S. Army Ordnance, was responsible for all the operations of these nonordnance plants that were brought into the ordnance picture during the war. He asked our chief metallurgist if he would release me to go to Tulsa to help in an ordnance program there, and of course he acceded, and I agreed, and, I think, one Saturday I was in Pittsburgh and the next Saturday I was in Tulsa.

After we moved to Tulsa, my wife concluded that she wasn't performing very much toward the war effort and she got a job at Douglas Aircraft Company, which was building the A-26 bomber. She became an inspector and worked the night turn. She would go to work at eleven o'clock at night and be home around seven-thirty in the morning so she was there when our daughter left in the morning and she was there when she came home in the afternoon. I told her that she could do it if all her earnings went into war bonds. This is what she did. It created a little after-the-war cash.

The war was not productive for our company financially. We had no regrets, certainly, but we used our equipment much more rapidly than we would have ordinarily in our regular production. The maintenance became high. When it was all over, we were renegotiated out of any profit we had made. I've heard some bitterness, but I'm not certain whether we actually lost money. I would say if one considered the abuse of the equipment, we probably lost some money. We did get recognition from the government—but extremely tardily, I would say. We were one of the last to get the navy "E," and we felt rather badly about this because we had been definitely instrumental in creating a new alloy that minimized the use of nickel and released nickel for other areas that required it. But a lot of us gained valuable experience in a short time that we might not have had at all. I know that I did.

John Nies had a master plan for avoiding the draft. Before it broke down, he spent some time in defense plants, working first at the Ford plant in Dearborn, Michigan; later at Willow Run.

I was on some kind of engineering system—a euphemism for a guy who doesn't know what the hell he's doing but has some formal education. I was doing the preliminary work on the manufacturing of the B-24. B-24s at the time were being made in San Diego by Consolidated Vultee, and they shifted all the drawings over to the Ford Motor Company. They were basic drawings of the airplane to be converted to the famous Ford mass-production line. That is what I was involved in, first at the plant in Dearborn, then, in early '42, I moved to Willow Run. I stayed there until the draft board got me.

I had a conscious plan and a subconscious plan that I have been trying to reconstruct ever since. Consciously I was trying to resist the draft, and subconsciously I really didn't mind going, because I think I could have avoided it.

What I remember most about Willow Run is chaos—total chaos. We had lots of big promises, with no one able to produce. We had a new plant manager every two or three weeks. It was filled with draft dodgers, draft evaders, relatives of plant managers. It was a haven from the war. It was filled with people who viewed it as that and not as a place to build bombers. That's part of the thing that made it not too difficult to leave. A totally unsavory atmosphere.

The B-24 that we had there was a mock-up, assembled and disassembled thousands of times, hundreds of times at least, into subassemblies, which the Ford people thought they could make like Model Ts or Model As. At the end of about the first year of operation at Willow Run they had to have something come off the production line, so they put that thing together for the final time and towed it out to the hangar doors for the newspapers. There were big stories saying, "The B-24 Rolls Off the Assembly Line at Ford." There was absolutely nothing behind it at all. They were still months away from the first production.

The main problem, as far as I could see from my low-level status, was, first, a lack of managerial talent; second, people who were doing jobs for which they weren't qualified; third, well, I think the thing was impossible to begin with. There was just a lot of people milling around not knowing what they were doing—a lack of organization. We had one major shortage—talent. It improved as the war went on. It had to.

The other thing I remember about Willow Run is Mr. [Charles] Lindbergh. At that time he was being excoriated by official Washington and President Roosevelt and by the American people. He tried, as far as I could tell, to help out the war effort. And there was only one place where he was accepted. It was the personal decision of Henry Ford to bring him in there as a consultant test pilot. And that is the only thing I can recall in the way of creative thinking in the factory. The workers were against it, but Henry Ford still had total personal control of the organization, and if he wanted Lindbergh in there, Lindbergh was in. That was a cause of tension. The Detroit newspapers said, "Ford Employs Nazi," and there were some overt demonstrations at the plant, but they were minor.

The draft finally caught up with me. I was registered in my hometown, which was in a small farm community in the western part of Michigan. The draft board there knew what was essential to the war effort, and it wasn't boys making money in the war plants, it was the farmer. And I wasn't a farmer. It was just that simple. I was in a nonessential industry, as far as they were concerned.

The mood in most homes was set by a wife's concern for her husband or a mother's concern for her son. In the Collins home in Bowling Green, Virginia, it was different. A young boy was concerned about his mother—as Herb Collins recalls:

My father operated a store, and after the war began, business started to slow down. So my mother took a job up at Dahlgren at the old proving grounds. She worked for about three years there. They had a bus that went from Carolina County to Dahlgren every day, and we got up at three o'clock in the morning, and I studied at that time by lamplight from three o'clock until time to catch the school bus and go to school. That would have been about eight o'clock. Then she would come home on the bus at night, and I would prepare meals and have them ready when she got home. I learned to cook that way.

Her job was to write down numbers off the shells they had there. I made some lamps out of some empty shells that mother would bring home. She also brought the little round containers the shells were packed in, and I made a table from them, and I kept that thing until I sold it at an auction down there two years ago.

Each shell would have a number on it to identify it, and they were packed in cases. In shipping them to the different installations you had to record the numbers. Several times the fuses would begin to go off, and the commanding officer there would throw them out the window. Some of them exploded. There were casualties; in fact, one woman was killed. I worried very much about my mother.

It was really her first opportunity since she married of getting out and working. There was a lot of car-pooling going on at that time, and there was no stigma attached to it. It was quite a letdown for my mother when they were all laid off after the war, because they didn't have any more work for them. But she went to Richmond and got a job—and she never stopped working.

When the company he was working for in Wisconsin, making pots and pans, went out of business, Joseph Clement went to work for Curtiss–Wright in St. Louis:

Curtiss–Wright was already making, I think, an aircraft they were selling to Russia. They had a plant in Buffalo and in St. Louis, and I came in under their training program to do production illustrations. I stayed there a year and a half or two years, until I got a letter from a friend with whom I had worked in Milwaukee. He had gone to a small bomb-making plant and felt that I could be of more use to him down there in developing target-identification bombs. It was called the Kilgore Manufacturing Company, in Westerville, Ohio. They used to make cap pistols. They were in gunpowder, so they were given contracts to make these identification bombs that would emit a light and color from a distance to be seen from high altitudes. For example, a lead plane would come in low over an industrial target in order to avoid the antiaircraft guns and drop an identification bomb that gave off a certain color smoke. Then the squadrons of bombers would find that particular colored smoke and just aim for that from thirty thousand feet or over. My job was to take one of these bombs, draw it up so that we would have a record of it, and send it to Washington so other people could make it as well as ourselves. We were mostly in the experimental end of it.

I had one close escape—it was a more dangerous job than I realized. I knew there were a lot of explosives around. You had to walk carefully, with no nails in your shoes, and you couldn't just walk around anyplace. I had a drawing board in a small cubbyhole and I had gone out into the machine shop. We were looking over some drawings out there, when we heard a tremendous roar—it just shook the entire place. The superintendent was there, and he said, "Oh, my God, I know what it is." We ran out, and my office, which was right across the courtyard from one of the bomb-loading areas, was completely ablaze. In my drawing board was embedded a huge piece of shrapnel right where my head would have been. They called the FBI in—it killed four people.

They had no idea what caused it. It was thoroughly investigated and found that it could have been static electricity. It's highly uncontrollable.

Rudolph Spitzer, a high school teacher in Shortsville, New York:

There were two years when I worked in plants in Rochester, and I had real mixed feelings about it. I didn't like the idea of being associated with manufacturing 16-mm shells, because I have a great antipathy toward anything military. I never thought of it as a way to solve problems and hated the idea of handling those ghastly things, thinking they were going to be packed with powder and that steel would blow up and inflict wounds on somebody. So most of the time I just closed my mind to the thought of what we were actually doing. I'm sure that most of the people working there did that. I have very vivid recollections of the people working there and of the women who, in many cases, were having the experience of paid jobs for the first time in their lives and were taking this silly kind of work very seriously, dressing in carefully selected work clothes, making a big deal out of a rather stupid job. It struck me that the only time I saw the capitalistic system provide full employment was during the war.

One summer I worked a four-to-midnight shift—I guess that was in the same plant—and the job there was to grind castings. Nobody ever did explain what castings were. They came out of the molds. They were about as big around as I could span with my arms, maybe bigger, sort of cone-shaped things, with a burr that had to be ground off. You stood in front of a three-foot grinding wheel, and every night your clothes caught on fire several times from the sparks. Of course, we wore goggles, but by the time I got through with that job at the end of the summer, my own glasses were so pitted, I took them to the personnel department, and the fellow there looked at them and said, "Well, go order a new pair and send me the bill and we'll take care of it," which they did. There were no women in that job. It was in the foundary, hot as hell, and the noise, I have a recollection of the noise! And I encountered the most ignorant group of people I've ever known. We had a break, I suppose at eight o'clock, half hour to eat, and there was another fellow who never did say anything, and he sat on the running board of a car. There was never any communication. He'd take a sandwich out of his bag and devour it in exactly four bites. Just like an animal, snapping at it.

There were large, heavy boxes, wooden boxes, in which they crated these 16-mm shells. And this one guy would come in, carefully arrange an old coat or something, lie down, and go to sleep. I'd be standing there putting in my eight hours, getting absolutely furious that this son of a bitch was getting paid and sleeping. I remember one day I finally went over and woke him, and I said, "You son of a bitch, you're getting paid the same as the rest of us, get up and go to work." He was so startled, he didn't know who I was, and he was too dumb to reflect that I didn't have any right to tell him to get up. He only had to say to me, "Go to hell," but he was so startled, he got up and started working.

The sheer monotony of the thing, oh, it was ghastly. These shells would come along the assembly line, and the job consisted of taking the shell off, inserting this thing into the mouth of the shell, and pressing a pedal which spun the shell—that was the way you checked the threading for the cap. Then you reversed the pedal and unwound the shell, and it went on. I used to type out on five-by-three cards poetry I wanted to try to memorize, and I would lay the cards on the corner of the bench. Then as I lifted the shell off and put it back, I'd glance at them. The dumb strawboss was very upset with this. I'm sure he thought I was doing something subversive or unpatriotic. He would make an effort to see what this was. So one night I had cards I had typed of "Kubla Khan" and deliberately walked away from my bench and out of the corner of my eye watched him. He edged over and picked the card up, shook his head, and put it down.

There were a lot of neighborhood drives for aluminum and that sort of thing. But I've heard that they were more or less to keep up the morale of the people. From what I gather—and this was from conversation in the aircraft plant—they couldn't use some of the material they got from the pots and pans anyway. They had to make their own aluminum metal. So it really wasn't that important.

John Rettaliata and André Hubbard work for the Grumman Corporation in Bethpage, Long Island. They also worked there during the war.

Rettaliata: I was assistant amphibian production manager, which sounds like a big job. There were only two of us in that department, my boss and myself.

Hubbard: I came under the engineering department that handled communications with the navy. Everything was coded.

RETTALIATA: The whole plant went from what you might call medium gear into high gear overnight. We were already in production on the F-4 Wildcat, which was fortunate because there were no other carrier-based fighters that were immediately available. We had problems with the draft, but I think on the whole the company probably was able to keep the people it wanted. We always have had outstanding management, especially in regard to the personnel situation. In those days Jake Swirbul was executive vice-president of the company. His name was Leon A. Swirbul, but everybody down to the lowest paid employee called him Jake. He was a great morale builder—very forward-looking in labor policy. We had no union. Didn't have then and do not have now. Andy, do you remember the time early in war when Jake asked us to work through a weekend, and we kept the plant open for forty-eight hours?

HUBBARD: That was done to assemble an airplane—I think it was the F-6. We turned out twenty or thirty over a weekend.

RETTALIATA: I think it was early enough in the war to have been the Wildcat. They needed two squadrons' worth of airplanes immediately, so we all stayed here around the clock.

HUBBARD: In early 1940 we were building about fifty or fifty-five airplanes every year. By late 1940 we were already building fifty a month. So you can see, it was picking up.

RETTALIATA: The aviation industry before that had been pretty well restricted to highly skilled mechanics who tended to know each other. They moved around a bit from plant to plant—the best type of mechanics. Today we couldn't find more highly skilled men in any industry. But the war meant fantastic training programs. We wound up with major training programs in every major high school, I think, in every town on Long Island. We were training women, lawyers, dentists, bakers, and just about every kind of person you could find.

People would drop their careers temporarily, often because they were motivated to do something to help out in the war effort. They were overaged or otherwise unsuitable for the armed services. They wanted to pitch in and help out. During the war I think you could walk down our production line and find any kind of skill that you wanted. A fine artist, a sculptor, dentist, musician, anything.

Thirty-some percent of the people were women, at the peak of our war effort. We even had women test pilots. I think we were the only company that had three women test pilots. They are still flying today; incidentally—private airplanes. They were not experimental-type pilots; they were production types. Which, nevertheless, was very

111

important. You have to bear in mind, we set the world production record for one month, for one single plant location. That was something over six hundred airplanes. In order to get that kind of production, you averaged three or four flights per airplane, because there are various small things wrong with a brand-new airplane. You have to have them corrected and fly them again to be sure they are corrected. That means we were busier than LaGuardia Airport. Hellcats came in like every five and a half seconds. And that was with other types of planes flying in and out of the airport.

HUBBARD: Women did a lot of electrical harness work and the detail and fine work.

RETTALIATA: The old-time fighters had miles of harness, that is, electrical wiring—very fine copper extended wire that winds up in a very complicated maze, because naturally everything you have to do in an airplane has got to be as light as possible. You don't have all the room you would like to have. You wind up with miles of wiring cramped into a space the size of a Hellcat or a Wildcat. Women were very good at that.

We set up what now you would call day-care centers. A mother could drop off her children on her way to work and pick them up on her way home. There were dozens of these around the Long Island area. We had what we called a little green truck service. If a woman came to work and remembered that she had forgotten to turn off an electric iron at home, she could call them and they would go home and take care of it. Or if she had a flat tire on the way to work, she could call them and they would take care of that.

We had fantastic orchestras and bands here. We permitted dancing during noontime. We had great athletic programs. This was all to keep the workers' attendance extremely high—almost make it fun to come to work.

Blacks also began coming into the industry during the war effort. We had a basketball team that was one of the finest in the U.S. We came in second in the national championship. The majority of our team members were blacks. This attracted other blacks to come to work here. We played the teams that formed the nucleus of the National Basketball Association. I think the morale at the plant was exceptionally high.

RETTALIATA: Quite a few of the boys who worked at Grumman went into the service—if they had not worked here long enough or they were too young. We worked out a system where if a fellow was drafted, we would give him a letter stating his skill so that hopefully he would be put in a spot in the army or the air force where he could use his abilities as an aircraft mechanic rather than being wasted handing out uniforms or something like that. If we had a really key person, then we would fight with the local draft boards as much as we possibly could.

HUBBARD: All I can remember of the war years was the long hours and just trying to catch up with the workload. Going like a whirling dervish.

RETTALIATA: The war years, to me, seemed drab and colorless; I didn't do any sailing or any of the things I have done in other periods of my life. It seemed like a gray, colorless time of going to work in the dark and coming home in the dark. I never had any incidents connected with my not being in uniform, but I remember generally feeling uncomfortable.

Margaret Oakham started the war working in an airplane factory and ended it joining the Army Nurse Corps.

Shortly after Pearl Harbor I went to school and took a short course in electrical work at night and went to work at Glen L. Martin's in Baltimore. I worked my way up until finally I worked on the B-26s. At one time I could wire the whole center section. The soldering that you did was very important because some of it was connected with giving signals and things. Sometimes I worked with girls who were not as conscientious about the work, and I became very annoyed, because I remember saying what if some of their own family were on a ship and they had done inferior work and things did not work the way they should. A lot of people could be killed. I was infuriated, because I was very conscientious about my work. If it took me longer than it took somebody else, it didn't worry me, because it had to be right.

When the last B-26 rolled off the line, they didn't know what to do with us, because we were first-class electricians, so they sent us to school, and we learned how to do sheet-metal work and riveting. We were first-class electricians, and they couldn't underrate us, but they didn't have any work for us to do as first-class electricians. So after they taught us that, they moved us to Plant 1, and we had two weeks to qualify as first-class assemblymen. There were no problems with the men—they just resented, like some men do today, a woman entering their field.

Stewart Hoskins was editor of the Lakeville Journal *and lived in the little western Connecticut town of Salisbury, but he spent part of the war working in the war effort, first in a defense plant in Torrington, later in Canaan, where they were making magnesium.*

I was thirty-five years old, and they were taking many people older than I was. So I said to myself, "What the hell are you doing here?"— doing nothing, so to speak. I thought I would help a little bit doing something reasonably intelligent. So I went and applied for a job, and they took me right away, which was all right. I didn't mind it, because I was energetic and used to working long hours anyway, even without the war work. But the burden of the *Journal* fell on my wife, Ann.

Most of the people I worked with were dedicated. They were learning as they went, including me. But a few months after I started working, the unions started to get on the ball. I had been reasonably pro-union because I felt in many ways they were needed to do a better job and get better pay and so forth. But during the war that didn't sit well with me at all.

I was sort of an all-around guy around the office down there. I would take magnesium in and out, drive the truck down to the railroad station to pick up something. And all of a sudden one day, they said, "You can't do this, you aren't a member of the union." I was a semi-executive. I said, "The hell with you," and went on doing it. But they sort of frowned at everybody, and the top people said you'd better go along with this. They didn't, to my knowledge, attempt to slow down anything, but they did attempt to organize and got a little nasty.

The same thing happened in Torrington. There I did get in, because it was a union shop. I paid my dues to United Mine and Smelters Union [International Union of Mine, Mill and Smelter Workers], God knows why. But I ran into another thing. I was in the grinding department, on a machine, part of the time—had to turn out so many thousand ball bearings, which were used in airplanes. The company wanted more production and better production without so many rejects. They started putting people on piecework, simplifying everything so there was no lost motion, speeding it up for the sake of the war and because it was more efficient. I love efficiency anyway, so I devised my own method of working. I got so I could produce a fair percentage higher than other people because I just stuck with it. I didn't fool around. And then, all of a sudden, the people on that machine said, "You're wrecking things here because if you turn out more, all they will do is set standards higher for the same rate of pay, so you will get nowhere."

I said, "Look, there's a war on. They need these bearings." And I know some of the men working there had sons in the army and navy. But even with sons in the service, this was their attitude, at least a fair percentage of them.

But most everybody worked hard, although there was a great lack of coordination. There was a lot of fumbling around, and probably a certain amount of mismanagement, because we worked so furiously. And there was a fair amount of friction. But as you look back, the exhilaration and the unification there was then was extraordinary.

Leonard Williamson worked for a construction corporation in Framingham, Massachusetts. He was its equipment superintendent in charge of equipment all over the world. He said that after Pearl Harbor they got started on war work "right quick." The first big job was the Limestone Air Force Base in Limestone, Maine.

We put up some new hangars and made some new runways and parking aprons. That was the first job we got related to the war. It was a government contract, and then the second one, the biggest one, was in Chambersburg, Pennsylvania, which was an ordnance depot. We leveled the land, put in housing, water system, hydrants, built roads and buildings. Most of these buildings had the railroads running right into them. It's still there today and still operating, although to not such a full extent.

Getting equipment was our worst problem. When we did a job in Red Bank, New Jersey, they gave us fifty-two scrapers. I went to look at those—somewhere out in Arkansas it was—and we shipped them all into New Jersey. But we must have hired about seventy mechanics to repair them before we could use them. It was the only thing you could do, because new equipment just wasn't available. That particular base was so important to the Normandy invasion that it was push, push, push. They started at one time to develop a strike there, and some big guy from the Pentagon came down, and he just laid the cards on the table: "There'll be no strikes." Everybody kind of buckled down, and we finished the thing in record time.

The war was very profitable for the company, but all those jobs were renegotiated. The government reserved the right to renegotiate after the job was done. If you made a little too much money, you had to give some of it back. And they had to give some of it back—especially on this job down in Chambersburg. All the help we hired down there really wanted to see the thing through. That was the best job, as far as labor goes and getting the job done, of any I saw before or after.

Genevieve Lewis, in Clairton, Pennsylvania:

I went into the steel mill at Clairton. When you go into a mill, they tell you you are taking a man's job. But I just kept the mills clean. When the mills were shut down, we would sweep up the wet scale that would come off the steel. That was it. We swept the mills. It wasn't so hard a job. But they told us we were taking a man's job, because the boys were all going in the service. We had quite a few coloreds, but the whites had the best jobs, working in the office and things like that. I don't know how the morale in the plant was because I didn't work around much with the men in the plant. Down in our department we didn't have any racial problems, and we got along real well in our neighborhood during the war. I didn't follow the war too much, but when I would come home, my husband would be talking about it.

Horace Hubbard was an engineering manager in the General Electric plant in Pittsfield, Massachusetts. Most of his work at GE was related to the process for manufacturing the materials that went into the atom bomb.

We did a lot of top-secret work at GE, and the thing that amused me was some of the methods that intelligence used to find out who was who and what was what. They probably properly should have scrutinized the people, but sometimes there were minor things, some remark that someone had made, or something that was blown up, and sometimes it hurt people who were innocent. We all make cracks that we don't mean, or shouldn't. I don't think security had to be that tight. Up here in the country it's a little different, too. It's not as easy for people to infiltrate. Everybody knows everybody. They keep together pretty well.

For quite a period we worked long hours Saturdays and Sundays, some overtime, sometimes nights. We had a foreman here who had a girl under him who the investigators claimed was not performing properly. Some little device, a coil or something she had worked on, failed. And they claimed that she purposely didn't put it together right. This foreman felt, as I did, that it was more or less a human error. So I went to some of the people who had received complaints about her and told them what I thought and told them of other experiences, how you always have errors in handling or in manipulation. And one night the foreman came down, and I thought he was going to kiss me. He was really pleased that I stood up for his people. He was a wonderful man himself and a hard worker, you get that in any construction work. He never let me forget it. I'd see him on the street after I retired, and he'd mention it. Those were the kinds of things that made you feel you did things right.

We had a lot of women there. They did light construction and intricate wiring on the controls, switchboards, and control devices. The women were very adept at that, and we had some who could really outclass the men. I think the men respected them—they did their part, and I think it worked out very nice. Women stayed on after the war, but of course the size of the force was reduced somewhat. I don't remember the exact figures, but we might have had nine or ten thousand normally employed over here. During the peak of the war, it went to thirteen or fourteen thousand.

I think war is depressing because it always seems foolish. At the same time, when you get involved in it and have to work on it, it goes a bit the other way. I must confess, I don't understand our philosophy with our so-called efforts to create peace. We never seem to be able to get together to settle things peacefully, do we? In the end, for all the knowledge we have and the sophistication and education, we really aren't where we ought to be in that respect.

Jack Lynch was manager of the Commander Hotel in Ocean City, Maryland, and he decided to go up to Baltimore and work in the Glen L. Martin plant building bombers.

I learned a great lesson up there. I wondered how we won the war. I used to go home so mad from there so many, many times that I said, "Well, if we beat the Germans, it's going to be an accident." It was the attitude. Not everybody. Some people there actually worked themselves down to a nub. They had twice as much work. Then other people were in there who weren't trying to do anything for the war effort at all. I can't say that I saw this, but I heard many times that there were a lot of people who came out of the shipbuilding yards and would come in there on second shift, go in the bombers, and go to sleep, and sleep the whole night out. They'd get up the next morning, hit the time clock, and go on back to the shipyards. They hadn't turned a peg all night. I never saw it, but I heard it so many, many times. If there was one thing you couldn't help but realize, it was the carelessness of people at that time. They seemed to be living well, and they weren't worrying about the rest of the world at all. They didn't have any attitude of personal pride. I remember one instance where we had a part that we had a lot of trouble with. The part was 162B48172, I still remember that to this day. It was a bolt about yea long, and it had to go through three or four different processes before it could be shipped out. I guess it was a very important bolt. They would write us that they had to have some of those bolts or they would have to stop production on the bomb hoists. Trying to get the bolts out, I went to procure some of these little cardboard caps that you put on a bolt to keep from scarring the threads. And there was one man at the desk where there was supposed to be two. He said, "I can issue the caps, but the guy is not here to put them on." I said, "You just give me the caps and I'll put them on." He said, "Well, you're not supposed to do that," and I said, "I don't care whether I'm supposed to or not but I'll do it, if you'll just give me the caps. I'm not worrying about getting fired." Here they were going to stop production on this bomb hoist, and it was when we were getting the tar beat out of us. So I put the caps on and carried them back to the fellow I was working under, told him the story, and we shipped them on out.

Another night I was going from one of the buildings over to B Building, when they pulled out a plane that was all completed. They would put a plane out in the yard and test-run it for so many hours before they'd even take it out to the field to be sent out. They were handling it so darned carelessly, turning this plane around in a very close area, and I thought, "If they don't hit something, they're going to be lucky." They should have had a man on the end of each wing. They were all at the nose of the plane, and the first thing you know, bang! they hit one of the wing tips into a pillar and of course damaged the wing tip. I walked over just to see what the comments would be. I didn't say anything—it wasn't my affair. They said, "Oh, hell, it just bent the wing tips. Pull it over on the repair side and they can put a new wing tip on." That was something of the general attitude. It was at the time when England was at its crisis. These bombers were going to England.

They had a lot of women working there, and by my observation I would say they were good. I really marveled at the way they could take it, the continuity. They'd take a piece of metal that's maybe a triangular shape, one by four, and sit down and work those things, not doing anything else but cutting those or drilling holes in those according to the pattern. I used to pass them and wonder how in the world they could just sit and do that one thing over and over a thousand times.

I don't think I was ever quite so mad as when I went to work one morning and saw about two hundred placards for people to go out on strike. Here people were dying everywhere waiting for that equipment, and then to see somebody out on the street with placards trying to stop you from going to work. They weren't successful, but they were trying.

Another thing, being a businessman, I know that you've got to keep things moving if you're going to be in business. In the department I was in, another fellow and myself were responsible for getting these numbers assigned to us typed up and out. We weren't overworked at all. I wanted to be busy or I wouldn't be there—I didn't want to waste my time. This other boy had put in a requisition for someone else to type. Well, I could type, and he could, too. We didn't need a typist, but he soon got a woman in there to type. So I went to the fellow that headed up the whole division and told him, "Have you got any other place for me here? The department I'm in, two is ample, and now we have three. I'm not going to sit here and waste my time. If you have a job, I'll stay and work, but if you don't have any more than I'm going to be able to do now with three in that department, I'm not needed." So he moved me out, because I was going to quit. You saw that. Some people did almost nothing and other people were overworked.

While in Florida interviewing for this book, I happened to be sitting with my friend Leo Hershfield early one evening, in the bar of the Columbia Restaurant, in Ybor City, which is part of Tampa, when I looked up and noticed a gentleman in his mid-sixties, or early seventies standing near our table; I asked him to join us. It turned out he had not been in this restaurant since he used to hang out here during World War II days, and he had come back now in something of a nostalgic mood. This, naturally, led to a couple of drinks and a somewhat rambling conversation. Believe it or not, he worked on concrete ships during the war. The gentleman's name is Clifford Eunice.

During the period of time that I was here, this was our so-called headquarters—not that we were heavy drinkers. We were heavy eaters. We drank light and ate heavy, this being one of the oldest and best established eating joints in America.

Mr. Hoopes, are you personally familiar with the origin or the advent of concrete vessels?

Well, they had their beginning, as far as we know, in World War I, when the British built the concrete barges used to ferry troops across the channel, and they were very successful. The government decided to build concrete vessels. McCloskey [and Company] was the third contractor to be awarded a program to develop them. They had a Scotch marine boiler and triple expansion, three-cylinder engines. They were maritime vessels, meaning that they were both cargo and men of war.

There is a material here in the state of Florida which had its origin possibly in Tennessee, Georgia, North Carolina—a form of red clay that was washed south and redeposited in the ocean. By taking this clay and burning it in a kiln, then running it through a ball mill and then out over a screen where it's powdered and droplets of water dropped on it, it forms a lightweight aggregate used to make concrete. So this concrete vessel was made from a very highly impervious aggregate in the first place, and the cement was manufactured in the state of Florida. Very few people realize the value of those ships.

Laddie Sadler worked in a shipyard in Tampa, Florida. He also helped build concrete ships, until he was finally drafted.

I was working for McCloskey and Company, located at Hooker's Point—it was called the Hooker's Point Shipyard. We built reinforced-concrete steamships. Actually, the ships we were building were for the merchant marine; they were cargo ships. There was a lot of feeling among unknowledgeable people that these were skyscrapers afloat; we got razzed about building concrete ships. But I sailed on the trial runs, and they were pretty fair ships. They didn't handle too bad. Some of them are still in use, down along the South American coast.

Why a concrete ship? Actually, there was more steel in a concrete ship than there was in a steel ship, by volume. But it was bar steel, stuff that was just cold-rolled. And there was a big shortage of steel plate, which was necessary for building steel ships. One of the advantages of concrete was brought home by one of the first three ships that we sent out of there. On its maiden voyage to the Philippines, with a full cargo, it took a Japanese torpedo, right dead amidships. It happened that it hit in a wing ballast tank, which didn't carry cargo—they filled these tanks with water to keep the ships level. Of course, it blew a hole about six feet in diameter in the tank. On a steel ship, this would have just ripped steel in every direction, and it would have destroyed the ship. But on this thing it just punched a hole, and nothing went beyond the confines of this tank. So they simply leveled the other tank, trimmed the ship, and kept on going to deliver their cargo in the Philippines, made a bee-line back to Tampa, put the ship in dry dock, put the steel men on it, and took airhammers and chipped away all the concrete that was damaged, cut out the reinforcing steel, welded in new steel, made forms for it and poured new concrete in the thing. All in a matter of a week or two. And then they cured the concrete for three or four weeks, threw a coat of paint on it and went back to sea again. But these ships were slow. They didn't do but about twelve knots, and they slowed the convoys down. The whole configuration of these ships underwater was quite similar to an LST, and the freighters up in the Great Lakes, the oar boats. It's just a great, long tube, rather narrow.

The people I knew who worked in the defense plants all felt that they had a job to do. We weren't running off to the front lines, but what we were doing was just as important because we were building the equipment and supplies. I was not particularly uncomfortable not being in uniform, because we were contributing our share to the war effort. In the shipyard, we were doing something that other people were not qualified to do. There were always goof-offs in every defense plant, of course. But I think the fellows in the lower echelon of management—the department superintendents, foremen—these people all were trying to do the best job they could, the ones that I knew, anyway. There was sabotage. There were people in the yard that I was in, for instance, who were working for the other side. They created slowdowns, and I think the biggest part of this was through union organizers. Their agents would come in and they'd try to set quotas for what the different guys could do, and they propagandized the fellows about, "You're only getting paid so much, so you can only turn out this much work," that kind of thing. I'm sure they were on the other side. There was a big wave of organizing for the sake of organizing—not to improve the situation, not to get the work done better, not to improve the abilities of the people who were doing the work. I think they just wanted to collect your initiation fee and your dues. And they tried to make it a closed-shop yard.

As far as social life was concerned, I was pretty well acquainted in Tampa, and there were groups among shipyard employees that you made friends with. While we were building a house, on Sundays, sometimes great numbers of these fellows would come out with their families, and the girls would cook up a batch of spaghetti, and we'd have a big outdoor dinner. These guys would all pitch in and help on the house. In turn, we reciprocated and helped others fix their cars and do things like that. A great deal of that sort of thing went on. It kinda went back to the pioneering days.

Later on, when things eased up, I filled in with a band, playing saxophone at a nightclub on Franklin Street in Tampa, patronized basically by air force officers. They were living it up—military personnel always pretty well lived it up when it came to night life. Their social life is necessarily fairly narrow. They are confined pretty much to their own group, and at that point they were even more confined because they had a lot of restrictions as to who they could associate with for security reasons. It was established that there were spies in the area. The pianist who was running the band was picked up for subversive activities. I don't know what came out of it, but he was a fine piano player. There were a lot of girls around. Tampa was notorious for having plenty of girls. They cleaned out Ybor City because of the prostitution there. But they all moved to Hyde Park, one of the nicer residential neighborhoods. They went from being prostitutes to being call girls.

Before the war, I had been in partnership in the sail-making business with a fellow named Clint. In fact, the reason Clint and I went into the shipyard was because the OPA had frozen what material we had on hand in the sail loft; we were not allowed to use it, and it literally put us out of business. But when the war was winding down and it looked like it was going to be over pretty quick, Clint and I started to look for another place to buy to locate the sail loft, because we figured the shipyard was going to start laying people off when they ran out of contracts. We finally negotiated for and bought a boatyard. We closed the deal, made the down payment on the yard on Thursday. On Friday I got my draft notice.

At the induction center I had finished the physical and was going through the routine you go through. One of the things you were supposed to have was a choice of service, so we went through a long line and at the end of this line was a table with a navy lieutenant commander, an army lieutenant colonel, and a marine master sergeant. As you approached this table, you handed your papers to the colonel who was sitting in the center, and he asked you if you wanted to go in the army, navy, or marines. The two young nineteen-year-olds ahead of me said they wanted to go in the army and they were going in together, and so the master sergeant said, "Well, I'm sorry boys, the army is full for today. You'll have to join the navy." So they accepted that and went on about their business. So I thought, "Well, that's good. At least I'll get in the navy." I handed them my papers, and he handed them over to the commander, and the commander looked at them and said, "Sorry, son. You're too old for the navy. You'll have to go in the army."

I said, "What do you mean I'm too old for the navy?"

He said, "You're over twenty-six. You're above the volunteer age."

So I said, "Well, if I'm too old to volunteer, I ought to be too old to get drafted," and I grabbed the papers from the guy's hand and started down the hall to the door. I got halfway to the door and realized I didn't have any clothes on. They had you before you even started.

When the war started, John Holton's company—the Carrier Corporation in Syracuse, New York—was making commercial air conditioners. But not for long. Holton soon found himself involved in the war effort—and with increased responsibilities.

Instead of making refrigeration equipment for air conditioners, we had a number of contracts for portable refrigeration units for the overseas operations where meat and other food were stored. It was primarily a large-size freezer or refrigerator, heavily insulated and carrying a refrigerator compressor, an air-cooled condenser and electrically driven, because as the forces moved up into the Pacific, they always brought their electric generators with them. That furnished the power for air conditioning the food supply. Then, of course, so much of the manufacturing required controlled air conditions. We found a great growth in the industrial air conditioning for manufacturing purposes.

I was responsible for manufacturing at the Carrier plant. We had probably two or three thousand employees at Syracuse. One of our first problems was to make bids on jobs, on contracts, and that kept everybody busy. We had to get all the angles that go into the cost, and of course we began to feel the shortage of manpower. I think one of the greatest helps I had was the doctor in charge of the industrial medicine for the plant. He was very helpful in sizing up the question of using handicapped people. And Carrier Corporation, up to the war, had never employed any women in production work. They had been in offices and clerical work. That meant training women, and we ran into the usual problems of putting women into the plant where they'd never had women. There was the question of the fear on the part of some of the wives that their husbands might not behave themselves when they were working with women. In fact, we found a couple of cases up in our storeroom; some of our employees made arrangements to hide themselves and meet others, which we had to break up. In general the women did very well. They were good workers, and after they learned the trade, it was no problem. Since then, women workers have continued. The war was a big break for them; it put women in the work force.

We had a number of miscellaneous contracts. I remember one in particular. It was a Greek submarine, which was disabled, came into Brooklyn, had diesel engines. They bent the engine housing up and we had to remachine it—something we'd never done before in our life. But we had a good heavy machine shop, and they worked it out and got it solved. It was absolutely unrelated to air conditioning. Just one of those emergency war jobs.

Then we began taking other types of governmnet contracts. I think it was a P-49 or P-48, a pursuit plane. We had to make an engine mount. Well, the quality control, the quality limits, the variation of accuracy of machining is quite important in making compressors, but when you get into welded frames for air conditioning units or anything like that, the tolerances were much more generous. When you come to an engine mount, you've got tolerances that are in the thousandths, and it presented quite a problem in working out the necessary jigs and in getting the employees up to that sort of quality. I've forgotten the figures on how many of these engine mounts we made—it was in the hundreds, maybe in the thousands.

I remember one thing particularly. It was awfully hard for us to stand by and see the British navy being beaten and sunk. My father died in 1942, and I remember so many times he mentioned, "Well, I can't see how we can pull out of this." Japan took over the whole South Pacific there, and we'd lost the fleet, of course, at Pearl Harbor, and they were sinking the remaining British navy, and he just was very pessimistic. He didn't see how we could possibly survive. Being younger, I didn't have quite that viewpoint; I knew we were in trouble and I think one of the amazing things as you look back at it, was how this country completely converted from civilian to war production. You read back about the number of planes that were built and involved in the invasion of Europe. How they built all of those thousands and thousands of planes and ships . . .?

4

KEEPING THE COUNTRY
INFORMED

The communications industry played a unique role in the war effort. In addition to providing the essential link between government and the people it was the source of what little information Americans had about the battlefronts where their loved ones were. And because of the nature of their jobs, reporters and editors often knew more about what was going on in their communities and in the country than anyone else.

After serving for about a year in the army in 1942-43, Studs Terkel was discharged when he tried to go overseas with the Red Cross. He has since obtained his army files, under the Freedom of Information Act and is sure he was discharged because of the things Army G-2 had put in his files. He says he was kind of "leftish" then, and he also made some cracks about his colonel, "that sort of thing." So he went back to Chicago and started working in radio again.

After I got out of the army, I had a call, in maybe less than a week, from some gal in the Arthur Meyerhoff Agency representing the Wrigley account. One of the first things I did was to go out to Catalina Island, which Wrigley gave to the merchant marine during the war as a training center. I lived out there in California for several weeks writing scripts for the merchant marine to be played on CBS radio for a program called "We Deliver the Goods." It was about the heroism of the merchant marine—the North Atlantic, the Murmansk Run. The shows were based on actual experiences and played over nationwide radio for the home front. For morale—but also informational. I was not in uniform then.

And I won't deny I had something of an uncomfortable feeling not being in uniform. I also went to Washington for a while and did a couple of things for a program called "First Line," about the navy and naval encounters.

I also did a news show about the war—heroism, pro–New Deal, pro-labor. For example, I did a show on Ernie Pyle. I also had a blue-collar news show—doing the human side of the news, from the other side.

Of course, everyone was conscious of the war. I was making speeches for the Office of Price Administration. And you were worried about the guys overseas, your friends. But there was an exhilaration, strangely enough, in contrast to the Vietnam War. You would follow the war and the argument about opening up of the second front and how they were doing at Anzio, the Battle of Leningrad, beachheads, Normandy. The war was always in the news and on our minds.

It was a very congenial time. Everybody was popping drinks for the soldiers in a bar. And sometimes the house would pop. Chicago was a great liberty town. And do you remember the Liberty girls? The little girls; they had a certain way of walking. They'd go arm-in-arm, three of them. And their feet wouldn't come off the pavement. They'd kind of shuffle like. Made them look a little sexier, more challenging. They were young—fifteen, sixteen, maybe—but they would chase after the boys, and the boys would chase after them.

If you want to know what it was like in a small town in New England during the war, the best person to ask, usually, is the editor of the local weekly paper. Stewart and Ann Hoskins owned and edited the Lakeville (Conn.) Journal. When Stewart went to work in Torrington in a defense factory, Ann took over the paper.

ANN: Our first reaction after Pearl Harbor was, "What can we do?" Stewart had registered for the draft, but could not get in because of his bad hearing. So he said, "I will see if they need me in anything else," and he went over to Torrington to register for war work. As he left, he said, "I don't think they will take me for months." I was down tending the paper and the phone, and the first call was from him, saying, "Can you carry on? I have to start today." So I did, although I had no real training in newspaper work at all.

Stewart would work at night and straighten out my mistakes, because I'm the world's worst bookkeeper. He also did a lot of the presswork; I got so I could make up the paper in a black apron and put the type together. Of course, it was all hot metal then. We had a linotype operator and a pressman, and then later we got an extra foreman, and we all worked together. I kept writing feverish letters up to the draft board saying they couldn't possibly draft my men, because we were communications and we were important and we had to keep them; and so we kept our men.

Stewart had to use the car for work, which meant that the *Journal* had no car. So I walked around the village, and we had to phone for ads and hope that they would send them in.

We sent the newspaper free to all the guys who were away in service. In the second year of the war we decided to do a special Christmas thing. This particular year we felt that the thing the ones who were away needed most was a picture of their hometown. So we asked the photographers in the six towns in the area if they would do the work for free. And we asked the Legion and other patriotic organizations if they would do the mailing. We did the editing and split it up into eight pages of pictures of people and places, casual pictures, funny pictures, candid-camera shots everywhere, and we got marvelous letters back. One boy wrote back, "I've taken down all my pinup girls and put up the *Journal*."

STEWART: People knew we were knocking ourselves out, and we felt that one of the things the paper should do would be to be a public service. We said, if you had any questions on anything, ask us and we'll find the answers. At one point one woman came in and said you're supposed to answer questions, what should I feed my dog when there's no meat? So I did a little research on the various kinds of dog foods and found one for her.

ANN: I would say, in a village like Lakeville the war was a waiting game—waiting for news of the men who were away and waiting for food. We were the last on the line practically, we were isolated, and the food trucks, when they came in, were half empty. Very often, to get food, people would gather at four o'clock in the morning with their boxes and sit outside at the First National, which was then in town, and wait for the trucks. I decided I'd try it, and by the time I came in the line, I was able to get one-quarter of a pound of hamburger. So I thought, the heck with that! I'll do with Spam and things we can get, and make dishes out of that, casseroles. I never could understand why we ran out of such silly things. I was sure the army wasn't eating an enormous amount of onions, but I didn't see an onion for six months. Nobody had onions. You'd think that everybody would grow them or something, but they didn't. And butter, of course, was an absolute rarity. It was very funny, we'd be sitting in the office, working feverishly, and someone would come along the street and say: "Butter is in," and everybody, the pressman, the linotypeman, everybody in the office would shoot down to the market and buy the butter. The *Journal* would stop at that point.

Of course, we had a little of that rumor kind of thing where somebody would suspect somebody of having German leanings. There was a restaurant up in Canaan, the Blackbury River Inn, run by a German family. They were refugees, poor darlings, and I understand they had a really tough time. Everybody suspected them. And there was this woman who had been an expatriate for years and came back here to live because it got too hot over there. She wanted to get news from Europe, so she built this tremendous antenna to get foreign news, but everybody thought she was sending secret messages. And there was a long thing in the paper at one point; a professor and his wife from Columbia University had a house in Salisbury. They had some Nisei friends and wanted to bring them up, so they wrote a letter to the paper asking how the community would react to it. One of the officers of the American Legion, whose son was in the Pacific, said, "Sure get any Japanese you can around here so I can knock them down." That was his reaction. Then John McChesney, a great Liberal, came out and said this is not what we are fighting the war for, this is exactly the kind of thinking that Hitler has. The fat was in the fire with everybody arguing about it back and forth, and the poor people who wanted to bring up their friends for the summer finally said to heck with it and brought them up anyway. And the people came and marketed and everything else, and nobody paid any attention to them.

Then, of course, there were the real concerns: The young men who were away. We would watch them saying good-bye to their girls in the little village restaurant at night, playing "The White Cliffs of Dover" and "When the Lights Go On Again All Over the World," sitting earnestly over a cup of coffee or a beer. And you'd see them go off and wonder about them, and they'd come back in different ways. Some of them never came back.

Bill Gold began the war with radio station WCPO in Cincinnati, as its news director. But before long, he was in Washington working for the Washington Post's radio station—WINX. Today he writes a regular column for the Post, *"The District Line."*

During the war Cincinnati was transformed from a very stable community, very steady in its habits, its growth patterns, its people, the old German community. It had a lot of milling-machine, machine-tool people, skilled blue-collar people but highly trained—pattern makers, die makers, people of this kind.

At the outset Hitler had not been quite as prominent in the news as the resurgence of Germany from a defeated nation to a nation that was making some progress. Cincinnatians took the positive aspects, a perfectly normal thing, and identified with this resurgent Germany— not resurgent in the sense of a military threat to world peace, but a nation that had lifted itself up by its own bootstraps after being crushed. Hitler's excesses they tried to overlook for as long as they could, and by the time war broke out, the German community was pretty well of the mind that this guy ain't for us.

In Cincinnati you had more of a sense of "Hey, aren't times good economically," whereas in Washington there was more of the patriotic note, people who had dropped what they were doing at home to come to answer the call of the government, which needed lots of new talent. Washington was exhilarating for me because I was just a rube from the country. I had never associated with top national figures. In Cincinnati you covered the mayor, the city council, the state senator, and people of this kind. If one of Ohio's congressional delegations or the governor was your assignment for the day, that was big stuff. Here people at that level of importance were a dime a dozen.

When you're news director, you're in a position to give yourself the best assignments, particularly when there's a very small staff. I covered the White House and the Pentagon and the major agencies. You have to remember that we were all working very short handed, and everybody worked an absolute minimum of six long days, and I worked a seven-day week. I didn't know what a day off was like.

You put up with an awful lot from your newscasters in those days because they knew it was virtually impossible to replace them. So I'd close the station up at 1:00 A.M. and stagger home and try to get some sleep. We went back on the air with the 6:00 A.M. newscast, and at 5:00

the guy who was supposed to open up would call. It was obvious he was hung over or drunk or whatever, and he'd say he didn't feel so well, you better get a substitute to put that 6:00 A.M. newscast on. You know who the substitute would be; you'd meet yourself coming back.

I covered Roosevelt's news conferences regularly. There would be two a week—a morning and an afternoon, so the morning papers and the afternoon papers would have an equal shot at the latest news. The morning session was supposed to start at ten-thirty, and I don't recall it ever starting before eleven. When Mr. Truman became president, that was a big upset, because people had become accustomed to arriving at five minutes before eleven for the ten-thirty newscast—knew they'd wait anyhow. When they arrived at five minutes to eleven for Mr. Truman, it was over.

When Roosevelt won his fourth-term victory, he had gotten the election returns at Hyde Park and came back to Washington a couple of days later. There was a big celebration, and Mr. Meyer [owner of the *Washington Post*] wanted his station to be competitive with the networks, despite the fact that he didn't have the facilities and we had no mobile equipment. It was important to Mr. Meyer that we participate and bring the news of this to the people, so we arranged with the telephone company to set up our lines, and the cord had to run through the thousands of people who were gathered at Union Station to greet Roosevelt. The closest outlet to the spot where the car would stop was several hundred yards away. We finally got all this set up, with people along the route to keep the crowd from trampling on our connections, and there I am with the microphone at curbside, my newscaster at my side, and he's got his instructions as to where the car will stop. The secret service man standing there gave me a very cold look and said, "What do you think you are going to do with that microphone?" I told him we would hand-hold the mike in the president's direction and hope that we picked it up, and he said, "No way." I said, "Don't tell me no way—I've got to have equal access to him with the rest of these guys. We're also a radio station, we have just as much right . . . ," and he said, "Don't give me a hard time, fellow. I have my instructions. You walk across here, you're going to be in real bad trouble. Don't cross this line."

I had a couple of minutes to ponder the alternatives: Is he going to shoot me? If he's just going to arrest me, that's okay, so long as my announcer gets to do his job. Finally we decided to hell with it, when the president's car stops, we're going to take those three steps and hold the mike forward. So it did, and we did, and the secret service man didn't do anything about it, except get mad as could be. And right at that moment a connection came loose, and I got a frantic signal from my announcer, who saw no point in our pushing forward because we'd just come undone. So I said, "Go back and plug it in," and in the meantime, I said, "Mr. President, could you hold it for a moment? We're unplugged." He said, "I suppose so." Then he turned to Truman and said, "Take your hat off, they want to see what you look like." The crowd was cheering; Truman had taken his hat off and was smiling and waving. Then I got the okay that we were plugged in again, and I said, "Thank you, Mr. President." And he said, "Young man, would it be all right if I start now?"

A small station had to use ingenuity. I remember one day we were waiting for V-E Day or V-J Day, or some big announcement, and I stationed Lew Aiken at a pay phone in the White House. He was the biggest newscaster we had, big barrel-chested guy and a scrapper, tough.

I said to him, "As we go into the press conference, just tie up that phone, get on the phone and stay on it." This was right outside the pressroom, where there were perhaps some fifty direct-line telephones.

I knew the *Post* reporter would have priority on that direct line. We could pick up that phone and say, "Give me the WINX newsroom," and she'd put us through at once. I said, "As we bust out of there, there are going to be some people who are going to try to yank you off that phone. When they do, just puff out that big chest of yours and growl, and keep talking, I don't care what you say, and in a few seconds I'll be along."

There used to be an awful scramble getting out of there. You'd have to come around that big Philippine mahogany table in the center of the room, and sometimes people got hurt trying to run around full blast. Once the newsreel guys had set up a ladder so that somebody could get up there and hold the floodlights to take pictures of us as we came racing out, and Smitty [Merriman Smith] wasn't expecting the ladder to be there. He tripped on the foot of the ladder, tried to regain his balance as he went along on that slippery floor for maybe thirty or forty or fifty feet and finally ended up knocking over some furniture and went just ass over teacup into the corner. He bounced off that corner like a billiard ball, knocked over lamps and ashtrays and things, picked himself up, got into the booth and dictated for an hour and ten minutes and then collapsed. He had a broken collarbone.

I don't remember life being very difficult during the war. I heard people say there were shortages and inconveniences. I just thought it was such crap that I would rather not talk about it. The inconveniences we experienced at home were so minor compared to what other people were undergoing in the armed forces. It seemed to me then, and it seems to me now, utterly selfish to think it an inconvenience to line up for cigarettes. What a helluva hardship! Really!

Occasionally somebody would say, "What's the matter with you, you look healthy, why the hell are you not in uniform?" But usually this came from a man who was in uniform and had had a couple of beers, and how can you get mad at him? You just pay no attention to that. Yeah, I felt bad myself; it was just awkward that I was at that age. It was like in bingo, my number was still in there when everybody else was called.

They actually didn't get to my number till almost the end of the war. I was in Washington at the time, and they sent me a notice from Ohio. I informed my boss of this, and he said, "Oh, that's no problem. We'll get you a deferral on the basis of the important work you're doing," and I said, "Thanks a heap, but I'd rather you don't. I doubt that they would take anybody as old and decrepit as I am, but if they want me, please don't interfere." So he gave me a lecture about how this was very foolish and there were a lot of malingerers out there who had gotten deferred and all the rest, but I said no. And that was the last of it. The war was over before anyone got around to calling me. So I don't know how it would have turned out.

I was working seven days a week, and I interpreted that as a form of volunteerism that was the most useful contribution I could make.

The thing that sticks out in my mind about the war years is the tremendous thrill of having a sense of participation in these things. There was a tremendous social change at the time to admit blacks and females to full citizenship, to accept them in terms of their own abilities, or inabilities, instead of in terms of the stereotypes we were accustomed to. We had no choice except to take anything that was alive and warm and see if we could use it. We learned a great deal. This was our reserve. And we found we had one hell of a reserve we hadn't been using.

The security was so lax in Washington at the time. I remember one session in one of the navy buildings attended by Forrestal, Nimitz, and the head of Eisenhower's air force, and a couple of other people of this sort. The reporters who covered the meeting were not asked to show any credentials. All they had to do was sign a book; you could sign "Mahatma Gandhi" in the book. And the smiling girl sitting there would have said, "Thank you, Mr. Gandhi," and passed you on. It was just fantastic what access the public had to terribly important people. The Pentagon was one of the few places where there was any meaningful security. The rest of Washington was very casual—and God was on our side. We just never got into any difficulty.

And there was no question about the country's unity. You just felt that the stranger sitting next to you, in a restaurant or someplace, felt the same way you did about the basic issues.

Don Baldwin began the war on a small weekly in Idaho Falls—but soon was working for the Associated Press in San Francisco, where he spent the rest of the war.

The weekly paper in Idaho Falls was not affected very much by the war. We had a small staff. I was the city editor. There were two men and some women. We lost some people in the composing room, and the first guy drafted was a forty-four-year-old printer. He couldn't believe it; he didn't think he was going to go to war, and his was the first number out of the fishbowl.

There was no defense industry in that area. The only thing that happened was that they began working on a project to make alcohol from potatoes, which we grew a lot of in Idaho. We covered that to some extent because the alcohol was needed in the defense effort. Idaho is a fairly isolated, insulated state.

I left right after Pearl Harbor and went down to Santa Barbara, California, and worked on the paper there for three months. I was there when a Japanese submarine shelled that petroleum dump outside Santa Barbara. The town was shaken up, and a lot of people left right after that.

Then I worked with the Associated Press in San Francisco, and for a while I wrote radio news. We would take news from the newspaper wires and rewrite it for broadcasting. Then I went to work for what was called the cable desk, processing material coming in from the Pacific war zone. It came in on the old teletypes at forty-five words a minute, and we'd process it and write roundups.

I never really felt that we ever caught up with the war news. I always felt behind. And so many things were proscribed. For instance, when the Japanese were sending balloons over with incendiary bombs—not over California, but over Oregon—we knew and couldn't write about it.

The censorship was voluntary. Anything that would telegraph some-thing that was going to happen was taboo. We, of course, were very con-scious of the Japanese in California, even though we had them all locked up. We were very careful not to telegraph the names of ships arriving and departing, troop movements. We did not play down U.S. casualty figures. We ran everything we got. I think there would have been censorship in the field, but if we got it from overseas, we would tend to use it, because it would have been cleared by the marine censor on Okinawa. We were more concerned with things we picked up from other sources than our incoming cables.

Early in the war, right after Pearl Harbor, there was some real fear of an actual invasion by the Japanese. Nobody knew how many Japanese ships were out there—there were all sorts of rumors. As a matter of fact, they would have had no great trouble landing. They would have had a great deal of trouble staying there, but no great trouble landing in the San Francisco area, or particularly south of there.

Late in the war, when you began to get the kamikaze pilots around Okinawa and that area—man, the ships that used to come into San Francisco were a terrible sight. They had been hit sometimes two and three times, and they were just coming in every day. Some were so badly damaged you wondered how they had gotten back. This made a city like San Francisco feel very close to the war.

To begin with, I didn't like the idea of the Nisei evacuation. In Idaho we had quite a few Japanese Americans. They ran truck farms, and I had been to school with some Japanese and liked them. I had had long talks with them, and the feeling around Santa Barbara was that the rich, white farmers were making a grab for the Japanese truck lands, and I think it's true. Among newspapermen, there was quite a bit of feeling that this was a bad deal. The trouble was in actually getting in-formation. Everything was so strained that we didn't really know, but you just don't take an American citizen and put him in an internment camp. But I think the general feeling in California was that it was neces-sary and a good thing. I think most people felt there was the potential for sabotage, telegraphing information about the movement of ships and troops. Fort Mason was there, ships were coming in and out all the time, so you had to get the Japanese out. This was a state of hysteria—in California more so than other states. There were continuing rumors of Japanese fleet movements in the early stages of the war, and I think a lot of Californians thought they were a risk.

I had a great sense of guilt being out of uniform, but I never ran into any problems with military men. My two sisters were there, both of whose husbands were in the service. They had an apartment near us, and I used to go to restaurants with three women with me and be very popular with young servicemen. We made some friends—one that we still hear from at Christmas. He was in the navy and came into San Francisco twice on destroyers that were really badly damaged, and it was a great boon for us because they would bring these damaged ships into the piers—we lived right down on the waterfront—and just dump everything off, getting them into the yards to repair them. So he would grab hams, underwear, shirts, and we ate well when he was there. We met him at a restaurant. He came and sat down with us—the young guys were so lonesome. We liked him and so we invited him out to the house to dinner. He was a first-class petty officer in communications.

My wife and I both gave a lot of blood and that kind of thing, but by and large we did not become involved in volunteer war work. I was busy all the time. Later in the war I was in the Coast Guard Auxiliary for about two years. I spent one day a week on San Francisco Bay patrolling what they called the degaussing area, where ships came in to get this antimagnetic belt around the hull that would deflect magnetic mines. I was on a fifty-two-foot patrol boat manned entirely by volunteers. Our mission was to keep other boats out of the way—this was right in the middle of the bay. They had some rather delicate electronic gear in this area, and we just patrolled around it, keeping fishing boats out. I think there were cables on the floor of the bay, so they didn't want any risk of hooks. It was kind of fun—we ate well.

San Francisco was a tremendously busy city. There were big shipyards over in Sausalito across the bay. Kaiser was building Liberty ships over there and dumping them in the water about every three days. A lot of the men and materiel going to the Pacific went out of San Franciso. There was a tremendous urgency. Some banks were staying open all night, theaters were open all night, bowling alleys—people were just working around the clock and catering to servicemen and shipyard workers. It was a twenty-four-hour city. With the time difference, the afternoon newspaper cycle fell from eleven at night until seven in the morning, so I worked nights for five or six years.

Mary McMurria worked for the Columbus (Ga.) Ledger.

Suddenly, from one day to the next, I was snatched out of the Women's Department and put in as city editor over this big newsroom. They had had trouble getting men to fill the post, and they had had a fellow, an unusual type, who wore purpley pink pants. When the editor told one of the newsmen that a new city editor was coming in, the newsman said, "I hope he doesn't wear pink pants." And the editor said, "Well, I don't think you'll be able to tell."

It was an experience for me. I was one of the first female city editors of that size paper, and it was exciting. I had to borrow a really snappy suit jacket from a woman—most of my reporters were women—to have my picture taken for *Time* magazine.

Henry, my husband, had arthritis, and it began to get worse about then, and we decided to go down to Homestead, Florida, which was almost as far south as we could go. So I quit the job in that first winter, and when I came back, I was a feature writer. The paper decided to sponsor tin-can and newspaper collections at the schools. Every week I'd have to visit the schools. We'd have the papers and the cans collected and keep a record of who had collected the most. There was a lot of excitement among the schoolchildren because about once a month our publisher, who was a colonel in the army reserve, would present a pennant to the school, which would be raised on the flagpole. I had to keep the excitement generated by writing features on this program.

Paul Kneeland was a reporter for the Medford (Mass.) Mercury. *But the war gave him an opportunity to move to the* Boston Globe, *and he is still there.*

From a personal point of view, Pearl Harbor didn't mean a thing to me. This sounds terribly callous, but I was 4-F. I had been classified October 16, 1940, because of a congenital defect in my left arm.

The editor of my paper was drafted, and I became editor of the paper. I had a small staff: one woman, and two men who were 4-F, for whatever reasons, I don't know. The woman was a middle-aged lady; she hardly was going to join the WACs. So the war didn't affect my working. As a matter of fact, when I became editor, I was given a fifteen-dollar raise, plus the glory of it all.

At that time the *Medford Mercury* was a provincial newspaper—printed no news about what progress the war was making on the eastern and western fronts. This was a common thing for many small daily and weekly newspapers at that time. If Dunkirk was invaded, you'd never learn it from the *Medford Mercury*. You'd buy a Boston newspaper or listen to the radio. In November '42 advertising was dropped because food stores didn't advertise. There was no necessity for advertising that a pound of butter was 49¢, with people standing in line to buy it. So financially the *Medford Mercury* was in straits, and instead of getting $37.50 a week as the editor, I was getting $15 cash and an IOU. Well, after a pocketful of IOUs I went to the manager and said: "What about this?" He said, "Well, we're doing the best we can." I said: "That's not good enough for me." I said I'd take it to the state labor board, and I did. The week after, I was fired—for wanting to collect my just and due salary. But they paid me off, over $200, and that ended my career at the *Medford Mercury*. After that I shopped for a job in Boston and was taken on at the *Boston Globe*.

I know for sure that I wouldn't have gotten the job had it not been for vacancies caused by the war. As a matter of fact, about a year after I went on the staff we were so short of people they would send me and other reporters down to the sidewalk to look for young boys to hire as office boys—just someone to bring up a cup of coffee or go downstairs and get some papers, it was just that short. They didn't want girls working at night. We were in not too good a district, on lower Washington Street, which was right around the corner from Scollay Square. Scollay Square, as any serviceman in World War II would tell you, is where you got what you wanted, whether it be wine, women, or song. It just wasn't the proper place for girls to work. But, finally, they did hire two or three women as office girls.

My early assignments were general reporting. I knew this war was going to end, and I had to do my very, very best to work up some sort of specialty so the editors would consider me when the returnees came back. And I was up against stiff competition. There were some fine reporters who went to war, came back, and they're still working there. They're my best friends. But I decided what I was interested in was personality interviews. So I came up with an idea of doing interviews with authors who spent their summers or winters in New England. Over a period of a year and a half I probably did fifty or sixty interviews with authors, some well known, some not so well known. And these made a big hit with Lawrence Winship, who was then the managing editor.

In 1943 I covered OPA (the Office of Price Administration) as a regular beat, five days a week. An OPA press conference was held every day at three-thirty with the codirectors of the information bureau, plus one of the men from enforcement, who might have a story on black markets, or one of the men in price, who might have an announcement to make about the fact that butter was no longer going to be two coupons but three coupons. It was nothing to walk out of that office and write a story which was guaranteed page one. Everybody wondered: Are they going to cut down on tire rationing? When are we going to get more nylons? After two or three months we all got to know the directors of each department. They would come down and be interviewed by the press. Well, the trick was not to wait for the press conference but to jump the press conference and talk to the directors the day before. So that's what we did. In all my years in this business—and I've been in it thirty-eight years—I never saw such rivalry. Everybody was trying to get the scoop, an extremely old-fashioned word, which is no longer used, about the fact that nylons were going to cost two coupons instead of one beginning on a certain date.

Boston was an extremely happy city during the war. We had the Charlestown Navy Yard here, and we had sailors on the streets, going to the movie houses when they had stage shows, and you could hear Vaughn Monroe or Harry James. People—servicemen and nonservicemen—were out for fun. The Charlestown Navy Yard was working nightly on three shifts, around the clock, repairing vessels and making equipment for the navy. At the time, I was going around with a girl who was a Boston University music school graduate. She was a church organist and piano teacher. She said this wasn't enough for her, and she went to a factory in Malden and asked if she could get a job in defense work. And they gave her the greasiest job, I think, that ever existed—we had a date, and when I went to kiss her, I said, "Go on, you smell like an oil can." She was dripping with oil. The price of war!

It was a happy town in spite of the tragedies, because every family shared that tragedy. "I lost a son"; "My daughter lost her husband." This travels up and down the town. A lot of that conversation was common in ration lines, swapping stories: "Is your boy here?" "Is he there?" "He's in the hospital, I hope he lives." "He lost his leg, lost his arm." Everyone had an interest in common, and that was: When will this war end, and what can we do? My mother religiously saved waste fats. I remember I brought some to a market once, I think I was given seven cents or something; my mother said, "It will help." And the clerk said: "I'm sorry, you have to put this in a coffee can." She had put it in some kind of cardboard container. I brought it back, she melted it down, saved the coffee can, marched back there with it. It was a pioneer spirit that hadn't existed for a hundred years. And it's never been the same.

Robert Bender started out working for the NBC newsroom in New York, but ended up down South.

At different times I worked with John Vandercook, H. V. Kaltenborn, Abe Schecter. I just kept up with the late news and fed it to Kaltenborn. Obviously the news was much more important then than it was in normal times. Everything was hectic, and we worked all kinds of hours around the clock. After a while I moved over into sports.

I remember the great army football teams at West Point—Doc Blanchard and Glen Davis during the war—1943. I think those army teams were probably the greatest ever to come out of a college, because they had the pick of the talent all through the U.S.

In 1943 I went to Norfolk, Virginia, as news director for station WTAR. If I had realized what was going to happen with TV, I never would have left, but I wanted more time on the air, and this opening came as news director, so I went.

You got a little more rough treatment in Norfolk, being a civilian, than you did in New York City, because it was a navy town. It was a very rough town during the war. I'd always been interested in swimming, so when I got to Norfolk, I was a water-safety instructor for the Red Cross. They, together with the navy, Y, and other organizations, organized this program where we taught swimming to the armed forces— to the navy, Marine Corps, and whatever else was available. Many of these boys came from the central part of the country and couldn't swim a lick. The navy attracts people from the inland. They're interested in boats and want to see what it's all about and travel. So I, along with a number of others, conducted swimming classes, at, I think, William and Mary. Years later, it filtered back to me that some of the fellows said that we had taught them something that had saved their lives. So I did feel I was contributing something. I got a certificate from President Truman, and to this day I'm not sure whether it was due primarily to my swimming instruction or whether it was due to the lives I had saved during my years as a lifeguard—I had saved something like twenty-five or thirty people.

They seemed such frantic days—I don't know. I don't have a great memory.

Gus Robbins was the owner and editor of a small newspaper in Hopewell, Virginia.

At the beginning of the war I had planned to make it a daily. It was the biggest semiweekly newspaper in Virginia—the *Hopewell News*. Of course, the war came along, and I couldn't get newsprint, so I went daily immediately after the war.

We had a National Guard company, Company E, which I was sort of godfather of—I had promoted it. In February 1941 they were taken into federal service and sent to Fort Meade, and the day after Pearl Harbor they were sent to Washington to guard the government buildings.

When the company left Washington, they went down to Fort Bragg. Then they were broken up, and the two hundred boys scattered all over the world. I must have had a thousand letters from them, which I had to go back at night and type, because I published every single one of them.

There was a great deal of sorrow over all the boys leaving. In addition to Company E, the draft started taking the boys, and, of course, that hit a small city pretty hard. But the general attitude was one of the utmost support of the war.

We are a chemical industrial city. The plants were still working twenty-four hours a day because everything they made went into the war effort.

There was never any doubt in my mind that we would win this war. We're too big and strong and powerful and too advanced in technology not to be able to do it. But there were some awful black days in 1942, when we were forced out of the Pacific—the Japs took Thailand, Burma, Singapore, Indonesia, and advanced almost to Australia.

When the first big scrap drive came along, the government did not run it or pay for it. I was president of the Virginia Press Association then, and I got five daily newspapers to put up the money to rent an office and get an executive director. We put on a statewide drive, and every single newspaper in Virginia, from the smallest weekly to the biggest daily, ran every release that I wrote and mailed out to them about the scrap drive—every one of them.

The public responded beautifully. We had a very wide boulevard in front of one of our schools—and the city roped off one full block, and we had that street full, piled as high as you could get it. The scrap dealer went through it, separated it, baled it, and shipped it out by rail to where it was needed. That was the way it was handled, not only in Virginia but across the country. We were proud of that. I've got four or five National Guard commendations for this effort.

Jack Altshul began the war working on a Long Island weekly newspaper but soon transferred to Newsday, *where he still writes a regular column.*

A guy I knew, who was working on a small paper on Long Island, decided he was very draftable, so he ducked out to South America and let me have some of his clients. This meant I was stringing on Long Island for the *New York Times* and the *Herald Tribune,* until, all of a sudden, they had a newsprint problem and stopped it. So I found that my most profitable vehicle for breaking news was at the new newspaper *Newsday.* After about six months they asked me to come work on the desk at night, in Hempstead, and six months after that, in January 1943, they asked me to become city editor.

I had this limited deferment because of my eye, and I felt that, at any time now, they would be calling me. So I said to Alan Hathway, who was moving up to managing editor, "I'd better not take this, Alan, until I get my army thing straightened away. I'm going to enlist, and if they take me, fine, and if they don't, they will probably make me 4-F, and I will take the job."

So they gave me a farewell party, and I went to Governor's Island. I got to the point where the examining officer, the final guy, looks at all the things that are right or wrong with you, and he picked up the "Accepted" stamp, looked at it, shook his head, and, ding, "Rejected!" That made me a 4-F, not very happily, I must say. But I liked the idea of being city editor.

The first impact of the war you felt was the boys going away. All of a sudden you had almost a full female staff, which in those days was a little innovative. My wife, Edna, for instance, was the first female photographer in the metropolitan area at the time. She walked in, a beautiful girl looking for a job. Hathway looked at her, and said, "We're hiring her." And she came out a hell of a good photographer.

Even then, the Island was a fairly prosperous area. They didn't have any ghettos in those days. It was a commuting community, and most people had white-collar jobs until the start of the war. Then, all of a sudden, you had Grumman, Republic, and Sperry in our own midst advertising for women machinists, welders, and riveters. They must have hired 100,000 people.

That was the first big influx of that kind of industry on Long Island. A lot of women had husbands away at war. I think they would have worked at these defense factories whether or not they were paid for it in many cases. In those days most people were making fifty, sixty bucks a week. Today you consider that a pittance, but fifty or sixty bucks a week then was good bread. But you didn't have a feeling of boom times. Even if people had a helluva lot more money than they had before, what could they do with it? They couldn't buy new cars, they couldn't buy appliances, they couldn't get gas, fancy cuts of meat, butter, or any of the status-symbol commodities.

Hempstead was a congested town because you had Mitchell Field two miles away, and the soldiers from Mitchell Field made it an army town. The theaters were booming, and the bars were booming. I can remember a bar up the street from the paper—it was our hangout in those days, and you never knew when you'd go there and see some airmen getting into a fight and cops dragging them out.

There were a lot of good stories from the war. I remember the case of the fifty super forts. Jimmy Jenkins was the wire-service editor, and it was his custom to bring the first paper of each new edition up to the balcony so I could peruse it. I had written the page-one banner: "Fifty Super Forts Bomb Tokyo." When the paper was placed on my desk, the first thing to hit me was that an *a* had been substituted for the *o* in the third word of the headline. I didn't look twice, and I suppose the whole scene resembled a Mack Sennett comedy as I careened down the stairs to the pressroom shouting, "Stop the presses!"

I stopped long enough to launch an invective at composing-room foreman Jack Schlegel for allowing the headline to get on the press. He joined the rest of the composing room and Jenkins in the horse laugh that followed. My friend, the indelicate wire editor, had asked a compositor to print up the phony lead and pasted it over the real one. And I had fallen for it.

Then there was the Brooks case, which had all the elements of a
movie scenario. The "pink" edition of the *New York Daily News* on
March 7, 1945, carried a small story saying that Grace Brooks,
Roosevelt, Long Island, a young bride, was trying for an audience with
Mayor LaGuardia that morning to plead with him to use his influence
on the navy, so that her husband would not be shipped back to Italy to
stand trial for seduction. LaGuardia had involved himself in the case
when he received a letter from Pizzo, Italy, in which a father charged
that Navy Chief Pharmacist Mate Frederic Brooks had promised to
marry his daughter and then "destroyed her innocence."

The easily outraged LaGuardia passed along the letter to the navy
with a recommendation that they send him back to Pizzo, where a court
was waiting to try him on the charges. Brooks had been thrown into the
brig, and his wife heard that he would be shipped out for the trial
momentarily. She turned to the *Daily News* for help.

Instead she got it from Hathway, who, upon reading the story, routed
reporter Bea Jones from bed and told her to get over to Grace Brooks's
house to find out what it was all about.

Bea's heart went out to the young girl, who tearfully maintained that
her husband was innocent of the charge but that his story would never
carry weight in a hometown Italian court. How, she asked the reporter,
could she convince the navy to conduct an inquiry into the case before
sending one of its most decorated heroes to an inevitable jail cell in a
foreign country.

Bea arranged to meet her at eight o'clock in the morning and ac-
company her to LaGuardia's office in City Hall. When she arrived at the
Brooks's home, the young bride was in a virtual state of hysteria; she
had just received a phone call from her husband, who had been told
that he was being flown over "as soon as an armed guard arrives."

Now it was Bea's turn to get Hathway out of bed to tell him the story
had narrowed down to a race against time. Hathway immediately sent a
telegram to the secretary of the navy detailing the facts of the case and
asking him to postpone Brooks's departure pending a navy inquiry. The
managing editor also made a rush call to Long Island Congressman
[Leonard] Hall, who promised to do everything he could for the sailor.

Meanwhile, the bride and the reporter had been refused entrance to
LaGuardia's office and proceeded to the navy receiving pier where
Brooks had been held in the brig since his arrival home. By this time a
dozen reporters had arrived on the scene, and while they were

clamoring for an interview with Brooks, Bea Jones calmly walked in with his wife and proceeded to talk to him.

Bea then managed to sneak into the office of the station's commanding officer and demanded to know why an American serviceman had been put in a position where he was virtually sure of being found guilty without benefit of fair trial.

The navy commander had apparently gotten word from his superiors by that time. He assured the reporter that the navy would conduct an investigation before turning Brooks over to civil authorities in Italy.

At two o'clock that morning, as the reporter was finishing the story of her day with the Brookses, Grace called, a happy note in her voice for the first time. A captain had visited her husband and told him that the flying orders had been canceled. Secretary Forrestal had ordered a further review of the case. A seek later the board found Brooks innocent of the charges, and he was restored to full duty. But first he would spend a month at Saint Albans Naval Hospital recovering from the battle fatigue engendered by months of treating and ferrying wounded GIs off Italian beaches under Nazi air attack.

The Brooks case became a nationwide cause célèbre. Veterans groups from all over the country offered *Newsday* money to help the young couple. New York's City Council officially rebuked LaGuardia for meddling in an affair that didn't concern him. When Leonard Hall flew to Europe immediately after V-E Day to view Nazi concentration camps, he was congratulated on all sides by servicemen who had heard of his fight to save Brooks. And *Newsday* received commendatory letters from Secretary Forrestal and Congressman Hall for calling their attention to the situation.

Ted Giddings was the city editor of the Berkshire Eagle *in Pittsfield, Massachusetts. He still writes a regular column for the* Eagle.

I think the war affected our community the way it did most. It was rallying around the flag, so to speak. Civil defense and war gardens, a lot of volunteer activity, and that sort of thing. I started my own garden. Also I was involved in civil defense, an air-raid warden.

We went in pretty big for salvage drives. During the war, a reenactment of General Knox's march down from Fort Ticonderoga was staged, picking up some salvage material—old cannons. A lot of the towns donated cannons, scrap iron that had been in front of town halls and places like that for years, practically back to the Civil War. Those were all lugged off to Boston and shipped out to be used for scrap iron, to some ordnance factory somewhere. *Life* magazine sent a photographer up here on that occasion.

One thing that stood out more than anything else in my own mind at the time that it happened was that we didn't seem to sense the fact that we didn't have, as a country, the capacity to strike back; we didn't realize the enormity of the strike in the Philippines. I think if you go through the files of the paper here, you'll find things like, "We're going to turn our navy loose, and we are going to catch them and show them a thing or two." But it didn't happen, because we had been disabled to a greater extent than we realized. It took awhile for that to sink in. I don't think I had any fear that we might not win the war. I guess I was enough of an optimist to think we were going to pull through, somehow, but it was going to be tough going.

Frankly, I was more aware of food shortages in World War I, as a child, than in World War II. As a child, in a family of five children, we had stricter rationing, it seems to me, as far as food on the table, and I was much more conscious of it at that time. At the *Eagle* we did have a shortage of paper, and there were times when we had to run smaller papers because of it. Gasoline shortage created some problems in this rural area. With what they called an A-ration card, you really couldn't go anywhere outside of the community very much. The length of the workday wasn't much affected at the *Eagle*, because before the Wages and Hours Law came into effect, we weren't too conscious of hours; we worked fairly long hours regularly.

When the first servicemen began to come home, they had a dinner party for returnees, and they didn't have too much to say. But one of their associates who had stayed behind in our composing room gave a talk on the hardships that he endured trying to have a war garden. It cracked them up. He was a very amusing guy. He told of the hoes he broke and the trouble he had with seeds. He kind of stole the show.

I think the war drew the community closer together, and the spirit was better during that period. There was less wrangling and a better spirit of cooperation, and there wasn't the infighting as far as the day-to-day operation, politically speaking. Their minds were on a national situation rather than the local. Not that they forbore altogether, but they did work together better. The morale in Pittsfield was pretty good. If anything, it tended to be an exhilarating rather than depressing time. People seemed to be able to roll with the punches pretty well.

Alison Arnold was society editor of the Boston Herald *as well as a mother with two children and her husband in the service.*

The war changed the pattern of social life in Boston, because all of the social affairs—the big events and parties, whenever there were any—were all to benefit some kind of war relief. The debutante parties were cut out. Everything was done for war relief.

Partly because the lighting was dim, people didn't go out much at night. The streetlights all had shields over them, and we had trial blackouts. You never knew when it was going to happen. You would hear this horrible siren blowing, and that meant you had to turn out all your lights and sit in the dark until the all clear blew.

All along the coast there was a great fear of submarines. They had barbed wire on the beach, and all our windows toward the shore were fitted with blackout curtains. I don't remember any real incidents, but people took it pretty seriously.

Downtown I felt uncomfortable. Sometimes the servicemen sort of got out of hand in Scollay Square, which is now the government center. In those days it was pretty bad. Sailors would come there on leave and cause havoc, and they would have riots down there. Nothing major, but the police were always down there. Young ladies were more or less advised to keep away from Scollay Square. I had a daughter thirteen, and I think she was at the age where she was intrigued that there were so many soldiers and people in uniform. Like all the girls at that age, she thought it was quite thrilling to see all the boys in uniform, but she wasn't allowed to date any of them. There was a war, and people were going off to war. She thought it was quite romantic. She eventually got over it. All the glamor went out of uniforms and war as time went by.

Leo Hershfield was working in New York for the newspaper PM *as artist and assistant art director until a job offer from the Office of War Information brought him down to Washington.*

The war was always with us long before Pearl Harbor, and we [at PM] came out forcefully for aid to Britain and France. I was doing cartoons, spots, charts, and sometimes diagrams of torpedoes and such under the direction of Willy Ley, who had been a pioneer with Opel in Germany in the field of rocketry.

I recall doing many cartoons and caricatures of Nazis, Fascists, quislings. There was one cartoon which brought plenty of fan mail—showed a toothy Japanese militarist with tank cannon pointing out of the page with the caption: "Maybe Honorable U.S. wish return of scrap iron, yes?" That was more than a year before Pearl Harbor. The U.S. had been a prime source of scrap metal for Japan for years. In fact the miles of track of New York's dismantled elevated had been shipped there.

PM's offices were in Brooklyn for the first two or three years. On fine days some of the staffers would lunch in nearby Prospect Park, and I remember the arguments over the opening of the second front. Some strongly urged an immediate opening of the second front to relieve the hard-pressed Russians. Other amateur military planners like myself were against it. Okay, the Russians were our allies now and were having a bad time of it, but we were not prepared. These arguments got pretty heated, and I was often outgunned.

A lot of folks couldn't get used to the idea of our being allies with the Russians, but we were. And there would not have been an Allied victory if they had not rallied from the Nazi push toward Moscow and with such battles as Stalingrad.

People, if they argued too strenuously for aid to Russia, were suspected of having Communist leanings or perhaps being card-carrying CPs, but I can't say truthfully who were or weren't. I never laid eyes on a red card. The Hearst press in particular baited PM as a Communist stronghold, and it was all a lot of hogwash.

I left PM in early '43 to join a group of good friends and former PM editors in Washington. My job at the imposing new Social Security Building on Independence Avenue, which the Office of War Information took over, was as art director/artist for the Domestic News Bureau. which meant helping put out a paper called *Victory Bulletin*—a sort of showcase for information and illustrations to be sent out to newspapers around the country, with drawings and charts to be mailed to the smaller dailies and weeklies in mat form.

I also had the job of urging editorial and gag cartoonists to contribute drawings, and they were most cooperative in wanting to help in the war effort. There was Ed Duffy, two-time Pulitzer Prize winner on the *Baltimore Sun*, and Dan Fitzpatrick of the *St. Louis Post-Dispatch*, to name a couple of the editorial artists. Among the gag cartoonists were Bill Steig, Garrett Price, Richard Decker, Chon Day, Sogolow—all *New Yorker* contributors—and many others.

There were messages in cartoons to buy bonds, save fat, and for safety in the plants, for silence against talking about things that might aid the enemy, for car pools to save fuel. Some of it may seem a bit silly now, but we worked hard to get the messages across. There was a letter of commendation passed along to me from Sen. William Fulbright, who was chairman of a committee overseeing the activities of the OWI.

In late '44 the battles of the budget and the funding of OWI got tougher on the Hill, and I had had enough of the constant threat of cutting down on the service, so I resigned. However, I continued on as a consultant.

PM liked the idea of having an artist-correspondent in Washington. During this period, the most interesting time in Washington, I was given some assignments but dreamed up many for myself. One was a double-page feature of "A Day at Walter Reed Hospital." Heading for the designated operating room, I went in the wrong door. Looking down at an operation in company of doctors and nurses, I learned I was watching a hysterectomy. The military hospital also operated on wives of military personnel. In another operating room, properly gowned and masked, I sat and sketched while the surgeon sawed away at a resection of a leg stump. Blood all over the place. The young soldier, with a local anaesthetic, seemed quite unconcerned about the whole thing. In the manner of standard TV correspondents' queries nowadays, I asked, "How do you feel?" "Well," he said, "It's like sitting on a board and somebody sawing on it." Went into another area after turning in the mask and gown and sketched a man being fitted with an artificial leg in the prosthetics department.

PM's Sunday editor, Bill McCleery, had me do a number of covers of generals and other notables. It's a long list. De Gaulle on the White House lawn; General Wainwright, after his ordeal at Corregidor and as prisoner, at the Pentagon; James Byrnes, director of war mobilization, in the East Wing of the White House—a shocking experience, that. Walking across the thick carpet to shake his hand, I built up enough static to light a bulb. Our hands crackled, and I jumped. He grinned and said something about his magnetic personality. Good guy to sketch. So was Dean Acheson.

There must have been thousands of young men in their thirties in America then who felt the way George Garrott did—not believing in war, not wanting to volunteer but feeling that you ought to do something, and not really objecting to being called. At the outbreak of the war he was working in New York for the New York Times. *But he was soon on the move in the army and out. This is the story of one man's World War II odyssey.*

I had seen other men at the *Times* go in and get these publicity jobs. A copyreader I knew had volunteered and been sent to 90 Church Street, and he told me, "George, if I were you, I'd just wait and see what happens. This is terrible to be transferred down to 90 Church Street; you get much less money than you do at the *Times*, and you're not really in the war and not part of it." So I just let it go.

I don't feel that war ever solves anything. I had followed a good deal of what Hitler was doing, and I felt as though he was just straightening out the borders there in Poland. And then the Sudetenland, the part of Czechoslovakia populated by Germans, it seemed as though this sort of belonged to Germany, and it was a straightening out, one of the applications of Woodrow Wilson's principles of each country determining its own language and nationality. But when he began taking over other lands and demanding everything, it became obvious that he was someone that had to be stopped. I felt that the United States was sort of being sucked into the war, but I don't see how we could have avoided it. I didn't volunteer, because I felt I was doing an essential job. But, of course, everybody felt he was doing an essential job.

Finally, I was drafted. I went over to Newark, New Jersey, on May 10, 1943, passed my physical, and was told to come back eight days later, May 18, which was my thirty-sixth birthday. I was put on a train overnight and ended up in Petersburg, Virginia, at Camp Pickett, an immense place, where we went through basic medical training, stretcher bearing, bandaging, et cetera. Although I could type faster than anybody could ever learn in the army—sixty to eighty words a minute—they decided that I was to go to typing school, so I spent six or eight weeks learning to type.

We didn't take the regular basic training, where you had to go under live fire. I went through that later. Frankly, to me it was like a picnic, because I'd been sitting on night rewrite for four or five years from six o'clock at night until four or five o'clock in the morning, and this was like going out camping. I remember we got up to an eleven-mile march; all the men under twenty-five dropped out, and all the men over thirty made it. I was with another man who was about my age, and we made the thing principally because we just didn't dare confess that we couldn't make a march like that.

I was assigned to Richmond, Virginia, the Quartermaster Corps, and worked in an armory there for most of a year, counting groceries.

While I was in Richmond, working an adding machine, I felt that I was just wasting my time, and my family had connections. I had a brother living in Washington, so I went up there and called on the city editor of the *Times*, Marshall Newton, who was down in the Pentagon as a lieutenant colonel. I just dropped down to see him and said, "Look here, I'm stuck down there in Richmond, and it seems like an awful waste of time just doing nothing. At least if I could get some travel and go someplace." He said, "Oh, God, we need you. We need you in publicity. I'll take you over to so-and-so." They immediately worked out a transfer to Rareton Arsenal up near New Brunswick. I learned later that was the biggest publications center around, where they published all the army manuals. I worked with a young lieutenant, Charles Collins, writing little articles about people who were being drafted into the army. It was part of a program to show that there was some kind of a social and human interest. I really enjoyed that.

My wife moved up to New Jersey, and we had this nice little house within walking distance of my office. Then came D day, the invasion of June 6, 1944, and everything was in complete uproar. It was a headquarters company, and we got orders to move to Aberdeen, Maryland, to be shipped overseas. So we moved out of the house, my wife went back to live with my parents, I got on a train and went to Aberdeen. Almost every day there'd be a big trainload of troops being taken up to Elizabeth, New Jersey, to be shipped overseas. But the ship would already be full, so the train would come back with them. Somebody told me that a trainload of troops from the East would be shipped to San Francisco, and they would pass a trainload of troops from San Francisco being shipped from the West. I wasn't doing anything except waiting to be assigned overseas, so I wrote to Elmer Davis, who was then head of OWI, and told him I was just sitting there doing nothing.

I'd never known him, but I got a personal letter from him in less than a week saying that everything was pretty well fouled up everywhere and that they surely could use me and he would see what he could do. The next week I got a long paper that I filled out for somebody in OWI. A couple of more weeks went by, and finally this thing came through—a Section 10 discharge for the good of the country, I think. As I recall, I went up as a buck private to the company headquarters carrying this thing which said something about at the request of General Eisenhower in Europe you are to be taken out of the army and transferred over to OWI for service overseas in the European theater. Within a few days I was out, with the understanding that I would technically still belong to OWI, although I was honorably discharged from the army, until the end of the war. I was on military leave from the *Times*.

While I was in New York, I was kept in reserve for service in London. Then I was transferred down to Washington, I think in February 1945, to a big new building at the bottom of Capitol Hill. First I did reporting. It was almost exactly like being a Washington correspondent. I covered Congress, and then I filled in at the State Department, White House, Agriculture Department. I wrote stories just like for a newspaper. Usually the first two paragraphs were picked up and used for radio, and then the rest of the stories were sent out on what they called a wireless bulletin. It was a file which was sent to embassies all over the world, which they issued as sort of a release. Nothing I wrote went to the home front; we were forbidden to do anything on the home front.

Washington, the last year of the war, was pretty crowded. We had an awful time finding an apartment. You just couldn't find anyplace to live. It was a war city, just full of people. I was kept busy. I really worked hard there for a while. I liked it.

When the war was over in May 1945, theoretically my military leave was expiring. Ed Barrett, who was head of the operation I was in in Washington, wrote a letter to the *New York Times* saying that they'd like to keep me to help transfer this into a civilian organization. They were going to keep OWI—they changed its name about five times in a couple of years, long before it became USIA. When my military leave did end and the war in Japan ended, I was supposed to go back with the *Times*—back where I'd been before, on night rewrite. I went back and looked it over, and there were other people doing the job that I'd been doing, and I thought I'd be sort of an extra person. I had had this offer at a fairly good salary in Washington with this new outfit, so I gave up the security of the *Times* for the insecurity of an organization that had to be authorized by Congress every year.

Melville Grosvenor, now editor-in-chief of the National Geographic *and chairman emeritus of the board of the National Geographic Society, was assistant editor of the magazine during the war and a graduate of the Naval Academy in the 1920s.*

Ironically enough, the war probably saved my life.

I was signed up to go into the navy, where I would have been a lieutenant commander and probably in charge of one of the destroyer escorts. However, I was turned down by the doctors. I had fibrillations of the heart. I myself didn't know that my heart was skipping and very irregular. In fact, the corpsman couldn't count my pulse. Looking at me strangely, he called the doctor, who, having no better luck, said, "You ought to be in the hospital right now; what are you doing here?" So I called my doctor, and he couldn't believe it either. I had had a physical a few months before. So they took me to the hospital. I was there two weeks. They gave me treatments and finally shook it down, and it saved my life. My heart, it seemed, had already enlarged double. And it would have gone on until something burst. I might never have known about it except for that physical.

At the magazine, believe it or not, my Naval Academy training came in handy. One doesn't ordinarily think of Annapolis as a good preparation for editorial work, but, for me, it proved to be ideal in the circumstances of the war.

At the academy we had been taught to think globally; I was used to studying maps to the concepts of strategy; I knew of battles and their place in history.

Our history courses at Annapolis had focused on the influence of sea power on history. We studied naval battles from the earliest days and what influence they had on the world and how the winning of a battle could change things radically. When it came to our war in the Pacific, I could sit down and figure out, "Well, now, they've got to go here first, then they've got to go there." And I could understand the general thrust of the strategy employed.

With this in mind, we could then prepare articles well ahead of time on those places that would figure in the news. But we weren't so much interested in the battles; we wanted to describe the background of the islands and archipelagos involved, and we worked very closely with the government.

It's no longer a secret now. For example, take the case of Okinawa. G-2 came to the *Geographic* in 1943 and asked in confidence to see all the photographs, maps, and material we possessed on Okinawa. I made a mental note of this. Then I studied the map, and it seemed obvious that our forces would have to hit Okinawa before proceeding north to attack Japan itself. It was an excellent jumping-off place for this final attack. At the *Geographic* we had very little in the files on the island— just a few pictures. But we learned of a retired member of the State Department who'd been stationed on Okinawa for seventeen years and lived out in Virginia.

He had an excellent collection of pictures. He agreed to do an article for us on the island, and our article was published in May 1945—and delivered the very month that the U.S. Marines landed on Okinawa. One of the things the author had told us about were the deep, elaborate tombs employed by Okinawans. He maintained that they would be very effective in a military defense, and that's one of the things the Japanese did on the island. They employed the tombs as defensive installations. We often managed, throughout the war, to be a jump ahead of the action. We felt at that time that our mission was simply to present the facts so that people could understand where our forces were operating.

For example, before the war we had had a wonderful series of pictures made of the Italian lake region and of Florence. I recommended at the proper time in the course of the war that we have another article on the region. We got the photographs out, had the plates made, and had them all ready to go. And then when the army was fighting up there, in the course of the Italian campaign, we published an article with twenty-four pages of color of that precise country where they were fighting.

The son of our minister at the National Presbyterian Church of the Covenant was a pilot. He was on a bombing raid of Florence, and he wrote in a letter to his mother and father how he had been briefed on avoiding all the historic monuments. He wrote a story about it, and we ran that with the article and the other pictures of Florence the way it used to be. Unfortunately, he was shot down and killed in the month just before we published the article.

We did have trouble with the paper shortage. We used special coated paper which was of premium quality. Things reached a point where the company that supplied us had so many orders that they told us one day, "We simply can't afford to make your paper. We have to raise the price." That was okay with us. So we joined the company in a petition to the War Production Board to increase the price of the paper. The board turned us down. It seemed that we would have no paper available. So, we had to buy the company. We bought it at a very good price, and then we sold paper to ourselves at a loss.

Throughout the war we felt that we were being helpful, not only to the American public but to the military as well. Soldiers and sailors would write letters telling us how they had *Geographic* maps everyplace they went. We printed them by the hundreds of thousands. We even had special printings of our regular maps, which were distributed all through the army, the navy, and the air force.

Just after the marines had landed on Guadalcanal, Adm. Chester Nimitz made an inspection tour to that island. He took off in an airplane from a New Hebrides base. The airplane, the only one available, was an army B-17 with a brand-new young pilot and a new crew just out from the states. They had never before flown in this area. All they had was a strip map showing the route up to Guadalcanal, with nothing appearing on the flanks before or behind. Well, after they'd been flying for several hours, Nimitz said, "Given this length of time and this air speed, we've obviously flown past the island and are now heading out into the Coral Sea." So he sent his aide up to ask the pilot where they were and when they would land. The pilot replied, "Quite frankly, I don't know; I'm lost. I'm off the track and I've not the slightest idea where we are." Nimitz said, "Does anybody here have any maps?" One of his aides said, "Yes, I've got a *Geographic* map of the Pacific in my suitcase." So they got it out, and the admiral plotted their course from the Hebrides. They discovered that they had probably gone right through some clouds and missed the island chain, and they were truly flying over the Coral Sea. So Nimitz plotted it out again and said, "We've got to make a 120-degree turn, and if we do, we're bound to hit the islands coming around like that. So he sent orders to the pilot saying, "Lieutenant, I'm taking command of the airplane now, and I order you to change to such-and-such course and fly that until we pick up the island chain." Well, they did that, and very shortly the islands were looming up on the horizon. From the map, they managed to identify the individual islands immediately. This enabled them to change course again, and they landed on Guadalcanal with only half an hour of fuel left. Nimitz told me after the war that the *Geographic* map had undoubtedly saved his life. This was no small thing, since he was commander-in-chief of the fleet at the time.

Before the onset of World War II, admirals and generals as a class had little use for air power. Even Pearl Harbor didn't shake them up much. I myself had always been enthusiastic about what a big fleet of carriers could do—particularly in the Pacific. My aviation friends said that it would be possible to take tankers, cover them up, and put flight decks on them, thus converting them into instant carriers. I wrote all of this in an article in the magazine. Not long before the war I was discussing this with Adolphus Andrews, who was chief of naval operations at that time, and he said, "Grosvenor, you've been out of the navy too long. You're out of touch with things. We only have these carriers to please the flyboys. They are very vulnerable, and when they fire their five-inch antiaircraft guns, the concussion damages the airplanes on deck." This, I repeat, was just a few months before the war. While I couldn't argue with him, given his position, I did go and write an article and got permission to publish it in the magazine. The lead of my story was about the German battleship *Bismarck* being discovered and disabled by carrier aircraft before battleships closed in for the kill. Then there was the sinking of *Repulse* and the *Prince of Wales* off Malaya. Then, before we went on press, the Battle of the Coral Sea was announced, which was a great naval victory, due largely to air power, and we put that in the story. We were on the press and down to the last few pages of the run when news came about the Battle of Midway. So I updated four or five times right straight along, just like a newspaper, changing the lead as the news broke. The article came out with the title "Aircraft Carrier: New Queen on the Sea," and pictures accompanied it. When it was in proof, the admiral in command of the naval air arm asked for sixteen galleys, and he sent them all around the Navy Department saying, "Look, the *National Geographic* is publishing this article, and they're a pretty conservative organization; there must be something to what they are saying." This was a time when the navy air arm was trying to put a bill through Congress to authorize one hundred new carriers. The admiral sent some galleys up to Capitol Hill, and President Roosevelt was told about it, and I think it actually helped to get the vote for these additional carriers. I'm very proud of that.

LOOSE TALK CAN COST LIVES

FOOD FOR FIGHTERS EVERYWHERE

5

THE WAR EFFORT— ALMOST EVERYONE WAS INVOLVED

You did not have to be in government, industry, or communications to be in the war effort. No matter what you were doing in those years, somehow you were involved.

Leverett Saltonstall of Massachusetts had a special view of the war from the State House in Boston, where he was governor.

The biggest problem up here was getting people working together. We had the Red Cross and we had a Public Safety Committee. The problem was to get those two organizations working together and making sure there wasn't duplication in effort. Occasionally we had rows to settle who was responsible. When a load of Germans landed down there in Wood's Hole, or a place like that, who would be responsible for looking after them? The same with people who had been bombed on ships— who should take care of them? I would get the two men together and say: "You settle it."

I was annoyed—that is a fair expression—at some of the federal agencies that were set up here. I thought there were an awful lot of people working and not doing anything. A lot of talk and no action. I tried to stop some of that, but without much success. Our people worked well in the war effort. We were proud of the ships that we built, the aircraft carriers, the battleships, and the destroyers. We were really in the army and navy "E" business. At one time we were second to Ohio in the number of "E" awards. I attended over eighty army-navy "E" awards in the state. I can remember going down to the Bath Iron Works in Quincy, facing fifteen thousand people who were launching a ship and getting an army-navy "E" award. Then they had other army-navy "E" awards where there might be only eighty employees. And the spirit of all those meetings was excellent. The workers and the management were all together.

We had a greater number of different races than any state in the Union; I guess we still do. We have Irish, Polish, Armenians, Jews. We have Turks, not many, and Yugoslavs. I think America got together during the war. After the war was over, the various districts and regions went back to their old problems in agriculture and industry—the South versus the North. In other words, when the war was over, we became much, much more natural.

John Lacey was a patent attorney for the firm of Lacey and Lacey in Washington, D.C. He had also been doing part-time work for the Carnegie Institution. When the war came along, he decided to leave his law firm and to work first for Carnegie, then for the Johns Hopkins University research program.

At that time, the Johns Hopkins operation was located in a garage in Silver Spring. It wasn't even a branch of the university. The university had a contract with the government. The whole thing was super secret. In fact, no one in Silver Spring knew what we were doing, and we were accused of carrying on medical experiments on prisoners of war and all sorts of crazy things.

Looking back at it in retrospect, my job wasn't very important in the whole scheme of things. It was to report all inventions through the patent system. At the end of World War I the government paid many millions of dollars to use inventions that were actually developed with their own money under government contracts. This patent program, under the Office of Scientific Research and Development, was set up to give the government an opportunity to protect itself for inventions under its own contracts. My job was to make records of all the devices that were invented by these scientists and send them in to the Office of Scientific Research and Development.

The basic project I worked on during the war was the proximity fuse. It was a radio device put in the nose of a shell or bomb which caused the shell or bomb to go off when it came within an optimum distance from the target, such as an airplane or ship. They even used them in the Battle of the Bulge in howitzers; the shells sprayed the ground with fragments and killed people in the trenches and foxholes.

The proximity fuse was not invented in this country; it was invented in England in its basic form, but the development started at Carnegie in the fall of 1940, and then it was transferred to Hopkins in 1942.

The Germans and the Japense were also trying to develop it. The big problem was the little radio tube that was necessary—we didn't have transistors in those days. The problem was to develop a tube which would withstand the shock of going off inside a gun. You have to remember that when a shell is fired, let's say a five-inch, 38-mm gun, the setback was on the order of twenty thousand g's or twenty thousand times gravity. There was also a problem with spin. To get a radio tube to stand up under that, it had to be very carefully designed. We started by dropping hearing-aid tubes—Western Electric and GE and a few others had already come on the market with them—from the top of a building over at Carnegie. Then they fired one from a smooth-bore cannon out in Virginia, and they finally got one to work.

The work was all top secret. This was down in Saint Mary's County at a place called Northern Neck. The fellows would load the station wagons in the morning and leave at the crack of dawn, go down to the proving grounds and be there all day. They had a draft board in Saint Mary's County, and one of these fellows was from that area, so our problem was to keep the draft board from drafting these men into the army, because they were highly specialized people. I remember going down with an attorney to try to convince those fellows that these men were necessary to the war effort. One farmer said to me: "Well, all I know is these fellows come down here, and they go in there in the morning and come out at night. I don't know what they're doing; they may play pinochle for all I know." But we did get most of them off.

The Reverend Harold Toliver was pastor of Grace Memorial Church in Pittsburgh. His wife, Elva, who taught Sunday school, joined us as we talked about the war years.

Being a minister, I realized it would not affect me personally, as far as going into the service was concerned. We had only one daughter, and she was very young. And Elva's brother was too young. Of course, war made us more aware of the rigid segregation in our armed forces. It became apparent that this was not going to be an easy problem to solve there, any more than it was in the national scene. So we listened to what the boys were saying and read what they were writing back. They were all loyal young men, as far as serving their country was concerned. They went where they were told, but they reported experiences that were very unpleasant. And it made us feel more and more that no matter what the outcome of the war was to be, we had to continue our efforts and our struggle toward recognition that blacks who served their country had a right to equality. This was one of the main issues we pursued all through the war and have been pursuing ever since. One thing that impressed me a great deal in the latter stage of the war, when General Eisenhower was in command, was that his attitude was not very favorable. It was President Truman—a southerner, a midwesterner—who took a stand and said, "Now, this thing has to change." I remember very well one speech he made somewhere in the South—I think it must have been a military group. He said very vigorously, in his typical style, that greater concern had to be shown for the black soldiers and that this rigid pattern of segregated units had to go. He was in the Deep South when he said it, and of course, it wasn't a very popular thing for him to say. But he didn't court popularity. And eventually the thing that he set in motion became a reality. He desegregated the army by Executive order, and Eisenhower went along with that.

ELVA: One of the things that, I think, helped the relationships between the races during that time was the organization in communities to get people together in case there was a disaster in our own country. I remember even in Schenley Heights, there were people who came together, organized, and did community things of unity and fellowship. Women began taking jobs they'd never taken before. Some wanted to operate the streetcars. I really wanted to drive a taxi or something.

HAROLD: I didn't let her, not that I was making any money as the pastor of a small church.

ELVA: So we organized nursing classes, and there were also women who were involved in trying to relocate the Nisei. They were very much disturbed by the fact that these people, who were American-born citizens, were uprooted because they were of Japanese descent.

HAROLD: They could have been kept under surveillance, if necessary, to see that they were cooperating. To root them up and say: "You're no better than the soldiers that are attacking our men," that's deplorable. There's no excuse for it.

ELVA: One of the things our relocation committee did was try to find communities which would accept them, and that wasn't easy. People were afraid of them. They were prejudiced against anyone who doesn't look white.

The morale here was mixed during the war. There were some people who were very pessimistic about the whole thing and thought that it was a useless war but that we were in it and we just had to go along and do what we could. But most people realized that this was a tremendous challenge to our nation. And no matter what our personal feelings were on the race question, we had to support the nation, because if we lost that, we lost everything.

One of the effects of the war among black people was the new job opportunities that opened up. There were openings that they'd never had before in some industries. They were making good money, and there were those who were happy to take advantage of that to buy homes they had been wanting to buy for a long time and send their children to college. There were many who didn't rejoice in the war but rejoiced in the opportunities that came. One thing that wars do is to cut down on discrimination.

HAROLD: For the time being. But then as soon as the pressure is off, things tend to go back just the same as they had been before. And those who had jobs are laid off.

You'd be interested in one young marine who is now a very prosperous dentist in one of the suburban towns. He was stationed in the South, I forget what city it was. He was a Presbyterian, so one Sunday he went to a white Presbyterian church in uniform. And he said that the first Sunday everybody was aghast that "here's this black fellow coming in here." And yet they didn't turn him away. He sat up in the balcony. After the service he met the minister and told him who he was and where he was from. So the minister invited him back for the next Sunday, and he spent several Sundays there in that congregation. Before he left, he was allowed to sit on the first floor. He said he integrated the church.

ELVA: Another thing the war did, it brought interracial marriage very close to many of our people. Because sons, when they were sent all over the world, brought home brides. One of them brought home a German bride and another a Japanese. We had young men stationed in Hawaii,

Africa, the Middle East, and in Germany, Japan, well, you name it.

We also had one young woman, a professional nurse, who went into the air force and was stationed in Greenland. I remember her saying how desolate and lonely it was. The commissioned officers were not allowed to fraternize with the noncommissioned. And being a black officer, she had no companionship.

But I was very impressed with what the young men who had been in my Sunday-school class and were sent to different parts of the world said in their letters. They didn't talk too much about the horrors of war, but they talked about the kind of things that brought them together in ways that they had never expected with other people. There were those who spoke of feeling that the only way that they could ever worship in a church was in a certain kind of building and how they learned that even in mud and rain they could pray and have a service. Or to have someone who was in Italy find that there would be people who would take them in, almost as a member of their families. And having a young man who was in the Middle East write back in descriptive words of places that he had only read about sometime in the Scriptures or sometimes in his geography book. And one young man who, during the eruption of the volcano Vesuvius, sent an envelope of ashes. I still have them in a little jar. And there were young men in Japan who would send some of their money. We've always been collectors. Some people call it hoarding. I call it save-itis. And they sent little things like that back they knew would be of interest. They talked about the people they met, some of the food that they ate, some of the children and things that they saw. It broadened their horizon. It deepened their feelings of worldwide community.

Margaret and Esther Dudley, sisters, lived together in Philadelphia at the time of Pearl Harbor. They were interviewed together at Leisure World in Silver Spring, Maryland, where they are now living in retirement.

ESTHER: I was a legal secretary in the office of chief counsel of the Internal Revenue Service—in the Philadelphia branch office.

MARGARET: I was a nurse in a dispensary for the treatment of tuberculosis. Having been turned down for the army's Nurse Corps—it wasn't the Army Nurse Corps then; it was under the Red Cross—I didn't feel the war would make any difference in my way of living. I was turned down several times by the Selective Service people. One of the things I immediately did was to go and take a course in first-aid nursing. As the war progressed and as things settled down—no, not settled down, because everybody was upset—I thought I had to do something. So I joined the civil defense, and during a blackout I would have to go down to the fire station on Chestnut Street and report in. After work I'd go to the Red Cross Blood Bank, and if we had an alert, I would have to leave there to go to my station.

EsTHER: We were located on the twentieth floor of the Lincoln Liberty Building, at the corner of Broad and Chestnut. And on about the eighth floor, the interceptor command had been set up. After Pearl Harbor an emergency call went out to I don't know how many government agencies. We, being located in the same building, and every one of us having been cleared by the FBI earlier, were asked to report to interceptor command, which at that time was under Major Quesada, who is now a general. My work was plotting. Of course, it was volunteer work. But while you were there, you were under the authority of the army, and there was no foolishness. Philadelphia was practically an arsenal, so it was very serious. You had the Frankfort Arsenal and a lot of heavy machinery plants making war equipment. Then you had the navy yard, and I think it was felt that Philadelphia would be a target of a suicide attack.

There was a big board in the center of a big room, and the plotters were around the board. Around the top was a balcony. The people there had earphones, and they were connected with people who watched outside, located all around the country. They would call in to the people on the balcony. Then these people would call down to the people on the board, and we would set up what represented airplanes and plot them across the board. Over on one side were the officers in command; they could look down and see the picture, and they would know what to tell the interceptor command, which was located somewhere outside of Philadelphia. The officer in charge could tell if it was a commercial plane or an army plane, and, of course, we were always on the lookout for unknown planes. One night it was very, very exciting. We don't know whether they were pulling an exercise on us to see if we were on our toes, or if it was the real thing. About fifty miles off the coast of Atlantic City a plane was coming. The navy was out there and started calling in. The plane was unknown. We didn't know whether it was a suicide squad. Major Quesada got his boys, and out they went in P-40s—you saw the P-40s going across the board moving out into the ocean; they chased the plane away. But whether or not it was the real thing, they didn't tell us. I took calls from the people out in the field, the spotters, and transmitted the information to the plotters on the board. Or I'd work on the floor. But I always worked in interceptor command. I didn't go out to call in. I thought it was very dramatic work. Very essential.

MARGARET: What was very painful to me was the feeling I had as the war went on, you know, your country right or wrong. I felt very strongly that I should be doing more. Here I looked good, and the Red Cross kept sending me letters, even though they had turned me down. So, finally, I wrote to the Red Cross—they were just about to be put under the Army Nurse Corps—and I said, "Please! Either let me have an examination and see whether or not I can make it or just stop these letters." It was a trauma to me; it made me feel like I was a slacker every time I got one of those letters. Finally, they did let me go for a physical and said I was okay, and I got my orders in August of 1943 to go. Then the sister who was in charge of our area of the Lutheran Dispensary got sick, and I couldn't leave at that point. The board asked me if I would stay. But I told them I was going to leave as soon as sister came back. After six months I went for another physical and nearly didn't make it. They sent me home to rest for forty-eight hours, and then they passed me. I really felt strongly that that was what I should do. I just wasn't going to be satisfied, particularly since I kept reading all the literature about the need for nurses.

ESTHER: After we had been on pretty strenuous service on that interceptor command for about seven or eight months, coming in every night, pretty rough, they organized the WACs. I was requested to take an examination for officer's training, passed, then came back and told my boss, and he got all up in the air. He needed experienced legal secretaries. He said, "After all, we've got to collect the taxes for the government."

What should I do, go in the WACs or remain on the job? In those days we handled the dockets for our men. I mean, we were real legal secretaries. My boss very much discouraged me from going. Some of my family didn't take to this very modern idea of women being in the army, other than as nurses. They were very conservative in their thinking, and they just didn't see it. So they also persuaded me not to go, and I stayed on the job.

MARGARET: Through a friend of mine, I met Nick, a British boy on the *H.M.S. Manchester*. The ship was in for repair. It had been hit in the middle. I dated Nick for about three months. It wasn't one of those terrific affairs—just fun. His interest was to get the war over with. He did think we were millionaires because we had a refrigerator. He couldn't believe it—the standard of living two women could have! I never saw him after the war. It was just sort of a wartime friendship. A lot of fun. He'd bring up liquor and cigarettes—you know, that was all rationed.

ESTHER: There were a lot of exciting times. It was a whole new way of life. I wouldn't say it was all sad or depressing. You would go through some very deeply emotional periods, either on a very high note or on a very low note, like the day my sister left to report to camp. You put someone on the train, say good-bye to them, and knew you might never see them again.

Elmer Louis Kayser was a professor of European history and dean of university students at George Washington University in Washington, D.C., where he is now its historian and a professor emeritus.

As I look at it now, it's a wonder the university wasn't temporarily closed. Take my own department—History. I was about the only man that remained. And so I found myself teaching eighteen hours a week. At the same time I was serving as the dean and busily bringing in part-time teachers who happened to be in Washington to take a great part of the teaching load.

As for the students, the graduate students moved out very quickly. But the V-5 and V-12 programs saved the day as far as assuring us a continuing body of male students. Our teaching problems were exaggerated by the ambitious war contracts we took. For example, the one that led to setting up our human-resources project here and the one that produced the bazooka. We had to furnish staff to keep the projects going. That pushed us very hard, but it had its rewards.

My idea as to the climate of wartime Washington is more or less colored by my experience here with university students. There was a lot of suspicion in Washington. The atmosphere was quite taut. I can mention one case that would illustrate that. A brilliant lad of great literary ability, liberal in thought, found himself faced with the need to be a patriot. And yet he was documented because he had written in the *Hatchet* [the GWU paper] and was active in this, that, and the other. There he was. Military service comes up. He has a fine mind, and he of course wants a commission. All of his documentation is brought up.

And I found myself in this case, and in many others, having to interpret, not always to understanding people, what a good mind, a free mind, would do in an intellectual academic atmosphere, and what he would do when faced with the necessity for military service—convincing them that he could develop a sense of command and dedication that was not conditioned by what had gone before. Because he had been an intense believer before, he could be an intense believer now.

Then I was harassed by interrogators—FBI, Civil Service. They would pursue me to my house to get information; they'd come before me with these stenographer's notebooks they'd pull out of their pocket, and they'd begin. As I say, the wave of suspicion was terrible. I dealt with thousands of young men. When they were asked to give a reference, they'd put my name down, because they had taken, say, Ancient History with me. I didn't know them half as well as I knew Nero. I'd never give any information over the phone. They'd say: "Oh, this is war, this is war, we haven't time. . . ." Oh, that pressure was awful. That's why my phone is still unlisted.

Neighborhood information can be just a collection of suspicions. This case will illustrate what I mean: Mickey Salkind—Mickey was his nickname—he never liked his first name. So he always wanted to have people call him Mickey, and he eventually began using Michael as his name. So here was Michael Salkin, officially known as, we will say, Isadore Salkind. He had a brother who occupied an apartment with him, and there were three Salkind names on the mailbox: Isadore Salkind, Michael Salkind, and the brother Salkind. Now, there was some woman in the apartment who reported to the FBI that there were three Salkinds and that one of them had disappeared. She said to the FBI, "He's a draft dodger," and the draft dodger was reported as Michael Salkind. A man came to me from the FBI, sweating, cussing, belligerent. And he said, "I have spent two weeks doing nothing but trying to find Michael Salkind, who's evidently a draft dodger. Can you tell me anything about it?" I said, "You're a damn fool not to come to see me first. You want to see Michael Salkind? You go over to Andrews Field and ask for Staff Sergeant Salkind, and there he is."

Well, that's the sort of thing that happens. It was a terrible atmosphere to have abroad.

Nelson Poynter spent part of the war as OWI's man in Hollywood. He said that Variety *quickly named his office "The Little White House."*

I made it clear—and they were most receptive, because it was a very patriotic bunch in Hollywood—that our office had utterly no authority, that we wanted none, that they could make a picture saying this whole thing was a mistake and that Hitler was right and we couldn't do a thing to them, and we felt that was as it should be in this country, that during wartime we could maintain freedom of information. So they would come to me and say, "What can I do?" They wanted material from Washington.

I dealt mostly with writers and directors. They would have an idea and say, "Is this going to help the war effort?" Probably one of the most helpful things I was able to offer was reminding them that after the war the pictures they were making would have wide circulation all over the world. No other country could even approach the influence that Hollywood had over literally hundreds of millions of people overseas, dubbed in with the native languages or with just titles, like our early silent movies. So scores of times, in consulting with writers, I would remind them, "How is this picture going to look after the war when shown in Italy? Or in Japan? Or Germany?" For instance, Dore Schary had just made a picture with an American in combat with a Japanese, who said something about, "You yellow-bellied bastard." And I said, "You know, China is our ally." I saw him a couple of years ago in New York, and he recalled that simple, obvious thing.

My job was to try to inspire some of the most gifted people in the world, and they were so eager to be of help. I remember Frank Capra went into the service, I think the Signal Corps, and made training pictures. He was in uniform, and many of them wanted to do that. Jack Warner—they're a bunch of prima donnas, of course, all of them—got himself made a colonel and wore his uniform around the studios on the Warner lot.

I think Hollywood's impact on the war effort was very good. In the first place, entertainment was curtailed as soon as they put gasoline rationing in, and we went on twenty-four-hour shifts in our factories, making munitions and war materials of all kinds. In places like Detroit, motion picture houses were open literally twenty-four hours a day, so that people coming off the night shift, if they wanted to relax and go to the movies, could do so. And before they went on the night shift. This brought enormous prosperity to Hollywood.

There were amusing incidents—one small producer, I've forgotten his name, who specialized in B films, cowboy films, came to me and said, "I make cowboy pictures. Do you know whether the government is going to continue to let us have film to do this?" I said, "Of course. You're making some of the most fundamental pictures there are, because it always turns out that law and order will prevail against the bad guys. That's all this war is about. We're fighting for law and order, based on consent." He brightened up and went back and made all kinds of cowboy pictures.

The government saw that movies were very important from a morale standpoint. The American people might not be able to drive their cars as much and take trips, but they could still go to the movies, and they did by the millions.

Hollywood had their blackouts, alerts. The wardens would be around, and if you were not observing the rules, they would scold you. People in Hollywood were very conscientious about rationing, giving blood to blood banks, doing all kinds of volunteer services for the Red Cross and other agencies of that kind. I would give Hollywood as high marks as any other part of our society in those war days.

Evelyn Keyes was a young star, working for Columbia Pictures in Hollywood. Two years before Pearl Harbor, there was the premiere of MGM's Gone With the Wind, *in which Miss Keyes played the role of Scarlet O'Hara's sister.*

Once, right after Pearl Harbor, I was awakened in the middle of the night. It was pitch-dark, the light wouldn't go on, and I thought they had pulled the main switch in Los Angeles. Outside it was like a newsreel of the opening of a movie with big searchlights—light jutted up in the air, and I thought, "Oh, my God, the Japs are coming." I was seeing what I thought were parachutes hanging in the air; they turned out to be puffs of smoke. They were shooting at something, and so I grabbed the poker and I was ready. I was cool and calm, and if some son of a bitch came inside, I was going to . . . it was interesting how I reacted, because I was going to do whatever necessary. I saw something in the light. I didn't know what it was, because they said the next day it was a false alarm. But something was in that big ball of light right overhead. I suspect it was our own planes.

I just worked almost steadily during the war. If it wasn't a picture, then it was in a portrait gallery making stills from pictures. They never stopped: War and star making—the war effort and selling bonds were a continuation of what we were doing. For publicity they'd send you out with other pictures, even if they weren't yours, just so your name got in the paper or on the radio.

There was a shortage of pickers for the crops, so they sent a bunch of us girls out, always combining getting your name in the paper and the war effort. We went out into the field and picked tomatoes all day. And the Mexicans complained because the girls were taking their work away from them. We gave them the boxes of tomatoes we picked so they could collect the money. But we did this with photographers clicking away.

We did what we were supposed to do. But we were so welcome everywhere and so eagerly sought. People were besieging us to come here or there. On the war-bond drives, the army picked me up and took me home again. They were happy to do that. It was all part of keeping the boys happy too. Our big audience was in the war, and the fan mail was enormous, and the studios were always conscientious about answering the mail. I spent a great deal of time in bathing suits for pinups. Even that was part of the war effort. It's funny when you think of it, because our careers were built on the war-camp walls.

We visited lots of army camps, saying hello or good-bye as they departed to go off to get killed. I was always escorted around by the brass—never an enlisted man. Once, I was supposed to have lunch in some mess hall; we got out of the car, went in, and there was a sea of black faces, because everything was segregated then. One of the officers escorting me said, "Oh, no, this is the wrong mess." The guys all looked up to see this movie star. "No, no, the wrong mess." We went out, and as we were going away, I felt guilty. I thought, is that why we didn't go in there, because they were black? Should I speak up, should I say, "Look here, men, don't do this; I'm against segregation. Can we go back there and have mess with the black guys?" And then I thought, well, who are you to think they'd want you for lunch; maybe they think you're a silly white thing they don't want to have any part of. How many years ago was that? Thirty years?

The hospitals were so depressing. I don't know how anybody could visit one in any kind of war. I went to one hospital, and they were all blind, not one single one could see.

I got a letter from somebody who had got his sight back—the first thing he did was to go see a picture of mine because he remembered my voice and he wanted to see what went with it. He told me how he got married, had children, got a job, and everything. That was nice.

When I was in California, I had a regular night when I went to the

USO, and so did everyone else. Every city had a canteen, and so every time I went to a city, I would go to that too. The boys always behaved themselves. They treated us with huge respect. Since television, it has changed, because now they know you're real people. But at that time, you weren't quite a real person. You weren't really a girl.

Most of the movies we made then supported the war in some way. We also made some shorts for the Signal Corps. The message was, "A slip of the lip may sink a ship," that sort of thing. I also did something about venereal disease, several of those.

The people in Hollywood wanted to help. If there were any who didn't, they kept quiet. The whole country was for this war. It seems funny now. I can't at all imagine being for war for any reason. I suppose it was because of the attack. And I suppose if another Hitler came along, a madman . . . that's the danger now. But it isn't the same, because we all have hydrogen bombs. There's no way it could go on, Hitler would have dropped one or two if he had them—if he could have gotten to New York!

It was a popular war. We'd been attacked, and Hitler was taking all of Europe, and we had a villain, unlike those latter-day wars. You didn't have dissenters and people like that. The war years were exciting, very exciting. I guess it was a way of life.

The novelist James M. Cain was a scriptwriter in Hollywood. His novel Mildred Pierce *had just been published, and although it had not made as big a splash as* The Postman Always Rings Twice, *which was published in the mid-1930s, it was a best seller. Cain is eighty-four and still writing novels. I interviewed him at his home in Hyattsville, Maryland, and he began the interview by telling me that he was "in the First World War, when the bullets were really flying."*

I have no recollection what I was working on at the time of Pearl Harbor. I may have been working on a book, but I very quickly became chairman of some kind of local committee. God knows what we did—I had to take courses under the Red Cross, some kind of air-raid stuff. My recollection of that is very vague.

My wife, Elena, was a Finn, and she had already been tremendously active in war work when Finland was invaded by Russia. The war to her was just a continuation. One time—this must have been around, I would guess, 1940—she was giving some party for Finnish war relief, and I said, "How many are coming?" and she said, "Oh, I don't know; I imagine about eight hundred." I said "Good-bye, rug." "What do you mean?" she said. "Nothing will be spilled on the rug. These people are Finns; they don't spill things on the rugs. That's an American custom." Nothing was spilled on the rug. When most of them had gone, I said, "How much did you make?" She said, "I forget, something like three thousand dollars." I said, "No more than that?" She looked at me, "About three thousand dollars we admit; actually about a hundred thousand dollars raised for guns. We'd be in great trouble with the government if we admitted how much was made."

My stepson, in 1941, was twenty-four. He was obviously tagged for the service, and it may be that he was already in some kind of aviation; if not then, he very quickly was. He was Finnish by birth, but they accepted him in the American navy—in aviation. And do you know what they regarded as important in deciding whether an applicant is right for training in the air? His ability to ride a horse! For some reason, a good horseman makes a good flyer, and he was a perfect genius on a horse. I mean, when he got on a horse, the horse just automatically knew that someone was up there who knew how to ride a horse. Anyway, he very quickly got his commission and was sent overseas.

I have no recollection of being pressed for money at the time or needing the money. At one point I was making $2,500 a week, not really giving up anything. And yet knowing nothing else to do. I was writing for pictures which the government said they wanted written, and when the agent would sell me for $250 a week more, who would I be to argue about it? For me to say, "No, I don't want to have any more money"— who's going to get that $250? I may as well have it, because the picture company was going to keep it, and I knew that they were not doing pictures wholly for patriotic reasons. Nobody even slightly pretended that even a war picture was not being done for profit. If it incidentally pepped up the morale of the country, okay. But plenty of money was also being made.

I think I was almost unique in the way I felt about it. I think most of them persuaded themselves that they were doing a pretty important patriotic work and deserved a great deal of credit. There was not much talk going around about it. You have to remember that Hollywood is a very peculiar place. You can be having a conversation with a writer and compliment him on some war work he was doing, and he would be very pleased to hear what you had to say, and you would be sincere. And his wife would say, "Give me a light," and you'd light her cigarette, and she'd say, "My, but he's self-sacrificing—at three thousand dollars a week! My heart is bleeding!" He'd be saying one thing, and the wife would be saying something else, mumbling into your face half stewed. But the general atmosphere out there was pretty high minded, pretty patriotic, and pretty quiet. Hollywood never played it noisy and never played it big, nor did they do any bragging. There was that general feeling about it. Keep it low; don't let yourself believe all the stuff about what an important guy you are because you work for pictures.

The only visible effect of the war you would see was, suddenly, every director, every writer had suede patches on his elbows. I was telling somebody about this, some writer in the course of writing me up, from the East, and he said, "Patches by Abercrombie." I said, "That's the idea." Of course, Hollywood wouldn't be Hollywood if they didn't do it big, their way. So that was the only outward visible sign of anything during the war.

The war didn't exactly impact on the industry, it impacted on nine hundred guys separately. For example, Clark Gable, he had the office up the hall from me at Metro, in the Thalberg Building, known as the Iron Lung. Gable was in a captain's uniform. I think, Air Corps. And he wanted to go to France and fight. But the government felt that he was so much more use being Gable for picture release and for publicity purposes right there at Metro than he would have been as one of a thousand combat flyers. There was only one Gable; making use of him was the main thing. Getting killed would have been very bad. So that's how the war affected him; it affected nine hundred others in different ways.

Most of them doing the pictures at that time were people like me— either too old or one way or another physically unable to take part in combat duty. You must remember that motion pictures had been declared an essential industry by whoever made the major decisions, the War Department maybe. They were so important for purposes of morale that nobody was knocking the picture business. But individual people in the picture business wanted to do their share. I knew dozens of guys that were commissioned, and some weren't commissioned, just enlisted. It left the picture business operated by older writers and directors and so on, and actors, of course, and women. There was no great excitement to it; you'd have scarcely noticed any difference in the way the lots functioned with the war going on. You must remember a picture lot is, in spite of all you've heard, a very efficiently run place. It had to be because there was a penalty for not being efficient. They found out that their employment of plenty of nontalent people who couldn't act, direct, or shoot, but who carried on the humdrum aspect of making a picture—getting the sets ready, getting them dressed, checking that everything that was needed for tomorrow's shooting was on the trucks ready to go out on location—was a great saving of money, although seemingly extravagant. So everything went on greased skids. The war going on didn't change anything. You'd have hardly noticed there was a war going on.

I don't think the war had much effect on novelists; of course, a war no sooner starts than two novelists out of three are writing war stories. And the magazines were still in existence, so they wrote plenty of war stories.

I don't see how we could have stayed out. We were kicked into it by Japan. After Pearl Harbor, whether we wanted to be in the war or not, we were in it. Because that was an act of war, and it could not be overlooked.

I have to say there was some concern about the Japanese. They talked about the monstrous injustice of herding them into concentration camps, but they had themselves to thank. Before the war, if they weren't a nation of spies, they were giving a hell of an imitation of it.

I remember down in the Palos Verdes Estates, somewhere, there was a hilltop restaurant. And a lady and I were having lunch down there, and the proprietor of this place stopped by to chat. We were sitting there looking down at the ocean, perhaps a quarter of a mile away. Between us and the ocean were hummingbirds. Beautiful, shimmering in the sunlight and darting in and out at flowers. And he sat there chatting, and he had a thick German accent, and he excused himself and went off, and she said, "Did it ever enter your mind what entered mine talking to him?" I said, "You mean that if there were submarines out there, this would be a very convenient place to give night signals?" She said, "Yes, that's what I mean."

That kind of thing—that suspicion of the Japanese and the Germans and what was going on under cover was fairly prevalent out there. Down below the border, in Mexico, there were Japanese concentrations. Obviously they would report on Mexican things and American things back to headquarters. And we had the feeling there was a great deal of that going on. Whether this was imaginary, I don't know. I'm not given to easy suspicion about people. But I remember having the feeling out there that the Japanese were reporting an awful lot to somebody who was smuggling a lot of information back to Japan. It may or may not have been unjust and monstrous on the basis of abstract constitutional rights, as they would be regarded in peacetime. The war takes precedence over everything. There was a general feeling that the Japanese were doing a lot of spying, that getting them all bunched together in one place and keeping them there for the duration was not such a terribly bad idea.

The other bad idea was that when they were swept up and put there, some people were profiteering with their property and taking advantage of them because they wouldn't be on the spot to look out for it. That kind of thing was very bad. But after Pearl Harbor it could not be assumed that an invasion of California was a farfetched, idiotic idea. Pearl Harbor was a farfetched, idiotic idea. But it put our fleet at the bottom of the harbor. So you couldn't take a chance.

Sid Luckman, the Chicago Bears quarterback, was married and had children. But he enlisted in the merchant marine after the season of '43. He recalls the years in pro football, just before he went into the service.

Most of the great players who weren't married enlisted in the service or were drafted. So even though there were still a lot of very fine football players around, there wasn't the caliber of football there was in the years 1940 and '41. The quality dropped.

The headlines every day were about the war, and people really needed an outlet. The outlet was to go to sports and to the movies to get their mind off thinking about what was in the newspapers. Football was very, very big in those years. A lot of people didn't want us to enlist, because they wanted football to continue. But eventually, I guess, all of us thought it was an obligation to go and do our part.

Hilda O'Brien took graduate work at Columbia University in New York City before going down to Washington to work in the government.

The biggest impact on Columbia was that the midshipmen were there. They were marching up and down all over the big malls, which were used as parade grounds, and the place was just crawling with midshipmen, so that it was not a normal university campus.

I was a hard-working and broke student. I worked a lot of the time at many different jobs. I worked in the employment office of the school, and I worked hard because I was very much interested in my academic work—political science, public administration, what they call public law at Columbia.

In New York at one time I lived on Riverside Drive. Every room was rented out to a different person, and we all shared the kitchen. One of the women had a room that looked out on the river, and we used to have our meals together in her room because it had a better view. We were always curious that at night the Hudson River would be filled with gray boats of all sizes and shapes and the next morning they'd all be gone. They would go out in the night, and the convoys would meet somewhere out at sea.

I got my master's in June of 1943, and I hoped then to go to Washington to work. I didn't know where or at what, but someone came up recruiting and told me that there would definitely be openings in the fall. So I took a temporary job in New York for the summer with the War Transportation Office. This was a federal agency that allocated tires and gasoline, and, being a woman, I was put into the pool of typists and clerks and all that sort of thing. The men actually interviewed the applicants who wanted these things. One of my jobs was to go out into a big room of applicants who had put their names down on a list and call these people for their interviews. I still remember one, a member of Father Divine's Church, whose name was Heavenly Thank Father, and I had to call out the name. This was a group of really tough New Yorkers who ran the outfit, and I was a bit more gentle, coming from the Midwest. I stood it for a few weeks, but we had a very nice supervisor, and finally she said, "Well, I think this isn't exactly your field." So I went into the regional office, which was on the floor above and worked there for the rest of the summer as a secretary-typist.

Benjamin Spock was practicing medicine in New York City during part of the war years, when he also began work on his book, Baby and Child Care, *which was to help the nation's mothers raise the postwar generation of babies.*

As pediatricians were gradually taken into the armed services, it left more and more work for those of us at home to do. From the time I started practice in '33 until I went into the navy, in '44, I'd been only partly busy during all those pre–Pearl Harbor years. They were depression years. In fact, it took me three years to earn enough money to pay my office and automobile expenses. Nobody needed a new pediatrician in New York at that time. But following Pearl Harbor, I gradually got busier and busier—for the first time in my career.

I was being called on for more and more work in my practice, but I wasn't thinking of the war years as a baby boom. I was thinking, rather, that other pediatricians were gone, so there's more for me to do. One thing I remember was how easy it was to drive around in New York City and to park the car. That was amazing. We got a C-card instead of an A-card. But still, they didn't give you a great deal of gas, and they asked you to conserve it. I was working also for the Public Health Department two mornings a week, holding staff meetings at baby-health stations all over the five boroughs, and I took subways when I went to Brooklyn or to Queens or to Staten Island or to the Bronx.

I didn't have any experiences with women losing their husbands and having to adapt. It was late on when fathers were taken into the service. Generally speaking, the mothers and children made a good adjustment, I would say. I don't mean it was easy. But I think human beings respond to a challenge like that. It makes them summon all their resources. I saw how children reacted to the absence of their fathers and how good an adaptation most of them had. In fact, the adaptation that was harder was when the father came home. The child who had mother to himself from the age of one year to three years was outraged to have this ogre come home and take over his mother. That impressed me. In fact, the interesting thing to me was not only how much trouble small children had accepting a father who had been away but how many fathers went through at least mild depressions when they came back out of the armed services. All the years and days they had been dreaming about coming out and when will this damn thing be over. And then they came home and had depressions. Somehow it didn't seem as marvelous as they'd dreamed. It all seemed to be related to the psychic reaction to meeting challenges. I think what alerted me was hearing these reports, newspaper articles, magazine articles, about how neighborly, loving, and cooperative people were in England, where war was brought right to them. After hearing about it in England, I saw, at least in a mild way, that we had the same thing. People feel good when they're making sacrifices and being cooperative, whereas in good times, in a prosperous country, the majority—and I always say "for the majority" because there's a minority that isn't having a happy time at all—begin to feel guilty, and get greedy and selfish.

I think, as in most wars, mental health for the majority of Americans improved. During wartime there is less suicide, less crime. People were friendlier; they took care of each other. It's a horrid thing to realize that during wartime people are mentally more healthy than they are during peacetime, especially in a country where so many people live relatively comfortable lives. This kept making me come back to the conclusion that our species is designed to cope with adversity rather than take it easy. In the depression, these same kinds of statistics prevailed: less crime, less suicide.

Judson Phillips, possibly better known to readers of mystery stories as Hugh Pentecost, was living and writing in Vermont at the time of Pearl Harbor.

I had two sons who did get into the war eventually. One of them in the air force, but he was sent to Syracuse University to learn to speak Russian for some reason and spent most of the war learning the language; and the other went in the navy and was in the weather service stationed somewhere off Alaska. Neither of them saw any action. Although the one boy in the navy was on what was called active duty, he was actually isolated.

At the time of Pearl Harbor I was writing magazine fiction: *Saturday Evening Post, Colliers,* and *American.* Those were your main markets. And I did a book a year at that time.

Everybody was urged to get in the war effort, and I tried to get into what was called Special Services. The air force offered me a commission as a major to go abroad and write letters home to the families whose fliers were killed in the war, and I said, "The hell with that." Because I was a writer, I suppose, that was all they could see for me. I was never able to get any other kind of an assignment, so I looked around to see where else I could be of service. I had a friend in the OWI and tried to get into that. It didn't work out, but he, in turn, got me into the Writers' War Board in New York, which was a propaganda agency. We did other things, but mostly my particular assignments were to promote for eventual recruitment. Subtly. I wasn't just writing blurbs.

One of my first assignments was to do a story on WAC camps. For the first time, women were in the army, so I was flown around the country in some kind of old crate with a bench in the back to write about WAC camps. As in most of the pieces I wrote for them, in the WAC feature I stressed how glamorous it was. The piece was placed in magazines and newspapers.

Then I got into something else. A friend of mine who was a radio announcer came up with the idea of doing a show about the great secrets of the war. And we did a show which went on every night from seven to seven-thirty called "Now It Can Be Told." We had a staff in Washington, and its job was to dig out the great secrets. Of course, we got stuff that was no longer classified. But nonetheless, we got a lot of interesting material about little-known stuff; and we did that right till the bomb. I regret to say this, and I would deny it with my last breath, but most of the stuff we had was pretty stale. But it did come out of government agencies, and much of it had not been revealed before, because nobody was interested. We made it interesting.

Unfortunately—or fortunately—it was a prosperous time to work. God knows. Except for people who had sons in the service who were in danger, it was kind of a lush time. Hardships were nonsensical. When you recall life in New York in those war years, you remember irritations, you couldn't get cigarettes. The deprivations, so called, that the citizenry had to bear were laughable. It isn't that you couldn't get cigarettes; you couldn't get *your* brand, and what you smoked was horseshit wrapped in paper. There was at that time an enormous amount of leftist excitement. This came out of the Spanish civil war. But in the process, something developed which became McCarthyism. I was very active in radio during this time, and there was a tremendous battle going on within the unions that had to do with who might possibly be an enemy. It was started then. And it led to McCarthyism.

I never had any uncomfortable feeling about being out of uniform. In '41 I was quite literally, as I say, thirty-eight; by the time I was involved here, I was over forty, I was married, I had children. I never had any trouble like that. I can remember much more of this as a young kid in World War I. Bear in mind, New York is a good deal more sophisticated than other parts of the country. I'm sure in a small town, if you are thirty years old and not in uniform, people might have wondered what was cooking. I can remember the horror that Jack Dempsey was working in a munitions plant instead of shouldering a gun, and there was also talk of certain privileges that people had, but I didn't belong to a privileged section of society.

I somehow see the war years in technicolor. It was a gay time, it was an involved time, and I personally wasn't hurt in any way. I didn't have people who were close destroyed. I didn't have property destroyed, and I suddenly was making more money than I had made before, and I was living in New York, which was a busy, involved place. I had a fine time.

I had no conscience, I hadn't ducked out of anything I should have been in. I thought I was justified in not going in the air force and writing letters of condolence; seemed to me I could be more useful, and I think I was more useful finally. I'm no real coward; I didn't want to go to war, but if I'd had to go to war, I would have gone. I had no conscientious objection.

We followed the war intensely, with interest and concern. I don't know anybody who ever thought we were in as much trouble as we were. I think everybody's attitude was: Well, we would take a little time to recover from Pearl Harbor, but there wasn't any question about the outcome. I never thought there was.

For the radio stuff, I was making what seemed like good money at that time—about fifteen hundred dollars a week. In addition to this "Now It Can Be Told" show, we did a dramatized news show for *Newsweek* called "You Make the News." It was a little like "The March of Time," except that "The March of Time" did several stories in its hour, and we picked one item in the news and made an hour out of it.

I was chief writer, and we had another writer and producer of the show. We would see the flimsies—the typewritten sheets that were going to be the magazine—and we'd sit with the editors of *Newsweek* and decide what story we were going to make into a radio program. And we went on the air with that story on Thursday, which was the day the magazine came out. I remember one story, just after the war was over. It was about Russians going into Berlin and kidnaping a whole number of scientists. This was an outrage, and *Newsweek* was outraged. It was a lovely story to dramatize; it had all kinds of detail. But I did what I usually did, which was to go upstairs after the conference and look at the taped ticker report from their correspondent, which was obviously much fuller than the piece in the magazine. And I discovered that the reporter said that nobody was making much of a fuss about it in Europe because we had done the same thing about three months before. There was none of this in the story appearing in the magazine, and I went downstairs to the editor-in-chief and said I didn't want to do this story because it could backlash on us. He said, "Go ahead and do it." I refused to do it. I was trying to protect myself. I was also outraged to discover that they would so slant a story. I hadn't believed they would do that. Hadn't been my experience.

There was also much talk in those days about what was called "hard news." There was a fellow named Joe Resnick who was part of the staff at CBS News. We conceived of an idea of doing a show which would be the Hard News! In other words, there would be blown up a piece from here and a piece from there about something. But what is the real truth? The hard news? We couldn't get anybody to look at it. In fact, people ran screaming when we presented the idea and a couple of tapes of shows to demonstrate. I thought, we're going to be in trouble all the way around. And I began to feel from that experience and the thing I was just talking about at *Newsweek* that news at that time and in that period was more controlled than I liked to believe. Maybe I was a little bit idealistic then.

Looking back on it, considering all the ties we had with France and England from World War I, I don't see how we could have let them go down the drain. They certainly were going to go down the drain without our help. England is pretty hard to let go. I think if there were judgments at the time that were incorrect, they had to do either with not doing enough, perhaps, in the early stages. Of course, Roosevelt was pretty well handcuffed; he had to do a lot of maneuvering to do what he did—I think the big issues of totalitarianism and all this was not so important as that France and England were threatened with total destruction and takeover. The big noise were the conservatives—the Wheelers and the Father Coughlins and all those people—who were opposed to helping or being involved in any way. This is an argument that goes on in this country all the time. For Chrissake, are we selling ten billion dollars worth of arms to Iran, or not? Surely if something blows up there, that will involve us. We got involved in Vietnam this way. Having lived for seventy-three years, well . . . I always used to say, we have no right to get involved in anything—I should be right back where Senator Wheeler was in 1938. And yet, I don't see how it is possible to live in this world—and now that it is only forty-five minutes to Broadway—wherever Broadway is—how you don't get involved is something I don't understand. Whether the involvement is wise or crazy, I don't know.

Coralee Redmond lived in Beach, North Dakota. She had a large family—a husband, nine children, and several brothers. Eventually, almost everyone in her family was involved in the war, some way.

I had a brother at Pearl Harbor, but he came out of it okay. He had been in the marines for about twenty years.

The girls were in high school, the boys were younger. My oldest child was a son, and he went in right after New Year's 1942. He was out of college. So he decided he might as well volunteer. I was asked how I felt about it, and I said I thought the decision was his. I'm quite a military-minded person. I had a lot of military in my family, and I felt like the decision was his. But I felt that we had a duty also. I didn't want to make it one way or the other for him. He did go in, and my younger brother went in right after. And by March, my younger brother was already overseas, in Australia. He survived the war. And my older brother stayed in thirty years.

We quit farming about the time the war began because of my husband's health. So then when the boys left and went into the service, I had my older daughter, who was teaching, and we decided we should do something to help too. So we went to Tacoma, Washington, to work in defense plants, and we worked in the shipyards. I worked in the cafeteria and office most of the time. My husband was what they call a fireman in the shipyard.

I felt my family and I were doing our part with things that had to be done to help our boys that were in the service. This is what it meant to me. I didn't feel that it meant that much to some others. To them it meant a job. You remember, this came right after the depression days, and people were thankful to have a job. And I would say the majority took their jobs seriously. They put in long hours and many hours a lot of times, because it was needed.

Generally, I would say the morale was good. We had some who were earning more money than they had earned in quite some time, and it was a good time. But to me it was a serious time. A time when you just felt that everything would help. You would do to the best of your ability what you thought would help.

One daughter married, and her husband went in the service at that point. The other daughter was married, and she went with her husband, when he was stationed in Louisiana, until he went overseas. Then she came back to Beach and lived in our home. We owned our own home there, and kept it set up. The next-door neighbors checked my heat and such things in the wintertime. Usually in the summertime I took the boys back home because they were younger and I wanted them off the streets. But I kept my home there just so that if someone was coming home, for furlough—my son-in-law, my son—all they would have to do would be to get the key from the next-door neighbor. There was food enough to get by till morning if they came in at night. I felt like when the boys came home, it should be to the home of their youth, and not to Tacoma, which was quite crowded in the war days.

I had two other girls. One graduated from high school in 1943 and the other in 1944. One worked at the shipyard, and the younger daughter went to Boeing in Seattle.

I suppose there were some people who felt we had hardships, but to me it didn't register as such because what would have been a hardship for some people wasn't for me. I didn't know how my son was having to live and what he was having to do. So whatever I and my family had to go without, I don't feel it hurt.

I had nine children, and those nine children went through the depression, and the older boy and daughter were in college during the depression. There was a lot of sacrifice on our part. I don't think any sacrifice or shortage during the war had that kind of effect on us. The welfare of my family was the important thing, and one didn't expect any more than the other. We all tried to provide equally. And we all took our thing seriously. The boy who was in grade school picked beans and all that. The money he earned, we bought savings bonds for him. We taught him that he earned this money but let's put it in something that might help. He would gain from it in the future, but at that particular time, it might be helpful for the war. We all set aside a certain amount to buy bonds. The boy who was in the service—when he came out of the service, he was just out of college—he would be wanting to go into business or something like that, and that was our part in helping him have something when he came back.

They were busy times. The main thing that bothered me was the many hours I felt like I wasted waiting for buses because the buses would be so loaded. One would go by, and you'd wait for another one, when you were trying to get home to get dinner for the family and to have time left to do some volunteer work. I felt that was needed, and the only resentment I ever had was having to wait for a bus.

Mary Dandouveris recalls campus life at the University of Wisconsin during the war and how the war helped her get her first postcollege job.

Because my family was a first-generation family from Greece, I had uncles and relatives in Greece who really felt the effects of Nazism. The Nazis were quartered in my uncle and aunt's house; they owned a transportation system on the Isle of Crete, so they had a rather nice home, I understand, and Nazi officers were quartered there. The children sometimes would do things to aggravate them, and I remember one time they said they had to hide the child in a bake oven they had out-doors to keep him from the wrath of the military. So we experienced the war not in a direct way, because my uncle who was in the U.S. was too old—he'd been in World War I, and my father, of course, had been in World War I.

But we didn't regard ourselves as aligned with the European side of the family; we just thought how important it would be for the United States to win. I do recall that my feeling was that this is our country, our home, and we felt sorry for those poor people over there, but we didn't feel like we were citizens of Europe. I mean, this was what we knew, and all we knew about Greece was what our parents told us.

I graduated from high school and was ready to go into the University of Wisconsin. I was a scholarship student, and it was easier for us to earn money to go to school because more jobs were available for students, as so many men had been drafted. A lot of the guys were gone, and women had their opportunity to take over in positions that formerly had been held by men. I was elected to the Student Council and was active in the War Council. We even had a woman who ran for prom king—Helen Finnegan. Prom king was an elected position on the campus: A man won, as it turned out, but the woman ran and had good support.

The other interesting thing was that we had a lot of military on the campus. They brought the V-5 program, and I forget what other military programs to the campus. Social life was good. And there was an army camp in Madison, with a lot of troops stationed there. There was the Red Cross and square dancing. I remember there were lots of Texas-type troops in the Student Union—that was a good meeting place—and there were the usual hostess Red Cross things and USO operations. Those of us who were in leadership positions would organize things like that. I remember being introduced to square dancing by the Texas troops.

We never had troubles. I remember it as a good time—except the hours were very severe. It wasn't in the days of the liberated campus. Girls had to be in at ten at night on weekdays and midnight on weekends. But there were student lounges. They used to call them the Passion Pits because there was an awful lot of passionate kissing—not the advanced petting they have today. But the fronts of the dorms would be just jammed at quitting time, ten o'clock or midnight, with the sailors and the marines and the army people—whoever was on campus—kissing the girls good-night. But beyond that it wasn't wild. The troops that were stationed on campus were pretty well regulated. They had their own classes—they weren't mixed in.

The war ended in Europe while I was still on campus, and by that time some of the boys who had been in the war early had come back on campus. In my senior year I remember some of the journalism classes getting some of the vets who were back. It was a very interesting class experience because they were so much more mature. By that time all of us had matured because the war really impinged on us.

Although the war was on, the university didn't suffer financially, because we had the troops on campus. We did suffer on football games; the players would get drafted just when we'd get a real good team going. I remember one dismal year in football, when our teams were being drafted and our fellows were sent around to other campuses, and we played a team that was made up of fellows who used to be on our campus, and everybody was just ripped apart.

I signed up for civil-defense training, and we learned the usual tourniquets and blackout practices. We even did some marching; I don't know for what purpose, but I remember they trained us in drills. The older people were the marshals, and we did have to turn out the lights at certain hours, and there were block marshals who certainly called it to your attention if you had any lights peeking out.

I don't really believe there was a fear of bombing, but we were right on the shores of Lake Michigan and the Great Lakes system, so there was a certain amount of concern that perhaps enemy planes could sneak across and over the Great Lakes, because this was an industrial section of the country.

When school ended in May 1945, I went down to Lake Geneva, Wisconsin, and took this job as news editor of the paper. I'll never forget the experience. It was a marvelous job, which I got because the fellow that had been doing it had been drafted.

Elizabeth Haslam spent most the war in Pensacola, Florida. Today, she and her husband operate the largest bookstore in Saint Petersburg.

First I was teaching school—a first-grade class. Then I transferred to the naval air station and got a job out there in the educational department. I administered tests for the men coming into the service. We were a depot for men from Alabama, Mississippi, and many areas in that section. They had already been inducted into the navy, most of them drafted, and they were getting placement tests. We gave them tests on general knowledge, mechanical aptitude, math, and a test in vocabulary.

The war had been going on for a while, and we were beginning to get older men—men with families, men who had been working on war contracts in various factories. The pitiful thing about it was that they had a sheet to fill out first with background information on them, and we had quite a few men who couldn't read and write. They were making big money at the job they knew how to do at home, but they were not able to read and write, except maybe to just sign their name. And some of them were pretty homesick. A lot of those men couldn't write letters, so we made collect calls home for them and wrote letters for them.

We had beginning pilot training there at Pensacola and boot training for a lot of the fellows. It's always been a navy town; it was just more so at that time. We had blackouts, but there wasn't too much fear. We did have one time when the commanding officer of our section came in and said, "What is today's date?" We told him, and he said, "Well, I can't say anything now, but ten years from now, you just remember this date." This was the day when the German submarines went up the Gulf Coast, right up close to Pensacola. We didn't know anything about it then. He, of course, knew about it, and I think just recently there has been a book written on that.

Carey McWilliams, best known today as the editor of The Nation *for many years, was in California at the time of Pearl Harbor.*

I was admitted to the bar in California in 1927, and I had practiced law from 1927 to 1938. From 1938 to 1942 I was in a California state job, and then when I left the state job in 1942, I did not go back to the practice of law. I began free-lance writing. I did give some thought to going into the services. I got letters from various people who knew my background, urging me to apply for a commission or something, but for a lot of reasons I decided not to. The major reason at the time was this damned Japanese-internment business. That dragged on well into 1943, and then we had the zoot-suit riots and all the rest of it.

My book *Factories in the Field*, about farm labor, was a best seller, published in 1939. Within a month or so, [John Steinbeck's] *The Grapes of Wrath* was published, and fortunately, the farm groups and growers were very indignant about both books and tried to have them banned in the libraries. They burned a couple of copies at public meetings, which was just perfect! So I started free-lance writing. I wrote for *The Nation*, *Saturday Review*, *New Republic*, *Harper's*, *PM*, *Christian Century*, and the *Baltimore Sun*. I wrote about the zoot-suit riots, the Japanese Americans, the consequences of the war in relation to the Dust Bowl situation. This was ironic no end. California had set up a border patrol to keep these people from coming into the state of California. You can imagine the end to it—*Edwards* v. *California* went to the U.S. Supreme Court when Earl Warren was attorney general of California. The issue was whether a migratory worker in a Farm Security Administration camp in California was entitled to vote if he had been there the necessary amount of time. Warren's position was that even if he had been there the necessary time, if he had been living in an FSA camp, he couldn't vote. This was the attitude! Then the war came along. The Dust Bowl migration was a godsend to the cities of California. There was a big supply of labor that went directly into the shipyards, into the aircraft industry. Overnight there was no problem. The labor was right there on their doorstep, labor that they'd been trying to keep out!

It seems to me in retrospect, and in part because I was involved, that race was put high on the agenda of critical national domestic issues in those particular years. To understand this, to appreciate this, you have to think what the general situation was pre–Pearl Harbor. As late as the 1930s the state of opinion in the United States on the subject of race was dismal. I used to go on lecture junkets to all kinds of groups from coast to coast, and you would be amazed at the attitudes that you would see, even on college campuses. The general ignorance of the dimensions of the problem and the latent, silly bias that would crop up in questions like "What you are saying is all very well, Mr. McWilliams, but how would you like to have your sister marry a Negro?" That kind of nonsense. And in the late thirties a group of scientists, sparked by Franz Boaz, the anthropologist at Columbia, issued a statement in which they said: "These are the scientific facts about race: This is what race is, this is what it isn't." Anyone today would regard it as commonplace, this kind of statement, but it was a necessity as late as 1939 because of incredible confusion about race. The statement by Boaz had a great impact, traveled all over the country. The fact that anthropologists and social scientists felt it necessary to issue a statement of that kind is an indication of the rather dismal state of ignorance.

At the beginning of the war California had a unique agency. There wasn't anything like it in any state of the union. It was called the Division of Immigration and Housing, and it had been set up by a distinguished California social worker by the name of Simon J. Lubin. His family owned the Weinstock Lubin store in Sacramento. A famous early family in California. Lubin was a great friend of Hiram Johnson, and he had been trained in settlement-house work in New York. He thought that California should have an agency to deal with the problems of immigrants, aliens in the state, because the Panama Canal was under construction, and when it was completed, there would be a great tide of immigration around to California. He didn't want California to neglect the problems of these people in the way the eastern folks had. So Johnson went along with this, and he set this agency up around 1916. The agency had the power to hold public hearings in connection with anything relating to the welfare and adjustment of alien immigrants in the state of California. It also had the power to inspect labor camps and agricultural labor camps. It did some very splendid work in its early years. Then it lapsed into a state of desuetude. No one paid any attention to it until 1938, when they elected the first Democratic governor in forty years, Culbert Olson. Olson had been a state senator in Utah, had come to California, been there for perhaps a decade, ran for the state senate from Los Angeles on the EPIC (End Poverty in California) ticket, and was elected. And four years later he ran for governor and made it. But the point about Olson was that he knew very little about the state. So with his backers he was going through the various patronage jobs they had at their disposal. They came to this division, and they were at a complete loss as to what the hell it did or was supposed to do. George Kidwell, Olson's key labor advisor, said, "What about Carey? He's done a book about farm labor; he knows something about the background." I had been on one of Olson's committees, so he said, "Sure. Why not?" So I was commissioner of immigration and housing from 1938 to 1942.

After Pearl Harbor we had a great deal to do. A succession of things happened that raised consciousness of racial discrimination. One, of course, was the mass evacuation of the Japanese Americans from the West Coast, citizens and aliens alike, 126,000 people, with no justification, no security justification, in my opinion. I don't buy the argument that we were protecting the Japanese from the citizenry, because even in the wake of the shock of Pearl Harbor there were no incidents. Furthermore we know that the Washington authorities shortly after Pearl Harbor had a very good report prepared, as I recall, by a man named Munson. He had cased the situation and didn't see any necessity for it. Naval Intelligence, which knew more about the West Coast Japanese than any government agency, because they had been watching them since the turn of the century, didn't think it was necessary. And the proof that it was not necessary really was what happened in Hawaii. If the Japanese were a security threat on the West Coast, they would be a much bigger security threat in the Hawaiian Islands. But there you had a district court judge who was a great man in my eyes—name of Judge Delbert Metzger—and, oddly enough, U.S. district court judges in Hawaii at that time were given term appointments. They didn't have life terms, but Metzger, in spite of this, wouldn't go along with this business. No! And he said to the naval authorities and the rest of them, "Nothing doing!" And they realized, when they came to their senses, that if they had tried to evacuate all persons of Japanese descent in Hawaii, they would have had no economy. So they just let them stay there. But this was near the end of Metzger's five-year term, and he was not reappointed, and this was the basic reason.

Anyway, the Japanese American evacuation program put race high on the agenda as an important issue. Oddly enough, there's more interest in the internment program today than there was then. The number of books is increasing. I wrote a book on it at the time called *Prejudice*. It's still in print. Young people would say now that that was a consciousness-raising thing, because we were at war with Japan. As a matter of fact, the man with the tam-o'-shanter, Dr. Hayakawa, who is running for the U.S. Senate* said recently: "Despite the hardships, despite the losses, it was a good thing for the Japanese Americans." And what he meant was, and he happens to be largely right, that it jarred them out of their ghettolike attitude and their me-too-ism. H. L. Mencken once referred to them as assistant Americans, and you know, in a manner of speaking, they were.

Before the evacuation I had worked closely with the staff of a Senate committee in Washington that had been investigating farm labor conditions in California. That staff had moved to another committee in the House which was interested in migration, so I got in touch with the staff and said, "God, schedule some hearings out here under some pretext or other, so we can exert a quieting influence." There was political agitation to remove the Japanese, but I didn't detect any passion on the part of people to get them out. They were getting along reasonably well with their neighbors, and the agitation was largely a political thing. Because of a vague grant of jurisdiction to be concerned with the welfare of alien immigrants I had reason to go to the authorities and say, "Now,

*He has since been elected.

look. I want to be heard about some aspects of this." They were delighted to listen, and I had excellent relations with the War Relocation Authority. The first director was Milton Eisenhower and the second was Dillon Meyer. When it was announced, some question arose as to who was going to have charge of this operation. Well, the army was going to have charge. This aroused great apprehension, and so we had to start a kind of agitation to set up a separate authority. Let the army move them out if you must, but we did not want the army running the camps. So they set up the War Relocation Authority, and they staffed it very well. It drew people who had backgrounds sympathetic to the idea of doing a good job, and I will say this to the army's credit, it handled the physical business of getting them out very well. But there is one very important thing to keep in mind. They never could have brought it off as well as they did if the Japanese had not been the kind of people they are. They were well organized themselves, responsible, cooperative, and they went along with it. To their very great credit.

After they had been removed, they went first to assembly centers and then into relocation centers which were scattered around—Wyoming, Arkansas, Colorado—and then at that point the then Institute of Pacific Relations commissioned me to visit the relocation centers, and I visited virtually all of the centers—all but two, I think—and that report was the basis of the book *Prejudice*. The camps were kind of chaotic, as you would expect; but again, the Japanese talent: They sort of found out what they were up against, and they adapted to it and began to do for themselves. And, of course, there were some problems. There were disturbances at Tule Lake in California, one of the relocation centers. There was some trouble there and one or two other centers, so it wasn't all peaches and cream. But by and large it went better than might have been expected.

And then came the final phase: At what point do you permit them to return? This was the hottest issue. Warren said, "Not one should come back until after the end of the war, absolutely none." He said, "A Jap is a Jap." And so there was great agitation on his side to have many nationwide radio debates on the subject and so forth. My position was that they should be permitted to come back before the war ended. They should be processed through relocation centers, and those released should be permitted to return, the point being that there was a battalion of Japanese Americans from Hawaii. The senator, Inouye, was an officer. He lost his arm in that battalion. That battalion had an incredible record in Italy. Our thinking was to take advantage of that and also to take advantage of the fact that the war was still on. It's your patriotic duty to accept these people back rather than wait until the end of the war, when this agitation might start up again.

The final decision was that they could return. They began to return before the end of the war. Robert Kenny, an old friend, was attorney general. He was splendid. He called the sheriff and local police officers together and said, "Look. This is the way it's going to be. I don't want any nonsense." And to his great credit, Warren backed Kenny up. He was opposed to him, but when the decision was made, he said, "There's going to be no trouble." And with the exception of two or three very minor incidents, there wasn't any trouble. They filtered back in, and that was that.

Another problem that relates to this had to do with Mexican Americans. We had, you may recall, the zoot-suit riots in Los Angeles. The naval personnel would go into Los Angeles on the weekend—you know how navy people are on the weekend, looking for trouble—and they would go into these various Mexican settlements just to raise hell. The zoot-suiters were Mexican boys who wore long hair and extremely long coats and long, peg pants. They were kind of weird looking for that time, like the hippies were when they first appeared. The navy boys on leave would go after them, and the police would tend to side with the sailors. The attorney general was my friend Kenny, a Democrat, and the governor was Earl Warren, an old political opponent. At that time we didn't see eye to eye. He was not yet the Warren of the Supreme Court, or we'd have gotten along fine. The question arose as to what to do about the zoot-suit riots. I got Kenny (I knew Warren would never do it on my recommendation) to appoint a commission, headed by the archbishop, to take a look at the facts of the situation. They issued a report that had a quieting effect. Many of their recommendations were carried out, and as a result, the Civic Unity Council was set up, and we were able to cope with some of the things that had caused the trouble and to quiet the situation down. As a result, we were commended by the officials in Mexico City for having played a constructive role.

I've always had pretty good luck with the timing of my books. Purely accidental. I did a book about racial minorities—all racial minorities in the United States—the Chinese, Japanese, Filipinos. As luck would have it, it was published in the spring of 1943. At that time there were racial riots in Beaumont, Texas, in Harlem, a big one in Detroit, and others elsewhere. About a half dozen racial incidents. And, of course, they gave the book a tremendous boost. It was a best seller for quite some time. As a result of that I got into a lot of speaking, radio programs, et cetera. I spoke all over the country; I was very much aware of what was going on in this field then. Because those riots came in the midpoint of the war and because of the Nazi attitude about race, the riots had a big, big impact. People suddenly came alive about this issue. They realized that something had to be done, and there was an enormous spurt of activity. Civic-unity councils were set up to oppose discrimination, that sort of thing, all over the country.

The riots relate to the war in this way. It was not as some people tried to imply at the time. It was not the result of any kind of agitation or anything of that kind. The minute the war started—any war will do this—you have a manpower situation. Then there was immediately an issue about segregated services. We've gotten over that now, but at that time it was a big issue. Segregation in the navy, segregation in the army, all the way down the line. And this began to raise the temperature, as you would expect, and people began to say, "Well, we're fighting the Nazis, you know." In addition, manpower was in big demand. For example, I served on a three-man board of arbitration at North American Aviation in Los Angeles. Some of the cases that used to come up to us for arbitration involved racial issues, and you could see what was happening. It was very, very interesting because many of the so-called Okies and Arkies (Dust Bowl migrants) were drawn into the aircraft industry and the shipyards. They were working with people from the minority races, and they didn't like it—at first. And there would be these incidents. We would examine the witnesses and raise the questions. We would say, "There's a war on, and you're objecting to working together?" You could see that you had them over the barrel, and after a while we didn't get any of those cases; the whole thing sort of faded.

Life was very hectic during the war. I was writing books, making trips, and was constantly involved in racial matters, this council for civic unity and all that kind of thing, so I was enormously busy, and I don't recall any hardships. It was a relief, in a way, to get those tensions of '39 and '41 out of the way, because they were very bad. Travel was very rough. I had all these lecture engagements, and there were travel experiences you wouldn't believe. Standing up, not being able to get accommodations, staggering out of trains with no sleep.

Los Angeles's attitude toward the war effort was amazingly cooperative. There was a very fine spirit there. For example, I had a dear friend, a very prominent Jewish businessman in Los Angeles, who was in the furniture business. He couldn't get some of the supplies he needed for the business, so he went to work at North American as a riveter. I never knew that fellow to be as happy as when he was working there. He was a millionaire. He felt involved, he thought it was great, had a marvelous time doing it.

I think the morale was very high during the war years. I was aware of very little black marketeering. Of course, everybody was fudging around a little bit for cigarettes—this, that, and the other. But the morale was extraordinarily high. Considering the contracts that were let and the amount of money involved, the defense program was handled very much on the up and up. I think Donald Nelson and those people did a splendid job, and the Truman Committee. It was a very different situation than it is now.

Cathleen Schurr was born in England and was living there when the war began in 1939. She came to America just before Pearl Harbor, and as she was approaching New York, the ship she was on was torpedoed.

I worked briefly for the Censorship Office. We were reading people's mail. Then I went from there to NBC. That was at a time when there were very, very few females working in any of the media. It was considered that women's voices were unsuitable and that biologically and for other reasons we weren't able to work as reporters objectively. I was writing news in the foreign-news section, which was a special area. It was beamed overseas. I thought at that time, and looking back, that it was an opportunity for me as a woman which would not have opened up otherwise. I didn't have the patience to stay there, because women were still not allowed on the air. But if I had hung on longer, there probably would have been a better opportunity. There were many cases where women were practically conscripted into all kinds of jobs for which they had been considered biologically and emotionally unsuited. It's like men going into the army: Those women who had the opportunity and learned from it went on from there.

We lived in Greenwich Village, and you barely knew you were at war. I don't know when the rationing came in, but I never experienced the war in this country as being a war. I don't believe, living where we lived, in a major city, that we really had any intensive experience of war at all. Rationing to me was a joke. You had to save up if you wanted to have beef, but there was so much of everything else available. Now, again, this may be because we were living in New York City, and I'm sure that's probably a unique experience. I don't feel eating fish and chicken and vegetables can be considered a hardship, and there was never anything that we lacked. We had a car, which we simply didn't use, and there was no need for gas. We arranged our vacations so that we went by train or by bus, or we biked whenever we could. We had the sirens going from time to time, and we had signs up saying where the shelters were. A lot of people went around complaining. I never could understand what they were complaining about.

After I left NBC, I went to work for a public relations firm. I had gotten into doing industrial promotion, and that was when I really began to get close to industrial areas and production. I was the first woman ever to be on the floor of the open-hearth furnaces at Republic Steel. I did a lot of traveling because I had a lot of industrial accounts for a small PR firm that hired women because it didn't have to pay them much.

War industries had problems in their communities, and they had no sense of public relations. One of the things, in my naïveté, I thought I could do in my little job was write about the great, big, fat company and tell the local community how wonderful they were and all the great things they were doing for the war effort and how they gave employment to people and the things those people did and the things the company did. They did a lot of things which were important and useful but which were not publicized or recognized. I went around to the plants talking to people and interviewed people on the various shifts, went through the shops and wrote about things they were developing, technical things.

I think that our attitude toward World War II was simply that it was absolutely inevitable. Inevitable, once it came. Having lived through it in 1939, I really could not believe that in my lifetime I was going to go through another world war. It just seemed inconceivable to me.

Sally Knox is now retired and living in Washington, D.C. During the war, she worked for the government in the Midwest.

I went to work in 1942 as a publications editor for the Central Procurement District in Detroit. That was part of the Army Air Force. They were responsible for procurement, at that time, pretty much throughout the Midwest and Canada. They were procuring war materiel mainly connected with aircraft, I believe.

My job was to edit or prepare publications to be issued by the publications officer. I did that for twenty-nine years in various places.

I worked in Detroit for a year and a half, maybe two years and a half. Then I transferred to Wright Field, it was called at that time, later Patterson Air Force Base near Dayton, Ohio. Dayton was just coming out of a bad depression, and the war certainly started it up industrially. I think that many people in Dayton of the old line, the old society, were distressed to see so many war workers coming in. They thought it would spoil their pretty little town.

Rationing affected everybody, of course, including me. I remember we couldn't get butter, so we bought oleo, and we thought it was awful and didn't eat it and left it in the refrigerator until it spoiled. There was rationing of shoes and gasoline. Travel was pretty bad. From Dayton there was a nice train that started in Saint Louis; it was called the *Jeffersonian,* and it had all reserved seats. That is, it was supposed to have, but it was just mobbed with people. People sitting in the aisles and standing up, and they served two or three meals a day, and I got in line for breakfast and waited for hours and finally got my breakfast and went right back in line to wait for lunch.

I don't remember whether it was in Detroit or Dayton, but somewhere I took motor mechanics. Women drive, but they don't know anything about the inside of a car. So this was to teach us how to make small repairs, if necessary, if there weren't any men around. Then we could do it. I probably forgot everything I learned.

We had an air-raid drill once, conducted by the Red Cross, in which each one was supposed to do something. A house was supposed to have been bombed, and there was a victim, and we were supposed to do things, and everybody did everything wrong. I remember the leader saying, "Well, you can imagine how I feel at this time." Then we had a review; we hadn't digested our teaching properly.

In general, I seemed very pessimistic because everything was going against us. The first thing that made me feel optimistic was when Germany attacked Russia. When that happened, I went out into the street and tried to get a paper. When 1944 came along, I felt maybe we were going to win the war after all.

I just remembered this recently in connection with all this talk about spies. A man came to see me when I was in the Central Procurement District in Detroit. I don't know whether he was in uniform or not, but he held out his pass and told me where he was from and informed me that we were in a very serious war with the Nazis and we didn't want any Nazi spies around, and he wanted me to keep my eyes open and see if I saw anything of that kind going on at work. He may have been with the FBI or Army Intelligence, I am not sure. He gave me an address, and I was to write a letter to him every Sunday night, and I was just to talk about my girl friends and what I was doing, and if there was anything of interest, I was to put it in. So every Sunday night I sat down and wrote a letter, and I never had anything to report. I was never to tell anybody about it; I couldn't tell my mother. She wondered who I was writing to, but I never told a soul until about a year ago.

Charles Keller was a professor of history at Williams College in Williamstown, Massachusetts, where he now lives in retirement.

The first military program came here in January 1943. It was a navy V-5 program. It meant that a lot of members of the faculty had to teach navigation, physics, mathematics. Then, I remember clearly the great group that went down to Philadelphia and had a cram course in how to teach navigation. I was in that group. It was between Christmas 1942 and New Year's.

I was aware of the fact that I didn't know very much, and that I was going to teach something and not explain it. If anybody asked me how that formula was derived, I would tell them it wasn't the point. The point is to learn it. The group was here about three months. I did feel a little uncomfortable knowing that if these boys made a mistake in the course I was teaching and they were out over the ocean, they would be in trouble. I thought of that all the time. But for a group of nonprofessionals we didn't do badly. We had navy people who guided us. We had tests that were standard tests coming from Washington. We had strict marking, and if we seemed to be falling down, we were told about it. But on the whole, we had some pretty good results. From here, they went on to the next set of steps, which was more intensive.

Another program came in the summer of '43. That was a V-12 program, and they were in uniform. There was no friction between the civilian students and the military boys. Everybody respected everybody else. The civilians were a small group, and their number went down steadily in 1943.

It was hard to get teachers during the war years, but we had enough. We'd lost some members of the faculty, but a lot of the teaching was done by navy people, particularly in the V-5 program. I taught history, I taught navigation, I worked as a facilitator—I don't like that word, but I'll use it—in the dean's office with both the V-5 and V-12 programs. You had to schedule very carefully, because you had a fixed program for V-5, and then you had V-12, and then you had the civilians. And you had to do a real reshuffle. We'd get through a term, have about two weeks for exams and a break, and then begin the next term. That started in the summer of '42 and kept on accelerating through '46. I taught seventeen terms straight without any break whatsoever. This was my way of doing what I could. We were teaching because what else could we do. I used to teach four classes in a row on some days on three different subjects. And that was tough, so I would huff and puff and get through, but that was that. And I know what other people were doing elsewhere.

The war years were exhilarating in the sense of: Well, here we are; something has happened, and what are we going to do about it? We have to do it as fast as we can.

When I began to see the war come to a close, I decided to give a course on postwar periods, so I was teaching it before the war was over, which I thought was kind of good. I was very much interested when the first veterans were coming back. What good students they were! I'm not sure when it was, but I think it was before '46 when the college resumed its full schedule. Somebody met me on Spring Street and said: "I hear you can't get a word in edgewise in your own classes." I thought that was wonderful.

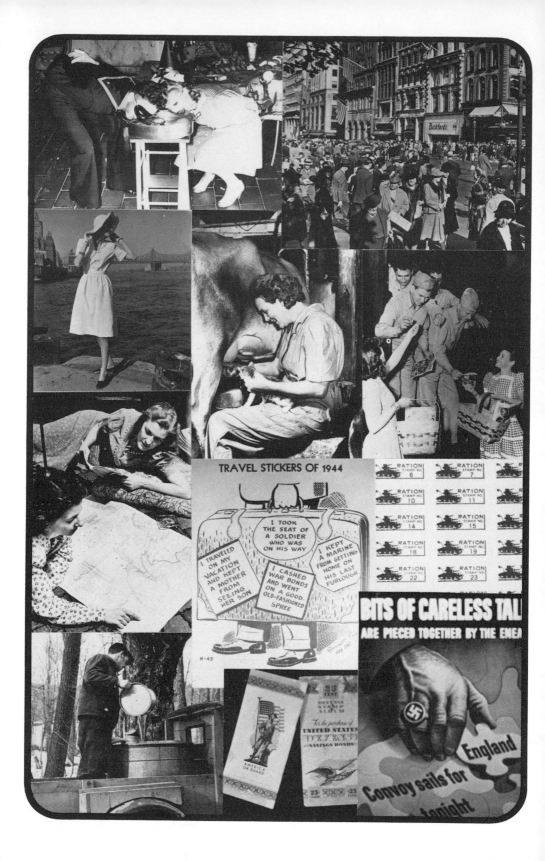

TRAVEL STICKERS OF 1944

I TRAVELED ON MY VACATION AND KEPT A MOTHER FROM SEEING HER SON

I TOOK THE SEAT OF A SOLDIER WHO WAS ON HIS WAY

I CASHED WAR BONDS AND WENT ON A GOOD OLD-FASHIONED SPREE

I KEPT A MARINE FROM GETTING HOME ON HIS LAST FURLOUGH

M-49

RATION STAMP NO. 6
RATION STAMP NO. 7
RATION STAMP NO. 10
RATION STAMP NO. 11
RATION STAMP NO. 14
RATION STAMP NO. 15
RATION STAMP NO. 18
RATION STAMP NO. 19
RATION STAMP NO. 22
RATION STAMP NO. 23

BITS OF CARELESS TALK
ARE PIECED TOGETHER BY THE ENEMY

Convoy sails for England tonight

6

"DON'T YOU KNOW THERE'S A WAR ON?"

Of course, some Americans were more Involved In the war than others. For a man with a physical defect, at the outer limits of the draft age, or with a wife and young children to support, the war did not have an immediate impact on him or on his family—especially if they did not live near Washington, one of the big industrial cities, or one of the many military installations around the country. Life went on as before, except for the shortages and possibly the concern about relatives or friends overseas. Millions of Americans were in this position. For them it was business as usual, except that every now and then someone would ask them—or they would ask someone—"Don't you know there's a war on?"

Although some people tried to avoid becoming involved in the war—and did not mind admitting it—most Americans did what they could to support the war, even if they were not directly involved. And most of the men, if they were of draft age, confessed that they were more than a little uncomfortable not being in uniform or in defense work during the war years. In fact, many men tried to salve their consciences by working, for awhile at least, in a defense plant. There were also the conscientious objectors who renounced war, and the men who were so engrossed in their work, or women so engrossed in their families, that they were not particularly aware that there was a war on. But they were the exceptions. Most Americans not directly involved in the war effort were very much aware of the war and affected by it. A few of them recall their experiences:

Americans Remember the Home Front

In Ocean City, Maryland, Jack Lynch, the owner and manager of the Commander Hotel, had his problems keeping a resort hotel operating during the war. He was married and had a family of four children, but he did take a job in a defense factory for one year, "just to clear my own conscience," as he put it.

We opened the hotel in the spring and closed in the fall. It takes a month to close it up, so when the war started, it was just about three or three and a half months since we had closed. Shortly after, we began to get submarine activity along the coast. We were put under the Baltimore region of civil defense. We organized a group of local people to try to work with the government and the region blacking out our town, because your being able to open the next season depended how you could black your town out. They felt that the lights from the various resorts would pinpoint everything for any submarine that might be operating offshore. A group of us got together and raised some money for the project by securing the Capital Theatre. The owner let us use the theater, and we showed the movie *Sergeant York*. That raised something in the neighborhood of two thousand dollars, which gave us a little cash for the blackout project.

They were asking us to blackout but weren't telling us a thing—there were no directions on it at all. After we organized, a group of boys went to the Jersey resorts to see if we could get any information about what they were doing before we started. Gee whiz, the theaters on the boardwalk in Atlantic City, you could almost see them in France! We didn't get any help up there.

Everybody had a front door opening out toward the sea, so we had to build a blackout and a turn. In other words, you entered and came out the doorway sideways and had to turn to the left, and the inside of it was all painted dull black.

Of course, that was before the days of air conditioning, so it was also quite a problem as to how you were going to have ventilation in a room with blackout curtains. What we did was to devise a standing rod which came out about six inches from the window, and hung a black oilcloth curtain. You didn't get direct ventilation, but you got ventilation coming in from the sides and over the top. We scoured the scrap heaps for number-ten vegetable and fruit cans, cut a hole in the bottom of each can, and did all the streetlights with those so there was no direct light shining; everything was right straight down.

Colonel Barrie of Baltimore came down and inspected us two or three times. The Coast Guard would take him out to sea at night to check us out. If they found a light somewhere, they told us, and it was up to us to see that it was corrected.

In the summer of '42 business was very good. It was really amazing. What few people did have the gas stamps came by car. There were a number of buses put on between Baltimore and Ocean City, and people actually crowded that bus so that they stood all the way—couldn't get a seat.

And I would say that after the first couple of years things improved. As we began to get toward the close of the war, more came.

One thing that was a help to the resorts was that people had money and they couldn't spend it. They couldn't buy a new automobile or a new refrigerator or cookstove or many other things they would normally buy in everyday life. We felt we did a good service, particularly with the medical profession. In those days we gave preference in reservations to doctors. There were so many doctors crowded in the cities; they were overworked, and to be able to get away to a resort put them back on their feet. We learned from experience over those years to give the doctors preference to keep them going.

The labor situation was terrible. Labor was so independent that you didn't know when you were going to have somebody on a particular post or not. As far as food was concerned, we did fairly well. Some of the farmers would just slaughter their own meat—they'd call you up and ask you if you could use a half a steer or something like that. So when we were caught without any provisions, we bought some. I never heard of anybody on the shore having any trouble. They wouldn't sell you something that they wouldn't want to use themselves.

I'll never forget one day during the war, on Good Friday, there was a lot of activity—planes and one blimp went by. A boat had been sunk the night before right off Chincoteague, Virginia, and the Coast Guard was called down there from Ocean City to help pick up bodies at sea. They brought them back here, and they had them racked up on the stern of the Coast Guard boat just like cordwood. Whether there was any truth in it or not I don't know, but we were told that the submarine, after hitting this freighter, came up and was circling around the boat, and someone in one of the lifeboats took a potshot at one of the officers on the submarine, and then they just turned their machine guns on these boats and they killed everybody except one colored man and maybe one white man.

203

The next day I was in Baltimore, and I heard this newsboy crying something about "Ocean City," so I went over and bought a paper. They ran a story about bodies drifting ashore at Ocean City—and they had the whole thing wrong. I went right straight to the *Baltimore Sun* building to try and get an interview with one of the editors to see if I couldn't get things straightened out. But I couldn't, so it just stood as it was printed—wholly untrue. It didn't particularly hurt business.

Anna Mae Lindberg lived in the Homestead area of Pittsburgh, where her husband worked for U.S. Steel's Irvin Works:

I was born on City Farm Lane, which was a ghetto street, actually, for people who didn't have much money. Mostly immigrants. My age group would be the first-generation Americans. The boys and girls that I played with, I think, all of their parents came from somewhere across the sea. The street we lived on was the last street of the town right next to the mill. I lived on that street from the time I was born until I married in 1936 and moved away. I didn't go very far. As a matter of fact, I've spent my whole life living within a three-quarter-mile area.

During the war Russell and I lived in a three-room apartment about ten blocks up the hill from City Farm Lane. He must have been in his mid twenties—but he had a job in the mill.

I was a housewife during the war. I had worked before I was married, and I hadn't been off work very long. I had a secretarial job, but it was a political appointment. When your side was out, you were out too, and I was out at the moment. We decided to start our family. I don't know if this was ever in Russ's mind, but I thought it was one more thing that would keep him out of the war. It was something we didn't talk about, but that was my idea.

I don't remember when this happened, and if it was just social pressure or what, but my husband has a master's degree, so he applied for officer's training. He didn't discuss this with me—he just came home and said that he had applied. As it turned out, he wore glasses from the time that he was in high school, so his vision kept him out of officer's training. And I was so relieved. I can't tell you how relieved I was about that.

We did all the things us ladies used to do: went to the Municipal Building and sewed nightgowns. I get angry when I think back on those days—like having to save the tin cans and go out and collect milkweed pods because they were used to make life jackets. So we'd be out in the fields collecting these damned milkweeds.

The morale in our community was the same kind you get when you find out somebody has a terminal illness. You keep it to yourself—you try to cheer up the other person, and the other person tries to cheer you. So we pretended there was all this tremendous morale. I did not find the war years exhilarating and exciting. Never; not for me. I would question that very many women felt that way. They pretended. Men may have felt an excitement about it. Maybe it was just me, I don't know. Women go a little deeper into the consequences, the human. There was always that pinch and always that anxious tension.

I remember a friend who was put in the hold of a boat with all these other soldiers. When they got to Europe, the European war was over, and without ever being reassigned, they were kept on this same boat and sent back over the Atlantic Ocean out to the Pacific. This fellow was on the ocean for God knows how long in the hold of this boat, longer than his tour of duty. He spent all his time on the ocean—not in the army. That starts you thinking.

Peter Scaglione was chief bartender in the Columbia Restaurant in Tampa, Florida.

I had some friends, young boys, eighteen, nineteen years old, who went to war and did not come back. I was 1-A myself, but they never did call me. I don't know why. They talked to my boss here. I don't know if he fixed it up with the board or not. Maybe he did.

When everybody was in uniform, we used to have a little more business on account of them. Sailors and soldiers would have a drink or two. Sometimes they'd fight, and I'd have to jump over the bar and get some of the soldiers out, because we didn't want no rough stuff, you know. I used to get my baseball bat and run them out. I didn't have much trouble, because they knew when they had a little too much. I wouldn't give them no more. They had to go somewhere else.

I was sorry, like I say, that a lot of good friends of mine went overseas and got killed.

Harry Hahn, then a vice-president of the Hahn Shoe Company in Washington, D.C. (now retired), and his wife, Elizabeth:

HARRY: Our shoe business was a Washington institution. It was family owned; I was the oldest of the third generation. We had seven shoe stores in Washington, and one in Baltimore.

I guess it was just after the war started that we got into rationing in the shoe business. We had no premonition of it at all. On a Sunday morning there was an announcement in the paper that shoes would be rationed.

ELIZABETH: You had to have coupons.

HARRY: Coupon number fifteen or seventeen in the sugar-ration book was designated as the shoe coupon. Leather was going to shoes for the military. The announcement came on Sunday, and on Monday morning, or evening, we had a meeting of all our employees and told everybody we had no idea what was going to develop. We had reasonable stocks of shoes on hand, but we didn't know how we were going to get more. The problem was not in selling them but in getting them. You had to go to the factories, travel all over the country. But we never went into the black market.

ELIZABETH: A lot of people did.

HARRY: Oh, I suppose there were offers for coupons. If there was hardship, you could go to a board and get an extra coupon or so. If you had a child, if you had an orthopedic situation, something like that, you could get extra shoes.

ELIZABETH: I worked at the D.C. ration board, where they gave out the stamps. I think I did a volunteer job every day as long as I had a cook. We gave out all kinds of ration stamps—for gas, for meat. A lot of people exaggerated their needs for gasoline, but they were thoroughly investigated before they were given extra coupons. And I was very busy saving my gas for our car, because I had a little boy who was always getting into trouble, and I never knew when I was going to have to dash to the doctor's or the hospital with him. So I took the bus and saved the coupons to use for him and marketing and that sort of thing.

The one thing people would complain about was the meat rationing. Fortunately, we liked a lot of the things you could get without the red stamps—liver, which you could buy without stamps; chicken, for which you paid maybe one stamp for two chickens. Red meat was the thing that was high in points.

HARRY: Scotch was hard to come by during the war, too, scotch and cigarettes. You had to queue up for them.

ELIZABETH: Butter was difficult to get. And Harry said to me, "Don't you ever feed me margarine." I said: "I wouldn't dream of it." He'd been eating it for about three months and didn't know it.

HARRY: Business was very good. I was merchandising women's shoes, and we were on a gravy train. We were selling most of the WAVEs and WACs and marine girls uniform shoes. They had to have coupons for them. We all worked kind of hard. Later on, to compound the aggravations, we had not only the rationing but also price control. I think at that time it was desirable. We didn't care what we paid for shoes when we bought them. We were anxious to get any we could. If people would give us some shoes, we told them we would try to do business with them after the war. I opened some very important accounts and made some good friends on that basis.

ELIZABETH: We were never afraid to go out in Washington during the war. We worked at the Pepsi Cola canteen. Anybody in uniform could be served free, of course. I was a volunteer soda jerk, and I loved it. The servicemen were so wonderful; never any unpleasantness, black or white. The second floor was a sort of game room, and the third floor was where they could shower and change their clothes.

Some of the boys came in regularly, and they got to know us. I had some of them up to the house for dinner occasionally.

I also used to go to work at the Bundles for Britain. I would knit and sew sweaters.

HARRY: I was an air-raid warden in Chevy Chase. Everybody pulled down their shades. The city was blacked out. To my knowledge there was never a threat. It was always a drill, about every three or four months.

ELIZABETH: We all went to Red Cross to take courses in survival. We had little packages of food in the basement in case we did have any difficulties, and we had a little Victory garden in our backyard, where we raised a few vegetables. Harry raised them. I can still see you sitting there shelling black-eyed peas. Really, the civilians in Washington did not suffer, believe me they didn't. I have it much worse now. I wish I had that dayworker I had then.

Newton Tolman lived up around Hartsville and Nelson, New Hampshire, where he still lives, the squire of Tolman Pond and an author of some note, having written a regular column for the Berkshire Eagle *and*

a number of books, including one which is now a collector's item, North
from Monadnock.

I would say that, accumulatively, the effect of the war years on me
was it aged me about twenty years more than I should have been; it confused my thinking. It confused the thinking of everybody in the United
States writing, and it still is confused.

Right after Pearl Harbor the government says my wife and small son
and I had to be self-sufficient. The government says to raise pigs. So I
got twenty-four hogs and plowed up six acres and got an old tractor,
and Uncle Bill and everybody got into the act. I built a barn and got a
stone and cut timber and spent altogether twenty-eight dollars on the
barn. It's a big one, and it's now lived in by my sister-in-law as a permanent house. And then they said: "We have too many hogs." That
knocked the bottom out of that, and we almost lost money on the
twenty-four hogs, but we bought a cow and chickens, so that when I
took off to save the country for democracy, my wife would be able to
survive.

All the girls, including my wife, were in the Red Cross because, they
said, "You got to be trained; the submarines are coming into Portsmouth." And they were all taught how to give baths. The whole thing
was great. Crazy. Everyone was frantic.

Then gasoline had to be rationed. A cousin of mine was a big-time
lawyer. He got sent to someplace in Washington and came out a full colonel. But he didn't want to suffer for gas when he came up here, so he
bought, surreptitiously, a five-thousand-gallon tank and had it installed
below his house and filled it full of gasoline. Sometime in the next year
or so it was discovered to be empty. The thing had a leak in it, so the gas
all went down into White's Pond.

Only the poor and ignorant people, I'd say, were 100 percent honest
about rationing. I had an old farm truck, and I took weekly pilgrimages
to Keene—fourteen miles. Everybody would pile in the truck to save
gas, buy their groceries, and come back. But the rich people, the ration
man, the one high up in the State Guard and all that, he was important.
So he didn't need that. He could buy black-market beef, everything
known to man. They lived high on the hog, these people. Mill owners in
Keene, Harrisville, Swanzey, and all over were great patriots. Their
mills were about to die, and some had been defunct for several years.
Suddenly, they got a contract with the army and the navy, and so they

were big patriots. "We wanted to go in the army, but we can't because we are essential to the war effort"—they all got out of it.

I was with the Guard, working my ass off, as I said, not because I really believed in the war under Roosevelt or this or that. My own view was that, well, God, it's happened, so we have to do something about it. I just hoped to Christ I didn't get into it. On the other hand, you have to follow the leader. I never told my wife, for God's sake, that I nearly broke my neck to get out of the navy deal. She probably wouldn't like it now, but I did. I didn't want to go. You have only one life to live, and if somebody wants to go and get themselves killed, well, let them go to it.

We slept three or four hours a night. It was a tremendous effort, and all these native people, the real people, were doing it unquestioningly. They were told that the Germans were coming into Portsmouth in submarines and so we had to have a drill down in Keene of antisubmarine attackers. And everybody took it seriously. Oh, it's unbelievable.

I made almost all of my farm equipment out of old secondhand parts, and I used old secondhand tractors. You couldn't have any rubber, everything ran on ironlike wheels. Christ, I farmed all the goddamned farms in town and hayed them with a tractor that went a maximum four miles an hour on iron spikes. I got so tired riding on that thing. There was no cushion on the seat.

I was in twenty-four businesses. But the two main ones were the family businesses of running a resort and a ski school and, in the end, renting twelve cottages down by the pond. Incidentally, during the war, my mother got letters from every damned country in the world. People would run into each other on a destroyer in the Mediterranean or in the desert somewhere, later in the Pacific, who had been to Tolman Pond.

The war was a tremendous concerted effort that brought everyone together in one way or the other—tremendous spiritual exultation. Then came Korea, and then came Vietnam, a tapering off to the bottom. But World War II, everybody was in it, and it didn't even matter if they were the crooks, like the guy who stored the illicit gasoline and got his great pay from the government for sitting on a desk down in Washington. Or the guy like my nephew-in-law's father—a great magician, a wonderful guy—who went out in the first carrier in the Pacific after Pearl Harbor, and the carrier was sunk. He was swimming—he was a great swimmer—with a carton of Camel cigarettes in his hand, and some rescue boat came by to pick him up, and he said, "There's some guys over there; they're in trouble; I'm fine." He was laying on his back holding his Camel cigarettes, and he said, "Go get them and come back." And when they came back, he was gone.

George Gloss is the proprietor of the famous Brattle Book Shop in Boston. During the war he worked for his brother as a salesman of ships' parts.

It wasn't until after the war that I got married and went into the book business. But I had accumulated a vast number of books all during that time. Every Saturday I would go from one bookstore to another, from Scollay Square to Huntington Avenue, and walk all the way to Cambridge, covering the entire city, getting books of various kinds. I just decided that I was going to read the best books that were ever printed, and since I had relatively little money, I would cover all the antique shops and furniture stores, especially the Salvation Army, the places that you could get books cheaply, even junkyards.

For the first few days of the war there was a rumor that some planes were about to attack Boston, but this wiped out almost immediately, and the people settled back into their work.

The war coming meant jobs for a great many who had been either unemployed or just starting work. The papers were filled with ads for all kinds of technicians. I remember how a lot of them were very worried about whether they were going to be picked for the army. Of course, many were volunteering. I had had a lung condition, and therefore I was 4-F, and I was working in a war industry; so those two factors left me out.

Boston wasn't so much a military town. The military that came here came to enjoy themselves. There seemed, to me, far less worry about going out at night then. You could walk around most anytime without the least fear of being mugged or robbed.

The main impact on Boston was a tremendous effort in war production and in entertaining sailors and soldiers who came to the city. Every industry was booming, going twenty-four hours a day. They were running on shifts, and the only ones who weren't working were people who were physically disabled. Morale was high, and it was the best of all possible worlds, despite the terrible holocaust of the war. The city was peaceful, everybody was working who could work, industries were booming, a lot of money was being spent.

"Don't You Know There's a War On?"

Helen Wilson spent the war at the University of Michigan in Ann Arbor. Today she is married to John Nies, and both she and her husband are successful attorneys in Washington, D.C.

We had a fairly normal world at the university for about a year, and then there was a sudden departure of all the males who had been in the freshman class. I was very much in love with a fellow who went off in the fall of 1943, and I was very concerned about him.

There still were many young men on campus, because we had the V-12 program for the navy, and there were lots of boys in that. Then at the law school there was the judge advocate general's program.

I had a roommate who was a professional dancer during the summers. She worked at the Grand Hotel up at Mackinaw Island. I was also a dancer, but not as accomplished—my mother had really wanted me to be a Rockette; that was her ambition. We also had a very beautiful red-head roommate, so we put together a song-and-dance routine to sell war bonds and stamps. We'd go around to the various sororities and dormitories at dinner time, and it was great fun. I'm sure we weren't very good, but we were well received.

I had been hearing since I was a child that Roosevelt was the worst thing that ever happened to the country, and starting with that, I think I had a basic mistrust of the Roosevelt administration and viewed the war with suspicion from the beginning. I was trying to remember when Roosevelt first met with Stalin, because to me that was the most significant thing that happened during the war. It made the whole thing false. Maybe that was the beginning of my basic mistrust of government. We were fighting for freedom, and everything I had been taught, particularly in high school, was that the Communist system did away with freedom. And then there was this great announcement following that meeting between Roosevelt and Stalin that we were fighting with Russia for freedom. When that happened, I considered the whole thing a power struggle and that the war had nothing to do with freedom. It was the most traumatic event I can remember, and to me it just meant that everything that happened was absolutely wrong, that the whole war was wrong. Simplistic, but it was probably the first thought I'd ever had politically. I never had really thought about politics or political systems or the basic ways that countries were organized.

One thing I remember is the nuisance of rationing. I never understood the need for it. Why wasn't there enough sugar? Why were fabrics scarce? Why did we have to have coupons for meat? Was that much meat needed for the troops? There weren't any greater number of people. I can understand why there weren't consumer goods like washing machines or automobiles, but I never understood the shortages of food.

And I can remember the crowded trains. I never understood where everybody was going. It wasn't just military; there were just as many civilians. There never were seats on trains; I sat on my suitcase on the train between Ann Arbor and Kalamazoo on every trip for three years.

I did get a job in a defense factory one summer; that was my first and only war effort. I applied at the factory which made musical instruments. They were then making bombsights, and I had the job of soldering little hairs across the bombsight. I think I lasted about three days. The monotony of the work and the sloppiness of the work really concerned me. People were not really concerned about making good bombsights—just in three days I got that—it was making the good wages. As much as I needed the money, I really couldn't stand doing it eight hours a day. I had previously applied for a job as a nursery school teacher for the children of the women who were working in the war factories, and I was so happy when that came through. It was a much better job for me, and I could make more money. I would work there from six in the morning until that eight-hour shift was over. And then I worked at night as a carhop. I did have to make a lot of money. Young people can't imagine now how difficult it was to make enough money to stay in school. A job at seventy-five cents an hour was about as good as you could do.

I remember summers in Kalamazoo, which was very close to Battle Creek, where a big veterans' hospital was always taking boys in and sending them back. Kalamazoo had a USO, and I went there regularly. Probably the biggest thrill of my entire young life was the night when a convoy from Battle Creek drove me home. There were six trucks that drove down the little street in Kalamazoo to take me home. I was very excited. It was like a scene from an Andy Hardy movie. I was probably a sophomore in college at that time.

I met a lot of soldiers in Kalamazoo. On dates then, the boys in the service were more demanding sexually than others. At that time, it's now hard to believe, we were really all very pure, and the sexual pressures were somewhat more than I felt comfortable with. There was a little of the attitude of "Well, I'm going overseas. I might be dead tomorrow," and some implication that you had an obligation because they were fighting the war. But surprisingly, the boys were either quite chivalrous or innocent themselves. They would have enjoyed having a sexual relationship, but if you said no, they would accept it. One word we used all the time was *oversexed*. Either you were afraid you were or someone else couldn't help herself because she was, poor thing. That's a problem no one has anymore.

Arthur Edmunds began the war as a student at Fisk College in Nashville, Tennessee.

I was a history major, a political science minor, and considered myself very well read. I used to read the *New York Times*. And I was a little bit amazed at the isolation of the students, at least the people that I came in contact with. Part of this was because we were in another world, so to speak. But I think, also, we were tremendously misled by our leaders and by the press. I would not have thought we were that close to war. Maybe it was a black reaction, I'm not sure, but there was no overwhelming desire to get a gun and go fight someone. Most of the students at the school were not southerners. I'm not—I matriculated there from Iowa. We considered the southern white to be as much our enemy as the Japanese five thousand miles away from us.

We were still rigidly segregated. Where our campus was located there was Meharrie Medical College, right across the street; Tennessee State A & I, and the state school for black youngsters was about eight blocks farther out. It was a whole subculture. We had a theater, we had stores, ten-cent stores and things like that. So until you went into the downtown area, you didn't run into much of that kind of stuff. But still, you felt oppressed, and no great urge to save democracy.

There were a couple of things that I recall happening that made an indelible impression on me. First, there was a notice circulated to all the men on the campus to carry their draft cards with them at all times. The Fisk campus is cut up by streets, and there are thoroughfares running through it. Police officers had been coming through and challenging students about their draft cards and roughing them up for not having them. I remember one student getting beaten for not having his card with him.

The other thing was that they instituted an Army Specialized Training Program at Meharrie. In effect, they took every student into the army and made them private, first class. Some did not want to do it, because this committed them to a certain amount of army service after graduation, but it gave them tremendous financial relief. At that time, I imagine, Meharrie Medical College was all black. White faculty but no white students. And when the ASTP went in, they paid the men sixty-six dollars a month basic pay for a Pfc., gave them a stipend for room and board, paid their tuition and their books. They were sort of like millionaires. And rather than the GI uniforms, these guys would go out and buy officers' uniforms. They all looked like General MacArthur, with these floppy hats and sunglasses and with this Pfc. stripe on their arms.

In the summer of '42 I worked with my roommate in a little bar on Washington Boulevard in Detroit. Several of the guys who came there to eat lunch were recruiting officers for the navy. The navy had two programs called something like the V-7 or V-12. They would give you two years to finish college, and when you came out of it, you became a gunnery officer, or a deck officer of some kind. By this time we were trying to analyze the war situation in relation to our own educational plans, and my roommate and I made the decision that we would try to get in this program. These guys had encouraged us, at least there in the restaurant, so we went down to the office and saw an aide there. The first thing that came up was: "What school do you go to?" He named a couple of schools. We knew Fisk was an A-rated school, but there was not a black school on the whole list. And they would not take us. At the time the only blacks in the navy were stewards. So that put an awfully sour taste in my mouth for the whole damned military. I'm volunteering myself, and I'm rejected.

After I graduated from Fisk, I went back to Iowa and started some graduate study at Drake University. Not too far from Des Moines, in Turinda, Iowa, they had a Japanese prisoner-of-war camp. They also had at Drake a large number of Nisei students. I got to be friendly with two or three of them and asked them why there were so many of them out here. They said: "Well, the only way we could get out of the relocation camps was to get into school. We couldn't go to any school in the coastal area. So we started applying. Every Big Ten school turned us down, and Drake accepted us." Drake was a Disciple of Christ Church school primarily.

Personally, I resented the action of President Roosevelt in relocating the Japanese Americans. They didn't do it with the German Americans, only the colored Americans.

Hezekiah Goodwin operated a dairy farm in the Canaan Valley just south of the Massachusetts border in Connecticut.

The war made hell with the help. Life as we knew it practically ceased. Oh, God, you have no idea. There were some wealthy people in the neighborhood, and they tripled the wages—more than we could pay 'em—and the supply of labor just dried up.

Well, we worked pretty hard, eyah, and we were able to get piecemeal help. We could get people from the incorrigibles—drinking people who were really good and broke—and they worked pretty damned good until payday, then that was the last you saw of them. We had this fellow who had worked for us for forty years; all of a sudden he was a widower, and then he married a fancy woman and moved out.

Eyah, some were involved in war work, some weren't. We always thought the ones that were were crazy, because it meant a trip either to Hartford or Torrington to go to work, and it didn't make sense for economic reasons. You couldn't tell them that. We could offer them more net income without travel than they could get in a war plant. But hell, they apparently didn't want the long hours on the farm.

Our economic position early in the war was very poor, as was true of all farmers. The political decisions regarding the price of food and the price of milk were very detrimental to us. And with the increased costs and the poorer productivity, low prices were close to being disastrous. But we were able to ride it out.

The first sign of improvement economically was in 1944, when we began getting a subsidy on our milk prices, and the price firmed up a little. The butchers made their money on both ends. They were crooked as a ram's horn, but it was necessary because of the government prices. People would line up at the stores on whatever day they had any meat, and they would have their points and their stamps, which was all right. But the prices were unrealistic in relation to the cost of production. The ceiling prices meant nothing. What good are ceiling prices when there's no meat? I think the government learned something we never forgot: Price controls are a good thing over a very short period of time. They can take the heat off. But as a permanent thing, they lead to anarchy, and we had anarchy then in some areas of the nation.

Americans Remember the Home Front

Rudolph Spitzer in Kenmore, New York:

Like all parents, we were greatly perturbed. We have four boys in our family, and at that time three of them were subject to army duty. We were apprehensive and abhorred the thought of our boys being called to serve. These were anxious days and years and gloom reigned over the entire nation.

Before Pearl Harbor I was in the sign and outdoor-advertising business. Almost immediately, due to the rationing of critical materials and curtailment of nonwar services, I had to operate on a very modified basis by using noncritical substitute materials whenever possible or available. The war practically terminated the sign business. The larger war plants had limited needs for signs and hired their own staff for this type of work.

Our whole manner of living took a disheartening turn. The nation suffered a blow that reached most every individual to some degree, but mostly it was the family breadwinner in his own business who suffered. There was less of a problem for factory workers or blue-collar workers. To them the war was a gift from heaven. People who had been engaged in menial occupations, earning minimal wages, flocked to the war plants. Even some who could barely sign their name earned more money than they ever dreamed of. This sudden, easy affluence had some disreputable effects. As many of these workers expressed it: "I hope this war lasts forever, this is the nuts."

In general, the morale of the country was excellent. Most people stood behind our leaders. The war was not of our making; we either had to fight or be annihilated. How the money was spent for planes, tanks, ammunition was something else again. The cost-plus war-plant contracts cost us untold millions. It was a free-for-all spending orgy for anyone who had a government contract. Wasted time in war plants was commonplace. I know from experience that to make employees look busy, they bluffed through, sometimes for days, doing nothing.

At this time, I operated my business on a part-time basis, but even that met with failure. I couldn't cope with all the restrictions involved. So, like many others, I went to work in a war plant—the Bell Aircraft Corporation in Niagara Falls. For commuting from my home to the plant I was entitled to gas-ration tickets, and from the very beginning I detested my job. I was placed on the 4:00 P.M. to 11:00 P.M. shift and eventually got used to it. But the strange activity, the unfamiliar surroundings, the misery of monotonous hour after hour doing the same thing,

216

the confinement, all these things—so contrary to my previous way of life—sickened me. But there was nothing else I could do except long for the day that I could work my way out of this situation.

Three of my sons were inducted into the service. Fortunately, except for one son's bout with malaria, they all got home safe and sound. My wife and I suffered the usual anxious periods—a letter from one of the boys was like a gift from heaven. Naturally, we were aware that some of the boys would never be back, or be permanently handicapped or meet the horrible fate of being taken prisoner. When our boys came back, our feeling of relief was glorious and indescribable.

During the second year of the war we formed a committee of businessmen and other citizens. Kenmore—Town of Tonowanda Boys and Girls in Service Committee was our title. We tried to make the departure of inductees as pleasant as possible by presenting them with pocket books, cigarettes, and other gifts. Sometimes a mother would cry on her son's shoulder. This had a sobering effect on the crowd. We were aware that some parents might be seeing their sons for the last time, which turned out to be the case.

Rudolph Spitzer's son Richard was teaching high school English in Shortsville, New York, thirty miles south of Rochester. It was a small school, with probably three hundred children in kindergarten through twelfth grade.

I had gone to teach at that school for a couple of reasons: One was that they paid a few hundred dollars more than I had been making; the other, maybe more important reason was that the principal of the high school was a very outstanding guy. I was teaching high school English, directing the dramatics, the school paper, and things of that kind.

I was concerned that I would face induction, although the birth of our first child on December 9 pretty well eliminated that in the beginning. It wasn't until two or three or four years later that I was actually involved with it. My memories of the school's reaction to the war are very vague, but one memory has stuck with me. I went to that school in 1939, and somewhere I picked up some very handsome wall posters that came from Russia. They were beautiful pastoral scenes. I put them up on the bulletin board in the back of the room, and the principal suggested that maybe I ought to take them down because Russia was a Communist country. So with some misgiving I did take them down. Then, when this country entered the war, Russia became an ally. And the very same principal walked in one day with some posters. He said, "I thought you might like to have these for your room." When he walked out, I looked at them, and they were similar to the ones I had before. They were from Russia. I threw them out. Why? I just figured that if they weren't suitable two years ago, they weren't suitable now.

For a lot of the kids in the school, in the kind of community that I was in, the service really represented a great opportunity. Suddenly it was, as the military always is, a solution, or apparent solution. They didn't have to make any more decisions for a while. Many of them had a very limited view of their opportunities in the world. If you ask girls what they thought they might do after high school, the stock reply was, "Well, I don't want to be a teacher and I don't want to be a nurse and I don't want to be a secretary, and what else is there?" For the boys, it was a very limited choice of maybe the machine shop or farming. A very small percentage went to college.

At times rationing was a hardship. Certain staples got short at times, and things got terribly expensive. I guess the greatest problem was the shortage of gasoline, the rationing. Finally in desperation we sold the car. This was probably in 1944. I was going to the University of Rochester, about thirty miles away, and at least one afternoon a week would go out and stand on the corner and thumb a ride to Canandaigua, five miles away. Then I'd take a Greyhound bus into the city and go to class. I'd reverse the order to return home, and I remember one night getting off the bus in Canandaigua about midnight, and it was about 0 degrees, and who was on the street? Nobody had any gasoline. I stood on that corner, and it finally came to a choice of freezing to death or walking, so I walked the five miles. Got home, I guess, about two o'clock in the morning.

My three brothers all went into the service. One had a pretty rough time in the Pacific. We were concerned about my mother. For years, I remember, she complained of poor health. Yet, during the years when the three sons were in the service, she seemed to be healthiest, tremendously occupied.

I think the war times were anxious times. They seemed endless. You'd read about the progress or lack of progress of the army in Europe. You had the feeling that Hitler was monstrous. There was great empathy for the British. Ed Murrow had a great effect on me. I also remember sitting in a room someplace alone and Roosevelt announcing D day and this voice coming on the radio in the dark room telling about how this great assault had been launched and asking the people to pray for success. I remember the sense of relief when it was over. There was a feeling that something was accomplished. Hitler was destroyed, Japan would never again be strong.

Esther Benson lived in Newport, Rhode Island, with her artist-sculptor husband and two children.

We lived in a navy town, and I was well aware of what the war was going to mean to Newport, because everything was already beginning to show signs of speeding up. It became crammed full of people, and we had a tremendous shortage of housing for navy families.

My husband, who was an artist and had a very bad heart condition and couldn't, of course, be in the war, was worried all the time about getting work. In wartime there isn't much work for artists. So he went on with his teaching at the Rhode Island School of Design. And he started very early in the war running the power squadron, a civilian set of courses for men in small boats. They started with basic navigation and ended up with quite complicated navigation. The idea was to teach these men so that in a situation like Dunkirk they would be able to help.

We had a very active Red Cross in Newport. We had difficulty with some of the navy personnel, and I'm not talking about the sailors, I'm talking about the brass—people who were not knowledgeable enough about what the navy was. So many complaints, and their wives didn't have anything like a serious point of view about what this war was. I remember feeling that they should just be thankful they still had their husbands, instead of complaining about where they were living. Everything in town was crowded with people.

Of course, Newport was a small town, and you met a number of interesting naval officers, men with broad points of view that came into your life for short periods. It was very stimulating.

We had sailors come down to the house. My husband and I were quite musical, and we had a wonderful bunch of sailors who came down and played music for us. We'd have beer and cheese and crackers, and I'd make pie.

My street was on the way to the naval hospital, and there was an awful lot of walking traffic, sailors late at night going back. You were inclined to forgive the sailors getting drunk, because they were under such strain. I found out if I polished my doorknob brightly, then sailors would knock on it when they went by at night. So I finally left the knocker dull.

I had three young boys, and being a mother was awfully hard. In the first place, you couldn't use the car very much, and I had all this marketing to do. You'd stay in line over half an hour to get a little bit of meat. The only meat we could get was a boned and rolled veal, and it was hard to make that interesting Sunday after Sunday, and the boys didn't like it. I'd have given anything for some good red hamburger.

Rationing was awful, awful. I was always losing the ration books, and you just couldn't get anything good, even if you did have the ration coupons. I can remember thinking a can of corned beef was just marvelous. We ate a lot of Spam. The boys liked Spam, and it didn't require any coupons. I was not aware of any heavy black market, and certainly none of the people I knew were on the black market. Sometimes a friend would give us a dozen eggs, and that was about all. Of course, my husband had a little sailboat and caught a lot of fish, which was a tremendous help to us.

We had blackout curtains all over the house. This made it so hot and stuffy in the summer. Another thing I remember are the searchlights. Sometimes they'd be all over the horizon, but they were in front of our house all the time because of the torpedo station nearby.

I don't think the war years were exhilarating. To me it was so serious. I was a member of the Society of Friends, and yet it did seem to me that Hitler was somebody we had to fight, because he was so lacking in any humanitarian principles. I didn't get involved in any defense work. The children were so young, and then, having a husband who was often sick, I just didn't get into anything. When you do it all by yourself with three small boys and a sick husband, you haven't got much energy. And I have the impression that I was just perfectly exhausted the whole time.

John R. Shepley, vice-president of the Saint Louis Trust Company:

I didn't figure the war would have much of an impact on our business, because we were primarily handling estates and trusts and things of that kind. I'd say, if anything, it improved our business.

I had two sons and a daughter, and the oldest son was a pilot in the air force, but my younger son was too young.

The principal effect on me was the inability to get enough gasoline. You see, we were at the bottom of the list, and I had a farm up in Pike County, about 70 miles north of Saint Louis, where we always spent the weekends. I had a Cadillac at the time which had close to 100,000 miles on it. The tires weren't very good, and one of the most difficult things was keeping the car in tires. You couldn't buy any new tires, and I remember once I had a flat at Saint Charles, on our way up to the farm. I ended up going up some back alley and buying one of the most woebegone tires in the world. Beggars weren't choosers in those days.

In order to save gas, I got a Harley-Davidson motorcycle to go to work on. I rode it for over a year, and in that way we conserved enough gas to go to the farm on the weekend. It didn't have a windshield like the modern ones. It did create quite a stir around the bank. As a matter of fact, my brother, who was a bit more prominent in Saint Louis than I, was featured in the newspapers because he had a motorcycle with a sidecar.

J. S. Smith, a St. Louis investment broker:

There were six partners in the business, and only one was overage— he was over forty-five—so we dissolved the firm, and most of the six ended up in the service. Other firms were "gutted" of personnel in Saint Louis, and one of them was G. H. Walker and Company, so three of us went over there. My application was never acted on, so I spent the war years there.

The war considerably slowed business down. Everybody was putting all their money into Liberty bonds, and there was quite a decline in Ford, General Motors, and Chrysler temporarily, until they got into tank contracts and military trucks.

As I recall it now, I'd say the Battle of Midway had a pronounced effect on our business, because, I think, that was the turning point of the Japanese. Also D day, of course, the market was up, very, very strongly. I think at one time during the Battle of Britain, there was a good deal of worry about England going under. Also, there was a period of stagnation, as I recall, when Roosevelt and Churchill were trying to work together.

I don't remember that any of my acquaintances suffered any great hardships. I worked on those drives for the sale of Liberty bonds. Cary Grant came one time. The movies were going great guns then, and I think Mary Pickford made an appearance at the Fox Theatre. With Cary Grant they had a parade downtown with a lot of banners. I think the movie stars helped the sales.

I would say the war years were fairly exciting times of whipped-up patriotism. I hated to lose friends and to see people wounded and all that. I had a real hatred for the Japs, even more than the Germans, I think.

At Leon Sylvester's gas station near Sedgwick, Maine, I asked Sylvester and two other Down Easters, Forrest Eaton and James Saunders, about the war years. Mainers don't talk a lot, but they had a little to say.

EATON: I was lobstering some up here during the war. Lobsters was selling at thirty cents a pound in those days. People ate them as much as they do now; course, they were more plentiful then. There was a time when you were rationed on gas, had to have stamps. You were allowed a certain amount for your boats. There was a lot of black-marketing of gas—you'd get it any way you could. There was no rationing on lobsters. I don't remember that the war years changed things too much.

SAUNDERS: There's been a lot more changes here in the last ten years than there was in wartime. A lot of the boys did go in the service. I had two friends that never came back. They were in the Pacific. I worked down in Portland at the shipyard for about two years as a cleaner—got the ships ready for the painter. Things were tapering off and quieting down, so I thought it was time to come home. Life in Portland was quite more exciting than around here. There was a lot of girls; they had brothers, fathers, husbands in the service, and they did their part. The morale was very good. In the two years, there were sixty thousand people employed, and there wasn't too much drinking and carousing and stuff like that. People behaved themselves pretty well. Forty percent of our workers were women, and they did good work. They were more conscientious than the men, they were more thorough. Naturally, the men got interested in the women sometimes. That's only human nature. But it was not so bad. The women made the same wages.

EATON: I don't remember any hardships. Everybody had enough. Just didn't have luxuries. Most people fished for cod; you couldn't get deferred for fishing lobsters, because they were a luxury. So all the young fellows went trawling for cod—so they could get deferred from war. The war didn't have so much effect on this area as the depression. We had a little place—an observation post—set up to watch for airplanes. But we never seen any. Never saw a German in the whole war.

SYLVESTER: I had two sons in the service. They both survived, but I was naturally worried about them. One of them was on a minesweeper, bouncing around in the Pacific Ocean. War didn't affect things around here too much. Some things were short; some things were better.

Lillian Williams lives in Sedgwick, Maine, but during the war she went down to Southwest Harbor, where her husband worked in the boatyard.

The first thing I remember about the war was the rationing of the food. And we had a hard time getting shoes for the children—we had two children. My husband was building PT boats. We had the Coast Guard and the navy there; everything was booming. We had a problem with gasoline, because people stole it all the time, siphoned it out at night. We had bought a new radio with shortwave on it, and we had it turned on in the evening. At a quarter past five every night it would come on that "Oranges are orange; coal is black; mashed potatoes are white." They'd repeat it over and over and over. So about the third night my husband told one of the Coast Guard officers that lived right next door to us, and he looked into it. Somebody on the shore was repeating this so that the German submarines could come in and fill up with gas. They had big oil tanks in an old cellar. Enemy submarines were getting gas; but they put a stop to it.

There were submarines sunk out there. One time they brought a lot of wounded soldiers into the harbor. They set up a place to give them coffee and doughnuts. Everybody was excited. Another time, on the back of the island some men were chopping wood when some German bodies washed up onshore. The men took their axes and everything they had and got out of there and wouldn't go back at all.

To us it was an exciting time. We moved down to Southwest Harbor from Sedgwick; there were dances and all kinds of things, so it was a lot different than living here.

J. Willard Marriott is the founder and retired president of Hot Shoppes, Inc. The drive-ins originated in Washington, D.C., where Mr. Marriott and his wife, Alice, still maintain a home. They are originally from Utah and are very active in the Mormon church. I interviewed them together in their summer home on Lake Winnipesaukee in New Hampshire.

J. WILLARD: The thing that worried us, of course, was using automobiles to get to our places. We were in a far better position for rationing and war controls than our competitors, like Howard Johnson. His places were all on the highway, and he was presented a real problem. He had to close up many restaurants. We had never gone to the highway business; we'd always gone after the suburbs, right around where people lived, so it never was a problem as far as we were concerned, getting to our shops. The big problem, of course, was rationing.

ALICE: In Washington more women worked than almost anywhere else, and I think they would stop on their way home from work or on their way to work. Because they couldn't get meat and a lot of things, they ate out more than at home.

J. WILLARD: They were working on war jobs, so we had a real problem getting help. They were being conscripted for war, and it was very difficult to get shop replacements. The war took all of our managers and a lot of our personnel in the business, so we had a management problem. I wouldn't say it was boom times, but then I'd have to go back and look at my figures. Wasn't a growth period, that's for sure, because a lot of people were moving from one factory to another or from one city to another.

ALICE: I don't think we went out as much. With the gasoline rationing you couldn't go very many places. We had blackout lining and blackout curtains on all the windows at home; I don't remember whether we had them in the shops or not; we probably did.

J. WILLARD: There was all kinds of black-marketing; I guess everybody was involved with black-marketing to some extent.

ALICE: Sugar was the worst thing to get, sugar and meat. We had coupons for sugar—could only get so much a week. I don't remember about the business, how they did.

J. WILLARD: I think that inasmuch as we were feeding the public and so many service people, we probably got more than some others, maybe. We were in a different area, and I think they rationed on the basis of need. But there were food shortages because they were shipping so much stuff overseas. There actually was a shortage; that's why they had to have rationing. I'm sure we were affected by rationing, but probably not as much as maybe a housewife would have been.

ALICE: It seems to me, Bill, that we put in a lot of dishes like macaroni and cheese and things like that because they didn't have to have meat in them.

J. WILLARD: The war didn't affect our way of life too much. We're not socialites; we're church people. I had a business that took a lot of supervision and really a lot of work. I was kept awfully busy. So it didn't affect my life as much as it would somebody who was going to parties all the time and had a high social life.

ALICE: I don't think we noticed the war effort as much as people living out of Washington. There were a few things you couldn't buy and you had to do without, but I don't happen to think we minded that as long as we were trying to help out and do something for the country.

David Soergal was an engineering student at the University of Wisconsin when the war began, and, as he says, engineering students did not feel "involved" in the war. They were exempt from the draft and more concerned with finishing their education. Soergal did end up in defense work, but he spent a year and a half on the campus during the war years before going off into industry. And eventually he even tried to enlist in the navy.

When the V-12 program appeared on the campus, the students who were in the army or navy would march up and down the streets of Madison, Wisconsin, singing. As I remember, the rules were that if you were in engineering school, you didn't have to take the V-12 program. I was exempt through all of college from the military-training programs. Every time I got issued a draft classification card, it was always marked "Exempt." I didn't apply for it, but I always got it.

The campus activities dropped down to a very serious tone. It was not all this frivolity. Most of the guys that raised a lot of hell around there were gone. The V-12s were based off campus. They had uniforms. They marched up and down the campus, kind of like ROTCs. The sports events were not as dominant. The people didn't go to football games as much, social events were way down. I remember some of the Wisconsin big gala events, like the Snow Ball, which had been a big thing in years gone by, were discontinued. We had a lot of turnover in our athletic groups because of the draft situation. But the engineering schools were doing their engineering as they had before the war started, and some of the poorer students did get drafted. I never had any discomfort about not being in uniform. Of course, I was only nineteen or twenty.

W. Clement Stone was the head of a selling organization—the Combined Registry Company, with offices in Chicago. It was an insurance agency, not a company, as he points out, although he did represent some eastern insurance companies. For most people the war years were a turning point, economically—the era in which we passed from the depression into economic prosperity. For Mr. Stone, who never had any trouble making money during the depression, the years from 1942 to 1946 were mostly just more of the same—hard selling.

I had discontinued school at the age of 16 and started to sell insurance. And I developed a system, which we call the success system— it never fails. In learning how to use one's brain power, particularly the powers of the subconscious, how to establish the right habits, how to aim high and to achieve high goals, it never occurred to me that we couldn't do as well at any period, peacetime or wartime, by turning a disadvantage into an advantage. Where others were having a difficult time during the depression, I was, through my own personal production, earning in the neighborhood of three hundred dollars a week.

Our business was not especially affected one way or the other by the war. We take advantages of disadvantages—war, or boom times, or poor times—so, really, the external influences have little or or no effect because of the philosophy.

Of course, there were things like travel problems. Many of my salespeople traveled by car. But like everything else in life, one who has a positive mental attitude gets what he wants. For example, getting reservations and sleeping accommodations on a train: All you do is make a five-dollar bet with the porter that he can't find a berth for you in the next half hour—and for some reason you always lose the bet. You have to use your ingenuity. Under the gasoline situation, we did have a problem. So what we would do was have several men team up and use, say, one car. If we're selling in a place like Virginia, the group could go out, and one individual could be left off at one town, another at another town, and so forth. We use one car and therefore pool the gas. There's always a way to do anything if you really want to do it. Actually, any problem can be solved if you use your brain power and if you believe that you can solve it. You may not have the answer when you start, but there's a solution.

Lois Raymond lived in Chicago and summered in Maine. Her husband worked for Swift & Company. She and her husband are retired and living in Sedgwick, Maine, where I interviewed her.

After you slaughter a lamb, you have a valuable commodity left over—wool. My husband would take the wool and sell it to the mills in various forms, depending on what kind of mill it was. He did a great deal of traveling.

Of course, his business was very good, because the synthetics hadn't been invented. I can remember that we had our first nylon stockings just about before the war. Most of the mills in the Midwest turned to making uniforms. A lot of them were blanket mills and were very busy making blankets for the service. He could sell all the wool he delivered.

My husband had been in World War I as an aviator and he had a 30-percent disability. He tried to enlist in World War II, but they said no. I did a lot of volunteer nursing in a University of Chicago lying-in hospital. My husband was away a lot, so he didn't have much opportunity to get involved in volunteer work.

Our daughter Barbara's fiancé, Paul, was a physicist. He was sent out to Alamogordo. I remember there was a test of the atomic bomb before the event. Paul wrote me a letter saying, "After what I have just seen today, I think all of us should become social scientists." But he didn't.

We knew that he was out there, there was no question about that. Also we lived right in the heart of the University of Chicago community, and half a dozen of my friends had said, "Well, we are going to have to go to Y-Town." It was a college name for Alamogordo. I remember having a dinner party and saying to Sam, "How is your cyclotron?" He said, "Oh, it is all packed up and put away." But we knew the Manhattan Project was going on. Famous physicists were coming from all over. There was a spontaneous code of honor in which you didn't spread the word around. You just knew they were with the Manhattan Project, although we didn't call it that.

The first war summer was 1942, and we decided to drive our car to our summer home in Maine. Gas was going to be rationed and we wanted to get the car back to Maine because you can live in Chicago without a car, but it is almost impossible to live here without one.

On the fifteenth of May gas rationing was going to begin, and so my husband and I started on Friday night before that, driving at thirty-five miles an hour. They had asked everybody to drive at that speed to conserve gas. We stayed at that, plodded along, and arrived here on the fourteenth, in time to be available for our registration for gas for the car.

I don't remember the war years as depressing. Except for transportation, it wasn't much different. I do remember that the last year, in 1945, I got down here quite early because the University of Chicago let out early, and I had enough gas to get back and forth. There was a lot of cheating on gas. Some people were always able to get it.

I remember how upset we were with so many Japanese being put into those camps—people who had been here for generations. During the war, when some of those camps were dissipated, many of those Japanese came to Chicago. A lot of my friends who had room took them in. We never had a finer group of people come to our city. They took pieces of property that nobody else would touch and fixed them up and made them handsome. Some of them turned out to be marvelous watch repairmen. The Japanese girls were darling. A lot of them worked at the University of Chicago as secretaries.

For forty-six years, Louis Speyer played English horn for the Boston Symphony Orchestra. I talked with him in one of the music rooms at Tanglewood, near Stockbridge, where he lives and spends part of his retirement years.

I came to this country from France in 1918, during the First World War. We came for three weeks with the band. And instead of three weeks, we stayed about six months, wandering around everywhere, in hospitals, in camps, at rallies. So they got me a position in Boston, which was wonderful for me.

In World War II we were very lucky because we could get anything we wanted. It was nothing; we were here and safe. We played quite a few concerts for the troops, and some groups from the orchestra went to hospitals or camps and play for soldiers.

I was an air-raid warden in Brookline, where I live, and I went to the Red Cross drill. The times were very quiet, a lot more than now. The real hardship was my family in France. I didn't know; we got some letters from the Red Cross. Of course, my father was dead already, my mother died during the war, and my sister was in the south of France, so she was safe there. But the rest of the family lived in Paris, and they escaped. I tried my best to send them something, you know, through the Red Cross, money or food; whether they got it I didn't know.

The war did not affect my life and career, because we were lucky to be with the Boston Symphony, and if you get in Boston Symphony, you can stay all your life. During the war, Mr. Perry, the manager, approached me and told me we have a black conductor—I wish I could remember the first name; the last name was Dixon—and he asked me, what you think, will the orchestra object to hire a black conductor? We never have one before. And my answer was, they are sending black people to be killed in Europe, I think the orchestra can accept a black conductor. And then he was good. We liked him because he was good.

Oh, yes, I forget. During the war, I gave blood to the Red Cross so many times they stopped me. Later, I learned why they would not let me give more. My wife was working at the hospital and had seen my name on the list of blood givers so many times that she added it up—twelve times. So she said, "That's enough." So they wouldn't take my blood anymore.

Jean Jepson spent the war years in high school in Bethlehem, Pennsylvania, and then at Smith College in Massachusetts.

When the war began, I was at Moravian Seminary, a Catholic girl's school. I remember a hayride that December, when everyone was home from school. It was a beautiful moonlit night, and I happened to be sitting next to a boy named Paul Couch. I remember asking him how it would be to kill somebody, what would be his reaction? This was one thing that really worried me about the war—you're going to kill somebody! I can't exactly remember what his answer was, but he became a conscientious objector.

After high school I went to Smith College. One reason I went there was because it seemed so lively, but by the time I got there, it wasn't lively at all, because there were no boys. But there was Westover Air Base. There was something about the whole army thing that was a little different from getting to know people another way. As the war was coming to a close, a lot of the boys who had been overseas began to come back to Westover, and we felt they were more interesting than the guys who hadn't been away.

One guy I was involved with came back after the war—he had been with the wave that went in for the Battle of the Bulge—and I remember him telling me all about Holland. They captured some Germans, and he told me how he interrogated one guy and he just picked the gun up and he jammed it down the guy's throat, and all the teeth went out. I was dumbfounded, because this was somebody I knew exceedingly well, and the violence wasn't like him.

Robert Wheeler, then—and now—one of the leading citizens of Great Barrington, in western Massachusetts. His primary business is real estate.

In my business, activity was reduced somewhat, not much. In a town of this size, I don't think you see changes as rapidly as you do in larger cities.

Incidentally, I did some work for the secret service, navy, locally. I guess it is still confidential, but I think it was helpful in some ways.

We were called from Washington one night—the president's secretary was on the line. They were seeking a place for a foreign visitor, a princess, and wanted me to send them descriptions of the rental properties we had, which I did. When I got a call that the princess was in front of the Red Lion Inn in Stockbridge, I sent an agent up there. Lo and behold, there was President Roosevelt and Princess Isabella of the Dutch family, and five secret service cars. I only wish I had been there.

Eventually they rented a house, and the Dutch government was here during the summer that year. I met them on one occasion. Queen Wilhelmina used to go into the drugstore in Lee for gumdrops, which she liked, and Mr. Pease, the druggist there, would always greet her, "Good morning, Queen." She got a kick out of that.

In the town everyone was anxious to do their part—the gray ladies at the hospital, activities that would help the war effort in any way; there was no question about everyone working when they were called upon.

W. P. Laws and his wife owned a grocery store in Ocean City, Maryland.

The war meant different things to different people. In our little church we were without a minister during most of the war years, and we had student ministers, mostly from Princeton. One Sunday, there was one from over near Japan—he wasn't a Japanese, but he had that coloring and features, you know. He was attending Princeton, and he was very well educated, spoke excellent English and everything, but one of our ladies had lost her son in the war, and just seeing him up there in the pulpit, she almost had hysterics. Some people had that attitude. They didn't send him back anymore, naturally.

We wouldn't have fussed about the hardships like some of the other people. I thought about some of those people having hysterics over butter and eggs. We managed.

We were younger then, and we had to work harder. Now I expect it would worry us a whole lot more, but it's been thirty years, and that makes a difference. If the help we got didn't produce what they should, and lots of times they didn't, we could pitch in and do their work. You couldn't keep help. The boys were going in the service and getting defense jobs with a lot more money. We like to have worked ourselves to death. I'd go down to the store at four-thirty in the morning and stay there until sometimes eleven o'clock at night. Then the government wanted to cut down on electricity, so we didn't have lights on at night, and as soon as it got dark, we'd close up and come home.

Mary Punderson today is the wife of Norman Rockwell. She lives in Stockbridge, Massachusetts, with her husband, who is in his eighties and no longer painting. In 1941 she was unmarried and teaching English and history at the Milton Academy in Cambridge, Massachusetts.

I had a niece whose husband was called into the service, though not immediately. Later I found that a cousin, not a close cousin, had been one of those who was on the ship that was attacked and was swimming for a while in Pearl Harbor. But he came out all right and is still alive, I think, and flourishing. I had a good friend who had fought in World War I, and he said right from the beginning that this war was being fought because we didn't finish our job in the First World War. He was in the navy, and I knew that he would go in. That's about what it was as far as my personal concerns. Oh, a nephew, a very favorite nephew, who never did get very much into it; he was still in training when the war was over.

I did little rationing jobs and things of that sort, and I was conscientious about not using my car. I walked to school every morning and rather enjoyed it.

Simon Greco is an Italian-born commercial artist who lived in Chicago at the time of Pearl Harbor. He is a conscientious objector to military service.

I was a commercial artist for a living, and a painter at my real job. Actually, I was doing maybe eight or ten days of commercial artwork a month. The rest of the time I was trying to learn how to paint. I wasn't selling any paintings at all, but I was becoming fairly successful as a commercial artist—a designer more than anything else.

How I arrived at a position of conscientious objector would be a little bit difficult to reconstruct. First of all, I think it had to do with my family. My parents were devout Christians. They're not very good Catholics in the real strict sense of the word, as most Italians are here. But they're very devout Christians. And I think that had a lot to do with it, and I think that being an artist had a lot to do with it, growing up trying to be one. Also, I think one of the things that probably led me to become a conscientious objector was a fight I had when I was a very small boy. I was going to be expelled from school because of the fight, and a very wonderful principal gave me a long lecture about what was the difference between me and an animal. That has always been in the back of my head. Men had an intelligence. They were made in the image of God and all the rest of that. Ironically, by the time the draft came, I didn't really believe in the image of God. The other part I did believe. Then, I think, it was the whole idea of who I was, what I was, what I was trying to do with my life. And somehow or other, killing people wasn't part of it. I really believed in the idea that somehow wars had to be stopped and that the only way they would ever be stopped is that the guy who had to fight them would simply have to say, "No, I'm not going to do it." I had a great admiration for Gandhi at the time and his pacifist method of trying to accomplish his ends. I did not think about being a member of a nation which was attacked. I think that that was not part of my makeup for the basic reason that I was brought to the United States when I was very young—three and a half—and although my father tried to make Americans out of us, he didn't succeed. I never really became an American in the real sense of the word, and ironically enough, I never became an Italian either.

I remember receiving my draft notification very vividly. Up to that point being a pacifist was a theoretical thing. And then, suddenly, you get this letter from Uncle Sam, and it's very real. I think that what most people don't realize is that you feel the weight of the government. Government is a really awesome thing when you're face-to-face with it. I remember that I filled out the questionnaire, but I didn't put it in the mail that day. I wanted to think about it because I realized what the consequences could be. I knew what the criteria were for judging conscientious objectors—primarily affiliation with a pacifist church or a pacifist organization, and I had none of these things. I had no record of being a pacifist anywhere except among a couple of people that I knew. So it wasn't a very encouraging situation that I was in.

At the same time I was being badgered by a friend who had signed up with the air force to be an art director and wanted me to be his assistant. He was very convincing about what a great time we would have, how we would never go anywhere but New York, how I wouldn't hurt anybody, and all that kind of baloney.

So another thing I learned very early is that being a conscientious objector meant that you had to make judgments almost daily. And I realized that he was asking me to make a judgment that really wasn't honest. If I were going to be an illustrator or designer for the air force, then I had no right to be a conscientious objector. I couldn't really play it both ways.

Finally, I sent the questionnaire, and I wrote them a letter. I had to give a reason for being a conscientious objector, and one of the reasons I gave was that I didn't really believe that I was put on earth to kill people.

Then I offered a deal to the government, because I realized I had very flimsy grounds in their eyes. I offered to go to war and do whatever they wanted me to do, with the provision that they would allow me to carry a gun after the war. If I were being asked to do what I considered committing murder in order to protect myself, I felt that after the war, if my existence was threatened by any enemy, even if he was the guy next door, I should have the right to shoot him down.

I felt the chances were better than average that I would end up in jail, but I really didn't resent the fact. I had a feeling—and this may sound like a contradiction—that societies are structured to protect themselves.

If you're outside the mainstream of your particular society, it's your own hard luck. I also knew that if you want to make a stand for something, you really have to be prepared to pay a price for it. I was really quite surprised when a few weeks later I got this notification that I was classified as a conscientious objector.

Life as a CO in civilian clothes wasn't bad if you stayed away from certain places. The hard times came from civilians, the hard-hat type of personality. So you learned to stay away from those kind of bars.

The girls didn't give a damn about my not being in uniform one way or another. I never really had any problem as far as the women were concerned. They couldn't care less.

I think what resentment I encountered was not so much against me. A lot of people had an antagonism toward the whole idea of being forced to go to war or their children being forced to go to war and the inconvenience of the war. They couldn't say, "the goddamned government." So they would take it out on a guy like me, or get a poor 4-F and badger the hell out of him.

After a while, I got a call from the draft board to have a physical exam at an army induction center, and that was real rough, because we were spotlighted. We had a band on our arm that was marked CO—in yellow, of course. What else could it be? And a lot of the examining soldiers really gave us a hard time.

I remember two incidents. One guy, I guess he might have been an army doctor, got very violent. He was going to "kick the shit out of us" or something like that. I was getting worried. You know, you're walking around naked, you've got a towel around you, and these guys start crowding in on you, and they're going to fix you. I just finally said to the guy, "Now, I've had about enough of this. The first guy that lays a finger on me—I don't mean a punch or a kick; I mean just touches me—you're gonna have so many lawyers down here tomorrow, you'll never know what hit you, because I am not in the army. I haven't been drafted, and you guys have no authority over me. Now, either this whole thing quiets down or I am gonna just walk out of here, even if I have to walk out naked."

The other thing I remember is the psychiatrists—they were really giving us a hard time. I don't know whether they were just trying to provoke us, but this one guy was particularly nasty.

He said, "Who do you think you are, Jesus Christ?" because I had a beard. Of course, in those days beards were very unusual. And I said, "No, I don't think I'm Jesus Christ. I've got a beard." And then I said something to the effect that "Seventy years ago it would have been weird not to have a beard. Today it's weird to have a beard. I just have a beard because I don't have to shave."

Finally, I got a letter ordering me to report to a conscientious objectors' camp in northern Michigan. I may or may not have gotten a ticket, but I know that we were not paid. All the expenses of being at the CO camp had to be borne by the individual if he could afford it. If he could not afford it, the Brethren Church, which ran the camp that I was sent to, fed you and found clothes for you. I shipped all my studio stuff home to Saint Louis and said good-bye to my two or three clients. I got an evening train and spent the whole night traveling up to this camp. It was a real bleak, deserted place, near Manistee, Michigan. These guys were standing there, and one huge guy—must have been six foot and a half—came up to me and said, "Welcome, brother. Are you saved?" And I didn't know what the hell he meant, am I saved? I thought, Jeez, I hope this isn't what I'm in for. The camp was an old CCC camp that had been used during the depression. A bunch of us lived in one big long room.

We had army cots, and no privacy except what you could concoct with boxes or pieces of wood or whatever.

The Forestry Service was supervisor of the work the camp was supposed to be doing. Our job was to go out in the morning at, I think, seven o'clock and plant seedlings. Two days later it would rain and wash the seedlings away; we'd go back after it stopped raining and plant more seedlings. It really wasn't a real work camp; it was a jail. Let's not kid ourselves about it. We were incarcerated, and there was this mythology that we were doing work.

I did this maybe a month or so. Then the guy who ran the camp realized that I wasn't really fit for outdoor work, and so I was assigned to the camp sign shop. We made signs; we had a silk-screen operation; we did posters and things like that.

I noticed that almost every month when I first went there, they would send inmates to Detroit for another examination. What they were really doing was weeding guys out, sending them home. Another thing I am convinced of is that the army and the government really didn't want the statistics of conscientious objectors. I think they did everything they could to give you a 4-F—mentally incompetent or physically handicapped, or whatever it was, just so that they didn't have these COs on their list.

Finally I was sent to Detroit for another examination. They didn't change my classification—I was still a conscientious objector—but they sent me home.

I went back to Chicago for a while, and I decided I didn't want to stay there. I went home to Saint Louis for the summer. The afternoon after I got home the FBI was at the door. "What are you doing? Where are your papers? How do you explain this?" and all that baloney. Neighbors had called them up saying, "There's a young guy here. What's he doing home?"

My mother and father were the ones that really suffered. The people in the neighborhood where I grew up, most of them refused to talk to them because I was a conscientious objector. By that time my brother was a conscientious objector also. There were people that I had grown up with that wouldn't talk to me, relatives that wouldn't talk to me, wouldn't talk to my parents. The guy next door, who was like a second father to me when I was growing up, refused to talk to me.

Now I have had time to think about those years. When you are in your early twenties, life tends to be black and white, especially if you're my kind of person. As you grow older, you get all kinds of shades of gray. And I've given a lot of thought to why I did it. Had I taken up that offer of the air force, I'd have been a captain; I would have a pension now. I have thought many, many times over the years whether I really should have done it. Not that I've ever doubted that what I did was right—that I really believe. But the question that has cropped up is whether a person can cut himself off from humanity. Some days I think I should have been part of it. I'm still part of the human race, and I think the experiences of humanity cannot really be sidestepped. This is an argument I used to have with my brother and with a number of conscientious objectors, because there was always that line that had to be drawn. So you say I don't work for a munitions maker, I don't do ads for a company that makes bombers. But I do an ad for a company that buys something from a company that buys something from a company. What the hell, it's all interrelated! And pure isolation is never possible. If you pay taxes, you're helping the war. And they make very short work of you if you don't pay taxes. I don't regret what I did, but it's given me a lot to think about in the years since. I put this with the things I can't answer, but it's an interesting question.

There are probably a thousand towns like Ridgefield, Connecticut, in America. But I am not sure how many citizens there are like Francis Martin.

I was in the gem jewelry business and president of the First National Bank and Trust Company. They made me wood coordinator for Ridgefield, because there was a shortage of oil. I also owned the telephone company, who were my tenants, and I had just put in oil heating the year before that. The telephone people came down from New Haven and told me that they'd pay the expenses to have my furnace reconverted back to coal because they were afraid of the poor operators out all night long without any heat. And I said, "You don't have to worry about that at all, I've got it all figured out."

At that time, you know, there were a lot of people who were hungry and out of work at the same time. I took it upon myself to buy a piece of land down by the great swamp and put twenty-six men to work cutting wood. For their wages, they got half of it in wood and half of it in cash, because they needed wood for their own homes. I needed nine thousand gallons of oil to keep me going for the winter, but the government was only allowing me a thousand gallons. I said, all right, and I brought my wood right up there—I carried it myself—and I put two-foot wood in, then lit the oil burner quick. The wood ignited, I got steam up good, and I'd feed it about every hour. Doing it that way, I got through with my thousand gallons of oil and kept everybody warm.

Ridgefield was not as affected by the war as some other places were. There was a lot of stuff you couldn't get. The Worcester School in Danbury had just started building, and they couldn't get any plumbing equipment at all. But I was just tearing down a building here, so they came to me and wanted to know if I could help them out. I gave them all the pipe and plumbing fixtures for the whole school. Then, certain foods were scarce, but everybody went right to work gardening in those days. We all had gardens. I was chairman of the Red Cross during the whole war. The ladies were just wonderful. Oh, they did a marvelous job. The people of Ridgefield weren't exhilarated. They were disgusted that Japan ever started the war, and some of them were scared. I know my friends in California were scared stiff. They thought California was going to be bombed. Naturally, we had a few people who would be scared of anything; but the town in general, no. We were so far away from New York, they'd be wasting their bomb in Ridgefield. We had our share of losses, though, which put a damper on things. Very sad.

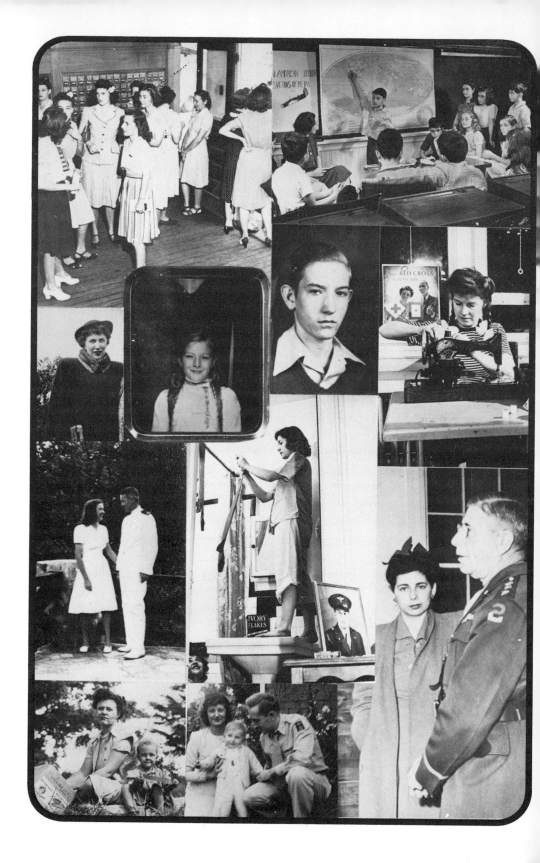

7

WIVES AND CHILDREN

The war had a special impact on the wives of servicemen overseas and on all children, regardless of how their parents might have been involved in the war.

Mabel Wiggins lived in Saint Paul, where her husband, Russell, was managing editor of the St. Paul Pioneer Press and Dispatch—*before he went in the air force as an instructor and then overseas to Africa and Italy as an intelligence officer. Her oldest son enlisted in the navy and spent most of the time on PT boats in the Panama Canal area.*

You really didn't let yourself worry too much about your husband being overseas, because everybody else was in the same boat, going through the same thing, and you wouldn't let yourself get down. I had three chilren at home, and I wasn't about to go to pieces. We had this mailman for several years, and then he stopped coming. I said to a neighbor, "Isn't that funny? I thought our mailman just had a vacation." And she said, "He couldn't stand all the women left behind who were always meeting him at the door and saying, 'You don't have a letter for me this morning?' He said he just couldn't stand all that worry, so he asked to be put in the office somewhere."

You kept right on doing what you had been doing, but adding more things to it. You helped in Red Cross. You volunteered wherever they thought there was something you could do; and the youngsters, too. It's quite fun to think how much really was accomplished. Saint Paul used to have a great big railroad station with a lovely big room and a big kitchen. Most of it had been taken out and turned into a nice recreation area. They had a pool table and counters for food, and there was a piano. Saint Paul was sort of central between Chicago and the West Coast for transporting troops. They didn't have equipment on trains to feed all these people, so when we got word that a troop train was coming in with three hundred starving soldiers on their way to the West Coast, we'd get ready for them. They'd be there maybe forty-five minutes. They'd come in and would want coffee and Cokes and whatever we had, sandwiches, doughnuts, and cookies. All these things were donated. It was really quite a project. You had to have quite an assembly line set up for getting three hundred lunches ready with a train coming in on a deadline.

I used to go down in the morning. I'd take that early shift because then I'd be home when the youngsters got home from school. And I would call home at seven-thirty to see that everybody was up and on their way to school. Of course, you had to ride the streetcars because you didn't have gas to trot back and forth. So, you'd catch the quarter-to-five streetcar, and it was perfectly safe. Now I think I'd be scared, because that wasn't exactly a pleasant neighborhood; there were a lot of warehouses down by the station.

When Russell was sent to the Pentagon, I went down to spend a day or two with him before he went overseas. They had to go in full equipment: the belt with the metal, the cuffs, the thing that opens for your plate, the canteen, full military garb, his typewriter, and one big bag that expanded. I said, "You look like a Boy Scout going off on a camping trip." We picked up this young kid who was staying with his brand-new wife over in Georgetown. He came out looking just awful, weeping too, with all his equipment, and when I took them to where they would be dumped at the Pentagon, I said again, thinking this would cheer this poor boy, "You both look like little Boy Scouts waiting for the scoutmaster." The boy just looked at me. The idea of a wife being so frivolous was just too much for him. Russell said afterward he asked how long we had been married. I admit I had some tears as I drove away.

Jane Malach's husband was a doctor in the army, and she began the war in the Columbia School of Journalism in New York but did not stay there for long.

My husband had been called up the preceding June. I had been accepted for the fall at Columbia, and we decided that I should continue and that he would just stay and do his stint. We were both stupid, because we thought it would only last a year. That's what the Medical Corps man said at the time he went in—six months before Pearl Harbor. He decided that he would get somebody to cover his practice for him while he was away, and I would go back and stay with my parents and go to school. I kept commuting between New York and wherever he was stationed. First it was Tennessee, and then it was a lot of other places.

When this blast came on December 7, I had a very hard time trying to decide whether I should quit school and go down and join him. It was obvious then that it wasn't going to be just a year. What I finally did was go to the dean of the school, Henry Pringle, who was really great. Then I went to Carl Ackerman. By that time I had decided I had better go, so I said: "Look, I would like to quit now, not finish the first semester, and go down and join my husband." He gave me a long speech: "This is a great big war. Some of the men who have to go overseas may not come back, but we have our job to do here, and what our job is is to see that we keep things going so that this country is just the same—just as good when they come back as it was when they left. Your particular thing is to stay here and finish your course in journalism. Furthermore," he said, "if you quit now and go down and join him, I won't ever let you come back and finish." I thought about that and decided that I would stay and finish. Then I went and joined my husband in June of 1942 at Camp Forrest in Tennessee.

There is nothing more insulated than a New Yorker. When I went down there to live, it was really an eye-opener. When I first went there six months before Pearl Harbor, Tullahoma was the center of the First Army manuevers. There were ninety thousand troops in the field in the area of Tullahoma and an explosion of wives and families. There was one little hotel in this town of about three thousand people, and people were sleeping on the floors, sleeping in the lobby. One of the things that shocked me was the fact that practically all of the women got married at eighteen right after they graduated from high school. It was an experience for someone who was as provincial as I was to meet people from Chicago and to meet the local people, really. I know this sounds absurd, but it was the first time I ever heard people use the expression "damn yankee."

I did not like the South, but the people were great. The social structure was very rigid, which amused me. I had a great deal of respect for the southern women. There were just inordinately capable—much more so than I or any of my New York City friends.

After I graduated and came down permanently, I wrote to the *Chat-*

tanooga Times and asked if they had any openings. They said they didn't have anything regular but asked me to cover the graduation of the First Army Rangers School. That was fascinating, because it was the first guerrilla training. They had been trained in judo, so I read up on that and really learned judo. I was the only woman in the press group. The rangers and reporters participated in a graduation exercise. We had to crawl, and they shot rifles over our heads. That was my first newspaper assignment.

My husband was transferred to Camp Jackson in Columbia, South Carolina, and then into the hospital in Augusta, Georgia, and there I was in Columbia waiting for him. I went to the *Columbia State,* which was twenty dollars a week, but because I had a graduate degree in journalism, they paid me twenty-two dollars. My beat was the police department, which was absolutely wild. I was pregnant. I must have covered the Police Department for about five months. When I appeared the first time and said I was the police reporter for the *Columbia State,* they all dropped, but they were very gentlemanly. I had to go over there every day; it was part of my beat. By the time I came back the second time they had cleaned out the jail—they really scrubbed it out. I think they were very careful that nothing happened while I was in the department; they felt I wouldn't know what in the hell to do if there was a murder, anything. They were darling, just darling! I was the first woman police reporter in the South. I was also the music and ballet critic.

Bob was in the hospital most of that time. After he had a gall bladder operation, we went to New York, where the baby was born in September 1943. After the baby was born, I stayed on in New York, living with my mother. She took care of the baby, and I worked—did some ghost writing. I was quite out of it. I worked, and my social life at night was otherwise. We played a lot of bridge.

I suffered emotionally from the war, and so did my marriage. It wasn't a good marriage to begin with, but it probably would have dragged on. I really don't know how the war affected him, because I never lived with him again. But if it had not been for the war, I am sure the marriage would have gone on . I don't know how long.

Anna Katherine Siemers had a husband on an LSM in the Pacific.
"Number 242, I still remember," she says. When I interviewed her at Leisure World in Silver Spring, Maryland, where she is now living, she

brought out the letters from her husband she had saved and her old, mostly empty ration books. Her husband is dead.

At the beginning of the war, right after the depression, my husband was working in New York City. I was working as a secretary for an engineering firm. We were living in Richmond Hills, Queens. My daughter was born in May of 1943, and my husband was drafted right after Christmas of that year. We probably would never have had a baby if we had known he was going to be drafted. We were both in our thirties, and we had kept postponing it because we didn't know whether he would be called or not. Finally I said, "Well, they are not calling anybody over twenty-nine." But it didn't work out that way. Of course, I am very glad we had the baby.

I remember that it was very difficult to get meat. You would have to stand in line. And we didn't get very much money—I don't think more than $125 a month. We had a coal furnace at the time. I had to go down and shake that up every morning, start the fire, and put coal on it.

We lived near a railroad yard, and it seemed all I was doing the whole time was scrubbing. That's what I remember most about the war. I just had my hands full existing. I still have my ration books. We would trade stamps with our neighbors. I didn't care much for sugar, so I would give my neighbor the sugar stamps, and she would give me coffee stamps. That is how we got along. I really felt the burden, besides not knowing where my husband was. I think that really was the worst thing—the uncertainty of everything. But he did survive the war. He said he was lucky; the fellow next to him had his head blown off at Iwo Jima. He said, "I guess it wasn't my time." They never talk about it too much when they come back. About that side of it.

ViCurtis Hinton was a student at Howard University in Washington, D.C.

I don't remember that the war affected my college life too much, but it affected the fellows who were in college. They were really afraid of not being able to finish; everybody was running to the draft board trying to get deferments.

In Washington I used to work with the service clubs. We had a little group that would go to entertain soldiers here, at Fort Belvoir, Fort Myer, and different clubs. We were trying to keep morale up. Some boys were in good spirits, some were really antiwar—but not as much as they were about Vietnam. The majority of them seemed happy. Some of them were bitter that they didn't have the opportunity to stay in college like others did.

My husband and I were married in '43. The night of my wedding reception he got his telegram for the army, which I'll never forget. He had finished medical school and had just finished interning. And all the fellows from the hospital . . . oh, they were so delighted to bring him this telegram! At that point, they were hoping to go because that was a way for them to get started in life.

When my husband went in the army, he went first to Fort Huachuia in Arizona. It was strictly an army base, in the middle of nowhere. That's where they sent most of the black officers. Everybody you ever knew at Howard University eventually got to Fort Huachuia. My husband was with the station hospital there. They had a party at the officer's club every Saturday night, and you just knew everybody because you'd been at school with them. The wives had a good time. This is terrible to say, but we had cars, we had coffee sessions every morning, we played cards all day while the fellows were working; it was a lot of fun. But the men didn't think it was fun. As the fellows say, whenever anyone tells them to "go to hell," they mean to go back to Fort Huachuia. Everybody was segregated.They had a black officers' club and a white officers' club, black swimming pool—that was really disheartening. The blacks just more or less accepted it at that time. We were there for a year, and then he went to the China-Burma theater.

I was interested in medical technology, and they didn't teach it at Howard at that time. So after my husband went overseas, I went to the University of Minnesota. It was really quiet in Minneapolis. In Washington you did get a little activity, but out there it was like nothing. You didn't get as much segregation there. The black population was small. One girl who was in school with me said I was the first black person she'd ever seen.

Heli Swyter lived in Houston, Texas. She and her husband were Dutch. He left her to join the army in Holland in April of 1941, while she was pregnant, and she did not see him again for four years. She is now a widow and lives in Silver Spring, Maryland.

We came to the United States in 1938 because of my husband's job with Dutch Shell. He was a research chemist, and they wanted to use him either in the Dutch East Indies, the United States, or Saudi Arabia. We said, "Why not America? A new adventure for both of us." So we arrived here in May 1938, and in April 1941 he joined up. We weren't even fit for our first citizenship papers when he shipped out. He had already decided to become an American citizen when he was here only a half year, because he liked it so well. I said, "Yes, I like it in so many countries. But it's not enough for me to become a citizen. It's not like taking off a jacket and putting on another jacket." So he said, "If you don't want to become one, why, just stay what you are, and I'll be married to a damn foreigner!"

I only decided to become a citizen when he came home alive. The war wasn't over, but he was called to this country to train the Dutchmen who had escaped, hundreds and hundreds, who had escaped Holland. Most of them didn't know a word of English, and they needed Dutch officers to train them, so he had to change uniform for the second time and became a captain in the Marine Corps. Our child was going on four when he came back.

One problem in raising the child alone was that I had no money. He started as a buck private. The Dutch government was in such a mess there in England, he didn't even get any pay. And so how did I have to live? The Shell Company, who knew about this, sent some delegate to my modest little apartment, and they told me I could borrow as much money of the company as I wanted, or needed, for my own upkeep and my baby's, but that it was a loan and later we'd have to pay it back. When my husband was commissioned, he was able to send some money home, but it still wasn't very much because he wasn't paid by the American government. It was still Dutch. That was the first problem, money.

So I went back to my art; I began making portraits. The trouble was, it was ten years ago since I had done that, and in those ten years I had lost the sight of one eye. It's a terrible handicap to have to make the portrait with one eye, because you don't see depth any longer; you only know that by estimation. You don't know how far the nose sticks out. But I had adjusted myself, and I did pretty good. How to get known, though, because I wanted to sell the things that I did. So, through a friend who was a Russian artist and photographer I did a portrait of Judd Mortimer Lewis, the president of the *Houston Chronicle*. He wanted to buy it, but it was the only thing I had to become known. It was shown in the Houston gallery, and then I got commissions after that, mostly friends of mine. It didn't help much financially, but the main thing was it helped me from being blue, morose, pessimistic. I was really feeling very low that first year.

All the food was rationed; linen was rationed, and toys. My son never had metal toys, never had one of those metal wagons; there were no little soldiers, either—everything he had was made out of wood. There was a big black market, but of course, only when you had money. That's a corrupt thing anyway; so I could never do that. The spirit in Houston was typically American. First, they don't want to have anything to do with the war—why would we want to get in the war? But then when they are in, everybody pulls together. I think that's very American; it is a very, very good feature. I made lots of different kinds of friends in Houston, because there were these big shipyards built there, and people from the rest of the United States all flocked down to the shipyards. They made big money there.

I lived completely for my child. I felt the responsibility of having to be not only a mother but also a father. I noticed that, for a boy, he was oversensitive. He was not an aggressive child. Of course, there are aggressive boys and nonaggressive ones, but with him it was definitely a matter that he had never had a man around to play rough with him. When his dad came home, he noticed that right away too. He wanted his son to be a real boy, so he started to wrestle with him, and slowly he became a different boy. I think he needed his daddy very much. Since I lived only for that child, I was always writing letters to my husband, whether he received them or not, about every little thing his son was doing.

While his father was away, it was hard for the boy. He used to play with the other children in the neighborhood, and they would talk about their daddies and how they were going to see them at suppertime. My boy would come in around five o'clock and say, "Where's my daddy?" I used to say to him, with a bright face, "Your father is far away, son, but he will come home. He is on a boat, that's why he can't come home so soon. That boat is far away." How many pictures he drew of the boat! And he used to say, "When I get bigger, I am going to swim out to that boat." I sent the pictures he drew of the boats in the letters to my husband. The letters from him took so long to come—six months, more. And they were so censored. And what kind of a censor that was! My husband was not a fool; he didn't give me any information about where he was.

When my husband finally came home, I got a wire which said, "I'll call you from San Francisco." I hadn't heard his voice in so many years,

I just about died! I couldn't say anything. I went in the car with our boy to the airport in Houston, and when the plane finally came in, from a distance I could see my husband come out of it, and I thought, is that him? He looked so much bigger in the uniform. When he came real near, I said to my little son, "There's Daddy." And he ran to meet his daddy, a strange man—but he knew him from the pictures. I had put in the back pocket of the little suit he was wearing, a package of Lucky Strikes to give him, and I said, "Don't forget to give Daddy his cigarettes." My husband picked him up, and with him on his shoulder he came to me and said, "My, I don't seem to be a stranger to this little fellow."

I was always very proud of the hair of my son. My husband never had very much hair. It was not curly or wavy, but my son had it from my side of the family—soft texture, plenty full, and it was curly—and I had always snipped the curls myself to make it kind of boyish looking, I thought. He'd never been to a barber. In these days it would be normal, but in those days, when the boys always wore the hair short, he must have looked to his dad like a girl, because the first thing he said after they became acquainted was, "Why don't you have his hair cut like a boy's?" I said, "He has such pretty curls, he is just so young, not even four; that can come a little later." My husband said, "That can come right now. He's a boy, my boy." And the next day he took him to the barber, and he came home like a little boy.

Regina Wilk lived in Albany, New York. Her husband was in a First Army antiaircraft unit. She had a son, born while he was away. Her son was later killed in Vietnam. She is first national vice-president of the Gold Star Mothers of America.

My husband was overseas at the time our son was born; he landed on Utah Beach, and he was in France, Belgium, and Germany. That's why I went to work; I wanted to get that off my mind. I worked in the payroll department of the New York Engineer Depot. I was one of the civilians working on a military base, and the morale was good. We had a job to do, and we had to keep busy. My mother took care of the child.

We all took the shortages in stride. I don't remember any complaints. I was married rather young, and maybe I really didn't get full realization as to what was going on. I had a son killed in Vietnam, and I think this war had more of an impact on me than World War II. It's closer to me. I suppose if my husband, God forbid, had been killed, I'd be feeling just the same way as I do now. But unless something affects you very closely, you just go on your merry way, which is an awful thing to say. I think I did worry about my husband being in the service, but it's not the same as the actual loss.

Mary Devereux Crist is a member of a Marine Corps family. Her brother was Col. James Devereux, who was captured at Wake Island. Her husband was a Marine Corps colonel who spent twenty-nine months in the Pacific.

The first thing my mother said after Pearl Harbor was, "What's going to happen to Jimmy?" He was captured on the twenty-third of December 1941, and held as a prisoner of war for four years. A lot of people criticized him because he didn't go down fighting with his men, but he was in command, and he had all the civilians under him, and he thought it was a better thing to do.

When my husband was sent to Camp Nyland in California, I drove out with the three children. We lived in a little house in Brawley, California, about twenty-five miles from the camp. My husband trained there for three months. Sometimes he would come in at midnight, and sometimes he wouldn't come at all. Then he went overseas.

After he left Camp Nyland, the Marine Corps paid our way to any spot in the U.S. that we wanted to go to. I had been in contact with a very good friend, and she suggested that we come to Clearwater, Florida. And I decided that the government might as well send me as far as they could. So I got on the train with the three children; copious tears at leaving. We landed in Clearwater with no place to stay, but we had one friend there, and she finally found me a house. My children were ten, five, and nineteen months. After a while the oldest boy got to be too much for me to handle, so I sent him to a prep school in Dade County, Florida, which was about a three-hour train trip away. I think the main problem was just growing up with female companionship alone.

One year I sent my boy to Porter Military Academy near Charleston, West Virginia. I came from Clearwater up to Charleston to see him one weekend, and the headlines were all, "Marines Land in Bougainville and Iwo Jima." I remember this woman who was in tears, an employee of the hotel where I was staying. Her son was in the Marine Corps, and we figured out that he was with my husband, and I said, "Well, at least you know he's under somebody who has had a lot of training." At the hotel they said they didn't have any rooms at all, and I said, "Well, I'm just going to sit here in the lobby until you find me someplace to sleep." Then I thought of a marine wife I had known who had made her debut in Charleston. Her husband had gone overseas, and I presumed that maybe she had come home, so I called the society editor of the paper, and she traced this woman to where she was rolling bandages. She made a phone call to the desk clerk at the hotel where I was, and he gave me a choice of rooms. So it just showed that if you knew the right person, you could get anything you wanted. Anyway, that morning they went into Iwo Jima, and I was able to comfort this woman employee at the hotel a little bit, though I was scared to death myself. My husband did see the raising of the flag—the first raising—remember there were two; one staged and one for real.

More and more wives who were in the same position I was in came down to Clearwater, and it ended up there were thirteen Marine Corps war widows down there, all with small children. We got as much liquor as we could. Not that we were alcoholics, but we certainly had our drinks in the evening. I was down there for nineteen months, when my husband came home on emergency leave because his father died. I remember when he called me and told me he was on the West Coast. The phone rang at two o'clock in the morning, and of course I screamed bloody murder and woke up all three children, and we all got on the phone and talked to him. He came to Clearwater, and one night he asked all the wives out for dinner—took eighteen of us to the country club. There were some Army Air Force men sitting at the table next to us, and they wanted to dance with us, but he said, "No, you can't dance with my girls. I've been out for nineteen months without anyone at all." Then he broke down and let them dance with them.

I don't think we wives complained too much. We all shared what parts of our letters we could, and none of us was sure of where our husbands were at any time. After my husband left New Zealand, he was allowed for maybe ten letters to tell me what had happened in New Zealand before they clamped down. He didn't write the full story in one letter, but then I had some idea of how nice and wonderful the people were to them. Their men were in the European theater, and they were without any troops until our men got there to augment their home guard. And they were not sure at all that the Japanese were not coming in there.

After my husband's leave was over, he went into Guam, and that's where he got hit. He was sitting in a deep cave, way in the back, so he thought he was safe enough. He took his helmet off and was sitting on it when a piece of shrapnel exploded just outside the cave, and it came back and grazed his head. I received a telegram—the telegraph office got mixed up and put the four black stars, which meant death, on his telegram. I was hesitant, to say the least, about opening it, and then I found the message was, "YOUR HUSBAND HAS SUSTAINED A WOUND OF THE HEAD," so I called Washington to try to get some word. I had a brother-in-law stationed at the headquarters in Washington, and I got him to try to find out how serious it was. He did finally, after several days, and said it was not a serious wound in the head. But you can imagine what was going through my mind. He was not even hospitalized.

I lived in Clearwater for nineteen months, then moved to Park Fairfax, Virginia. To tell you the truth, the people up here were still having a good time, and they certainly didn't talk about the war much. No one ever asked what I heard from my husband. They seemed to have the same cocktail parties. Life went on pretty much as usual. Gas rationing didn't seem to affect them much, as I remember. If they had enough money, they would have two or three cars, and they would buy the gas.

The war years were like a haze. I think I was restless for something to get my mind off it and see new people or cry on my mother's shoulder and let her cry on mine.

We were all service oriented in my family. My mother had twenty-seven stars on her flag—that was counting sons, sons-in-law, a granddaughter, and three or four grandsons. She had a special commendation from the navy. All my relatives survived the war—I think my husband was the only one who was hit. We all kidded that if the government ever folded, none of us would eat.

Mary Hoehling's husband, A. E. Dolph Hoehling, was an officer in the navy. Many years later he wrote a book titled Homefront, USA. *As with so many women during the war, Mary Hoehling's life centered around taking care of two small children in a peripatetic existence:*

Dolph was in the states about two years before he finally went overseas. From Corpus Christi he went to sea school in Boston; and I came from Worcester, so the children and I stayed there with my mother. Then he went to Newport.

The big problem was moving every few months. But it was kind of fun. By that time, I had begun to realize what could happen, and things had begun to happen to friends of ours, so I was more and more thankful that Dolph was still at home. As far as the children were concerned, neither was in school, and of course they just loved being with grandmother. But my older daughter has told me since that she had had dreams during that period and afterward because she thought something might happen to her father. I don't know that she clearly realized it when he went away: He was just going to Boston or to Newport. Later we came back here [to Bethesda, Maryland] and he went overseas, and that was very bad.

My daughter was about five by then. That was the winter that we got the flu. We were way out in the country, and people thought twice before they came out there, because of the gas rationing. Doctors didn't want to come out, there was no bus service, so we were pretty isolated.

Incidentally, I might not have brought up one of our children if we hadn't been in the service, because penicillin was just coming in and was almost impossible for civilians to get. The youngest girl was sick with a terrible pneumonia when we were at a naval station in New Jersey. I don't think they would have pulled her through without penicillin.

I don't think it ever occurred to me that we would lose the war. Probably any thought of not winning was something I wouldn't entertain, because it was too frightening.

During that winter Dolph was in Boston, I worked at Massachusetts General three days a week in one of their big clinics. I did secretarial work as a volunteer. So many people had gone, they were always short of people. And at Corpus Christi I worked for the Red Cross, probably doing bandages. It was a disruptive life, even though, as I said, it was kind of fun moving around. Of course, after Dolph went overseas, it was pretty grim. The winter we were out in Maryland I remember as being very bad. Not only were we all sick a lot of the time, but it was just terribly lonely.

I think, on the whole, the morale was good. I felt that everybody tried to do what he could to help the war effort. There were a lot of complaints about the rationing and so forth, but I don't think they were terribly serious. I myself was terribly frustrated because I had several friends with whom I'd grown up who got into the Red Cross and went overseas, and it was all very exciting for them. But I had to sit back and see them off and stay home with the children. I would have liked to have been in the thing, too. There was a lot of that feeling that everybody wanted to be in on it.

Celeste Kavanaugh, now living in Bradenton, Florida, was just finishing at Florida State College for Women, in Tallahassee.

I remember Founder's Day at the Alpha Delta Pi House. We had a beautiful lawn party, and all the girls dressed in long dresses. That was in May of 1942—it was so peaceful and so lovely, and yet there was this overtone of all the girls trying to decide whether they were going to go ahead and marry the boys they were pinned to or whether they were going into the war effort or what they were going to do. It was such a contrast, because May in Tallahassee is so lovely. I remember the phonograph was playing "Don't Sit Under the Apple Tree with Anyone Else But Me," and I said to myself—and I've thought about this so many times—"Will life ever be like this again?" Things were so different after the war. It was never the same again.

One thing always amused me, looking back. I was a political science major, and I had been reading *One World, Union Now with Britain* and all these books, and I remember before Pearl Harbor—it must have been, maybe, the first part of the 1941/42 school year—going to the president of the college with several friends. We wanted to organize a One World movement, and he looked at us very peculiarly and stopped it in a hurry. The war came so closely thereafter that it's really strange to think that you still were idealistic about the world.

There were lots of air bases around Tallahassee, and the officers would fill the sorority houses. They were always there, coming and going. I had some good friends at the Jacksonville Naval Base who were learning to fly; they were cadets. I remember one boy who was killed in training—by his friend, incidentally. He was following too close behind the other plane. His plane was hit, and he couldn't open his parachute in time.

I took the civil service exams for administrative assistants before I graduated in May. Then I went to Fernandino and was waiting for an assignment—I had no idea it would take so long in coming. It was a year and a half before I heard from the exams. My father was in the marine hardware business, and he was flooded with forms to fill out to requisition materials for the fishing and shrimping fleet there. I helped him with his office work and helped with the civil defense in Fernandino.

Ponte Vedra (just north of there) had had German spies landed from submarines. I was there when that happened, and from then on, we couldn't leave the island without identity cards, which we all had to carry. To get into Jacksonville we had to take the bus and cross the bridge to get off the island, and when we boarded the bus, everybody had to take out his identity card and be checked out to leave. They did catch the spies, who got up, I believe, as far as Kingsland. It was in the early days of the war, and the spying technique was really amateurish. Someone heard them speaking German, I think, at a gas station, and they picked them up.

I can also remember tankers burning off the coast. We had oil slicks and debris all over the beaches. There were horse patrols on the beach every night. I used to ride for pleasure on and off, and I remember seeing the tracks of the horse patrol when I would come down in the morning. The lighthouse at Fernandino was extinguished, and the houses were strictly under blackout rules. We had civil defense uniforms, and I believe that there was an airplane-spotting watch on the island. I think I helped to set up the time schedule for the volunteers.

They were exciting times. You would just see uniforms everywhere. In trains you'd sit in the aisles on suitcases because the trains were so full. You weren't supposed to travel unless it was necessary. There were signs Is This Trip Necessary? everywhere. It was exciting. We were very united then. Everyone was doing anything he could to help, no matter what it was. Whether it was rolling bandages or addressing envelopes, civil defense, or anything that came up, everybody was pitching in, going about cheerfully, not complaining, patching up old tires, stretching the gasoline, going without sugar; because everyone had part of his family in the military. They were doing it not just for the country; they had a personal stake in it.

Everything was very uncertain—what the news was going to be from overseas, what you were going to be allotted, whether you would find what you wanted at the stores, food or anything else. You just sort of adapted to it and accepted it as it came, but still you never quite knew what was coming next. And I remember that every night when Kaltenborn came on, everybody listened. His voice was a very caring voice, and the overtones of sorrow were so strong. Any family that had sons or sons-in-law in the war were so concerned about any news from day to day. I remember hearing Kaltenborn on the night that Dunkirk was being evacuated and what a terribly depressing time that was. But it was also exciting, you know, hearing about the boats and how many of them were going to get there and worrying about whether those little boats were going to get back to England loaded with men.

Eunice Yoakum lived in Chicago. Her husband, a retired minister, was too old for the military service, but he wanted to do something for the war effort, so he went to weather school and then taught weather at Chanute Field in Illinois. She had a young son, Robert, who could not wait to get into the air force. She took a job working for Liberty Mutual Insurance Company.

Bob was in college at that time, in his second year at Northwestern. Very soon after the war began, he called up one night and said he wanted to enlist. He was an only son, an only child. It was, I'd say, in January or February 1942—before the school year was up. I thought that was terrible, but his group was very patriotic. His whole crowd of friends enlisted in the Air Corps. When Bob went away to school, I was very conscious of the war coming on, and I wanted to do something, so I took a secretarial course, a whole-year course, and then I went right out and got a job. I could have had every job I applied for, but I took this job at an insurance company. My work really didn't have anything to do with the war, except that they did need help. I had two girl friends who were also working in the insurance business, and it was really loads of fun. I was on my own in a way I hadn't been since I'd been married. We did everything together. We took in shows when we wanted to, and it was a very independent life. Except for worrying about Bob constantly, I was enjoying it very much. There weren't a lot of men around to bother us. We really didn't do anything else in the way of war work. I didn't knit and I didn't sew or sell bonds. We didn't have a Victory garden; I was living in the middle of the city. I did not do volunteer work. Everyone didn't have an opportunity. We got up early in the morning and home late at night from our jobs because it took three-quarters of an hour to get to work. By the time we got ourselves cleaned up and our nails fixed and everything, we were ready for another day. We didn't have really any time.

The war had quite an impact on the company. We had a great deal of trouble getting help, and what help that did come was very mediocre. The good ones were leaving because they were all getting jobs that paid twice as much. The starting salary was $18.50 for file clerks. I guess it was $21.50 for typists. You could get double that in the defense factories. So the average efficiency was down because of the types of people we had to hire. There was a great deal of crabbing by the heads of the different departments. They would make snide remarks about the kind of people we were sending to them. But the morale was good. There was much enthusiasm.

I was constantly worried about Bob, just constantly. I would wake up in the morning with an awful feeling that something terrible was going on; and, of course, it wasn't just poor Bob, it was the whole situation. But being the only son, my whole life, almost the only time I had him off my mind was when I was working. That's one of the reasons I was very thankful to have a job; I could forget about it all through the day. I think any mother went through that. I had one real scare—the Battle of the Bulge. He had written to me where he was, and when we heard about the Battle of the Bulge, we looked on the map and knew he must be in that territory. That was terrible. It seemed like at least six weeks, but it was probably three weeks, that we didn't hear a word from him. Then he finally wrote from Paris that he was having a wonderful time. He met Moira Shearer—the dancer in *Red Shoes*, the ballerina. He had been sent by his colonel to publish a little pamphlet on what they were doing in the Nineteenth Tactical Air Force. So there he was, having the time of his life in Paris, and I'd been worried about it.

Except through Bob and the fact I was working, I don't know if I had enough direct contact with the war to have it affect me—except through my emotions. My horror was the Jewish situation. I'm not Jewish, but I kept thinking of all the wonderful Einsteins and Danny Kayes and all those people who were being destroyed in such a horrible way. It was my feeling all the way through the war that we were fighting for that cause. It wasn't so much the political as it was the humanity. I was conscious of that all through the war, and I don't know—maybe I was unusual that way, because so many people nowadays don't seem to realize this. In fact I was just listening on television to somebody who didn't even mention that as their reaction to the war.

Gertrude Blassingame lived on Anna Maria Island, near Bradenton, Florida, with her daughters, Peggy and April. She died a few months after I interviewed her.

My husband, Wyatt, came home and said he had applied for a commission in the navy. April was born in January 1942, and I don't think

Wyatt told me about this until after she was born. I was mad; I guess it was a woman's normal reaction. We had very few conveniences, and the pay for a lieutenant in the navy was very small, even though we didn't have inflation.

I felt terrible. I felt alone. But I would say it was one of the best things that ever happened to me, because I learned to depend on myself. About a year and a half later, Wyatt was transferred to Quonset Point, Rhode Island, and I just walked in on him with the kids. He didn't have anyplace for me to stay, but I was going to be with him if he was in this country, so we slept in pretty crowded quarters, the four of us. When his training there was up, he was going to South America, but he went someplace else first. So he said, "Look, I'll pay your fare back to Anna Maria if you promise me you'll stay there for the duration." Wyatt was sent to Hawaii, just living it up. But he made up for it in Okinawa.

I followed the war by listening to three commentators. I didn't want to get confused with too many people who had different points of view so I kept to about three that I respected—H. V. Kaltenborn, Edward R. Murrow, and I can't remember the other. I followed the Battle of Okinawa on the radio. It was my first experience with following a map. When the radio would announce where there had been a battle, I'd say, "Well, Wyatt was just there." I thought he must still be alive, and he was. Of course, I was worried, but I think I just believed. I remember one time I sent him some martinis. They weren't supposed to receive alcoholic beverages, but I went to the canning company here in Bradenton. Two quarts and a pint bottle just fit in the package, so I made the martinis, put them in the bottle, and then the bottle of olives fit in the side, and I took it to the canning company. They sealed it for me in the form of a can of orange juice—Tropicana. The man that is there now would not have approved of it, because he's a teetotaler. Wyatt received it, and he was sending his men out on a mission that night to bomb Shanghai. It was just enough to go around, and the mission was successful.

I remember some things with pleasure. I had no fear; I didn't feel like I feel now. We didn't even have a house key. We had a radar station up on the north point. I think they may have had about eighty men there. They'd come to my house, and if I had beer, they would drink it. I finally made it clear to them that they were welcome, but beer was scarce, so they'd have to bring their own, and they did. They were nice, and there weren't any older men—I was in my thirties, and you didn't have to fight off passes or anything like that. We'd have parties, and they would come to our house on Christmas and any holidays. That part of it was good. I found out that if you don't want to be lonely, you share your facilities with other people. I learned to be cautious, but not to be afraid.

Her daughter, Peggy, was eleven years old at the time of Pearl Harbor. Then her father went into the navy.

He was a lieutenant in the navy. I remember thinking how wonderful he looked in that white uniform. I don't remember thinking necessarily of his being a hero. He was home one Christmas, and that was a dismal time, because he must have been leaving immediately, maybe the next day. So instead of being happy, I felt low. I couldn't take the day for what it was worth; I was too worried about tomorrow and having him go back again. I missed him very much, and I got along with him very well—at that time I got along with him better than with my mother. Now, in retrospect, I see that so much of the irritability that she had and her terrible tension was due to the fact that they were separated and that she had to fear for his safety.

I was too young to have any personal friends who were servicemen, and when strangers would whistle as I went by with my girl friends or they'd come up and say something, I'd want to slug them with my pocketbook. I could romanticize about them as heroes, and it was all beautiful.

The war years had a tremendous impact on young Herb Collins. He lived in Bowling Green, Virginia, a small town about thirty miles north of Richmond. Camp A. P. Hill was nearby, and he remembers the war years and what they meant to his town.

Camp A. P. Hill took over one-third of Caroline County area; it moved in in 1941, and that made a real impact on me when that happened. I had relatives there, and it displaced them. The army bought up land in adjacent counties as settlement land for people who were dispossessed and couldn't find houses of their own. People don't realize that happens in the twentieth century. They moved all those families at A. P. Hill, and I remember them moving the bodies. They moved every cemetery out of there at the time. They found one casket, which, they said, was filled with silver. It probably was buried there during the Civil War, when a lot of silver was buried like that.

I remember the USO clubs at Bowling Green. They were segregated at the time; the black USO club was down by the black high school, and the white USO club was up in Bowling Green, the county seat. Many of the old maids at home who went to these USO clubs met service guys and married them. On weekends the troops completely took over Bowling Green. There were no bars, but restaurants served beer. Here was a little town with five hundred people, and you couldn't even get your car through the streets; both sides of the streets were just lined with army trucks and Jeeps and all kinds of army vehicles. Even tanks would be driven in, so that you felt like you were in the middle of warfare. This really made an impression on me.

War is a time of social change, and the girls were supposed to be nice to the service guys. They dated a lot of the local girls. You know, you didn't have that attitude that was felt after the war: "No sailors or dogs allowed on the grounds." That's more of a peacetime thing. Soldiers had real support and backing in World War II.

We had a lot of patriotic songs, "Nathan Hale and Colin Kelly, Too," "There's a Star-Spangled Banner Waving Somewhere." That was one we used to sing all the time. "In a distant land so many miles away, / Only Uncle Sam's great heroes will ever get to go there, / How I wish that I could also be there one day," and it just goes on and on, and it lists all the patriots, from the Revolutionary Army on. "Green Berets" was about the only war song that came out in the Vietnam War that was a success. There were no heroes in the Vietnam War; the prisoners became the heroes, actually. In World War II you had a lot of heroes.

I remember the gas rationing, because we were on the farm at the time, and the school buses had to consolidate routes. Children had to walk several miles to board a school bus, and I was very fortunate, because the pickup point for the children was at my house. My mother was very good about it, because she used to observe all the children's birthdays. When they'd get off the school bus before they'd go home, she'd have a little birthday party for each one. So it brought the community together more than you'd ever dream of.

I think the gruesomeness of the war certainly made an impact on the children at the time. I saved a clipping about how they had taken the Jews and burned them in Germany, and they had heaps of ashes with bones all mixed in, and I saved the picture as a child because that made an impression on me.

I also learned who the generals were. I went to war pictures and saw the newsreels. You had this growling lion head that would come on before the news, and then the news would come on, and they'd tell what was happening in the war, and then they'd go on to the movie. I went as much for the news as I did for the movie because we didn't have any radio at home.

I never had any fear of losing the war. For some reason, we had almost as much faith in the country as in the church—until I came to Washington and actually saw that people weren't supernatural. I think that children, especially in a rural area, grew up with the feeling that Washington know all the answers, that the Great White Father, as the Indians used to call him, would take care of you, and you didn't have any fear.

Democratic Congressman Norman Mineta was ten years old at the time of Pearl Harbor. He was a Nisei Japanese living in San Jose, California.

My parents were born and raised in Japan. Dad came over in 1902 as a boy of roughly fourteen years. He and my mother were not American citizens because the laws prevented Asians from becoming U.S. citizens. The Chinese weren't able to get their citizenship until 1944; the Filipinos didn't get theirs until 1946. The Japanese got theirs in 1950. We were leading a comfortable life; we were not a wealthy family, but I think we were above average.

Immediately after Pearl Harbor a curfew was imposed on all people of Japanese ancestry. You couldn't travel in groups of any more than five, and you couldn't travel distances of greater than twenty-five miles without permission from the FBI. My sister got married in February of 1942 in San Francisco, and so we had to get a permit to go to the marriage ceremony. My brother had to stay home because if he had gone, there would have been six of us.

My father's business just went down. His clientele was 100-percent Japanese, anyway, and at that point the insurance companies would not insure anyone of Japanese ancestry either. On the nineteenth of February of 1942 the president signed Executive Order 9066, which established zones in Washington, Oregon, and California and indicated that within thirty days those people in zone 1 would have to be removed to camps. The army took over racetracks, and the early ones being evacuated from their homes had to go and live in stables.

We were fortunate in that we were able to lease our home to some friends. My sister was the secretary to the head of the Speech and

Drama Department at San Jose State. One of the professors there, Lucy Lawson, was looking for a place to live. She was living with her mother, and we asked if they would like to rent our place after we were evacuated. So our house was never confiscated. It had been in my sister's name, who was an American citizen. Children born in this country were automatically citizens. The property, when it was purchased, was in the name of an attorney, and then when she became old enough, it was transferred to my sister's name.

In the San Jose area we were very fortunate in that we did not have any acts of violence. Toward Stockton, toward Salinas, toward the central valley, there were many arson attempts, bombings, and a number of incidents.

Because they had a phased evacuation schedule, we did not leave San Jose until the twenty-sixth of May. My dad had just purchased a 1941 Packard—he had probably bought it for fourteen hundred dollars, and he had to sell it for seven hundred dollars. There were other people, who had businesses and grocery stores. What do you do with a grocery store? In thirty days? A lot of them just padlocked their businesses and had to walk away from them. They just lost thousands and millions of dollars totally.

We left San Jose on big trains and were taken to Santa Anita, a racetrack in southern California. We were fortunate in that we didn't get placed in one of the horse stables; we got put in barracks buildings that had been built in the meantime. In a room about the size of this [a Congressman's office, which is not very big] there were six of us. We were there from May until October of 1942. They tried to keep friends and families together as much as they could. From Santa Anita we went to a camp at Hart Mountain, Wyoming. These camps were all barbed wire, guard towers, searchlights. They were concentration camps. There's no question about it. In roughly May of 1943 my dad got a job teaching at the University of Chicago, teaching Japanese under the Army Specialized Training Program, so he was able to leave Hart Mountain, Wyoming, and go to Illinois. My mother and I stayed at the camp. Camp life was a very Spartan kind of existence. Morale was low. But, you know, despite what happened here—to show the resilience and the loyalty of the Japanese Americans—at Santa Anita they were making camouflage nets for use by the troops during that whole time. Behind barbed wire enclosures and in a concentration camp, American style, they were still making camouflage nets.

These places where the camps were, were not vacation spots. In the summer they were extremely hot and in winter extremely cold. They put them in isolated spots so that even if you jumped the fence and got away, you'd still be twenty miles from any community. We stayed there until the latter part of 1943, and on Thanksgiving Day of 1943 we were able to leave and go to a home my dad had rented in Evanston, Illinois.

In Evanston I think we were treated as well as could be expected. There was always that curiosity among the kids at school about whether or not I was Japanese. I remember during the war they said things like, "You can always tell a Japanese because they can't pronounce their v's and their l's, because v's come out like l's, and the l's come out like r's." So the kids would try these rhymes on me, and I'd go sailing right through them prouncing the l's and the v's, and they'd say, "Are you sure you're Japanese? Are you sure you're not Indian?" Evanston being a university community, I think there was more tolerance in our being there.

My brother-in-law was in the army with the 442nd Regimental Combat Team, the most highly decorated outfit of its size in the annals of U.S. Army history, and my brother was learning Japanese to go to the South Pacific. So as a twelve-year-old boy, I followed the war, read the papers, and watched the maps of the battles. I remember following those things very closely.

Hugh Sidey was in high school in Greenfield, Iowa; population, 2,500:

We had a boy in town who was killed at Pearl Harbor. He was on one of the battleships. His mother worked for my mother. So, instantly, the war was brought home. And I think the mothers understood it, but we kids didn't look that far ahead. When my brother turned eighteen he enlisted, ended up in the medical corps, and was over in Europe in field hospitals that followed the troops. It was kind of exciting. I didn't really understand it, but it began to come home. We had a bunch of fellows that were lost. Red Oak, Iowa, nearby, lost more men than any single town of its size per capita or per unit than any other place in the United States in World War II. Their boys made up a good part of the 34th Division that was hit hard in Tunisia. That was our National Guard division. And then, curiously enough, there was a bunch of guys who ended up in that glider infantry, and that was brutal. A bunch of them were wiped out in England when they were training. Then they went over to take part in the D-day invasion—using gliders—and a whole bunch were lost over there. From our area there must have been twenty guys who were bunched up there.

To understand the effect of the war on us, you've got to remember that we kids all came out of the depression. It was a deprived existence by today's standards. We didn't understand that. Nobody had any money. We had been through miserable times economically: businesses folded, the drought, soil dried up and blew away, no crops, mortgages foreclosed, there was just a lot of suffering. My family was never cold or hungry and we had clothes, so we were relatively all right. But we had nothing else. My dad never took a vacation, we never went out of the state, there was no travel at all. This little town was all you had. In many ways it was a marvelous life. We made kites; we'd buy a nickel orange crate and cut the lumber up and make model planes; hiked; we swam in the old creeks around there. We were totally happy, but there was no money. Out of that we just went from one kind of restriction to another—gas rationing. I remember we canceled some football games. And we canceled music contests; and there were no vacations. You stayed right there. Our diet was affected a little, not much, but you had the rationing—meat stamps, shoe stamps, sugar stamps. My dad had a pretty good gas ticket—a B-sticker because he was a country editor and got to drive around. But in those small towns, you walked or rode your bike, it didn't have that much impact on us. We never went any place anyway. So we didn't feel deprived.

Fortunately, we had just gotten a swimming pool from WPA before the war, so we had that in those years. But there wasn't anything else built around the town. There was another benefit, though, in human relationships. In my graduating class of thirty-three people about nineteen had gone all the way through kindergarten and high school, and we were thrown together through the depression and the war so closely that it's a bond that still exists today. When we have a high school reunion, almost all of those who are still alive—about fifteen of them—come back from wherever they are to see each other,—Paris, New York, California, they come to that little town. Our activities were in the school—school plays, basketball, football, baseball, walking around the square on Saturday night, church groups. Then there were other things: aluminum drives, paper drives—about every other month there would be one of those.

My father's newspaper business was good. We began to come out of the depression because of the war contracts. So now it became very difficult to get help. He needed linotype operators, he had machines that broke down, presses, that sort of thing. But he was a handy guy and he improvised a bit. He had to work awful hard, but he made more money, and one of the reasons he made money was that there wasn't any help to hire. I worked at the paper in the mornings and after football practice.

I took pictures of all the draftees leaving and by this time, when I was in high school, they were friends—only two to three years older than I. The old Trailways bus would come to the hotel, which was right beside my dad's newspaper, to take the draftees into Des Moines, and dad insisted on a picture of every guy. Almost every day, it seemed, there would be another ten or fifteen, and they all lined up in their farmer's clothes with their cardboard suitcases. I'd go out there with my speed-graphic and shoot a picture of them lined up. I'd see them go off, and a year or so later, in some instances two years later, suddenly would come news that so-and-so was lost in a bomber over Britain or killed in the Pacific.

So I was very much aware of the war. The social mores were also affected. There were sexually deprived women around and there were some wild scenes. Young wives, with their husbands gone, took the boys in high school out and introduced them to the joys and sorrows of sex. There were divorces after the war; there were bizarre and exotic tales.

Then there were the boys coming home. They'd come around to the high school and, oh God, we thought they were the greatest guys in the world. There was even a flyer or two who came back and buzzed the high school—and then they'd write about it later. Airplanes were still novelties and everybody would go out to look at these guys flying over. One guy flew over in a B-25. They'd be ferrying these planes and they'd come low, you know, circle a couple of times. It was a marvelous thrill.

We did have a little bitterness in our part of the country. They deferred farm boys. A lot went, but some took those agricultural deferments to work on farms. Quite legitimate, but it caused a bitter feeling, no question about it.

There was a sense of exhilaration during the war that brought people together. There was no real hardship and there was no fear, like people on the West Coast. Nobody was going to get to Iowa. There was no deprivation, despite the rationing. So we didn't have enough stamps for meat—my uncle butchered a cow. There was no problem except for those families that lost sons. Even there, there were some people who took that as part of their duty, the lost sons. It was a sense of pride, in some way.

Anne Relph remembers what it was like to be evacuated from her home in California and go to another country—Louisiana.

I was in an elementary school, and soon after Pearl Harbor my mother got very worried about the possibility that the Japanese were going to attack the coast of California, because a submarine was sighted or something like that. So she sent me to stay with relatives in Louisiana in the little town of Bogalusa, which is about eighty miles outside of New Orleans. As a child, I didn't realize why I was being sent until I got there, because my mother was so frightened about this that she didn't even tell me. She simply said, "You're going off to spend a vacation with Aunt Gladys in Louisiana."

My mother brought me home in about six or eight months. Of course, it had become obvious that the Japanese were not circling Los Angeles and were not going to come and drag us all off. But the psychological effect of that attack on Pearl Harbor created a kind of war hysteria that took awhile for people to get over.

To me as a child, though, the war never had any reality. It was like a story that someone was telling me. One day the Japanese were there, and the next day they'd simply disappeared. I can remember going to a friend's home and seeing that suddenly her bedroom was just filled with beautiful toys, and I said, "Where did you get those?" She said, "Macimo (or whatever her name was) gave them to me last night before she went to the internment camp." A lot of the Japanese children had done this, given their toys away to friends rather than have them confiscated.

We lived in North Hollywood, and they had big searchlights on those hills, I guess to look for aircraft or something. I can remember going up and taking hot coffee to the soldiers in uniform. I was a member of the Civil Air Patrol, which was something they organized for kids. We bought WAC uniforms from the army surplus and were given wooden guns to drill with, and we were taught Morse code and the different kinds of airplanes to watch for. We were never actually used, but we did have a sense of being prepared for something, for some time in the future. That was the only time that to me the war seemed real.

Ray Hartman lived in Chicago, where his father was in the restaurant business. He says, "I was probably his number-one dishwasher, on a part-time basis."

When I wasn't in school, I'd be working for him, so I used to go with him to purchase supplies and things, and I remember the rationing. On gasoline, of course, he got a C-book, or something, because he needed it for the business. Rather than use individual stamps like families had to do, they gave restaurant owners something like a checkbook. He would write them up for butter and meat, and that checkbook used to be guarded like it was money. If anybody stole that checkbook, he could go out and buy all kinds of butter or meat and sell it on the black market.

Everybody was campaigning to sell war bonds. The school set a goal. They were selling stamps. Each kid would buy stamps and try to fill books to get an $18.75 bond. We were using our allowances and paper drives and whatever way we could to get money to purchase the stamps. In those days we were going around selling war stamps similar to the way children now sell chances on raffles. We'd go door-to-door and ask people to contribute dimes and quarters and fill up a book of stamps and buy the bonds. The goal of the school, I believe, was somewhere in the seventy-nine-to-eighty-thousand-dollar range, and we were told that this would be sufficient money to purchase a P-38 fighter plane. We reached the goal. I was the student chairman of the drive, and after probably eight or nine months of work, we were successful, and there was a P-38 named after the school. Alphonsus was the name of the school, but they named the plane The Spirit of Saint Al's. We went to some Douglas Aircraft Company when they painted the name on the plane, more or less christened it, took pictures. I was thrilled, being the chairman of the student drive. I did the ribbon cutting or something like that. We received a letter of commendation from some general for the school. There were pictures taken with a couple of air force men who were pilots dressed in their uniforms, so it was a thrill.

Dorothy Whitaker had a brother in a prisoner-of-war camp and a husband who spent most of the war trying to stay out of the army. He was unsuccessful.

My husband had been babied all his life, and he had parents who clung to him like grim death, I guess because they didn't want him to go in the service. It created an embarrassing situation for me and my family, because his family didn't make a secret of it. Everybody knew it. He had had rickets when he was younger, and he was very skinny. As far as I know, he had probably as good health as anybody else, but he was exceptionally skinny. He decided to go into a war plant in Pascagoula, Mississippi, where they made ships.

It was a really small little hick town that nobody ever heard of until the war. Then it turned out to be one of the three largest shipyards in the United States, and they just poured class 2-A men in there. If they didn't know anything, they trained them. When my husband first went up, I was told not to come there because there wasn't any place to live. But I got tired of staying here and wondered if he was just giving me the runaround, or what. So one day I took my little three-year-old daughter, got on the bus, and went up there. I found out what a mess it was. There just wasn't any housing at all. It was a pain in the neck, but I didn't complain about it because, after all, we were well and healthy.

They had a hotel for men, and that's where my husband was. He appealed to the people who owned the hotel, and they told me if I would take care of their little girl, they would give me a small room. That's what I did. They sectioned off part of the porch—it was cold, too. I was there for about two and a half years. For entertainment, I rode a bicycle.

We didn't have a car. I finally got in a project house—one of the project homes that they threw up as fast as they could—but there was no entertainment. I never went to church so much in my life, just for entertainment, just to see what the neighbors were doing.

Food was so hard to get up there. You couldn't get any fresh milk at all. My husband was a welder, and they told him that he should have milk, but I just couldn't get it. The day came when he got sick of lead poisoning, and he had to stop working there and come back to Florida. He went into commercial fishing. He was under a doctor's care all that time, which put him in 4-F for a while. But then that cleared up finally, after about six months, and he was back in class 1-A. That's when he was drafted—about a year before the end of the war. He had had a college education, and they sent him up to Fort Dix, in New Jersey. He worked in the personnel department.

When Germany surrendered and the boys kept coming back so fast, there was just pandemonium at Fort Dix. Everything was getting sort of frayed at the edges. He worked in an office with one other Pfc. and finally, one of the officers came in to his office and said, "No one in here is supposed to be doing this type of work as a corporal or private or Pfc. You are supposed to be higher rank. We're going to have to give out a promotion."

I doubt whether either one of them had been there long enough to be eligible for staff or tech sergeant rank, but one of them was going to be promoted anyway. They flipped a coin to see which one won and my husband went from Pfc. or corporal, or whatever he was, to tech sergeant.

My brother had spent the war in a prisoner of war camp in the Philippines and Japan. The government gave everybody who survived prison camp an automatic promotion to whatever rank they would have reached had they been fighting and in a position to get a rating. So they gave my brother a staff sergeant rating—and when he and my husband got together after the war, they really batted that one around. My brother said, "It sure is a heck of a note when you have to spend three-and-one-half years in a prison camp to earn staff sergeant rating and you get one on the flip of a coin."

Anne Rippery, then nine years old, was living with her parents in Bloomfield, New Jersey.

I lived in a neighborhood of all boys, and a German girl was the only girl of my age in the neighborhood. Prior to the war, her family had been very loyal to Germany. Her older brother had been sent to Germany by the family when he graduated from high school. He was considerably older. He fell on his head, I think, the first week in training in the German army, and he came right back, so we had this young man living down the street who had been crippled after he had enlisted in the German army.

One of the things that was really nice about my German girl friend was that her father ran an ice-cream store—I think it was Strube's Ice

Cream Parlor. The two of us would go down there and get ice cream. Our family traded with her father quite often. Then I came home one day and said, "Mr. Strube has a picture of Hitler on the wall." And I remember my grandparents saying, "You can't play with her. This is the end, we can't deal with him." So it cut off a basic friendship with the one girl I was able to play with in the neighborhood. I didn't understand it, and it was hard on me. I had been very happy that she was in the neighborhood. But a little later, when my uncle, who was a few years older than I, about as close as a brother, went into the army and was fighting, there was enough suspicion in my mind so that I didn't want to have much to do with her.

We used to go to Manasquan Beach in New Jersey, and I can remember a lot of coastal defense. We weren't allowed to have any lights on the front part of the cottage, and lights at the amusement parks were shut off. I can also remember Coast Guardsmen going up and down the beach on horseback, I guess to make sure lights weren't shining out toward the ocean.

I remember occasional oil slicks, when a ship would be sunk, or some kind of destruction. I had a great-uncle who was in Naval Intelligence all during the war, and he would tell tales, and I would never know whether they were scare stories of his or what. Manasquan had an inlet to a very shallow bay, and he claimed that German submarines would go in that inlet and down to Tom's River, which was a very pro-German community, to get supplies and daily newspapers.

I was an only child, but I sort of lived half time at my house and half time at my grandparents, so my youngest uncle and aunt were very close, like a brother and sister to me. He was in the Pacific during the war, and she was an army nurse in the Atlantic. I was very concerned about them.

As long as my uncle was in the Pacific, which was a good, long time, we never lived without fear, because often they'd say the Ninety-sixth Infantry is doing so and so, and we knew darned well he was with them.

My aunt was in what I guess you'd call a second-line hospital in France. I can remember her getting home before he did. Apparently she'd had some rather harrowing experiences. But I always felt she was having a marvelous time, a very easy time of it, which was not true at all.

I was a rather dedicated student; I threw myself into work rather than worry about things. I corresponded a lot with both my uncle and aunt, and at one point I became a nurse's aide at Mountainside Hospital in

Montclair, New Jersey. I really went into that because I knew Florence was overseas.

Mercedes Fritzching is an American citizen of German parents who lives today in Washington, D.C. At the time of Pearl Harbor she was a Venezuelan citizen, and she had just started college at American University in Washington. Her father was the economic attaché at the German Embassy. As she says, the war "absolutely split my life in half."

I remember the summer of 1941. My girl friends were dating American boys—I was too—and all of them said, "Oh, no, there's not going to be any war. We don't want war." None of the young teens, and I knew lots of them, had any idea of "lets go in there and beat the Germans."

But even before Pearl Harbor, I'd say a good six months before, my very closest friends—two daughters of an American army doctor—were a little strange when they came to see us and didn't come as often. Finally mother called their mother and said, "Is there something wrong? My children feel some kind of change in your children." And their mother said, "Actually, yes, there is. My husband is in a high military position, and it's a little embarrassing for us to have any contact with Germans." And so we stopped seeing them. When mother or I would run into the girls downtown, they always embraced us, and so forth. They felt badly about it, but apparently that's what their father felt was important. And then, after Pearl Harbor, that was very, very pronounced—I mean, our neighbors of fifteen years, everybody was afraid to talk to us on the phone. And we were very, very aware of the most incredible rumors circulating around the neighborhood—that we had made a tunnel to the White House and were sending radio transmissions from our attic—this ridiculous stuff. For instance, we had a black cat, and one time the daughter of one of our neighbors came and asked whether her cat was there. Mother said we hadn't seen her cat, and she said, "Well, folks told me he was out with Hitler." Mother said, "What do you mean?" The girl said, "Hitler—isn't that the name of your cat?"

At some point during the year before war was declared, the naval attaché at the German Embassy told my father that he needed a social secretary and couldn't hire anyone from outside and wondered whether I would be interested. I was just twenty years old then, starting out at American University in all kinds of languages. At that time it never occurred to me that I'd ever have to earn my own living, so the courses I had signed up to take were totally useless from the point of view of life today. They were in line with my life then, Advanced French Literature, Spanish Literature, this sort of thing. I could type, but I didn't know any shorthand, and at that time I couldn't write German very well—I could speak it, but I couldn't write it. Daddy thought that experience would be better, that I could catch up on my education later.

So I started there as the admiral's social secretary, which was very simple work for me, because I had the background—arranging his table seating, doing his place cards, sending out his invitations, receiving his visitors, and that sort of thing. Then, just before Pearl Harbor, his main secretary got sick, so I had to take over her functions. He would dictate telegrams to me into the typewriter; I would write phonetically, and he would laugh like crazy. He was not a Nazi. He was a very charming, lovely gentleman of the old school who had an American wife. He was very tolerant, whereas, in the other areas of the German Embassy—for instance, the military attaché downstairs—there was real Nazi atmosphere.

When the admiral realized his secretary was not going to get better (among other things, she was suffering from paranoia), he said, "I don't think she's coming back to work. Why don't you every day carry some of her stuff over to her apartment?" So I started trooping back and forth, bringing her coffeepot, her teapot, and other stuff. I wasn't aware that for those last four months before war broke out, the FBI was sitting in the building across from the embassy and was photographing me. Years later, after I came back here, I was told by my friends: "I saw you in a film about the FBI, *The House on Forty-second Street.*" Eventually I saw that film on TV, and, by golly, if they didn't have me, coming in and out of that embassy door with this secretary's teapot and everything. In and out, in and out, they photographed me.

After Pearl Harbor everyone in the embassy was interned at the Greenbriar Hotel in White Sulphur Springs, West Virginia, where we stayed five months. First it was just the members of the German, Italian, and Hungarian embassies from Washington. Then, very slowly, came Germans, Hungarians, and Italians from Mexico, Central America, the Caribbean Islands, and from Venezuela. They were all brought up to White Sulphur Springs. The Japanese had been treated differently. The day of Pearl Harbor all the Japanese diplomats had been put into the embassy building, and until they were interned at Hot Springs, they were not even allowed to return to their homes. After we had been in

White Sulphur Springs about three months, the Italians were moved to Hot Springs, and the Japanese came to White Sulphur Springs.

Some of us took care of the little children. I gave English lessons to some of the diplomats coming from South and Central America who wanted to get accustomed to American English. White Sulphur Springs lies in the mountains of West Virginia, and the radio reception was very poor. We got no newspapers, no mail, so we really didn't know what was going on. Of course, there were constant rumors all through the hotel about our being interned in Texas for the duration. Most everybody wanted to stay in the States, and every time a rumor like that came around, we thought that was great.

The people who worked in the hotel went home every night—they had special passes—and of course they brought in all kinds of news. My sister and I, being devils, young, and not really aware of the hardships that were ahead of us and the real significance of it, had a big ball. We were always starting rumors. We'd start a rumor in the morning and then see what shape or form it would come back to us at night!

For the first three months we were locked up in the hotel. Then they opened a little walk and two tennis courts, so we could get out of the hotel. All of us were suffering from allergies and colds because we were locked up in the building with those deep rugs and the dust that came up, and we never had any fresh air.

The Italians and Germans got along beautifully. I would say there was much more friction between the Italians and Italians and between the Germans and Germans—the holier-than-thou Hitlerites and the old-guard Germans. On New Year's Eve we wanted to dance. We didn't have any music, but there was a beautiful ballroom there, so we all got together and hummed waltzes and danced Viennese waltzes in a big circle. Then in came the first secretary of the German Embassy and said, "There's a war on! We'll have no dancing here!" We thought he was a big old crank. After all, they were dancing in Germany during the war. That was just ridiculous.

Of course, all the while we were there and dreaming about going to Texas, they were working on the ships to take us to Europe. In May 1942 the first ship was arranged—the Swedish ship *Drottningholm*. We went by special train from White Sulphur Springs to New York. When we arrived at the pier, there were police guards all around, holding hands so that we couldn't escape, and when we got on the ship, there were our Italian friends from Hot Springs.

Here we were, twelve hundred people, loaded on a ship that had a capacity for five hundred people. So all the young folks slept on deck. Fortunately, we had good weather; and we were the only lit ship that crossed the Atlantic—great big *Diplomat* written on the outside and lights glaring in all directions so that the submarines wouldn't catch us. When we got to Lisbon, they decided that my father had to be on the first train going to Berlin, so we only had one night in Lisbon, where other Germans had two lovely weeks there at the expense of the German government.

It was interesting how the different people in the embassy acted. Some kept saying they just couldn't get to the fatherland fast enough to serve. But when we hit Berlin, those were the first ones to try to find a way to not go into the service. It was so funny. I'd run into them on the streets in Berlin and say, "Well, what are you doing? Where's your uniform? I thought you were so anxious to get into the war." They'd all try to find a way out. It was all just big talk.

Mary Studwell was thirteen years old at the time of Pearl Harbor and living in Stamford, Connecticut.

In my junior and senior years in high school a lot of the fellows went in the service—most all the boys I went to school with. We had a USO there, but you had to be eighteen or over [to volunteer services]. I used to hear a lot of stories about what went on, but, of course, you only hear the bad ones. In fact, it wasn't very popular for the hometown girls to date sailors, because they figured you were being a bad girl or something like that. But I dated one. I knew three of them altogether—met them at church. I used to write to a lot of them. One would tell his buddy, and then his buddy would write to me. Most of them just wanted a letter from a girl, I think.

Tony Taylor, jazz impressario and a member of the Washington, D.C., Commission on the Arts and Humanities, was only twelve years old at the time of Pearl Harbor.

During those times people looked at soldiers like saviors of the world, and they got away with a lot of shit that nobody else would have gotten away with. I think there were a lot of times when they were very lax.

One thing really stands out. Where I lived, it's about a block from the railroad, and, man, we used to always see the trains come through. During the war it was the troop trains, and sometimes they would have to stop in our area. All of the families, man, like my mother and our neighbors, would always take things to give the guys. There was a very strong feeling when they saw a soldier, and he didn't have to be their son, because they are thinking like he's somebody else's son. And I think that made people come together, made people come out of their shells a little bit more, be more aware of other people. Everybody's relatives were going into the service somewhere. I lived in a predominantly black area, and on most of the troop trains that came through, you know, there were more whites than blacks. But it ain't none of that bullshit. They just went on out to the train.

You see, it takes a major disaster to make that kind of thing happen.

Richard Lingeman was a ten-year-old boy growing up in the little town of Crawfordsville, Indiana. Many years later he would write a book about the home front in America called Don't You Know There's a War On?

My father was a doctor. He was too old for the service but was quite active in community affairs that were war related, not all with a specific civil-defense organization or anything like that, because it was a small town of about ten thousand. And he took over from other doctors who went away, which was an added burden for him.

He also helped start recreation centers where young people could dance and play pinball. There was one for soldiers and navy boys in town, too. There was an ambivalent view regarding servicemen. I remember having Sunday dinner for a soldier. It was a great thing, and we would do that for navy boys, too. At the same time there was a dislike of the servicemen, especially among the high school boys, because they were taking away the girls. I remember, as we were walking along, a friend and I saw some sailors. They were called turtles because they didn't go to sea, and we said, "Hello, turtle, you land-going sailor." My friend was much younger than the sailor, and the sailor was very angry. He said, "If you were half my size, I'd knock you down," and my friend said, "It's too bad I'm not half your size." I think there were probably some fights, too. The sailors had a sort of risqué image, anyway, and the girls who went out with them were looked on as sort of bad girls. These were college boys—V-12 students at Wabash College—who would probably go out as officers. It was a small town, and they were sort of foreigners. At the same time people would have them over for dinner.

The war would often enter into our games. I had a lot of war toys, toy soldiers from England—Dinky Toys they were called—and they were really good representations of tanks, personnel carriers, and everything. They were considered the status-symbol toy to have. And there was a sense of hero-worshiping the boys in the service, especially my cousins who were in.

I remember taking paper to the local junkman and scrap metal, too. My brother and I would put it in a wagon and take it there. There were campaigns at school, too.

My mother was not much of a participant of community groups, but she did join the Motor Corps, driving a car around, learning how to change a tire; ferrying people to give blood donations was one of the main projects they had. I think the community was pretty much in support of the war, but there were certainly isolationists there. And there was dislike of Roosevelt and criticism of the way the war was being run. Even in Sunday-school class there was talk about Roosevelt being a Jew, this sort of thing—pretty far out.

Netei Degen was a fifteen-year-old girl living in Malden, Massachusetts, a suburb of Boston.

I was a plane spotter at the local school, where I spent every Saturday morning with a telephone that never rang and with maps that were never used. After the first year I began to look on it as a bit of a joke.

At that time I met a lot of young people who were in the navy, and that was a very interesting part of my young life. There was a great sense of danger and a great sense of romance in the immediacy of the moment, the kind of thing that ensues from a wartime climate. I remember having a tremendous number of dates with young men from all over the country. It was interesting and exciting, if you could put that apart from the actual war, which was far away.

My mother's family was in Lithuania. She did manage to get one brother to Canada a year before the war, but the rest of them—six or seven sisters and brothers—were all lost in concentration camps during the war. They had been communicating up until 1939, but after that no word was ever heard from them again. We lived with that very big worry in the life of our parents.

The radio was the main line of communication. We listened every night. Radio had a much greater impact on our lives than TV does today. You were removed from having to contend with the faces and interpretations that are forced upon you by TV. They gave you the news, and so much of it was imagery for yourself to develop. I think TV has taken away, what shall I say, a good bit of the thought process that should go into interpreting the news yourself.

In school I remember we would collect things for the war effort. People would bring in melted-down fat. They would bring in tin and aluminum for recycling. Even things I don't know what in the world for—paper and string. People were simply into recycling, making do, and being careful of things generally.

We also used to go every week and visit young men in the hospital who were seriously wounded. That was very sobering.

Sally Lucke remembers the things she did for the war effort in Columbus, Ohio—and how it affected her attitude toward the Japanese.

I spent all my waking hours outside of school collecting tires and organizing the whole neighborhood for collection of scrap materials, and my parents very kindly put up with all the miscellaneous objects in our garage for quite some time. I don't know whatever happened to all these objects, but we certainly had the spirit. Also, we collected all kinds of magazines and books for the Red Cross. The only real awareness of the war was in blackout curtains.

My feelings for the Japanese people had been very loving. We had had Japanese houseboys in my father's family, and after Pearl Harbor it seemed like we had been attacked by people that I considered friends. Then they became a frightening image. It helped me in exploring psychologically the Japanese character structure, and I spent quite a bit of time and effort doing that.

We had had one Japanese houseboy before the war named Kay, who loved to take his camera all over the United States, and we often wondered if he could have been a spy and if he was as friendly toward our family as he appeared to be. We have no way of knowing whether he was a spy. He went back to Japan, and we only heard from him once, so I still have doubts. I think the war made me want to understand how a people could be so sensitive in their art and culture and still commit atrocities.

Erwin Hargrove is director of the Institute of Policy Studies at Vanderbilt University and the author of The Power of the Modern Presidency. *At the time of Pearl Harbor he was nine years old and living in Saint Joseph, Missouri.*

I got the idea that people might get conscripted to work in war production of various kinds and that I might have to go off and be separated from my family. My mother had died about three years before; I had a stepmother, and I was very concerned about losing my family. But it took the war to project that into a kind of anxiety about the family being broken up. This was in Missouri, the middle of the country; the thought of the enemy coming never bothered anybody. I had no immediate concern about my father going to war. He was in his early forties at the time, and I had no brothers or sisters.

We had a Victory garden that almost killed my parents. I can remember to this day my father out there on a summer evening in the dusk, staying to the very last minute. He had to do everything after work, and he was working himself to death on this big, stupid garden. My father also ran the USO in Saint Joe. He found a building, leased it, and hired a director. There was a man who had sold suits in a clothing store for years in Saint Joe, kind of a smart fellow, and Dad hired him to be the director. That man told Dad later that those were the greatest years of his life. That made some real contribution. Selling pants and suits was not very rewarding work.

I remember knitting squares. I think, maybe, they were used to make blankets. I don't know whether they were for soldiers or refugees or Bundles for Britain, but I remember learning to do that, and it was a big deal. All the boys were learning to knit. But the thing I remember most vividly was getting out of school to go on scrap drives. That was the thing that was the most fun. You would take the wagon and go pick up scrap—old newspapers and things like that.

The war was really fun for a boy. We used to follow it in the paper and the newsreels and on the radio. I remember Lowell Thomas. We followed the movement of the troops and all the war movies. My God, the number of John Wayne movies I must have seen. You see, it was fun in the sense that there was just so much raw material for an adolescent to fantasize about.

The war brought Eleanor Neuland romance; a husband, Edward Kuhne; and a new way of life.

In 1941 and 1942, I was living with my father and mother in Glover Park in Washington, D.C. I was working as secretary to the vice-president of the gas company.

A lot of my friends and acquaintances had gone into military training. My parents became very active in feeding and housing problems under civil defense. They helped form a unit with the neighbors to list available emergency sleeping spaces and arranged for using the basement of an apartment nearby for a feeding center. Everyone contributed coffee, canned goods, coffee urns, and other equipment.

I remember we had meetings of the first aid group from my office in our recreation room. Once we were all practicing artificial respiration, lying face down with some of us straddling others, when my father came downstairs and said: "What's going on down here?"

I did not have a serious boyfriend at the time. I was kind of between romances. A friend of mine in the office was going with a boy named Mickey, a marine at Quantico. That was how I met my husband. She would meet Mickey at Quantico on alternate weekends when he couldn't get leave to come to Washington. She asked me if I would like to go down with her one Sunday. Her friend knew me, and he would get me a date. Of course, this was very easy to do at the marine base. They met us at the train. We went across the parade ground to the Hostess House, where they served food and drinks and the servicemen could take guests. When the four of us went in, there were two Marines sitting across the room, and one was definitely my type. Mickey said, "Hi, Ed." So I whispered to Marie, my friend, "Let's sit with them." There was no reason for us to sit there since there were plenty of empty tables, but she whispered to Mickey, "Eleanor says let's sit with them." So he took us over and introduced us. I sat right down next to Ed as fast as I could and started talking to him and he to me. The boy I was supposed to be with finally got up and left. It wasn't very nice of me treating him that way, but we had nothing in common anyway. Anyhow, poor Ed was not financially prepared for an unexpected date but he didn't seem to mind too much; he borrowed some money and we went on from there.

We spent the rest of the day together, and he kept saying, "I'm snowed, I am." At that time I was not bad looking. I had golden-red hair and I was dressed in a matching "Eleanor" blue dress and coat, and a white flower hat. He was taken with me. He put me on the train at midnight, but we had been talking so much that he had forgotten to ask for my phone number until the last minute, as the train was pulling in. So I wrote it down quickly, with the paper against a rough brick wall. He put it in his pocket without looking at it. The next day, he was going to call me, and when he got the paper out he couldn't read it. He called what he thought the number was. It was the wrong number.

I waited for him to call for three days, and all this time we each thought the other had been handing out a line, so we both were very depressed. Mickey finally talked to Marie about what Eleanor had done to Ed, and she straightened things out. Ed called me, and everything was lovely from then on.

We had only about five or six dates before he had to go overseas. We were very much in love, but I knew that Mother and Daddy wouldn't have any part of me getting married when he was on his way overseas.

He was away thirteen months, in the Ellice Islands. They were without adequate supplies and the food was very poor. Ed was a big fellow—six feet and heavy chested. He went from about 250 down to 165 pounds.

I signed up to be a lady Marine while he was overseas the first time. I took the aptitude test, passed, and went down to be sworn in. There I was in my mink scarf and high-heeled shoes, and the man said, "Are you sure you want to do this?" I said, "Yes, I am sure." So I was sworn in, which meant I would have to go into training camp. I barely got home when there was a letter from Ed's buddy saying that I might get a big surprise. Of course, I knew that meant that Ed was on his way home. I had to get out of the marines as fast as I could. My uncle knew somebody who knew somebody, and they finally got me out of it. I hadn't actually gone to boot camp, or I never would have been released. I was in the marines for three days.

When Ed came home, he was assigned to San Diego as an instructor in communications. We were married there in the marine base chapel by the Catholic chaplain. Ed was not a Catholic at that time, but he had arranged everything. I was so blithe. At that time, I wasn't afraid of anything. But when the time came to get married, I began to shake. I had little curls on the back of my head, and my mother said they were going like steel springs. The more scared I got, the calmer Ed got. He took my hand and steadied me, and we made it through the ceremony.

Things seemed so unreal then. San Diego had camouflage over all the streets. There was artificial foliage on nets. From an airplane you were not supposed to be able to tell that there was any city there. It was very strange to drive along under all that camouflage, as if you were under seaweed and water.

Ed was there for ten months. When he went overseas, I didn't have any social life. I just wrote letters. I didn't mess around. If I had been younger, I might have been tempted to, but I was twenty-eight years old—I had gone with a lot of different boys, and had found the one I wanted. But many of the other girls, with their husbands overseas, did mess around. People react differently to war. Sometimes they can't adjust to it, that's all.

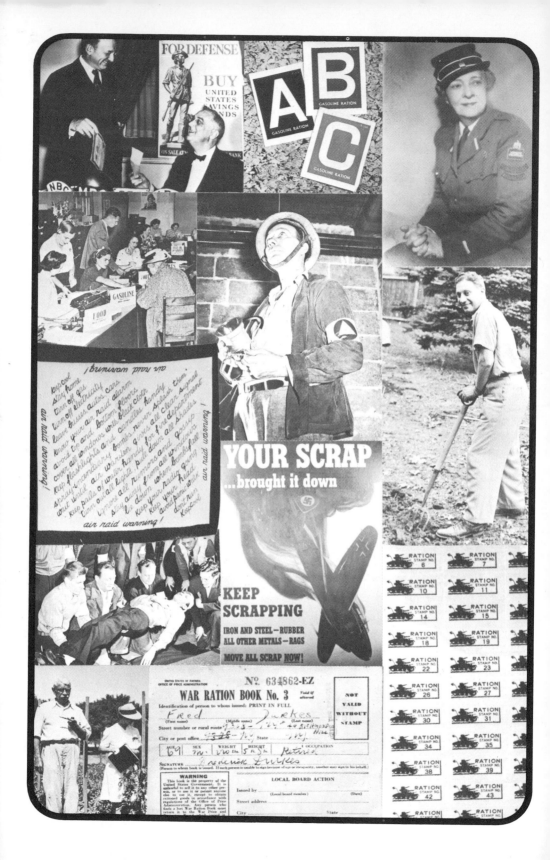

8

THE HOME FRONT

With the Atlantic Ocean between us and Germany and the Pacific Ocean separating us from Japan, America was never in any real danger during the war. But we could not be sure. The civil defense units organized as if attack were imminent. Elaborate systems for spotting enemy planes were developed. Coastlines and big cities were blacked out and coastal waters were watched for enemy ships and submarines, which we knew were out there from the number of ships that were sunk off our coasts. And although Americans may not have had it as rough as they did in France, England, and Russia, where battles were fought and bombs dropped, we had our hardships. There were shortages of almost everything—food, clothing, houses, gasoline, tires, and services. This led to rationing—and consequently black markets. And every backyard, vacant lot—and occasionally even window boxes—had a victory garden. Some people remember life during the war as being hard and unpleasant but something we had to put up with "for the duration." Others recall their tribulations as something of a joke. But almost everyone I talked to had vivid recollections of the home front, which, in itself, is significant.

Ann Hoskins in Lakeville, Connecticut:

I was always writing letters to the government, because I got very teed off about a lot of things—including the observation posts. They were absolutely ridiculous. We'd get up at dawn to go on down there, and we'd do our level best, but Stewart was hard of hearing, I was nearsighted, and between us it was the best of luck that we would recognize a plane, whether it was his, hers, or ours. The dear woman who took over after us in the morning was eighty-six years old. She couldn't read a menu her eyesight was so poor. They made no attempt to screen or train people. They would show them charts and that was it. It annoyed me. I wanted to help, but I didn't want to help just because somebody thought it was good for me to help. So I wrote to the government and said, "If this is as important as you say, why don't you train a few people to come into these towns and pick people who have all their faculties, their hearing and sight and everything else? Train the young ones. They're gung ho on planes, and they know them already." I got back a stiff little form letter saying that it was very important.

We had air-raid wardens who were very strict. Boy, they never missed a trick. If we were at a town meeting or something and the siren suddenly went off, which meant a blackout, we would race home, because the kids would be alone. Right next door to the house was the church that rang its bells when there was a blackout alarm. The bells made a heck of a noise, and we were afraid that they might be afraid, so we would drop everything and run back to the kids. Usually, they would sleep right through it. But those things were part of the war.

Alida Pierce was working as a secretary in the chamber of commerce in Dunkirk, New York. She lives now in Bradenton, Florida, and when I interviewed her there, she had a scrapbook from the war years, which included copies of letters she had received while she was with the rationing board.

Almost immediately, we were involved in administering the rationing program. A chairman was appointed, and we organized committees, made up mostly of businessmen in town and chamber-of-commerce members. Soon we were swamped and had to take over larger headquarters because we had thousands of volunteers working for us. Whole plants, their office staff, would come in for an evening. We interviewed people almost every night of the week on fuel oil, foods, or shoes, or whatever was being rationed at the time.

Of course, our board had a soft heart for the boys from the service, and sometimes they managed to get extra stamps. One of the most interesting cases involved a full-blooded Indian from Oklahoma who came every summer to sell perfumes and this type of thing. He told our board that he would have to go back to Oklahoma as a permanent move. After quite a little discussion, we decided that he was honest and gave him a lot of gasoline stamps to get to Oklahoma. He got all these stamps, let's say on a Friday, and on Monday he came back with them. He'd gotten as far as Cleveland, and the snow was so bad that he had to come back, and he returned all the stamps.

Rationing and its supposed hardships made up a lot of the conversation. You would hear this sort of thing: "Thirty-five cents for that little basket of grapes? Ridiculous! They were grown right here in Fredonia, weren't they?" Or, "My neighbor just *drove* to New York, all that way. *Where* did he get the gas?" And, "I thought they were checking on prices, but my wife paid $1.86 for three dozen of eggs. Who's checking?"

And so, on and on. Let me read you a couple of the letters I used to get. I think you will enjoy them. I had a few of them reprinted for a speech I used to give to Rotary clubs and places like that.

Here's a letter and bill from an indignant farmer who suffered a loss because his request for fuel oil was delayed two days:

Dear Miss_____

We received no certificate so we could buy kerosene for a stove to warm a house in which to keep little pigs. The pigs were born last night; they are all dead. Enclosed you will find a bill to cover the loss. We hope and pray you may influence the board to grant us our request for kerosene to keep the house warm for the other sow who will have her pigs during that week.

We are sorry your board was delayed in their acting on this, for it means eight pigs that will not be raised to help win the war. Please act as soon as possible.

Yours truly,

Rationing Board
Dunkirk, New York
To: Mr. _____

8 pigs	at	$7.50	$60.00
$7.50 is the price these would have sold for when old enough.			
		Balance due	$60.00

And what would you have done if you were a board member and received this letter:

Dear Sirs:

This morning a card came to my home stating that my husband may have booklets for more gasoline. I want you to know the truth. My husband does not need more gasoline. He takes the bus to work on his day shift. When he works nights, he uses the car only three times a week; on Tuesdays and Thursdays he drills at the armory and works days. You can figure out for yourself if three gallons a week is enough for twelve miles. The reason why he needs more gasoline is for pleasure. He likes to go out with women. I'm sorry to tell you this, but I'm sure you will help from breaking my home. You can come to my home any time and talk to me personally. I am keeping the card. If he appears before the board, you can show him this letter. He will tell you I'm crazy.

Sincerely,

Mrs. _____

P.S. I will probably get a beating for this, but it's the God's truth.

One lady even sent us a poem:

I can't send my husband to market—He'll order some meat for
    a stew,
And then when the points are requested, insist they be torn
    from the blue.
Or if it's canned soup he has chosen, or pineapple, ketchup,
    whatnot,
He'll count up the number of red ones he plans to give up for
    the lot.
He'll pick up the greatest collection of vegies, in big cans
    and small,
Although I've repeatedly told him the fresh ones aren't
    rationed at all.
And when from those rules he's untangled and able to just
    muddle through,
He's likely to offer some coupons from strips which have not
    yet come due.
I carefully list all the items, essential we need to replace,
And then he buys plenty of extras he wants to have handy "in
    case."

I can't send my husband to market—he worries me into a huff,
For when he adds points up correctly, he never has money enough.
So now we've a frank understanding; he's "sorry" (the wily
    old elf)
He stays home and plays with the children, while I pull the
    boners myself.

We were very fortunate, perhaps, in the type of men we had on our board. They were so dedicated—in winter, summer, or the worst weather, they would show up every night for our board meetings, which lasted many times till twelve or one o'clock in the morning. And most people were really behind us.

It took a lot of planning, too, to arrange for as many volunteers as you had to have to get out a notice that a new book was coming out. They tried to keep shoe rationing secret, so we had to rush at the last minute to get the volunteers to get the stamps out to people. We had also a large commissary there that supplied something like thirty thousand meals a day to industries in Buffalo, and we would have to see that they got their stamps for supplies promptly, because it was important that the men in the plants be fed.

The stamps had to be kept under lock and key all the time. But we were very fortunate in that people could be trusted. I had just one case, a little girl who hadn't worked long in the office. Her husband or boyfriend was home from the service, and she finagled somehow to get tires and stamps for him. Of course, I had to let her go. Too bad. If it had been necessary, the board probably would have given the boy enough of whatever he needed.

From Alida Pierce's scrapbooks, here are the Eleven Commandments of Rationing:

1. Don't try to buy rationed goods with loose stamps.
2. Don't lend your ration book to a friend.
3. Don't swap ration coupons.
4. Don't give your unused stamps to your dealer.
5. Don't try to buy rationed goods without coupons.
6. Don't try to use ration stamps after they have expired.
7. Don't try to use a ration book that doesn't belong to you or that should have been returned to the board.

8. Don't use a ration book that is a duplicate of one you already own in your own name.

9. Don't pay over top legal prices.

10. Don't let any dealer make you buy something you don't want to get something you do want.

11. Don't use your gasoline rations for anything except the purpose for which intended.

Evelyn Keyes in Hollywood:

America didn't suffer at all during the war. We went on rationing—of what? I had plenty of gasoline. So I kept the same car during the war. Big deal. We had coupons. You can't get around California without a car, so I suppose California got more.

Amy Bess Miller is the director of the Shaker Village in Hancock, Massachusetts.

I was really apprehensive that the Japanese would infiltrate, perhaps not get as far as Pittsfield, but certainly into California. There was fear of bombing, so we blacked out every single night.

We had to be careful of food, so I plunged into working on a war garden. We had more than an acre under cultivation at our house; we supplied five families, plus ourselves, plus providing space for other people to have gardens, plus growing a lot of material to be sent up to Canada to be canned. Then we sold our surplus, and during the summer the children had a little store on the street to sell eggs, honey, and all kinds of things. That was the first project, to be able to feed people.

Freezing was in its infancy then—but we managed to get hold of an ice-cream freezer, and whenever the power went out, as it did often, it seems to me, we'd have to bicycle up and get dry ice, because our gas was rationed. You should have seen us biking with a huge parcel of dry ice and trying to see over it! And transportation was funny. Sometimes the buses didn't run.

We had guaranteed to supply fourteen acres of carrots, beets, and beans to the Canadian government. They were going to send flatcars for them and can them up there. The vegetables were just in marvelous shape, all ready to be called for on the first day of September—and we had a killing frost on August 26! The beans were ruined and the beet tops and carrot tops. The following business day, we got a letter from the Canadian government saying, "Sorry, we can't send our flatcars." What were we going to do with fourteen acres of produce?

We thought it was a crime to deprive anyone of all that food, so we got in touch with hospitals and that sort of thing, and they said they'd buy it at cost. So we didn't have to plow it all under; just what had really been damaged.

The morale and attitudes of the people in Pittsfield were just marvelous. We're considered to be overorganized, anyway. Even before the European war was announced, my husband, Pete, went to Fort Devans because he was sure there was going to be conscription; he thought they would take volunteers, and he wanted to be one of the first. After he got there, he found he couldn't wear a gas mask—they were still thinking in terms of gas masks—because he had this terrible asthma. He was in the infirmary most of the time, though he did manage to fill out his two months. Then they said to him, "We'll give you a job in Washington or someplace. In the army you'd be a liability! The enemy would hear you coming for miles, the way you're sneezing."

After the war started, I joined a group to sell war bonds. We had our monthly quotas, and if I found that the business sector was not meeting its quota, I'd try to prime it. At one of the meetings, I'd have a banker stand up and say, "I want five thousand dollars worth of bonds." And the businessmen would, hopefully, follow suit. A good meeting would produce five or six thousand dollars, and we'd have something like six meetings a year.

During the war I think everybody ate better and fared better, because the emphasis was on keeping the home front healthy, not being a drag. I don't see how the doctors managed, so many had to go to war. That's why they taught us preventive medicine. If a neighbor was sick, you went right over to see what you could do about it so she wouldn't have to call a doctor. There were a lot of babies born at home.

The most dramatic thing about the war was D day. The office in Washington got in touch with me to say that when it was known that we had landed, they wanted me to notify the clergy—all the churches in Pittsfield. They thought people would want to go to the churches and pray for success and pray for the lives of the boys on the front. The call from Washington came late at night. I called our minister, Mr. Hayden, who had agreed to notify all the others, and at 5:00 A.M. all the church bells rang.

Anna Mae Lindberg in Pittsburgh:

I suppose there was some cheating on rationing. We had a neighborhood butcher we had been dealing with as many years as I could remember. Somehow or other, every now and then, he'd forget to collect the red stamps for beef, and so we were able to get more meat than what was really allowed on the ration allotment. Now as I look back on this, I don't think I feel any guilt whatsoever. I didn't know whether other people could do this or not—it was the kind of thing you really didn't talk about. We didn't want the butcher to get in trouble.

Paul Kneeland, a reporter for the Boston Globe:

I did a series of six articles on black-marketing in various fields. The mechanics of black-marketing were no different then than they are today. Seller A wants to get a good price for some beef or nylons—wants to get more than the going price. Remember, we had price controls then, and you couldn't get more than x cents for a pound of butter or x dollars for a pair of nylons. Buyer B wants the scarce item—butter, beef, nylons, whatever—enough to pay two or three times the controlled price for it. The distribution is usually done privately, not in an open store, and you hear about it word of mouth.

With rationing it was a common sight to see people waiting outside the stores where they had scarce products for sale. Butter was a scarce commodity, and the word was quickly passed from person to person: "Come down to Cowles' Grocery; they have butter!" Immediately there'd be a line of shoppers who'd come from out of nowhere—sixty, seventy-five, or one hundred people—with their ration coupons, waiting for an opportunity to buy a pound of butter. I was in those lines many times.

Something I'll always remember about the war were the air raids in Medford and how strictly they were enforced. There was no such thing as not pulling down shades or not dousing lights. At the time, we had streetcars running, and there was a tie-up on the streetcar line one night—nothing to do with the blackout. Six or seven streetcars were stalled, automobiles were honking their horns, flashing their lights. And the air-raid warning sounded. I had a press card, so I was allowed on the streets. Immediately all the streetcars on the line turned out their lights. All the automobiles, maybe 150 on Main Street, turned out their lights, and there was total silence for half an hour, no one getting out of their cars. It was as though they expected that within ten minutes a bomb was going to drop.

I remember when there was a false air-raid alarm in New England and we were listening to the radio. My mother was in tears; my aunt, shivering under the dining room table in our house, said, "I hope if it hits, it hits us direct." We were never in danger, but the fear was there.

Lillie Bernstein, who is now eighty-nine, had four sons in the service, and she knew what her duty was.

I was born and raised in Chicago, and I'm in the Hall of Fame in Chicago for sixty-four years of community service. During the First World War, I remember my next-door neighbors were a senator and his wife whose son was killed in action. That was supposed to be a war to end all wars. She would talk to me about it frequently, and I said, "Thank goodness, when my boys grow up, there won't be war anymore." I had four boys, and I never dreamed that they would all be in the Second World War, but they were.

At the time of Pearl Harbor my sons were thirty-one, twenty-nine, twenty-seven, and nineteen. They all went into the service, and they were in every spot that you could think of. My youngest son was in the third contingent to land in Europe. My second son, a civil engineer, was a lieutenant commander in the Navy Seabees. They sent him first to the Aleutian Islands. My next son, Sheldon, was a special assistant to the attorney general of the United States when he enlisted. My oldest son had already gone overseas, and so I said, "Three of you are gone already; you're the fourth. It wouldn't be so terrible if you didn't go." But he went anyway. He thought any day they were going to send him overseas, but they never did.

I was on the management committees in the Chicago USO and of the Jewish Welfare Board. I'd start out early in the morning and wouldn't get home until midnight every blessed day of the week. I worked day in and day out. My husband would meet all the trains that the boys came in on, and I would work at the USO. You know, Chicago was called the serviceman's city. They got everything free; they didn't pay on buses or streetcars. They could go to any show or any restaurant in Chicago if they'd just come and ask me. A number of them would say—it seemed to me that nine out of ten were from Brooklyn or New York—"What can we do to repay you?" And I'd say, "One thing you can do. When you get back home, you can tell your parents that everybody west of New York isn't an Indian." Sunday they would come in, and we'd give them lox and bagels and cream cheese. That got to be a standard breakfast in all the USOs all over the world. It started in the city of Chicago. They all liked it—the Irish boys, the other boys, we had all kinds. They're all God's children, the white and the black and all of them.

I didn't realize how weak we were until I went to England—we'd cry if we couldn't get an extra piece of butter. We're so spoiled; we're so used in this country to having everything, we take everything for granted. When I went to England, I saw everybody getting along on practically nothing, and nobody was complaining. That was immediately after the war, and they were still being rationed. One piece of meat a week per family—they could make it go so far—and one egg a week, and here we were crying because we couldn't get a little piece of butter or something else.

But I don't know, there's something in the American spirit that when the need is there, they all come and get together and do something about it.

The only tape that was broken in the course of this project was the one of an interview with Alice and Daniel Rosenbaum of Tampa, Florida. It was unfortunate. The Rosenbaums, who owned and operated a fruit-canning plant that did a lot of business with the armed forces, had a vivid recollection of the war years. But I was not able to return to Florida to repeat the interview. However, I could not forget this story:

We had a cousin—he was about fifty-five years old—who was in the Civil Air Patrol. He flew one of those little Piper Cubs, and his duty was to fly at low altitude up and down the coast off Palm Beach and look for German submarines. If he sighted one, he was supposed to radio the Coast Guard. One day he sighted a submarine surfacing, and he circled around and swooped down to identify it—and it fired at his plane. It was a German sub. He was so badly damaged that he was forced to return to his airfield in Palm Beach—thus becoming, perhaps, the only

American plane in history to be downed by enemy action in the continental United States.

Herbert Collins is assistant curator of the Smithsonian Institution, and at the time of Pearl Harbor he was a nine-year-old boy in Bowling Green, Virginia. My interview with Herb Collins took place in his suburban home in northern Virginia. It began with him showing me his collection of souvenirs and mementos saved from the war years.

I was in the fourth grade in 1942, and we would all buy war bonds and war stamps to support the cause. When you filled a 25-cent-defense-stamp album, you'd turn it in and get a $25 war bond. I think it cost $18.75 at the time you bought it. The school-bus driver would take orders from the children who wanted to buy war savings stamps, then go to the post office up in Bowling Green, get our stamps, and bring them back to us the next day. He did that to encourage the school-children to buy war savings stamps.

This pledge on the stamp book says: "To every soldier, sailor, and marine who is fighting for my country. For you there can be no rest, for me there should be no vacation from the part I can play to help you win the war. I therefore solemnly promise to continue to buy United States War Savings Stamps and Bonds to the limit of my ability throughout my summer vacation and until our victory is won." It is signed Herbert Ridgeway Collins and witnessed by Cora V. Kay, my fourth-grade teacher, May 29, 1942. At one time I had it in a little frame on the wall.

Then there were war ration books. You had all kinds of rationing— meat, sugar, gasoline. I remember going down to my great-aunt's, and she would say: "You should bring us a sugar stamp." It was very embarrassing to visit more than once or twice and not take a sugar stamp. I also remember going into restaurants, and they'd have signs up that said, "Use little sugar and stir like hell. We don't mind the noise."

Different-color stamps stood for different products that you bought. If you didn't use the whole stamp, you got back little red tokens and little blue tokens, depending on what type stamp you used. Each member of the family had a ration book.

There were different gas allowances for pleasure driving, business driving, and farm use. They put little tablets in farm gas to color it, and if anybody caught you driving an automobile with gas that was colored, you were fined right heavy for it. That was really enforced, and I think people forget that worked well.

During the war a lot of people had this little button. It showed Uncle Sam, and when you pulled a string, Uncle Sam pulled Hitler up on a tree limb and hanged him. The slogan was: "Let's pull together." You'd wear it on your lapel like a campaign button.

One thing we looked forward to when the boys came back home was that they would bring some souvenirs of foreign money. I was given some Japanese occupational money, and some money from the Philippines, and that started me collecting foreign money.

Newton Tolman in New Hampshire:

We had this one fellow who had a row with the mailman shortly after gas rationing came in, and he said, "Don't bring the mail. I will get it in Marlboro." So he got extra gas rations from our friends down there in Keene, and for the entire war he would drive, not once a day, but usually two or three times, twenty miles to get his mail at the post office because he didn't like the RFD fella. While everybody else was breaking their asses really living up to it and using as little gas as possible, he's going twice a day at least twenty miles to get his mail because he doesn't like the mail carrier. But he was telling everybody, "I'm all for the war!"

Everything was regulated by the government to some extent. The county seat, Keene, was the center of distribution, so that's where everything went that we raised—to the market there to help the war effort. At the market where all the mill owners and the wealthy people and everybody else dropped off their things, here were these guys making a million dollars selling black-market beef. People were really cashing in on the war. Everybody was for big, fat wages and everything, except for the poor buggers who were out there getting killed. I never bothered with the black-market beef. I'd go out and shoot a deer every year and use that; but the black market, no.

I was interested in the State Guard, because I knew a lot of these young kids who had never gone through the sixth grade, and I thought, "Jesus, they'll get drafted, and they don't know how to kill or drill; they don't know nothing." So I went all over the area, not only in my town, telling the young kids to get into the State Guard. They'd say, "What for? And I'd say, "Well, you're going to get drafted. Don't you know there's a war on?" Well, I talked a lot of them into it. A fellow who was here this morning got into the marines; he has only one eye now. He had a terrible time, but he made out. If he hadn't had this State Guard pre-liminary training, he wouldn't have. These guys could hardly read or write or anything, but they learned to drill, they learned the routine, principally the phony part of it, the military, but you have to learn it. Once a week we'd have encampments, and then we'd go out three or four nights and have sham battles in the woods and that kind of stuff. All the officers got drunk as hell. These kids remember that training to this day. I saw one yesterday who I hadn't seen in about fifteen years. He said, "You know, you saved my life with that State Guard thing."

Merlo Pusey in Washington, D.C.:

The thing that hurt us most, of course, was the gasoline shortage. I remember one occasion I spent two and one-half hours in a line trying to get to the service station. I got about two cars from the pump, when a fight broke out in the service station, and they closed it down. It took almost every bit of gas I had to get up to the pump, and then I didn't get any. There were some distressing things of that sort. The chief difficulty was you couldn't go anywhere. You had to vacation in West Virginia or someplace like that if you got any vacation at all. But there weren't any great hardships.

Martha Wood lived in Raleigh, North Carolina, with her husband, who was then a professor at North Carolina State College. Her present home is in Bradenton, Florida.

We were restricted socially. I remember that we had a LaSalle sedan, and because of gas rationing we sold it. Dr. Wood rode a bicycle to N.C. State, and I was working within six blocks of our home, so I just walked.

We formed a neighborhood Victory garden, plowed up the backyards of three houses, and planted beans, corn, tomatoes, okra, squash, and all the things we could use. When the crop came in, the two wives who were not working used a pressure cooker and canned all day. I'd come home at five o'clock, fix my evening meal, and then I was given the pressure cooker. So I was canning until midnight and later, night after night, and I frequently said, "I wish I had Hitler in that pressure cooker."

We raised chickens in our yard, too, for the three families. At noon it was my duty to walk home and make the warm mash to feed the chickens. We didn't have home freezers at that time. We had a community freezer, and on Saturdays, when the men would kill the chickens, we'd help pick them and clean them; then they'd take them to the freezer. These three families shared everything.

My husband plowed, because his classes would be over early, and the other two men who were working for private industry didn't get home until late in the afternoon. So he was the chief farmer.

The morale was real high in Raleigh. Rationing was hard to live with, particularly silk stockings. I can remember that if you had a run in your stocking, you took a needle and thread and worked it back up, because there was no chance of getting any. One time at a Lion's Club meeting I won a pair of hose, and I remember what a great surprise it was. But, you know, you just learned to live without lots of things. We started drinking coffee black; we didn't have children, so I never was a cookie and cake baker. It was a long struggle, and it was awfully tiresome at times because of the six days' work a week and gardening and the fact that we didn't have a car. Occasionally Dr. Wood and I would make a trip to Birmingham to visit our parents, and the trains then were miserable—the accommodations were so poor because they had pulled off all their good equipment. There was no such thing as a Pullman; you sat up all night, and sometimes you were full of cinders and soot because there was no air conditioning.

We took vacations when we could down on the coast of North Carolina. The family we stayed with had to black out the house at night. We ate our supper by daylight and didn't even turn on a light at night. German submarines had been spotted within sight of that house. Of course, the area was always patrolled by the Coast Guard, and it was an eerie feeling. Everybody was suspicious of everybody else. My husband would walk at night to a little grocery store at the crossroads to hear the news on the radio, and until they knew that we were from Raleigh and that he was a professor, the men in the grocery store were a little apprehensive, because we were strangers.

You would work for months and months and have a dismal feeling that, "This thing's never going to end, and I'm getting tired." At times it just seemed hopeless. Then you'd have a ray of hope when something good came through.

James M. Cain in Hollywood:

I remember there was rationing—I lived on turkey and chicken because there was no ration of those things. When I was writing a script for the Signal Corps, a technical advisor, a Colonel Lawson, was assigned to me. And he got very upset and indignant that I, working on a war story, didn't have more gas-ration tickets. He took a whole sheet of these things and handed it to me, and after that I had all the gas that we could possibly need. I was still using that sheet of ration tickets, in addition to my regular rationing, until the end of the war.

Alice Newcomer Baker, a student at George Washington University, spent a summer in Orlando, Florida, and another in upstate New York.

As a student, the war didn't really make much of an impression. But it had a lot of impact when I went home to Winter Park, Florida, where I lived with an aunt and uncle because my parents were in South America. We were near Orlando, Florida—a huge air base.

My aunt was a very energetic sort of person who started a community center for soldiers. I remember the wonderful dances and the slot machines. The ones in the officers' club paid off at such a wonderful rate, so I wanted to be there playing slot machines and going to the dances, and my aunt wanted me to be at the community center for the enlisted men. We kind of compromised on that—I was at her place sometimes and sometimes where I wanted to be.

One summer, in Delaware County, New York, my aunt was involved in the American Women's Voluntary Service, the AWVS. The national chairman of that organization was a very rich woman who had set up an organization to do war work of various kinds. One of her plans was to organize a women's land army! Somehow or another, I, the genius student who didn't want to join the women's army because I thought my brain would be wasted, was dragged up to Delaware County and plunked down in a victory garden. She put a bunch of us into a house that she had bought. I suppose her idea was that we were going to be a pilot program. We had one cow, but none of us had any idea how to milk a cow except this nurse, who had milked a cow as a child. Her nursing training obviously had overtaken her childhood training on the farm and she carefully sterilized the cow's teats before she milked them. And the poor cow got so chapped and it was so painful that she kept trying to kick this woman.

Americans Remember the Home Front

Jack Altshul, city editor of Newsday:

Miss [Alicia] Patterson decided it was time that *Newsday* grow its own Victory garden. Assigned to the job were two staff photographers who knew nothing about gardening, which was the idea of the whole thing. Herman Klappert and Jim Martenhoff were to go out like Mr. Average Nassau, buy seeds, plant them in a small plot, and watch the tomatoes, corn, radishes, and cucumbers grow. They were to photograph the progress, and the end result would appear in a weekly page of how-to-do-it pictures.

The idea was a wonderful one, and one ghastly incident would have been averted if the war had not worn the photography department so thin. Since Klappert and Martenhoff had been allowed to work on their garden on office time, there wasn't a photographer in the office one noontime when Harold Davis got a call from Miss Patterson that she was the guest of the president of Arnold Constable at a country-club luncheon and wanted a camerman to record the event.

Davis got Klappert at his home, the backyard of which was *Newsday*'s Victory garden. He told him to drop everything and shoot over with Martenhoff to get a group of pictures at the luncheon. Klappert tried to explain it would take some time, because both were dressed in dirty flannel shirts, jeans, rubber boots, and chicken manure. The managing editor had no time for argument. "Get over right away or else," he screamed through the phone.

They looked at each other. "I will if you will." Off they went to the country-club luncheon, following instructions about not bothering to change.

They walked solemnly into the impeccable grill of the club and up to the U-shaped table, at the head of which sat Alicia Patterson and Isaac Lieberman, whose department store had recently signed *Newsday*'s biggest advertising contract.

Noses wrinkled and heads turned away as the photographers wended down opposite sides of the table to the head table. Miss Patterson blanched as she saw her men, but remained poised, though cold. When the photographers finished taking the pictures, Mr. Lieberman turned to her with obvious distaste and asked,

"Who were those men?"

"I never saw them before in my life," Miss Patterson replied, deadpan.

All of us had to worry about getting enough gas to get to work, and photographers had a tougher time than most, because they had to cover the whole of Long Island. I think they got what was called a B-coupon, which wasn't essential for the war. So all of a sudden you found yourself standing in line for things. After a year or two, you'd find black-market gas stations, and some people took advantage of it—also black-market tires, black-market food stamps.

I remember one thing that shocked the hell out of us, and the paper made a big crusade out of it. Some socialite in Garden City was marrying off her daughter. She was marrying a Philadelphia boy, a mainliner, society people. One of our society reporters who was covering the wedding called the managing editor and said there were an awful lot of big limousines from Philadelphia over there, and where did they get the gas to come to this wedding? This wasn't a military wedding. We looked into it, and it turned out that, sure enough, the father of the bride had influence, and he was able to get gas stamps. This was the kind of story newspapers kept their eyes open for.

Hathway got on the phone to Augustus Weller, Nassau's rationing chief. What was the rule on cars going to weddings when all pleasure driving had been banned to conserve gas? Weller told him that only the principals were allowed to drive to the ceremony if they could find no alternate transportation. Hathway informed the rationing boss about the nuptials that were to take place in a few hours, and Weller promised to get in touch with the Garden City police to take down the license numbers of the wedding guests. The city editor's next call was to the mother of the bride. He was checking on wedding details: what the bride was going to wear, the bridegroom's education, names of the wedding guests. The lady was in a hurry, but cooperative. She even gushed about the help she had received from a friend of her husband's, a senator who had wired them a special dispensation allowing all wedding guests to use their cars for the gala event.

So Hathway roused rewrite girl Deborah Lane from her Saturday afternoon off and had her in the office in a few minutes. She called the senator and she called the Nassau congressman who also had helped get the dispensation. Both admitted their part in the affair and claimed it was all legal. Hathway knew otherwise, because Gus Weller had told him so. By the time Lane and a photographer were ready to cover the wedding, Hathway had an apology from the congressman, who admitted he had misinterpreted the rationing rules.

Monday morning the story broke on a gas-pinched public, complete with copies of the telegrams sent by the senator and the congressman, the official wording of the rationing law pertaining to weddings, and pictures of many members of the wedding who had been invited to attend and told not to worry about rationing restrictions. Some whose licenses were taken by the police eventually forfeited their ration books and blamed it all on *Newsday*. The paper accepted the blame—and the flood of congratulatory letters from readers who had no friendly senator to get them special gas privileges.

Elmer Louis Kayser in Washington, D.C.:

I remember rationing, but I must say that it never made it impossible for me to get what was adequate for my needs. It did lead to some very strange incidents. I might mention one: My daughter was married to a marine officer just at the end of the war, when rationing was still on. And for the reception at the Mayflower I wanted the traditional wedding cake, of course, My friends on the Mayflower managerial staff said, "We can't give you a wedding cake. We haven't any sugar." So I began going to places where you would normally go, and finally I got hold of Clement's, a very good confectioner, and they said, "We'll make you a cake if you'll get us the sugar." I got the sugar. I like sugar myself, and when I was sure that was one thing that would be difficult to get, I built up a supply of it. And that supply of sugar made possible my daughter's wedding cake. That, I think, is the most grotesque of my experiences. I'll tell you, I had a very good technique on gasoline. I live on a hill, and I mastered the technique of coasting down Wisconsin Avenue to the station at Q Street. That saved coupons.

Fourteen-year-old Peggy Blassingame, living on Anna Maria Island in the Gulf of Mexico, did her duty.

We always would hear nice, delightful, scary rumors about somebody seeing a U-boat out in the gulf. For a while my girl friend and I were plane spotters. The plane-spotter station, which looked like a fire-watching station, was built right up on the gulf. We had a special assigned time, I forget how often it was—a couple of days a week for two or three hours, I think. We were given charts and taught the shapes and silhouettes of the planes, and we were supposed to tell how many miles away they were. It was terribly confusing in the beginning. At first, we were lucky to distinguish between an airplane and a seagull. But eventually we could identify every plane we saw. We learned to estimate distances and direction—north, east, south, and west. I never had the remotest idea which was which before, but we learned it fast. As soon as we saw a plane, we instantly reported the type and direction. We were certainly under the impression we were watching out for a possible enemy plane that might have infiltrated our airspace, but of course, we only saw domestic planes. We would have recognized a plane that was not American. We were terribly confident.

I don't ever remember feeling one minute's suffering for something to eat, though we did have to stand in long lines, trying to buy canned food with the little coupons. And you couldn't get much meat. Shoes were rationed, and my mother had given me a coupon to go to the shoe store—I must have been fourteen by then—to buy some shoes. I went with a girl friend, clutching this little coupon in my hand; I picked out the shoes I wanted, opened my hand, and the coupon was gone. There was no way, although he was friendly and nice and a friend of the family's, that he could sell me the shoes without the coupon. Not only did I not have the shoes, but I had to go back and face my mother.

Before my father went into the service, he was one of the air-raid wardens. He would patrol the beach every night to make sure everything was completely blacked out, and my mother would walk with him. One night when he was doing his patrol, he saw a glaring light; he hightailed to it as fast as he could go, and the closer he got, the more he began to realize it was our house, and I was the culprit. I was home with my baby sister, and I had left the bright bulb burning in the bathroom with the shade up. The only light on the whole island! It was the first time I ever remember his being angry with me. He was furious. I was forbidden to go to the movies for months and months. During that time *Mrs. Miniver* played and I never got to see it.

Max Bassin was the proprietor of the famous Bassin's Restaurant, on Pennsylvania Avenue in Washington, a block from the Treasury Department.

I chose that year—1942—to remodel the restaurant, and instead of taking three months, like it was supposed to do, it took a year. And instead of steel, I had wooden rails. Business was very good. In addition to running the restaurant, I was making sandwiches for Fort Meade and a couple of other army camps in the vicinity—Belvoir and Arlington Hall. We'd work over the weekend, making them after the restaurant was closed, and shipped them out the next day. I got seven cents apiece for them and made a profit.

I wasn't drafted. I had children at the time and a business they felt was essential. There were a number of times when I felt uncomfortable not being in uniform. Being in the restaurant business was hectic. You couldn't get any labor of any consequence. We were working so hard that subconsciously I wished I had been drafted. I had two brothers-in-law working with me. They went in, and two brothers went in. One of the brothers-in-law was a partner, so I had to take over his portion of the restaurant and run the whole thing during the war. I used to average twelve to fourteen hours a day working. With the rationing and the stamps, it was a very complicated process just running the business.

A situation came up that was very peculiar. When I started making sandwiches for the army, I went to the local OPA and told them what I was planning to do—open a different place, put my manager up there, and run the sandwiches out of this one shop, on Georgia Avenue, called B & B Commissaries. They told me that it would just be a continuance of what I had been doing and gave me a letter to that effect, so I could use the volume I had there to get the stamps. Ration stamps went a lot further when you just served sandwiches than when you served steak. It took ten, fifteen, twenty times as many stamps to get steak as it did to get sandwich meat. After I had operated the commissary for six months to a year, I got a call from the head of the main office of OPA, and when I went up there, they told me I wasn't handling it right, that I had to have institutional stamps for one and regular restaurant stamps for the other. I explained to them that I had cleared it with the OPA before I even opened the place and had a letter to that effect. He said, "Leave the letter with me, and I'm sure we can get it straightened out."

About six months later I got another call. Come to the OPA. Same thing all over again with somebody else. Explained it to them, and they said, "Oh, we'll take care of it." A little while later, I got a third call. This time I was told they had no record of the letter, no file on the case, and according to the law, I had to close both places until I had absorbed the hundreds of thousands of food stamps that I used and they said I wasn't entitled to. So I asked if it was about time I got myself an attorney. The fellow I was talking to said, "Yes, you ought to." I said,

"You don't happen to know anybody that's familiar with this thing?" He said, "Yes, there's this Chinese who's familiar with the operation. He's a very good man." So I went to my attorney, and he said I should go see the other one. I did and was told it would cost fifteen hundred dollars as a retainer and an additional fifteen hundred dollars if he got it straightened out for me. He did. I got a call a few weeks later saying it was all straight. I suspected something fishy, but couldn't say anything about it. There's no way to prove it. But as soon as I went to this attorney, there were no problems. I sold the commissary on account of that. There was so much aggravation going through those things, being threatened with closing both businesses, so I sold it.

Black-marketing was prevalent then, no question about it. You could get gas if you paid for it; in fact you could get some meat if you paid a little higher than the market price for it. You and to go out and look for it. I didn't resort to that nearly as much as other businesses did.

After V-E Day, the army started selling meat. I never did understand this—you could get a package of meat, frozen, solid beef, all boned, cut up, and put in one package; you'd get sirloin steaks, choice; chuck to make hamburger out of; but there was no distinguishing what you got. It was a little bit of everything, a grab bag. They were in fifty- or sixty-pound packs. You paid a standard price for them, and they turned out to be bargains once you broke them down.

There were times when things were exciting and times when what was going on was depressing. It was exciting operating a business then, and with the handicaps you had, it was a challenge. At the same time, with your brothers and brothers-in-law in the army, it worried you.

J. S. Smith in St. Louis:

I guess to a certain extent there was black-marketing. Coal was sold by the bushel basket to the blacks in town at rather exorbitant prices, maybe $2.50 or $3.00 a basket, or something like that. This was sort of fly-by-night stuff, individual entrepreneurs, if you want to call them that.

I had gotten some new tires for my car just before rubber rationing went in. And I had them on about two days, when they busted down the garage and stole them right off the car, wheels and all. I remember paying thirty-six dollars in those days, when I guess the average casing cost twelve dollars, and they were absolutely bald. Prices up to forty-six dollars apiece for used tires when new tires were twelve dollars. Somebody would tell you who you could see, and he'd tell you who to go to, and it was sort of subversive.

There was meat shortage, yes, but it didn't make much difference to us. As to sugar, we switched to saccharine for coffee, and I would say that we lived very comfortably through those years. Some people worried about food; I don't think any of them worried that the war would reach our shores. They worried mainly about the little inconveniences that might crop up in their lives.

George Garrott, working at the New York Times:

I don't recall any really bad shortages in New York. We had pretty much what we wanted. The only thing I remember was the shortage of cigarettes; I was a chain smoker, and cigarettes almost disappeared. All of us at the *Times* bought these little gadgets for making your own cigarettes. Then you bought tobacco by the pound, and of course you smoked twice as much as you would ordinarily.

There was a lot of fear. I remember one fellow on the *Times,* a reporter about my age, was scared to death. He lived in Greenwich Village in an apartment on the top floor of his building, and he immediately canceled his lease and moved into a cellar right after we got in the war. I knew a few other people who did that kind of thing. And then there was the civil defense: people running around in hats, getting in everybody's way. Personally, I just felt, when it comes, it comes.

Hezekiah Goodwin, a Connecticut dairy farmer:

A lot of people cleaned up. The black-market activity around here was considerable. We never traded with them. They would come out and prey on the local farmers, who would butcher the legitimate quota and kill the rest in the woods, stamp it, and peddle it. They used to do it pretty openly. I was kidding a fellow one day, and I said: "John, I'd like to get a nice quarter of beef tonight." He said, "Hessy, I can give you any kind of meat you want," and he pulled out a five-gallon pail all full of rubber meat stamps: Swift's, Armour, all government inspected, choice. It didn't faze him a bit to take a Jersey carcass and stamp it "Choice Swift." It was a great business.

Potatoes were high at certain times and hard to get. I'll never forget, before the war we had a nice crop of potatoes, and they didn't sell very well. Hardly any customers; nobody had any money. I stopped at this old Italian food store where we traded, and I said: "Mrs. Divarre, could you use a few nice potatoes?" And she said, "We got Maine potatoes, and the Maine potatoes are nice; the potatoes around here no good." So, needless to say, she didn't buy any. Then sometime in the middle of the war I was in there, and she said, "Mr. Goodwin, you got any potatoes?" And right in a flash it occurred to me I got a whole cellarful, and she didn't have a damned one. And she said, "Would you let me have a few bushel?" And I said, "Well, Mrs. Divarre, I'd like to, but I can't. I have to think of my steady customers—you know, the people who bought potatoes from me years ago when they could have bought Maine potatoes." And I got her so mad she was jumping up and down.

Mary Devereux Crist, whose husband was in the Pacific with the Marine Corps:

I was up in Washington one time visiting and wanted a ration book to get some liquor because I was going to see a friend in Virginia. I went into the ration board, and they said, "Sorry, we can't give you a ration book when you're just visiting." I said, "Well, nobody wants a visitor who has a drink or two if he doesn't furnish his own liquor in this day and age." They said, "Well, haven't you got a letter addressed to you here in Virginia, or anything that would show that you are going to be here a while?" I said, "Yes, I have. I've got a ticket from a shoemaker, where I've taken my daughter's shoes to be resoled." They said, "That's enough to get a ration ticket for the whole month, because you'll never know when you'll get those shoes back."

In wartime Washington, the worst thing was the cigarette shortage. I remember one time standing in line with this little baby of mine and after three hours getting up to the head of the line and being told they didn't have any more cigarettes. I got in a cab in tears, and the cab driver gave me the rest of his pack. He had only taken about two cigarettes out of it, and I've never been so grateful for anything in my life.

Americans Remember the Home Front

Marquis Childs in Washington, D.C.:

We planted a Victory garden and canned a lot of vegetables, most of which we threw out later, they were so terrible.

Pauline Christensen, a widow with two young sons, worked in the educational publishing business in Chicago. Her contribution was to drive for the Red Cross.

I was a member of the Red Cross Motor Corps and spent a good many thousands of hours convoying. Of course, I was working, but on weekends and evenings I would go into Chicago and spend whatever time I could driving convoys. The young recruits would be sent from one camp to the other, and we would drive them from the train, as they arrived, to Lake Bluff or into some of the other areas. We'd also drive the blood bank, entertainment buses, and things of that sort. Or we would pick up an admiral and take him wherever he wanted to go in the Chicago area for a whole day. I don't know why that was a Red Cross responsibility.

When we were on duty, we wore our Red Cross uniforms. That protected us a great deal, because we were all over the city, back into some of the areas I had never known were there—the Polish community, the Greek community. Sometimes it was a little bit scary, but the uniform protected me. We drove all hours of the night. There were some black and white problems in the area at that time. Once, I knew someone was following me as I got off at the station in Evanston on my way home. Finally the person caught up with me—a young girl who said, "Oh, Ma'am, you walk so fast, but I knew if I got close to your uniform, I'd be safe."

The war affected my business, which was one reason I had time to give the Red Cross. Paper was limited, and the president of the company was in the navy on one of the first ships to land marines on Guadalcanal. We just kept the business going; you couldn't do much with it. You only had so much paper allotted to you; you could only print so many books.

It's now about thirty years since World War II, but we still are not out of the controversy of the war. And I think that's a tragedy for the human race. The last drive I made, I thought, "Well, the war is over now, and I've done my duty." I took a busload of young high school entertainers up to Great Lakes to entertain the hospital residents, people who had been brought back, and the road was a complete sheet of ice. I thought,

"If I ever get these young people back safely, I think this is the end of my driving." That was New Year's Eve 1945.

Lois Raymond in Sedgwick, Maine:

Do you remember punching oleo up in a bag to make it look like butter? Our first summer in Maine the neighbors asked us if we would be willing to go on the watch as airplane spotters. We said, "Sure." It was right up at the head of the hill in an old chickenhouse which had been cleaned up. We would go up there with a cribbage board, a lantern, a book or two, and a pot of coffee. Every fifteen minutes we would go out and look, but we never heard a thing. It was just as well, because the telephone hadn't been put in. Anyway we did our duty. The next summer they shifted the watch to the schoolhouse. E. B. White wrote about being on duty up there. I don't remember ever having to report anything very suspicious. There were a good many rumors, though. Fishermen would say that they saw lots of what they took to be insulation material, as if a submarine had been sunk. Then there was the time a German was put ashore on Hancock Point. As I remember the story, it was in the wintertime, February or March, when a young lad, the son of the sheriff, was driving along the road and saw a strange-looking man carrying a briefcase. He told his father, who immediately became very suspicious and called the FBI in Ellsworth. They apparently were able to get on his trail, and he was followed for quite some time. He led them to a group of people who had been put ashore on Long Island and in Florida—there were eight of them. When they all got together at some central point like New York, they were arrested.

Alice Marriott in Washington, D.C.:

We had a grocery store right close by that had all the black-market stuff in town. We could get anything we wanted from those people. We paid through the nose. If we wanted a roast of meat, we had to buy two cases of canned goods, but they had it. They only gave it to their charge customers, and we would get a bill at the end of the month. We bought all kinds of stuff we didn't need just because we needed to get a little meat.

Americans Remember the Home Front

Dorothy Currier in Waltham, Massachusetts:

You don't think of Massachusetts as a farming state, but there are a lot of small farmers up there. And every farmer would can and stock his root cellar for the winter. I canned extensively; I had a small backyard garden, and I canned every vegetable we ate for the entire winter. I had a big stock—then along came the rationing, and you were supposed to declare every single edible you had in the house, and that had to be deducted from your food stamps. The Farm Bureau rose up in wrath. The secretary of the bureau, for whom I was secretary, put on a mighty effort to have the farmers excluded, but he was not successful, as I recall. I imagine the farmers did not tell the truth, and I sure didn't blame them, because they had done just what they had been doing all of their lives, and all of a sudden they were being penalized with food stamps. So it was an active time for the Farm Bureau, because they were fighting hard for the farmers, who were having a pretty rough time.

I also went into civil defense. I don't know what year, but I'm sure it was an offshoot of the bombing of England, because we patterned our civil defense activities on English defense activities. I hadn't realized what I was getting into, but I very shortly was a zone warden. You had to spend hours on the telephone trying to sell civil defense. "Why do I have to walk up and down the streets and be a post warden?" people would say. "Why do I have to be a district warden?" "What's the point of all of this—nobody's ever going to attack us here." It was an awful selling job. There were five or six zone wardens, and I had the biggest zone—I was kind of pleased they thought I could do it. I chose a man for an assistant, but I think I was the only woman zone warden. Of course, as we progressed in the civil-defense effort, with practice drills and night blackouts, people became a little more aware that the whole country was getting prepared for the war. We all made curtains for the windows that we put up for the night blackouts. I was allowed to drive my car, because I was in civil defense—not that a zone warden had to drive much—and had to get to my station quickly to get things under operation. I remember one time a runner suddenly appeared at the door and handed me a piece of paper that said: "You have just been bombed out." So we had to think quickly what we had to do then. There were exercises like that that made the people realize that perhaps these things could happen. I'm sure a lot of people regarded it very lightly, but when we began to give out helmets, then there was a fight. "Why can't I have a helmet?" people would ask.

Food stamps were a big problem, because we were just a family of two, and there was no way you could stretch it. When you signed up, you had to say how many were in your family, and you were given so many food stamps for a week or a month. Gas stamps the same way. You had to go down and declare why you needed a car at all.

I think we were mostly concerned because we couldn't get what we wanted to eat. We couldn't drive where we wanted to. It was a light war, in a way, to those who did not have anyone in the family in the fighting. We could get butter all through the war if we had the stamps for it. Then after the war you couldn't get an ounce of butter. They just froze the whole thing, waiting for the price to go up, because prices were way down at rock bottom when the war started. Then there was rent control. We had a two-family house, and the rent was frozen at some ridiculous figure, like thirty-two dollars a month. We couldn't raise it, we couldn't do a thing. We just had to sit there and maintain the place. That went on for years too.

Arthur Edmunds in Des Moines, Iowa:

I can remember Senator Taft trying to get price controls removed. At that time the issue was pork chops. I think pork chops were something like 38¢ a pound, but they were hard to get, and Taft's argument was if they removed price controls, which they did, everybody could have pork chops. Then you could get all the pork chops you wanted—at $1.08 a pound. I was newly married—I've forgotten what my salary was, maybe $3,600 a year or something like that—with a baby on the way, and things were just tough. I regretted immensely the relaxation of price controls. That was, as I recall, in the period immediately after victory in Europe, but before victory in Japan.

Ted Giddings in Great Barrington, Massachusetts:

Federal charges were brought against a few men that were involved in selling gas-rationing tickets. I think they counterfeited them. They were convicted and, I believe, given sentences and put on probation. Unfortunately, one of the men, a family man, committed suicide, and that really shook the community.

9

THE ULTIMATE COST
OF VICTORY

As we have seen, there were few physical hardships for Americans at home during the war. The real hardship was in the anguish, the tragedies, the constant worry and concern for loved ones overseas. War may not have affected America the way it did other countries, where the battles were fought, but the loss of a son or a husband in the war is the ultimate hardship and something from which some people never recover.

Celeste Kavanaugh on Fernandino Island, Florida:

I think the hardest thing about the war was not knowing where your loved ones were, when they were going to be sent into battle next, how they were making it from day to day, and whether they would come home. We weren't too far from Camp Blanding, the big induction center. It was a terrible thing to see them go. I can remember going to meet one of my brothers at Blanding. It was an induction center, but you really told them good-bye.

Jack Altshul, city editor, Newsday, *Long Island, New York:*

The most popular feature on the paper, which almost broke your heart, were the casualty lists—every day a new casualty list. And often you had to send reporters to families who had just received the news that their son was lying on some beach, or whatever. It was a tragic period, and it did get to you. It got to me. I hated to read those casualty lists for fear of finding friends on it. And you often did.

Marquis Childs in Washington, D.C.:

One of my son's closest friends, a hell of an attractive young fellow, was lost in the Italian campaign. And suddenly, it brought home to you that—well, the casualty list was just figures. But when that list included a human being you knew, had seen grow up, had seen develop, you realized the terrible waste of the whole thing.

Betty Bryce had two sons, Dalton and Kenneth, when the war began. She lived then, and still lives, in Mount Pleasant, Michigan.

Dalton was eighteen years old and valedictorian of his class. He had an American Legion scholarship, but he went down and applied for immediate induction as soon as he graduated from high school. He went overseas—I think he was gone seven months from the time he enlisted.

I was out raking the yard when I got the telegram. The man who brought it went next door to my neighbor and asked if she would come over with him, because it was the third one he had delivered that day in our town. When he handed me the telegram, I just looked at it. He said, "It's bad news." I guess I was kind of in a state of shock, until I read it, you know, seeing he's gone, that was it. The police went to the high school and brought my younger son, Kenny, home. We had a terrible time getting him calmed down, and of course, my ten-year-old daughter took it awfully hard.

Dalton was home once after he went in. I knew, when I put him on the bus, I'd never see him again; I just had this feeling. And while he was home, he got rid of everything in the house that belonged to him. He must have had a feeling too. He received the Silver Star, and there was a citation that came with it which told about it. They were in Germany, six miles past the Remagen bridge. He was a medic; he went to help some fellows in a burning tank and was killed by a sniper on his way back. It took me about a year before I could really get a hold of myself. I think I cried day and night for three or four months. It was a terrible thing to happen to anyone. He was so young.

When his company was traveling through Belgium, they had stopped at one point, and some local people had given them things to eat. A little girl remembered him, and when she was going through the cemetery in Liège, she saw his name, and so she wrote to the War Department, and they sent the letter to me. I answered the letter, and she wrote right back and sent me pictures—she kept flowers on his grave. And that's how I found out where he was buried. She informed me when they were closing the cemetery—I knew before the War Department even told me. In every letter he wrote he always said, "Oh, Mama, I can't wait until I get home." So we brought him back and buried him in Mount Pleasant. His brother was his escort, and I felt that I had done the last thing I could possibly do for him. I did a lot of visiting after my son was killed to other mothers in Mount Pleasant who had lost their sons. It was very depressing.

My youngest son went into the paratroops, and while he was still in training, I wrote to the adjutant general in Washington, D.C., and had him transferred out of that. I just felt that I couldn't take a chance with him, too. I didn't want Kenny to be where he would be in danger, and so they put him behind a desk, which he didn't like. He never talked about his brother, never even mentioned his name. He just seemed to clam up inside, and he's never unclammed. I think it had a tremendous impact. We mention Dalton's name real often; we talk about him a lot, but Kenny doesn't. And yet, when his son was born, he named him after his brother.

Mary Moore Lacey was the wife of a naval aviator assigned to the carrier Yorktown. *After the* Yorktown *left Norfolk, and later San Diego, early in the war, she settled down in Coronado, California. She had two small children.*

We had built a small house in Coronado, and I was glad to have a place that I could call my own—sort of as though I had roots. It was not long before we heard that Jack had been lost in the Battle of the Marshall Islands. They didn't know what had happened, so he was declared "lost" all during the war.

My son was a year old when Jack was lost. My daughter, Sandy, was born six months later. Occasionally a friend of Jack's would come through and take the children to the beach or something like that, but there wasn't a lot of masculine contact. We were all in the same boat in Coronado, and it was comfortable for me, because I didn't have to keep explaining. When I went into family situations, I got a lot of "you poor dear" kind of stuff. I found that very difficult to take. I understood that I needed to be real about what was happening and say that it hurt and, yes, it was hard. But the minute I began getting sympathy, it made me feel awfully sorry for myself, and I'd break down. It didn't seem to heal anything. It just opened the wounds.

The allowance Jack had allotted wasn't enough for me to live on. Everything else was frozen, so I went to the officer's club at North Island and worked. My job was making sure that the kitchen staff had food ready for service at the snack bar. I was also a Red Cross nurse's aide and worked in a civilian hospital in San Diego and in a military hospital at North Island. In nursing duty I felt very much part of the war.

I stayed in Coronado around nine months or a year. Then I was called to Texas, where my father was an army doctor at Fort Sam Houston. My mother was sick with cancer, so I packed up the children, found somebody to rent my house, and moved to Texas. I stayed with my family for a little over a year.

By the time I went back to Coronado, Jack had been gone long enough for me to feel that he probably wouldn't come back. The one hope was that he might be found in a Japanese prison camp.

So what do you want to do? You want to end the war! and you buy what they say about the atom bomb.

Patricia Megargee in Pelham, New York:

I had one boyfriend who was killed. He flew a torpedo bomber, based on an aircraft carrier in the Pacific, and I really expected him to come home. He hadn't been reported killed, he'd been reported missing. It took me about a year to get over it.

Another one wanted to get married before he went off, and Mom said she thought I was too young and he was too young, and, really, there wasn't a lot of point to it. It was kind of a panic situation as far as he was concerned, I think. His parents were divorced, and he just wanted something that he could hang on to. He finally married someone he'd known just for a very short time. I heard from his mother later that he too was killed. So it was really good to work, I think, and have something to do. When you weren't working, it was very depressing.

The Reverend Harold Toliver and his wife, Elva, in Pittsburgh:

ELVA: There were tragedies. One of the cases in the congregation was very pathetic. We had a young couple, and the husband went to war and became what they called a "basket case." He was in a hospital in Washington, so depressed and bitter that he didn't want anyone who had known him before to see him.

HAROLD: I had performed the marriage several years before he went into the service, and they were happily married. When he came back, he would not see his wife. We never found out whether it was just his physical condition—impairment from all his injuries and all that—or whether it was something deeper than that. I don't know. He wouldn't talk, and I never got down to the camp to see him or get to talk to him. They eventually separated.

ELVA: He told her he wouldn't have anything to do with her, and she got a divorce and went on and carries the name. But she grieved just terribly. She was brokenhearted.

Mary Hoehling in Bethesda, Maryland:

I had a cousin lost during the war, though not actually in combat. He went down in the jungle in South America, and they never did find him or the plane or anything. His father never did resign himself. He kept waiting for him.

My husband had an accident when the freighter he was on was rammed and burned in the North Sea. It was not by enemy action. He was going into Antwerp with war materiel—they had oil drums all over the deck. That was the one experience I've ever had with ESP—I woke up and knew something had happened to him! It was about midnight, and in the same moment I knew he was all right. I called two or three of my friends, even at midnight, to say that this had happened. It was such a strong feeling; and, indeed, the letter came a month or so later bearing out that it had happened and at precisely that time.

313

Governor Leverett Saltonstall of Massachusetts:

I had four children in the service. One son was killed—in Guam—after Guam had been declared safe. He was with the marines who landed on the island and was put in charge of a patrol. They were supposed to be safe, but there were still several hundred Japs hidden, and they fired. Two were killed, and three got back. My son was one of those killed. It was three o'clock in the afternoon when I heard. They always sent the top Western Union fellow up, so when I heard he wanted to see me, I knew it was trouble. It was hard, especially for Mrs. Saltonstall. My oldest boy was in the air force, an air marine. My third son was in the navy, and he was up in Newfoundland. My oldest girl was the first enlisted WAVE in the country. She enlisted at Smith College.

Mary Speir lived in Westminster, Maryland. Her only son enlisted in the air force when he was a sophomore in college. Her husband was also in the air force. The Speirs now live in Leisure World, a retirement community in Silver Spring, Maryland.

At that time I had a different feeling than I have now. I thought maybe people should go, but I didn't want my son to go. My husband also went, but he was a grown man and knew what he was doing, and that was different. I had a very bitter feeling about taking these college boys and not training them, which they didn't do for infantry. My son was only in the infantry six weeks when he was put in the lines, which I thought was very bad.

When my son enlisted in the air force, he went to McDill Field in Florida. So I went there until he shifted to the infantry and was sent to Fort Gordon. Then I came back to Westminster, which was a big mistake. I should have stayed in Florida. I found that people who didn't have someone overseas were not too concerned. They were interested in bacon and sugar and gas, which I was not. I even had people make remarks to me that we ought to do war work because we had men on the front. I felt the others lucky enough not to have men on the front should be doing it. However, I did a lot of war work—not after I came back to Westminster, but when I was at McDill, I worked in the hospital and at the USO. In fact I got decorated for the work in the USO in Tampa.

I started to do some volunteer work in Westminster, like rolling bandages, but I couldn't make it. The people I was doing it with were not in my situation at all. They were more concerned with what they were having to give up than with what was happening in Europe. I had people call me up and ask, "Do you have coupons? We can get butter tomorrow." I never stood in a line for a thing. I thought that if the men could do without it, so could I.

I was alone and was terrifically upset the morning the Episcopal rector arrived at my door and said, "I have very bad news for you." I said, "Has my son been killed?" He said, "Yes." He was twenty—my only child. It ruined my life. I can assure you of that. On Friday it will be thirty-one years since he was killed.

I hadn't seen my husband for nearly two years; he had been overseas. He was able to get leave for fifteen days when our son was killed. The minister who brought the telegram was young enough to be in the service. Instead of trying to be of any help to us, he wanted money from us. He even came and asked me for money as a memorial to my son before my husband got back from overseas. I nearly left the Episcopal church; in fact, I didn't go to church for five years after the war. I had been on airfields, and I knew they needed chaplains, and I didn't have much respect for him for staying out. I told him so.

Four boys who had been with my son during the war came back, and we call them "our boys." They've been very close to us.

We don't fly a flag. The flag that came back on my son's casket was given to his school. He was president of his class, and they asked for the flag. I was standing here on my walk one day when everybody had flags out, and a man said to me, "You're not very patriotic, are you?" And I said, "What have you done?" He didn't get it. He walked up the street and told one of the neighbors what he had said to me and that I had reacted very violently to it. They said, "Well, you certainly talked to the wrong person." I said to him, "It takes more than waving a flag to win a war."

Sally Lucke in Columbus, Ohio:

My cousin was in the war in Europe. He was badly wounded in the Battle of the Bulge and died soon after the war as a result of those wounds. When we would visit him when he was home on leave, some-

times we would be awakened in the middle of the night by his screaming in German. From his death, his father had a heart attack, and from
his father's death, his mother became ill.

*Dorothy Whitaker's brother was on his way to the Pacific when the war
started.*

We didn't hear much from him after Pearl Harbor, which upset the
entire family. Several months later we learned that he was at Corregidor. Then we heard from the government that he was missing in action. They were pretty sure he was a prisoner, but that's all the message
said. Then we got two letters from him over the next three and a half
years. He said he was in prison, but his letters were so censored that
they didn't make much sense. Eventually he was transferred from the
Philippines to Japan, and I don't believe we got any more information.
The worst thing was that when the war was over and the peace treaty
was signed, we still didn't know anything. That looked bad. We had
gone to meetings set up by the Red Cross, and the boys that came back
from Germany told what they knew of prisoners still over there in Germany, but very few had any knowledge of what was going on in the
Pacific. None of the prisoners in Japan had come back. We kept calling
the Red Cross, and they contacted the government; they were doing all
they could, but they couldn't locate an awful lot of them.

It had a very bad effect on my mother. She tried to have a good
outlook and did, but it affected her more than any of the rest of us. She
was sort of withdrawn, not herself.

It affected me, too. You just went from day to day wondering if it was
ever going to end so you could stop worrying about it. You didn't in-
dulge in your usual pleasures; you were just thinking about the war all
the time. I about gave up hope for my brother for a while; my mother
never did, but I think my dad and I were prepared for the worst.

We didn't have a telephone, and my mother wanted one installed so
the Red Cross could call as soon as they heard anything. Finally, when
they did get news about him, they called, but they wouldn't talk to
anybody except my father, and he wasn't there. They wouldn't tell
Mother anything. Evidently one of the rules was that they could give the
information only to the person whose name happened to be on their list,
and that was my father's name. Finally she called back and said, "Look,
this is my son. I've been waiting to hear from him all these years, and I

am entitled to know one way or the other what has happened." They said, "We can't give you that information, but we will tell you this. He's all right." So she started calling around and got neighbors to take her to my father on the job so he could get home to find out the rest of it. All they said was that he had been located and that he was ambulatory and that was it. Then it wasn't too long before we began getting all kinds of messages.

As it turned out, he was in a prisoner-of-war camp in Japan. There were no roads up there, and he didn't know what was going on. Then these American boys came up in Jeeps and tried to tell the prisoners about the atom bomb, which was so far out, they didn't believe it. When they found my brother, he weighed eighty pounds. He had a heart condition, beriberi, dysentery, and malaria. He was not in good shape. When he came back, he was in Staten Island Hospital and then in another one in Coral Gables, off and on for about two years.

Elva Newman in Washington, D.C.:

My son never got a furlough to come home after he went in the service on March 4, 1943. He took his basic training at Camp Wheeler, Georgia. He was scheduled for a furlough after the basic training, and we were sitting at home waiting for him to call. My oldest daughter was with me, and she said, "I'm going to call Camp Wheeler." And she got him immediately. He said the furlough had been canceled; they were leaving the next morning but did not know where they were going.

That was on Sunday. On Monday they were sent to Shanango, Pennsylvania, a replacement camp. They came right through Washington, the train laid over two hours at Union Station. Of course, I didn't know anything about it. He did call me from the embarkation depot. That was the last time I talked with him.

He went to England and took all his training there. I heard from him regular, and, of course, they weren't supposed to tell where they were, but in my husband's family, way back, they had a saying that his great-great grandfather was chased out of England for stealing sheep. So, when my son wrote, he said, "I'm in the same place where my great-great grandfather was chased out for stealing sheep."

He was there until the D-day invasion, in the 115th Division—I think the 116th went in first, and then the 115th followed. That was June 6, and he was killed on June 12.

I heard the news by telegram, but I wasn't at home at the time. My mother had had a stroke, and I was taking her home by ambulance that day. The ambulance came in the afternoon, and right behind it I recognized the cars from my home. My husband came, and the children who were at home, and my son-in-law, who was in the marines stationed in Washington. I wondered why they were coming in two cars, but thought, "Well, I guess they want to leave one here for me." But they came to bring me the message that they had gotten the telegram that morning. He was killed instantly. I heard from one of his buddies. They used to correspond with me. He was buried temporarily in France. Later they asked whether we wanted him brought home, but we decided not to, and he was buried in Saint Laurent, in the Normandy cemetery.

Ten-year-old Ray Hartman had an older brother whom he idolized.

My brother immediately volunteered for the air force, and, I believe, he failed his first entrance examination because he was lacking in math. So he went back to school and took several courses in math, which probably took about a year. Then he took the examination again and successfully passed as an air force cadet.

On August 24, 1944, we got a call saying that he had one more practice mission to fly and then he would get a furlough, before going overseas. He was in the Eighth Air Force. We were elated that he was coming home.

The following day when they took the last training mission, there were 100 planes flying in formation; two of them locked wings and tore each other's wings off. Both planes just crashed to the ground with no survivors. We got a telegram around four o'clock in the morning. I was sleeping, so I heard about it in the morning. It was quite a shock to me. I was about thirteen, going on fourteen, when that happened.

Naturally, being a young boy, I blamed it on the war, on the Japanese and the Germans, because if it hadn't been for them, we wouldn't have been involved, and he wouldn't have been killed. I did idolize anybody that was in the service—my heart went out to them.

Margaret Oakham had left her husband. She had a son in the service and a daughter.

My son was seventeen when he decided to go into the service. I didn't want him to quit school, because he had won a scholarship, but he wanted to join the marines. When he was at Paris Island, two boys committed suicide during basic training because it was so rough. I remember him writing to tell me that he would never again do anything that I told him not to do, because he realized he didn't know as much about the military as he thought he did. He was assigned to ships going back and forth overseas and, of course, I was concerned, but he did come out all right.

My daughter was going with a boy who was in the air force. They were quite serious about each other and had planned to get married after she graduated, and then he went overseas. After his orders came, his mother wrote and asked me if my daughter could go out to Iowa to see her son before he went overseas. I scraped the money together—about $135, which was quite a bit of money at that time. I received a beautiful letter from him thanking me for letting him see her. He wasn't overseas very long, just a few missions, when he was reported missing. I guess he was on a B-26. My daughter took this very, very hard. I think it made a big impression on her. I still have the letter that she wrote to me about it.

Anna Mae Lindberg in Pittsburgh:

The war had immediate impact, at least on my family, because one brother had just been out of high school about a year and was in the service within a couple of weeks. He went immediately overseas, and he was in combat from the time they invaded the tip of Italy until they got all the way to Germany. And there was the constant waiting for that telegram.

My second brother was called almost immediately after he graduated from high school, but he was a little more fortunate in that he got into the intelligence service, and while he was also overseas, he was never in active combat. He was either just ahead of it or just behind it. Nevertheless, we never really knew where he was or what was happening.

I remember getting one letter from my brother, and all he said was that he was broke. That was somehow traumatic to me—my poor brother over there, involved in all this holocaust, and broke. I remember calling the Red Cross and asking them if there was any way I could get the money to my brother, because he was broke. Well, they didn't laugh.

Americans Remember the Home Front

Helen Wilson at the University of Michigan:

I was concerned about a boy I was interested in, because he was with Patton's army. They were always moving into the fore, and anyone attached to that group was in danger most all the time. I remember giving him a sort of a macabre gift before he went off—a lighter that smoldered rather than flamed, so you wouldn't be seen. Thinking back on it, it was really a terrible gift. But it did save his life. He was carrying it in his breast pocket when he was shot, and the bullet was deflected off the lighter. He was a delightful, gentle person, and I doubt that he ever got over the effects of combat.

Joseph Clement:

I had a nephew who was killed in Anzio. I remember him well and it was a shock to me, because he really didn't know what it was all about. He was all of eighteen—the family's only son, and they never recovered from it.

Herb Collins, who was nine years old at the time of Pearl Harbor:

Raymond Barlow got killed in service, and I remember going to the funeral as a young boy. I expected the body to be there, and instead they had Raymond's picture up on the communion table, with flowers on either side of it. It struck me as being very funny that they didn't have the body there. Then they had a second funeral when the body arrived, and it seemed tremendously odd to have two separate funerals for one person.

I remember the curiosity we had about the bodies when they were brought back. In some cases they wouldn't let the undertakers open the caskets up—they said for health reasons. There was much talk in the neighborhood that they just put sand or rocks in the coffin and didn't have bodies in a lot of them because there wasn't anything to put in. So people whose loved ones were brought back always had a doubt as to whether there was anybody in the coffin, indeed, and if it was the right person in there.

I also remember this one boy and his sister who were in school with me, and their father was reported as killed in service. Their mother married a second time after about a year or so, and then the father showed up. I never will forget it, because I think nobody on earth would have done what he did. He visited with them and talked it over with her and her second husband; he said that obviously they were very happy together and that he didn't want to disrupt their life. So he went to Florida and came back periodically to visit the children. But he never interfered in any way with her second marriage.

Eleanor Kuhne was married and living in California.

I was very worried about Ed all the time he was overseas, although he never did get wounded. Twice I saw pictures in the newspapers of someone who was wounded, and I was positive it was him from the back. But I think that is what everybody went through. Looking back, it seems everybody has a tendency to remember the good parts. Ed would never tell me about the dark parts, all he would tell me about the service are the funny things.

It was a horribly lonesome time—the anxiety, the worry about Ed, wondering whether he was dead or alive, and all the other people that were hurt, wounded. So many of my girl friends lost their husbands and boyfriends. And others came back so changed. Marie, a friend of mine, was engaged to a boy who was in Guadalcanal through the whole thing. He went away a carefree, handsome, laughing type of Irishman, and he came back a wreck, a mental wreck. I think he went into a mental institution.

The scars from the war were very deep. My husband was not the kind of person who could talk out his traumas and troubles very easily, but there were a few times when he blurted it all out. And he saw some things—in fact, he saw somebody get his head cut off right next to him.

Leo Hershfield in Washington, D.C.

In December of 1944, they were busting out of the Bulge. My younger brother, a Pfc. in the infantry, was killed in action on the twenty-fifth. Sam had gone after the job. He could have had himself rejected for active service because of an eye problem due to an injury in a Golden Gloves match. But he volunteered. I'll never forget the phone call from my older brother in Chattanooga about the War Department telegram.

A few weeks later his widow received a letter from the colonel commanding the 290th Infantry and one from his good friend and sergeant, who described the action. He said, "Sam was very cool-headed and brave" and that they had "wished each other good luck and Merry Christmas" before moving out.

There were many such telegrams and letters during the war. Telegrams were delivered by hand in those days, and the odds were it was bad news when the boy with the yellow envelope came up and rang the doorbell.

Mabel Wiggins in Saint Paul, Minnesota:

I remember going to a luncheon, and one of the guests was late; she was on Red Cross duty. The hostess had just started serving a lovely casserole when this lady opened the door and said, "I'm sorry I'm late! Have any of you heard the news?" The *Royal Oak* had blown up in the Pacific, and no one was saved. I was sitting at the right of the hostess, and I could see her hand shaking. She went on serving and said, "I have two nephews on the boat." It was shocking. But she changed the subject, and that was it.

The fellows were so nice. Whenever anyone came back on leave, to be transferred someplace else, they'd put in long-distance calls to all the wives. I was awakened so many times at three o'clock in the morning— my W was down on the list—and someone would say, "I had dinner with Russell two nights ago, and he's just fine." One day the telephone rang, and the operator was so gay. She said, "Mrs. Wiggins, where are you?" and I said, "What do you mean, where am I?" She said, "Are you sitting down?" She wanted to tell me my husband was calling from the East Coast, he'd arrived; they had such times, she said, with people who'd faint. And they used to have an older man who had some understanding and sensitivity deliver the death notices, the telegrams. They couldn't do it over the telephone, because people just fell apart.

In Fort Collins, Colorado, Dorothy Schenck's war years were dominated by the fact that her son had been captured on Bataan.

He was in any number of camps there, and then, eventually—it must have been a year or so—we got the austere, typed card that said "I am well" or that sort of thing. But it was his signature. I knew it. And we were allowed to send one box to the Red Cross. Some of the boys who came back said that he had shared some of the things he had.

I think I was practically the only mother in town who had a son who was a prisoner of war. I did get one letter. It hadn't been opened—there was no cancellation or anything—and I always had a feeling that it went out with MacArthur when he left there.

It wasn't until after the armistice was signed, quite some time after, that I had word that he had been killed. The Japanese were sending the prisoners of war by unidentified ships to Japan to work in the mines, and they were bombed by the American troops because, naturally, they thought these were Japanese troops. They didn't have them identified as prisoners of war when they were transferred. He lived through the bombing of the first ship, one of the boys that came back said, and everyone who lived through that was put on another ship, plus others. They couldn't sit down; they couldn't lie down; they were just body-to-body standing up. The boy who came back told me that. It was January before I was notified that he had been killed.

War ages you very fast, I can tell you that. You go through a nervous strain. No night did you sleep, because you knew your son was a prisoner of war.

Lillie Bernstein was living in Chicago, Illinois.

One of my daughters-in-law said to me, "Mother, do you see anything different in Sheldon?" He looked good, he's a very handsome man, and he looked the same and everything. I said, "What do you think? How can a man who has never hurt a fly kill people?" A kamikaze attacked them, and the first person killed on the ship was the doctor, and my son had to cut off legs and do other things that he never dreamed of doing. How could it help but change him? But only a mother and a wife would know it. It surely harmed their nervous system—every one of them—I could tell it.

I'll tell you, the war work helped me keep my mind off my sons. My husband was so beside himself that his four boys were away that in order to brace him up, I was very courageous. Of course, I had a four-star flag in the window. I had to succumb to it, or rise above it.

Laddie Sadler:

It wasn't long after V-E Day that I learned that a cousin who was a frogman had been killed in Normandy, and of course, that kind of colors your reaction. I had another cousin who started out right at the beginning of the war in the infantry. He went all the way through Europe into Berlin, came home for a twenty-one-day furlough, went back through all the island invasions, and worked his way all the way to Tokyo. After the war was over, after Japan had surrendered, he was there for a while in the occupation. He was married, had a couple of children, and had accumulated enough points and was looking forward to getting out on points, among the first ones. Then just a week or two before he was destined to come home, he and a group of his friends went into Tokyo in a Jeep to go to the movies. On their way home they were hit by a train, and all five of them were killed.

Henry McMurria, in Columbus, Georgia:

My brother was a prisoner of war in the Pacific, and the government didn't know where he was. One night, a Sunday night, about midnight, the night editor of *The Enquirer* called. The day editor had gotten a bulletin about a British ship going into Rabaul and taking off a number of prisoners, and it mentioned my brother's name. He didn't read the article, but he slipped it back into a drawer so the night editor would find it. When he did, he called, and that was the first we had heard. The war had been over for several weeks, and that was the first we had heard. My father just put on an overcoat over his pajamas and went down to the paper and got a copy of it. Of course, the story came out in the paper the next morning, and we had friends coming in before breakfast.

They took him from Rabaul over to Port Morsley and then to the Hawaiian Islands. He stayed there, I think, overnight; then they shipped him into Seattle, Washington, and put him in a hospital there, but he wouldn't stay. He got out, thumbed a ride down to San Francisco, and caught a ride on an army plane to Washington, D.C., where he met a friend of his, a colonel in the air force, who put him on a plane to Atlanta. He was grounded in Greenville, South Carolina, and it took him longer to get from Greenville to Columbus than it did from San Francisco to Greenville. The whole town turned out to welcome him.

324

He called my parents when he landed in Seattle, and we had to call the State Department to tell them that he was here. They didn't know a thing about where he was. They had tried every way to find out what had happened, but he was home before the government knew where he was. They let him stay home for a day or two, and then he had to go back to the hospital. He had scars all over his legs from the plane catching on fire before he was shot down.

Martha Wood in Bradenton, Florida:

My husband's brother was sent to Europe and ended up with the OSS on the island of Corsica by the time the war came to an end. We never knew where he was. Several times he was sent out from a camp and didn't come back. So they sent his clothes home twice to his mother in Birmingham, and, of course, that terrified her. But when she would get in touch with the Red Cross, they would tell her that everything was all right. We can laugh about it now, but at the time it was not funny.

We were in Raleigh, North Carolina, when the news came of V-E Day. Our church was open for prayer, and that day I went in with a woman who said, "My son is in Europe, and I'm just happy to come today to pray." He was killed the next day, because the war had not actually ended in some of those remote areas. I remember that woman well when she prayed that day.

Mary King lives in Providence, Rhode Island. I interviewed her in Washington, at the headquarters of the Gold Star Mothers of America, of which she is president.

My son loved the navy. I really think he would have stayed in after the war. He would love to have made a career, because he was trying very hard to get a rating and go right up. He wasn't one of those "ninety-day wonders." He was working his way up, and I don't doubt he would have done it, because he was a very smart young fellow, if I can say so.

I first got a telegram that he was missing in action; that's the way it came through. And it came to me at a very bad time. My daughter was making her wedding gown to be married to a man in uniform, and here I was reading this, and it wasn't sinking in for a while. You know, you read something and you don't read it. Then suddenly I broke up, crying.

He lost his life on March 19, 1945, on the U.S.S. *Franklin*, fifty miles off the coast of Japan. All the boys were ready for a takeoff when this lone Jap—how he got there nobody knows—a kamikaze, hit the ship, and all of them, there were four hundred and some, were lost. There was a book written about the U.S.S. *Franklin*—*Big Ben* they called it. I have turned the pages to read it, but I just can't go far, because my son's picture is in there. He was taking his initiation as chief petty officer, going through this foolish ceremony where they had dirty whites on and they had fellows kneeling in front of him. I never saw him with the uniform on.

I have two other sons. They took it very hard. And of course, my daughter did too. She thought I was going to stop the wedding. I debated in my mind, should I, and I thought: No, if she had it all planned, then let her go through with it. But it wasn't an easy thing to do.

Since I've been in the American Gold Star Mothers, I have really felt that I am not alone in the world, having lost a son. Back home in Rhode Island we have one mother who lost three sons. You have a different outlook belonging to this, because you just try to forget. We try to brush it off, and I feel myself that would be as my son would want me to be. We all have something in common: We don't have to go around bewailing ourselves.

One of the things that used to annoy me during the war was that there was lots of work going on, people were getting good money, and when it ended, some wished we were in the war again for the money they made. That was the attitude of the working class. It really was an awful thing. The fellows would go out there and lose their lives, and then for some people to feel that way. That hurts.

My general feeling about the war is why did it have to happen? You just have to learn to accept it; it's a bitter pill to swallow, but I think I relieved myself of a feeling of bitterness when I went into the hospital to do some volunteer work. When you're around the hospital, you see some amputees, and you have to say to yourself, "Thank God, he went as he was—if it had to be—as we remember him." That's the only consolation you can give yourself.

The Reverend Edward G. Latch is the chaplain of the House of Representatives. During the war he was the minister at the Metropolitan Memorial United Methodist Church in Washington, D.C.

I tried to keep the war, as such, out of the pulpit, because I felt people had read enough and that when they came to church, they wanted something with meaning to their life, something that would support them, some idea they could use during the week in this state of confusion and uncertainty. That is the thing I tried to do, and, to a degree, I think we succeeded. But you never know.

Any number of my people had folks in the service—always hoping things would turn out well. All I did was try to be a steadying factor, persuading them that God is good and not that he was on their side or the other side; I avoided that; I just stressed that his will will be done, with truth and goodness coming out of it.

Once in a while I would have a call in the middle of the night if a family had just learned of a death. But usually they would wait until morning, and I would go and just let them talk. There is nothing much you can do. It is a fact, and they have to adjust, which is not an easy thing to do.

Most people took it exceptionally well, tragic as it was to them. The church plays a very important role in a moment like that. People need someone to turn to, someone to talk to, someplace where they can come.

The morale during the war years was good. People were busy, working day and night. I had some people in the parish who worked too hard, some with family problems, but because it was during the war, they seemed to get by. In the war effort the wives had to work—there were jobs that had to be done—but that always creates a family problem, particularly for the children. I think that is one reason why some of the kids have grown up with problems. They have not had the warmth and affection they should have had.

War begins to turn you against the fact of war because of what it means to people and what it does to people in terms of personality problems, domestic problems, neighborhood problems that arise out of war. You begin to see how, actually, in the long run, war is useless. But I didn't find many people opposed to the Second World War. Pearl Harbor came, and people thought there was only one thing we could do and that was stop them from doing what they were doing.

THE WAR ENDS
Victory Over Japan
An American Victory
(Special)—Page 6

The Berkshire Evening Eagle Extra

Pittsfield, Massachusetts, Tuesday, August 14, 1945.

JAPS SURRENDER;
WAR IS FINISHED

WIPE OUT HITLER

A Prayer of Thanksgiving · · · · Nips Accept Unconditional Terms

10

1945—THE END

The year 1945 was possibly the most significant year in American history, certainly in the twentieth century. In April, President Franklin D. Roosevelt, who had been president for twelve years, longer than any president in our history, died. It was not only a traumatic experience for many Americans, it symbolized the end of an era. And his successor, Harry S Truman, symbolized the beginning of a new era. In May, the war in Europe ended, and with it the most destructive human force in modern history—the German Nazis. On August 6 and 9 the United States dropped what, by today's standards, were small nuclear bombs on Hiroshima and Nagasaki, and on August 14 the Japanese surrendered, which ended one era and launched a new one—an era dominated by the existence of nuclear weapons and an ambiguous, uncertain condition marked by an absence of war, at least not all-out world war, but certainly not peace. Winston Churchill summed it up best: "a balance of terror." Some of the Americans we have heard from in this book recall their reactions to the events of this momentous year and to the two men who dominated it—Franklin D. Roosevelt and Harry S Truman.

FDR

Jack Altshul, at Newsday:

I personally thought President Roosevelt was a hero. I thought everything he did about the war was right. You couldn't understand how these Japanese, who didn't consider themselves our military equal or threat, could wreak the havoc they did. All of a sudden, for the first time in our generation, we were underdogs. You didn't know what was going on about Roosevelt's conduct of the war, except that after two or three years all of a sudden we're getting those islands back and we are winning battles on the seas and we're landing in Italy, and then, of course, D day. I will never forget that. I think that story broke at two o'clock in the morning.

Hezekiah Goodwin:

We hated him, Roosevelt, because we saw what he was doing—this went back before the war. He had nothing to offer us. He had ability as a war leader, but we certainly hated him and his ideas on domestic affairs.

Stephen Ailes:

Roosevelt did a helluva lot better job in the war situation, just like Churchill. Churchill was a bit of a problem in peacetime. But, my God, he was heroic in wartime! And I think FDR was the same way.

Anna Mae Lindberg:

My feeling about Roosevelt at that time was that he was my leader— and take me to my leader. But I wouldn't feel that way today. At that time I was caught up, I felt admiration. Actually, some of us were intelligent enough to wonder about Pearl Harbor, but it was like committing a sin; the minute doubts would come into your head, zoom, get those thoughts out of there! They don't belong there. But there was always the thought, how could it be such a surprise?

Melville Grosvenor:

I was not a Roosevelt man before the war, but he converted me when he started the lend-lease assistance to Great Britain and followed with the deal leasing fifty destroyers to England. Being a navy man, I knew that was a particularly intelligent move. Britain was in danger of losing control of the North Atlantic to German submarines. As for our destroyers, most of them were literally sinking at the moorings. I was aware of this because I had a friend who commanded one of them. They were built under a crash program in World War I, made of steel that was less than first quality. With the passage of time, the hulls were rusted, and the navy had actually put new bottoms in most of them before they went to England. Furthermore, in the conference at Quebec that outlined allied policy in World War II, I thought the president was just marvelous—and I still think so.

Francis Martin:

I had no use for Roosevelt. None whatever. He caused class distinction in this country. And when he met with Stalin and Churchill over there! We had a Ridgefield boy who was the head of a group to help Russia out against the Germans, coming through the back door with trucks by the hundreds full of ammunitions, food, and everything else. And he told us at the Lion's Club meeting that we were fighting the wrong enemy. When Roosevelt sold out to Stalin, it was too bad, because they should have let Patton go right on through. I think that was most people's opinion.

Congressman Ray Madden (D-Ind.):

If it had not been for Roosevelt, God help us. You could go back before the war, there were fourteen million idle men in 1933, and if it had not been for Roosevelt taking hold of things and putting people to work, we would not have the kind of government we have today. There were riots around here—food riots. There was no Social Security, no protection of bank deposits. There were very few people who owned homes then. The banks, back at the turn of the century, every five or six years had a panic. They didn't call them depressions then; they had panics. They would foreclose farms and homes and start over again. Roosevelt did more to revolutionize this form of government and let the people have some say about the government than anyone since maybe Lincoln. Maybe history will give Roosevelt credit for being one of our greatest presidents. He had the ability and power and personality to do things.

The late Congressman Wright Patman (D-Tex.):

On January 20 of that year—1945—at the time of Roosevelt's speech to Congress, he came in on the arm of James, the oldest boy. And instead of going up the ramp to the podium, as he had done in the past, they went up in front of the Speaker in the aisle that led to the Senate. And as he took his seat, he said: "Well, I guess you fellows have wondered all the time that you've seen me walk in here under surveillance how I could possibly get along so long? I carry 112 pounds of steel on both of my legs, and that's quite a burden for me, which you realize. But I've enjoyed every bit of it, for I felt like I was doing something."

Leverett Saltonstall Governor of Massachusetts:

The last time I saw him was when he came before the joint session of the Congress after his trip to Yalta. He came back and spoke from a wheelchair in front of the podium. He looked an awfully sick man.

Marquis Childs:

I remember the last private phone call I had with Roosevelt. His assumption, partly spoken, but implied, was that he would be around to mastermind the peace. It was just exactly one year almost to the day he died. He was then, I think, a tired man; I remember his hand shaking when he was lighting a cigarette.

Bryson Rash:

He had the ability, and I've seen this seldom in men, to come into a room and, depending upon his mood and attitude, light it up like an incandescent bulb or throw it into complete gloom.

Toward the end of his life Roosevelt lost weight. He looked terrible because his clothes didn't fit properly as they had before. I was talking with Adm. Ross McIntire, his personal physician, and told him the president didn't look too good. He said, "He really is in fairly good shape, but he's a stingy Dutchman, and he won't buy any new shirts.

The result is that he's wearing all these old shirts, and they're too big for him, and his neck looks dreadful. If I could get him to buy some new shirts, he'd look a heck of a lot better.''

I had seen him the night he left for Warm Springs. He made a little speech in the diplomatic reception room, which is a relatively small room. He came in with three dogs—Fala, and Elliot's mastiff, and another big dog that looked like a Labrador. He was in great spirits, he really was. I went to him and said, "Mr. President, let's get these dogs out of here, because if you're on the air and right in the middle of your broadcast, these dogs get into a big fight or we start a big barking contest, it's going to sound dreadful." He said, "That's great. Let 'em bark. I think that would add a great deal to the broadcast." So the dogs remained, and nothing happened. It was a very short little speech—on war bonds, I think—but he was in fine spirits. It may be because he knew he was going to have some time off at Warm Springs, which he loved, and just be alone and rest.

Bill Gold in the WINX radio newsroom in Washington:

I was standing in front of the line of teletypes in our newsroom urging my newscaster to please look at the goddamn copy before he went in. It was twelve minutes to six; he was going to do the big evening newscast at six o'clock. Lou Aiken was a hell of an impressive newscaster, but I couldn't get him to look at the copy before he went in. I was standing there saying, "Lou, for God's sake, will you look at that copy," when the INS machine stopped, which indicated that a bulletin was coming. Somebody said, "What's this going to be now?" I said, "Oh, probably an announcement of how many tons of shipping MacArthur's air force has sunk," since that report was about due. The machine remained stopped for a few seconds longer than I could stand, so I kicked the leg of the thing and said, "Come on, idiot, tell us something!" And it did. The bells began to ring, and it said, "FLASH, FDR DEAD." Boy, you should have seen that newsroom at that point. Oh, man! Everything went out the window, and we got on the phone to the White House to confirm.

By the time we got confirmation from the White House, all the wires were carrying it. Now you could take your six o'clock newscast and throw it in the wastebasket. We had eleven minutes in which to get up a new newscast—a brief summary of all the other stuff, and almost all of it on Roosevelt. In the meantime I was sitting at a typewriter, writing just as fast as I could, and somebody was taking it out, putting it into some semblance of order, fitting in the other stuff, and carrying it into the man while he was on the air—and he was doing a beautiful job of figuring out what went where. I know I was crying as I wrote; the people on the desk were crying; and the newscaster on the air—although he wasn't crying, he was shaken.

Leo Hershfield:

I was down on the Potomac River at the boat slip, and somebody had a radio going, and it came over like that. I dashed back to the house, then went into town and did a drawing that evening of the vigil—people in Lafayette Park just standing there looking at the White House. It was very moving.

Jack Altshul at Newsday:

Roosevelt's death broke after our last edition was out, and I felt like sitting there crying. We had to get out an extra edition of the paper, and all our carriers were out with the earlier paper, but we went back to press. God, there were people in the office who were professed Republicans and may have come from stockbroking families who have never forgiven Roosevelt and still, during the war, were blaming him for bringing on the war, getting us into it. But I can remember going with some of those guys to the bar where we used to hang out after we put out the new edition, and the guys were crying.

Mary McMurria in Columbus, Georgia:

We're so close to Warm Springs—just thirty-five miles. Everybody was stunned. The news came in the afternoon, and we just felt like we couldn't stand it. Fort Benning, of course, went on an alert, because everybody who flew into Warm Springs came to Fort Benning. In fact, two or three planes landed before Mrs. Roosevelt arrived, and all of the brass was lined up at this one particular plane, which maybe had several newsmen on it and one young pilot who had hitched a ride.

When he walked out the door, there was an entire contingent of generals lined up. There were several false alarms before Mrs. Roosevelt's plane arrived.

Kay Halle, working for OSS in Washington:

I was walking home from Q Building, near the old naval hospital, where we worked, with Geoffrey Hellman, another OSS colleague. We were crossing the park at Dupont Circle when a friend approached us shouting out the news. We couldn't believe it. Odd how everyone remembers exactly where they were at that moment.

Ann Hoskins:

I was coming home from the office in the late afternoon. It was one of those lovely spring days, the children were biking up and down the street under the elms, and suddenly my little girl, with her pigtails flying, came running up, and said, "Roosevelt's dead, I just heard it on the radio." I felt as if the bottom had dropped out of me, and I couldn't imagine what was going to happen next. But it never occurred to me that he wasn't mortal.

Tony Taylor, a young boy working in the Cosmos Club in Washington:

I remember the night Roosevelt died, because all the news commentators were coming into the Cosmos Club. They were shocked, crying, screaming. It was really an unbelievable thing. And you know how everyone felt about Roosevelt if you was a black person. He was a savior, man.

Anne Relph:

That was a terrible, terrible afternoon. I can remember riding my bicycle back to the playground after school, having just heard on the radio that Roosevelt had died and feeling, as a child, that this was going to be the end of the world, because he was the only president I'd ever known. I was almost not aware that there could be another president. He had always been THE PRESIDENT, in capital letters.

Betty Bryce:

I remember it. It happened in April. My son Dalton was killed on the fourteenth of March, and his citation was signed by Roosevelt.

Barbara Smith (pseudonym), Summit, New Jersey:

I was having dinner with a very good friend when it came over the radio, and although she and I were both Republicans, we thought that Mr. Roosevelt was doing a superb job, and we could hardly finish dinner. After that, I was in the food market, and two women were chatting. One of them put her arms up and said, "Thank God that man is gone!" It struck me so that I stood there, and all I could say to them was, "God help you for having such thoughts." And I walked away.

Mabel Wiggins:

Somebody told me up here [in Maine] that when she heard President Roosevelt had died, she rushed home to tell her husband so they could celebrate. Just cruel, sick people.

Lillie Bernstein:

I was on the corner of Wabash and Randolph Street in Chicago, and I stood and cried my eyes out. I thought the world had come to an end.

Studs Terkel:

I remember meeting with a sponsor in the Stevens Hotel; we were having some drinks, and somebody said, "The president is dead." I didn't know what the hell he was talking about. "The president's dead." "What are you talking about?" "Franklin Roosevelt." Everybody left. I'm walking south on Michigan Boulevard, and I can't stop crying. Everybody is crying. I was doing a series for Mutual of Omaha called *Freedom of Opportunity,* dealing with Americans—John Huston, Ring Lardner. Somebody said do a program on Roosevelt, and I said, "I can't." It was too much. But I did do one finally, for my news program. I may have played some music.

Mary Dandouveris, a student at the University of Wisconsin:

I'll never forget the gloom that we felt at campus on his death. When the news came, I think I was in journalism class, and one of the fellows I knew came by and said, "Did you hear?" And I thought he was joshing me, because I was a strong supporter of Roosevelt. I remember later clustering around the radio and hearing about it. The thing that was predominant was that the churches all stayed open, and there were special memorial services, a lot of quiet music on the radio stations, and we all went to church. In the evening people seemed to congregate in the churches, and nobody knew much about Truman. It was a great sorrow, not unlike the sorrow that was felt for President Kennedy.

Richard Lingeman was fourteen when FDR died and living in a small Indiana town.

It was a very Republican community. My parents were rather liberal. They were Republicans, but I don't remember them as being Roosevelt haters. There were a lot of those in the town, and I sort of imbibed that, but not from my parents so much. It seems to me my father would read the liberal magazines, like *The Nation*—he subscribed to that—but he didn't want to go too far, it being a small town. Anyway, I was very anti-Roosevelt. When he died in '45, I was on the Boy Scout color guard that raised the flag every day at school, and we were sort of joking about the possibility of flying the flag at half-mast. Then we said, "Aw, we're not going to," and raised the flag. The art teacher came out, obviously a Roosevelt supporter, and she said in effect, "You awful boys, put that flag at half-mast!" We immediately sobered up and put it at half-mast. I later completely changed. But at that time I was like the rest.

Elmer Louis Kayser:

There is one thing about Roosevelt's death I will never forget. You remember trivia, you know. Shortly after the president expired, I and everyone else who was on the radio with news commentary got a long telegram from the morticians' organization, saying, "In your references over the radio will you please be sure to observe the following rules: Never say *coffin*, say *casket*; never say *funeral procession*, say *cortege*." They were instructing us to use this fancy nomenclature. It was one of the most macabre and grotesque things I have ever seen. It has stuck in my mind, or maybe I should say, my craw.

Hilda O'Brien:

My first reaction, I remember, was "Truman is our vice president." And somebody said, "No, he isn't. He's our president." It was just a terrible feeling of being absolutely leaderless. Actually he turned out to be not that bad, but my feeling was that he was totally inadequate. The next day when I went to work I put on an entirely black outfit. It was hot—it was in April, and I can just see myself now, but I was just that much affected.

Mary Punderson:

I was reading College Boards at that time, and I remember coming out—I can see the surroundings of buildings and trees and things—and hearing that President Roosevelt had died, then meeting someone, looking rather gray and grim, and saying, "What do we have; who is Truman?"

TRUMAN BECOMES PRESIDENT

The late Congressman Wright Patman (D. Tex.):

There's a place over here at the Capitol that's called the "Speaker's Hideaway." On the afternoon of April 14, 1945, Vice President Truman had just come over to the Hideaway from the White House, when the telephone rang. Mr. Rayburn answered it and said, "It's for you,

Harry." It was the White House, telling him, "You are requested to come down here at once, just as quietly as you can, without talking to anyone if you can possibly do it, and it's required that you come now." He left there and told Mr. Rayburn that he would hear from him pretty soon so he'd know what was going on. In a few minutes he called Mr. Rayburn and said, "I'm instructed by the people in charge to ask you to come down here to give the oath of office."

Under the Democrats, three people had keys to that place, the Speaker, Lyndon Johnson, and myself. I've got my key, same key I had then. Of course, Mr. Rayburn had one just like it, and it went to his grave; Lyndon Johnson had one just like it, and it went to his grave. There were only three.

Mr. Patman died about a month after this interview—and, presumably, took his key with him.

Marquis Childs:

I think it was one of the great moments in history. I will never forget. I got home, and the office called to say a bulletin had just come through that Roosevelt had died. And I thought, "My God! Harry Truman is president." I had known him through his whole career. I had known his connection with Prendergast and how Prendergast had made him a senator sort of by accident and all the rest of it. And how his first election was one of the most rigged elections in American politics. Kansas City always waited until the rest of the vote came in, and then they voted as many as were needed. I had had a casual enough friendly relationship with him on the Hill, and I was dismayed. But I came to feel that he was certainly doing the very best that he could. That he had not been clued in to anything. And, of course, the revisionist historians now tend to blame him for the whole war.

Professor Charles Keller at Williams College:

I went on the college radio that night to say something to the effect that a man of great stature had died, a man who had carried us through the period from 1932 to 1945—three terms plus—and now an unknown kind of a person was taking his place. I guess I went on to moralize a bit, saying that this was the kind of situation where we had to be better people, to make up for the change in leadership.

Bill Gold:

When President Roosevelt's funeral took place a few days later, the body was brought to Washington, and it passed us on Pennsylvania Avenue, headed for the White House. I was there as a reporter, and I was trying to remain objective. But this is an experience you never forget: There were tears in everybody's eyes—white people, black people, old people, young people, males, females, it didn't make a damn bit of difference. This was the father figure, the guy who had seen us through the war, for better or for worse. You knew his strengths and his weaknesses, as a man and as a president. The nation was shaken, but I think here in Washington we felt it harder than anybody, because we knew him best.

Carey McWilliams:

I had mixed feelings about Truman, and in retrospect, I must say that I'm not a Truman fancier. I don't go along with this latter-day adulation of the gentleman from Missouri. I think he was a dreadful president. A nice man, understand, but he wasn't Roosevelt, and I don't think he understood the situation as Roosevelt did. Then, of course, he was also the victim of circumstance, because, I think, one of the unavoidable things that happened was that the fervor of the antifascist rhetoric and ideology spilled over into the postwar period, and they just changed antifascist to anticommunist. Because you apply the same name to two things doesn't mean they are identical. Nazi Germany was a dictatorship; the Soviet Union is a dictatorship; but they're not the same. The Soviet Union poses one kind of problem, which I think has to be coped with politically. The Nazis posed a very different kind of problem, which had to be confronted militarily.

Richard Spitzer:

In the beginning, I thought, my God, this is the end of the country— this poor political hack who was part of the Prendergast machine, who couldn't make it in a men's clothing store, is president. I had this feeling for a long time; then I began to gather some respect for him.

Anna Mae Lindberg:

I liked Truman. I always liked him—maybe because he was like the mailman. He gave you the feeling that us common men are going to show them what we can do. I guess I'd have that same feeling today.

Alison Arnold:

Like everybody else, we thought he was a little necktie salesman. Everybody had the same idea.

Helen Wilson:

I remember Truman taking over and what a pitiful sight it was. I must have seen it in the newsreel. He just seemed so inept and struggling for help. You could tell. This man was not prepared to take over as president. You had the feeling that Roosevelt obviously hadn't prepared this man, even though he must have known he couldn't last another term.

Bill Gold:

People thought that he was a small-town politician, a Prendergast man who just couldn't cut the mustard. Well, the war was pretty well won, and I think from the moment Mr. Truman came in, he began to project an entirely different image to the American people. I remember at one of the very first press conferences, Merriman Smith asked, "Mr. President, are you going to go to a conference with Mr. Stalin?" And Mr. Truman pulled his arms across his chest very complacent, and satisfied. He wasn't at all impolite about it. But it was just beautiful the way he said, "Why, the president of the United States would always be happy to see Mr. Stalin if he came here," turning it around very adroitly. And we began to get a sense that this was no little country boy, he was a very solid citizen.

Ann Hoskins:

I thought: That little ginky guy! I don't see how he could possibly handle it. I really didn't care for him. I didn't realize that he had been a great president until almost now.

Bryson Rash:

He was a remarkable guy. He had this great capacity for homework. He was a very deep student of history and had a humility and an approach to the problems that were just refreshing.

Former Speaker of the House, John W. McCormack:

I was a strong supporter of Truman—I supported him in the convention where he was nominated for vice president. He and I were very close friends. We were in constant contact with one another. He was one man who impressed me as having what the feminine sex has—a powerful sense of intuition. He'd make judgments, and it seemed he could look into the future and see what was going to happen.

Edward Stuntz:

A lot of newspapermen knew Truman as a senator, and they knew that Truman was one guy who said what he meant and meant what he said.

Stephen Ailes:

I was greatly sympathetic toTruman, as a guy who was in a mile over his head, to all appearances. It's always been my view that there was a rare form of patriotism which you find in congress—guys like Sam Rayburn—who really are concerned about the future of this country and who would do almost anything if they thought that was their role in connection with the future of the country. I always put Truman in that category.

Louis Speyer:

I liked Mr. Truman. He was simple but intelligent. People thought he was a little peasant; he might have been a peasant, but he knew what he was talking about.

Frank Waldrop:

Truman was a relief, because you can't imagine the intrigue. God, talk about a corrupt court. You see, you had a president who had been sitting there a long time, and it was rather like Versailles in the last six months of old Louis. So Truman was a breath of fresh air, a great relief to everybody. We got along with him fine. He was, in every way, a better president for the time at hand than Roosevelt. I was reading just recently a review of Harriman's memoirs, and I was interested to see that Harriman now—thirty-two years later—is willing to say that Roosevelt didn't do the country any favor by running for a fourth term. But it's one thing to say it in 1976 and another thing to say it in 1944.

V-E DAY

Paul Kneeland in Boston:

On V-E Day everybody was covering it. It was really great. Every reporter took off. We were all out getting color stories—interviewing girls who had taken off their blouses, taken off their shoes, were dancing, standing on their heads, hanging out of hotel rooms, sitting on ledges of hotel rooms fourteen flights up and waving down, pouring water down. Crazy. World gone nuts!

Ann Hoskins in Salisbury, Connecticut:

On V-E Day the church bells rang out all over town, and everybody dropped what they were doing and went to whatever their church was. And those who didn't have a church went to any church. They came in overalls, they came with babies in their arms. And all they did was just say a few words and sing a hymn, the choir kneeling, and it was one of the most moving, simplest services I ever heard. I'm not much of a churchgoer but this did me in.

Harry Hahn:

We happened to be on a little vacation in New Orleans. We went down to the French Quarter that night expecting hell to be exploding, but nobody had gone to the bar at all. It was an amazing thing. People went to the churches; they didn't go to the bars. The churches open, people went in and knelt down and said a prayer. There was no festivity in the streets.

Anne Relph:

I can remember being on a train with my grandmother and hearing bells ring as we went through little towns in Louisiana. I didn't know what was going on until the train stopped, and someone told us that the war in Europe had ended. There was rejoicing, people sort of dancing in the street and church bells ringing in every little town we went through. In New Orleans people were literally dancing in the streets. They were singing, dancing, jumping in and out of fountains, and people were kissing and hugging each other. It was like Mardi Gras, and just this incredible sense of relief that part of the war, anyway, was finished and that people would be coming home again.

Anne Rippery on the New Jersey shore:

We were at our beach house. My aunt was a nurse in the army and had been sent back to the United States. She'd gone home and found out we were at the beach, and just as the news came, Florence came up the walk to the house. That was such a sheer delight for the whole family. We were in the midst of celebrating, when one-half of the family we worried about so much just walked in the door.

Don Baldwin:

They had a major disturbance in downtown San Francisco on V-E Day. Servicemen particularly, but also some civilians. They really ran amok, broke windows and looted right down at Fifth and Market around the Emporium and that area. I went to work at about midnight, and it was really exciting. The police had made one of these cordons. They had some armored cars, and they were just sweeping Market Street. Servicemen and civilians—just sweeping them ahead with all those big bullhorns: "Break it up—Get off Market Street." It took them the better part of the night. People turned over streetcars and some taxicabs. And of course, all the liquor stores had their windows broken.

THE BOMB

Former senator from Vermont, George Aiken:

When Truman got in as president, the Pentagon was not telling him what was going on in the war. I told him so one day, and he said, "I know it." His big objective was to get out of the war. Japan had then made an appeal to us through a third party, wanting to get out of it, but the president didn't know if the people of this country would stand for letting Japan get out of the war without our invading the islands. It was estimated it would cost us about 200,000 casualties. Then, finally, there was the bombing of Hiroshima. I'm not sure how much he knew about it. The military faction didn't tell him any more than they had to. But he had to make the final decision.

Tom Page at the War Production Board:

We had a request once, related to the refinement of rare metals in Germany. "Rare metals?" we all said, "what the hell are rare metals?" Well, they said, things like plutonium and uranium and named four or five rare metals. We started calling around the country and went to see metallurgists who we knew were familiar with occupied Europe. And we'd get answers like: "We can't talk about that. Why are you asking about that? You mustn't go around asking questions like that."

Actually, we were asking about the atom bomb, but we didn't know that. We were asking guys who were working on the Manhattan Project about the refinement of plutonium and uranium and, Christ, they wanted to get under the bed, they didn't want to hear any part of these questions. After we went through this, a guy I was working with said to me: "You know, there's something about these rare metals—honestly, if I had any money, I'd invest it in rare metals!" As a matter of fact, he was right, because there was a company that did a lot of refining of rare metals, and, God, it took off in the postwar years like nothing you ever saw.

And there was a newspaper story about Oak Ridge, Tennessee. Some congressman said that's where they're producing the front ends of jackasses. The government has spent millions to produce the front ends of jackasses to fit to the rear ends of all those jackasses they have in Washington. He was complaining about the hundreds of millions that had been spent at Oak Ridge for reasons they never stated.

John Lacey, who worked for the Johns Hopkins Research Laboratory:

I remember attending a meeting down at the Office of Scientific Research and Development, and something was said about Oak Ridge. When I said, "What's Oak Ridge?" everybody sort of recoiled in horror, and somebody said, "Oh, it's just a wide place in the road down in Tennessee." I got the message.

John W. McCormack:

I remember being in FDR's office on some matter. We knew that the Philippines had been recaptured, and there was some organized resistance on the part of minor segments of the Japanese army. A mopping-up process was going on. FDR said to me, "John, I have before me now three plans from the Joint Chiefs of Staff as to our next military campaign, and I've got to make the decision in the near future." Two of them were in different parts of continental China, and the other one was through Japan. And he said, "If I make the decision that the next campaign will be right straight to Japan"—and I knew he would—"the Joint Chiefs of Staff have estimated that there would be one million American casualties." That was what faced Harry Truman when he dropped the bombs on Hiroshima and Nagasaki. I would have done the same thing, and I was next in line to succession when John Kennedy was assassinated and Lyndon Johnson took over. I'd have made the same decision. I would have disliked hurling bombs on noncombat camps in the city. There was a moral question involved in that. But on the other side there was a moral question in trying to avoid a million American casualties.

Horace Hubbard, an engineer with General Electric:

We knew we were working on something unusual. But at that time I did not have a feeling of the devastation of this weapon. And when the bomb was dropped, I had a feeling of satisfaction that what we worked on apparently produced results. It seemed to me at that time that, regardless of the subsequent criticism, the United States had almost no alternative but to use it. I don't know if that was any worse than a whole lot of other things that were going on. I don't think I had so much time to think about it.

R. W. Danischefsky, with the Defense Plants Corporation of the RFC:

I worked on the Manhattan Project for about eight months and didn't know what I was doing. Nobody did—the greatest kept secret in the world. I was helping to equip plants to make small parts in Detroit. All we knew was that it was for the Manhattan Project, and nobody knew what that was, and there was no way you could find out. But we didn't care. You had other things on your mind. So it was for the Manhattan Project. So what? Go ahead and let them have it. If it's government sponsored, it's gotta be all right.

Hilda O'Brien, who worked in the Office of the Censor:

I was in the office, and somebody said there was a notice up on the board. We walked down, and there it was posted on the board—the dropping of the atom bomb. It was no secret anymore, but this was something that we had, quite by accident, picked up in a letter. We didn't know the details, but it had been picked up by our division that something very special was going on in Nevada. Of course, it had been treated with great circumspection.

Marquis Childs:

I had known about the building of the bomb and had written a column saying that, of course, the United States and Germany are competing to see who will come out with it first. I was in the dentist's chair, I remember, when the censor's office called up—maybe it was the head guy himself—and said, "This is very bad, you will have to kill that," which I proceeded to do.

Jerome Thirion:

I had a friend who worked at Los Alamos, where they developed the first atomic weapons. He was a young chemist—never drafted into the service, but he was drafted into this work and was one of their top directors down there.

The power of the bomb was made clear to us through him. When he visited us, he brought us samples of the tower—they must have had a huge tower that they had set off. The samples he brought showed just how this tower melted right into the soil. It was highly radioactive, but it was permissible to bring it. It was a souvenir encased in plastic. It made me realize what a thing the bomb must have been. When we saw what it could to to a tower, all of us realized this thing could tear the whole world apart.

George Garrott, working for OWI in Washington:

I was called at home to get over to the White House for an important announcement. I think it was about noon. So I got over to the White House, and we waited around. Nobody knew what was coming until finally the secretary came out and just handed us a mimeographed announcement which said that the atom bomb had been dropped, and its force was twenty thousand tons of dynamite. There was no briefing of any kind, but they did give out the so-called Groves Report on Atomic Energy. We looked at it, and it was just so much flute music, fanciful mathematical writing. So we did what any newspaperman would do— wrote a story saying the report was out but that it was very difficult to understand and then quoted two paragraphs from the frontispiece by the author of the report, and that was the official story of the first atom bomb. I mean, none of us could understand it. Weeks later the experts began to interpret what it meant.

Gus Robbins, editor of the Hopewell (Va.) News:

I was in the back shop when my girl Friday came running back and told me they had dropped the bomb on Hiroshima. I stood there with my mouth open, and I said, "Oh, my God, they've destroyed the world." I remember those words just as well as if it happened yesterday. You see, I had a brother-in-law in the Manhattan Project, so I knew what was going on, and I was praying they'd never do it.

Judson Phillips, who was writing a news program for radio station WOR in New York:

The day that the bomb was dropped I had already written my show when the radio station called and said: "You've got to change the show." I asked them why, and they said. "Come down here. They dropped the bomb on Hiroshima." So I went down, and they had listened to the tapes. I had no more idea what they were talking about than the man in the moon, but, for a show that had to go on the air at seven o'clock, I wrote a story about the dropping of the atom bomb, not having any idea of its dimensions or its importance or anything else. The people at WOR didn't know what the hell it was, but they figured it must be important, so much was being made of it. I guess the show I wrote was the first dramatized program on the air, because it was three hours after it happened. And I never had a tape of it. At the time, it didn't seem like anything. We weren't really aware of the significance. Truman's speech seemed like double-talk.

Erwin Hargrove, who was fourteen years old in 1945:

There was a series of dramatic announcements, and, as I remember, the atom bomb was a kind of decisive event associated in my mind with the end of the war. A great sense of release. But there was no reaction that we were doing something horrible.

Dorothy Currier:

Horror—complete and utter horror! That something like that could be made by man and that anything like that could happen to a city—wiping out so many people at once! And why couldn't it happen here? At that point, we all stopped and took a long, deep look at Russia.

Dorothy Whitaker, whose brother was a prisoner of war in Japan:

It just left everybody in a state of shock. It was so foreign to anything we had even thought about. It left everybody wondering, what next? When we got the pictures, it was sickening. But at first everybody thought, "Oh, this is great! We've got something the others don't have, and it's enough to stop the war." I was thinking of my brother and all the other prisoners and those boys who were over there getting ready to go into battle. It seemed like such a great thing to have it cut off just like that. The churches all were open that day, bells rang, and everybody left their shops and jobs and went to church. My brother was in Osaka at the time, and it sounded so much at first like Nagasaki.

Helen Wilson:

It just seemed like another weapon; nothing particularly traumatic about a larger size weapon.

Anna Mae Lindberg:

My husband's parents had a place in the country with no electricity, no water, no nothing. Consequently, we had no radio or telephone.

Every day we would go down to the village and buy a newspaper. Well, the day the bomb dropped on Hiroshima, we were isolated. We had no visitors, so we didn't know anything about it when we bought the newspaper. I don't remember exactly what the headline was—but 100,000 people killed by a bomb! But I could not absorb that, getting it for the first time on the written page. I thought, this must be a joke newspaper or a misprint, or the headline is wrong. I couldn't conceive that 100,000 people would be killed in one blast. They were the enemy, but they were people. And actually, they were innocent people, the same as if they were to drop that bomb on Homestead [Pennsylvania]. You could put yourself in their place, because if they dropped a bomb on us, then it would have been me.

Celeste Kavanaugh:

When I look back on it, I'm rather ashamed. One of my dear brothers was in the Philippines, getting ready to invade Japan, and I knew that it probably spared his life. I had another brother in China at the time. After four years of wondering from day to day where they were going to be, it was a great relief to know that things were speeding up. It was a terrible way to end it, though.

Hezekiah Goodwin:

We thought it was great.

Newton Tolman:

Christ! Oh, my God, don't ever mention it! I haven't been sane since. Hiroshima to me was the most total defeat of the whole progress of humanity that I have ever seen. I'm a pessimist—that's why I'm happy. Pessimists are always happy, because we only have one more day to live, and that's the end of that. Optimists are always horribly sad people. Well, anyhow, my reaction to that—I remember so vividly, more than any day in my whole goddamned life—was, this is the end! This damned stuff can't be! Jimmy Doolittle's best lifelong friend had come back from the Greek army, and he was all excited. "Isn't this wonderful! Jimmy has done it!'' Well, Jimmy did it all right; but Jimmy never knew what the hell he did. It was disaster. Don't mention it.

Eleanor Kuhne:

I thought it was great. I still think it was a good idea. I think we would have lost a great many more men if we had had to end the war by conventional means. I probably would have lost my husband. They had to invent the atom bomb. They would have used it eventually. It is not the kind of thing that you can keep under wraps forever.

Sally Lucke:

I had a very strong reaction to the dropping of the atom bomb. I remember I made a gigantic painting, which we still have in the attic someplace, of an atom bomb, like a figure of a mother holding a child, trying to protect him from the flames. I was very aware of the human beings who had been bombed, and the fires. My godchildren's mother was in the bombing at Hiroshima. All of the family became radioactive, and the mother eventually died.

Carey McWilliams:

I had been downtown in Los Angeles; when I picked up an afternoon paper and saw this, I was really shaken by it. I didn't think of it as I now do, because it was so sudden, shocking, and the war was on. But what I've read about it since makes me believe that it was a dreadful mistake, that Japan was really knocked out of the war, didn't need the bomb to complete the process. But there should have been a specific warning. It was actually aimed at the Russians, and they got the message. I wasn't thinking in those terms at the time.

Frank Waldrop:

About dropping the bomb—I felt just like everybody else did who had any sense. I didn't give a damn how many Japanese were killed; it was

Americans who made the difference. And if the Japanese didn't want to get bombed, they shouldn't have started the monkey business they did.

That's not saying I go 100 percent for the doctrine of the Japanese as aggressors. I think the United States provoked the Japanese extremely and severely. But Truman was doing what was ordained by the time he came to the presidency. Churchill once said a line I've often thought was applicable. He said, "The Second World War should be called the unnecessary war." This is an involved proposition, concerning the mistake of trying to appease Hitler, beginning in '36. We'll never know whether Churchill was right. But *the unnecessary war* certainly is a phrase to be applied to the United States in the Pacific. Now, I am not going to hash up all the arguments about whether we could have avoided war in Europe or not, but we sure as hell didn't give the Japanese any corner to go into in the Pacific.

That has nothing to do with the question of dropping the bomb. The president of the United States has an obligation to the corn farmers in Iowa, never to mankind. Nobody knows who mankind is; that is one of those great big juicy generalities that is an alibi for not doing your job. Yet he knows who the people of the United States are, and it was their sons who were out there getting killed.

Marquis Childs:

I remember the next-to-the-last session we had with Marshall, in which he repeated what had been the provincial wisdom of the attack on the Japanese mainland: It would cost 500,000 American casualties. The Japanese—man, woman, and child—would fight with pitchforks or guns, or whatever they had. I think that was probably a terrible overstatement of the situation at that time. The Japanese were beginning to make overtures for peace. And I thought Truman was so unwise when he was interviewed by Murrow, remember? Truman said: "I would do the same thing tomorrow."

Richard Lingeman:

I didn't quite understand it. It seemed another one of those wondrous weapons that you cheered on, much like you cheered on the other raids that you read about, the fire-bombing raids and the raids on Japan and

Germany. It was sort of awesome, hard to understand. But it was another weapon. It never occurred to me to question the morality or wisdom of Truman's decision to use the bomb. You heard casualty figures all the time—so many thousands were killed. As a boy, you were a war fan, and you kept maps with pins and flags on them and watched the advance of the Allies. It was something a bit glamorous.

Kay Halle:

   The dropping of the bomb came as an utter and complete shock. I shared Herbert Elliston's view that we should have demonstrated its terrifying power by dropping it first on an uninhabited, remote place—before a group of heads of government and, of course, the Japanese.

Eunice Yoakum:

   I have always felt that Mr. Truman should not have dropped the bomb. I think Japan was really ready to give in anyway. And he should have given some kind of warning or dropped the bomb somewhere else to let them see what it would do—especially the second one. I never understood why they dropped two. I always felt that was the beginning of our moral decline. I don't see how a country could do a thing like that. I feel very strongly about that. But otherwise, I admired Truman.

Arthur Edmunds:

   I reacted to the dropping of the atom bomb almost exclusively on a black-white issue. It was dropped on colored people, not on white people. I tried to accept the rationale of the leadership at that time that if we had not done that, it would have cost so many of our soldiers' lives, and so forth. And I have some appreciation for that. But I never quite understood it.

Mary Devereux Crist, whose husband was a Marine Corps colonel:

   I was delighted. There are very few service people who would say that. I have a good friend, a writer, and a retired marine general, who thinks it was perfectly awful that we dropped the bomb. But he was not out there when we did it, and I felt: Why shouldn't we? My husband and I discussed it many times after the war was over, and he said, "Well, if it hadn't been for that, I would have made the landing in Japan. We were all prepared to make it."

As a matter of fact, I think we should have done more to them, and I have a very difficult time holding my tongue when I hear about those poor Japanese—like that film they had on TV of the Japanese being interned. I have some close friends here who are very pro-Japanese, and I said to them, "In that whole film it didn't say anything about what the Japanese had done to us." I realize there were isolated cases, and that they shouldn't have *all* been gathered up. But on the West Coast, where I had a niece whose husband was overseas, they were terrified of the Japanese making a landing in California. I have a sister who was married to a general in the Marine Corps, too, who was out there, and they were in a rush to get as far away from the coast as they *could.*

Dorothy Schenck:

I had a feeling of horror that so many people were killed. But I also had terrible resentments against the Japanese. There were some Japanese going to school at the college, and I had a lot of hard resentment against them.

Tony Taylor:

Dropping the atom bomb didn't scare me, 'cause I said: "Now, wait a minute, these people are fucking around over there, you know. Like, let's end this shit and just drop a bomb and wipe out a whole lot of people." But then, later on, my Christian side came out. I said: "Hey, I could be very aware of those people, the innocent people over there. They don't want bombs dropped on them." I almost feel that the tempo was such that Americans wanted to show their dominance at that time. They had all the technical know-how, and they wanted to really display it. I think that everybody thought the same way. They didn't look to the other side, the Christian or humane side of it. They thought: "Hey, we're being faced with something, and this is a shortcut, and if this bomb is dropped and we let those people know how powerful we are, we can end it right there." I don't know how it was among the heavier politicians, but the average person walking through the street and in backyard-fence conversations would say, "We've got this big thing that's going to end all of that shit, and then we won't have to go anymore." That kind of thing.

Necei Degen:

The dropping of the atom bomb was a question of morality. It was an immoral act, as far as I am concerned. I knew that day something ungodly had happened. The American government had unleashed this vile thing, and it has haunted me personally from that point on.

Studs Terkel:

Well, this is my moment of confession. At the time, I felt—wow—the war would be over. I remember that night I was on the radio, and I said, now the war would be over. Later on—the horror hit me! Remember when Einstein heard the news, he is reputed to have said: "I wish I were a locksmith." His secretary said on a program many years later that she met him coming down the stairs, and he said something like "oh way." She wasn't Jewish and, of course, what he was saying was "*oye veh.*"

David Soergal, an electrical engineer:

My reaction was then and still is that I don't know why we didn't tell the Japanese we'd demonstrate this thing at some unpopulated island, and they could come over and watch it. I don't know why we didn't do that instead of kill over 300,000 people. There's no point in using science to kill people. Science can do wonderful things, but it can do a lot of bad, too. There was a great revulsion among the leaders in the atomic energy business at the use of this thing. Robert Oppenheimer got labeled as a Communist just because he was philosophically against it.

Lillie Bernstein:

When Truman dropped the bomb, I thought it was the most courageous thing. I felt terribly bad about the people in Japan. But I felt that it took a lot of grit and courage to say it should be done. At that time, two of my sons were en route from Europe to go to the Orient, and it looked as though there would be millions more people killed. I really think it kept the war from going on.

Francis Martin:

I could see why they had to do it. It was terrible, but just look at it— we probably saved thousands and thousands and thousands of lives on both sides by doing it. It was a terrible thing.

Don Baldwin:

I don't think I had any sense of foreboding. We had all been fairly well toughened to death figures and the sense of killing and the fire storms in Tokyo, so to announce that another forty thousand people had been killed was not the shock that it might have been.

Anne Relph:

A very terrifying thing, the feeling that the world had somehow changed and that it was never going to be the same again, that some kind of scary, terrible force had been set loose that nobody had any way to contain. I can remember having bad dreams about it for weeks— about building shelters in case of an atomic attack and there not being anyplace you could go to escape. I was old enough by then to be going to movies, seeing newsreels, and being aware of what was going on, rather than having it filtered through the grown-ups. My family tended to keep a kind of optimistic attitude about things, but I think this was one of those secret terrors that children have that the world had changed, that there was no way you could ever go back to the time before that bomb had been dropped.

Ann Hoskins:

I was stunned at first. Nobody knew what to make of it. Afterward, when we realized what it had done, the reaction was, why didn't they drop it on an empty mountain so people could at least see and have a look and then they could save all those people? It was that kind of a feeling; at least it was with me. I never felt happy about that.

Jack Lynch:

   Whether you liked Truman or not, he made many good decisions, and probably the most debated one was the decision to drop the atom bomb. I agreed with him 100 percent, 1,000 percent, because I think he saved many thousands and thousands of American lives. We didn't start the war. If they paid a price, I think it was their own indebtedness. I never heard any reaction against it. The way we had entered the war with the sneak attack on Pearl Harbor, I don't think there was much sympathy for the Japanese in those days.

Harry and Elizabeth Hahn:

   ELIZABETH: Horror! We have seen Hiroshima since then, and it was ghastly. My first reaction was, that's going to end the war, great! But then, when I thought about it, I thought, my heavens, it could happen here! And I was just frightened of it, really.
   HARRY: I think I approved of it. The president said we saved a lot of lives by taking so many at one time. Had we had to invade, the casualties in Tokyo and all the other cities among the Japanese would have been stupendous and the loss of American lives would be untold. As bad as this was, I think we saved lives.
   ELIZABETH: Well, we went there and saw the memorial and museum and, oh, just horrible.

Peggy Blassingame:

   I didn't think of it as horrible. I thought of it as being fantastic—this means the war is going to end. Of course, I didn't understand the destruction. But today I still refuse to feel the sense of guilt that some Americans feel simply because it happened, because of the number of people who died. I agree that it was terrible, but, God, how many more would have died had the bomb not been used? So I still think that it was the right thing to do. I felt at the time, without knowing the enormity of it, "This is the end of the war!"

John Lacey:

I think it was the wise thing. I still do. I must say, I share the opinion of some others that it is a terrible shame the thing was ever developed. But if we hadn't developed it, the Germans would have. In fact, you know the story of the heavy-water plant in Norway. One of my friends, who recently retired from Hopkins was, I believe, on the team that helped destroy that German plant in Norway and thus postponed the development of the atom bomb. I'm sure if Hitler had had it, he would have used it.

The Reverend Edward G. Latch:

My reaction to dropping the atom bomb was that it was a tragic thing to have to do. I question, sometimes, whether we had to do it, yet who am I to know? I can't answer questions like that. I'm just an ordinary citizen like anyone else. It took a lot of lives, but it saved a lot of lives that would have been taken if the war had been prolonged. I think that was the hardest decision a president has had to make, and yet I think it shortened the war.

An interesting thing about the Japanese. In Nagasaki they have observed the anniversary of the atom bomb. But then, they never said what they did to Pearl Harbor. Not a word, and I don't think we did either. We ought to say a little more about it: Yes, we did that, but look at what you did here at Pearl Harbor to cause that. But that's never recognized, for some reason.

V-J DAY

Bill Gold with radio station WINX in Washington, D.C.:

We had a couple of false alarms. A cuckoo walked into the United Press office in Memphis while the machine was unguarded and typed out a bulletin saying that the war was over. That went out for a few minutes and threw the country into a tizzy. This was in the last month, as I recall, and it was at a time when people could sense what was coming and were ready to believe it.

Later, we had another one while I was on duty in the White House. Joe Short, Truman's press secretary, would come out at night and say, "The president's gone to bed, and I'll be around till midnight. We put the lid on at midnight, and you can all come back at eight o'clock tomorrow morning and start standing by again." So that night the president had gone to bed around nine-thirty, nine-forty-five, and we had a poker game going in the pressroom. All the desks were pushed back in the corner to make one big poker table. I was way in the corner in the middle of a hand when my phone began to ring, and I said: "Oh, hell, I wonder what that is. Let it ring for a minute until this hand is over." And then another phone rang, and another phone rang, and something inside me said, "Hey, never mind the hand. Go." I had to walk across the tops of the desks, right through the pot, to get to my phone, and by the time I got there, every phone in the room was ringing. They were all diving for telephones, and my guy was saying, "Well, we beat the world with that one!" I said, "You beat the world with what one, Danny?" And he said, "Oh, Jesus Christ, you mean to say it isn't true? The White House didn't announce that the war was over?" I said, "Danny, you know I have been sitting here eighteen hours a day waiting for it. I'd have called you!" He had seen it come up on the wire and zuppp! He was on the air with it, and then his brain turned on. First he reacted automatically, which is what he is trained to do: Get the goddamn thing on the air. Then he began thinking, of course it's a phony. This sort of thing happened at a lot of radio stations. Some of them were pretty slow putting a correction on.

When the real one came, I was at the White House. We pretty well knew that that was what it was going to be. There was a press conference, and Truman announced it personally.

Frank Waldrop, managing editor of the Washington Times Herald:

I remember V-E and V-J Days. All these great events, as far as I'm concerned, were the same—looking at type upside down and backward!

Celeste Kavanaugh:

I don't remember V-J Day because, I think, the atom bomb sort of ended the war for everybody. That was the end.

Ted Giddings, city editor of the Berkshire Eagle *in Pittsfield, Massachusetts:*

V-J Day was our last extra. After that, radio and television wiped out the extra edition of newspapers our size.

David Soergal "just happened to be in Times Square on V-J Day":

It was wild; you couldn't walk through the streets—Forty-second and Broadway was just a mass of humanity.

Simon Greco, a conscientious objector:

When the war ended, I expected some great religious feeling to take over. In other words, I really expected all the wheels to stop, theaters to close, bars to close, trains to stop running. Something irrational. Nothing happened. A bunch of people gathered in Times Square, some gals getting laid. And that was the end of it. The wheels were going, the bars were open, the pool halls were open, the factories were running, almost as if nothing had happened. It was really just kind of a psychological shock.

Tony Taylor was a young boy in Washington, D.C.:

I remember working at the Cosmos Club on V-J Day. I wasn't that relieved, because I was really not aware what we were into. But I knew that it had to be something heavy, because there was so much joviality around me. Oh, yes, something very heavy.

Cathleen Schurr:

On V-J Day we were on holiday at Orleans on Cape Cod. We didn't have a radio, but somebody had one on in a car, and I remember going out and sitting on the ground alongside the car and hearing the news. We all looked at each other and said something about church and went to a service in a little traditional New England white chapel. It was a tiny place that probably didn't hold more than forty to fifty people, beautifully white. It was run by an elderly gentleman and his wife, who kept goats and made bracelets. I remember during the course of this belabored sermon that the so-called minister made celebrating the end of this awful holocaust—he couldn't remember the word for the bomb. He stumbled over it, and the wife, who obviously was the intelligence of the family, called out from the back of the chapel, "Atom bomb." I can't remember that he said anything important, we were all so relieved and so happy. It seemed to me that his attitude was that the atom bomb had "saved us"—that this is what it took to end this terrible war.

Lois Raymond in Sedgwick, Maine:

My younger daughter had been spending that summer with a friend of hers. They were coming here for the last two weeks before school. The girls caught the train in Boston, got off at Bangor, and then took the bus. As they went through Orrington, there were people out banging on washtubs and covers and whatnot, and they knew the war was over. A young serviceman on the bus popped up and kissed Rosemary, saying, "I always swore I would kiss the first pretty girl I saw when the war was over."

Martha Wood:

When V-J Day came, we were in Eastern North Carolina; my husband had been fishing. In the little town there they whooped and hollered a little.

Mary Studwell in Stamford, Connecticut:

They just stopped everything, including the buses. I lived about three miles outside the main body of town, and a whole bunch of us teen-agers walked down into town and formed a big conga line all through the town. It was just a silly thing, letting off steam. They called out the Home Guard, and they just cheered.

Alison Arnold in Duxbury, Massachusetts:

I remember distinctly driving home from work one night listening to the radio, and all of a sudden it came over that the thing was over. And at almost every house the doors opened, and children poured out waving flags. The church bells were ringing. Everybody got in their cars and drove them around town with the horns blowing.

Gertrude Blassingame, on Anna Maria Island, near Bradenton, Flroida, was with her daughters, Peggy and April. Her husband, Wyatt, was in the Pacific with the navy.

My neighbor next door came running over to say they had announced the armistice. It was just at dinnertime. I grabbed April, and I cried and cried and cried. April kept asking me, "Why are you crying?" and Peggy would say, "Because she's so happy." It was about three months before Wyatt got home.

Regina Wilk:

I know we were eating dinner at the time when we heard about the war ending, and we all just went hysterical. We didn't finish our meal; the family all seemed to get together, and we just went downtown. Everybody was one family there, the streets were packed and all. Everybody was so glad. My husband happened to be home at the time, and there was jubilation, because he was slated to go again. He didn't tell me until after that he was on rest-and-recuperation leave and that he was going to go back.

Eunice Yoakum's son, Robert, was on his way to the Pacific with the air force.

When the European war was over, Bob was supposed to go over to join MacArthur, whom he despised. He had eighty-four points and needed eighty-five to be sent back to this country. I knew he was on his way to the South Pacific, and I was not at all happy, because that meant another war. Then, all of a sudden, the telephone rang; I answered it, and someone said, "Mother." He was in Norfolk. The ship he was on had heard the news that the Japanese war was over and had turned around just before they went through the Canal, and returned to Norfolk. Of course, we were delirious; we couldn't believe it.

Esther Dudley:

We were working, as usual, and when the news came, they let us off. Everybody went home, and a couple of friends came over, and we sat there and had a couple of good ones.

Mary Dandouveris, working on a weekly newspaper in Lake Geneva, Wisconsin:

Our weekly didn't have a ticker, so when the end of the war came, the story was of how the local folks celebrated—it was a wild celebration. Snake lines all over town, and, because it was a resort town, there were lots of bars and places where you could dance—they were wide open that night. Everybody went in and out. I don't think anybody asked if you had money or not. It was joy and pandemonium in that town. The chap who used to be the head of the composing room was home from the service, and I followed him all around and did the color story. I remember the poor hung-over editor coming in the next day. But we got the paper out on schedule in spite of the celebration.

Because I knew that the Milwaukee and Chicago dailies all came into this town, I wanted a different headline for my paper. So I decided I would do it in French—"La Guerre Est Finis"—but the editor said, "Are you sure that guerre is feminine, or masculine?" He really rattled me, so I decided I had to call around, but I couldn't find anybody. They were all out of town that weekend. I finally decided to go with it and trust my instincts that it was a feminine noun. When I got back to my last year in journalism school, I found that with all the papers the journalism department had put up on the bulletin board as examples of how the dailies had treated the end of the war, mine was there, too, as an example of how a weekly could compete with a daily in covering local color.

Heli Swyter:

On V-J Day we were at Camp Lejeune, and I remember the shouting in the streets when it came. I picked up one of those firecrackers. And also there was shooting, all the guns. I found a bullet in the street, and I put a red ribbon around it; we have it on our Christmas tree always every year since then.

Peggy Blassingame:

It meant he would be coming home. By that time I was fifteen, and I was more able to understand what was going on. It meant that this horror was over, people would stop getting killed, and my father would come home.

Sally Lucke in Columbus, Ohio:

I can remember going downtown; everybody was jumping and screaming and yelling, and there were balloons and fireworks. Somehow, although I was very happy that the war was over, it also seemed very sad—a lot of people dead.

Margaret Dudley on an east-bound cross-country train:

The trains were loaded with boys returning from the West Coast. From Chicago we were on an old train with old-fashioned square seats. I didn't mind that. But when we got into the dining car, honestly, I could have taken several of the people there and boxed their ears: "Oh, these service people always taking over. Why can't we have something now? The war is over." They never gave a thought to the fact that some of these kids had been out of the country three or four years, and they were anxious to get back. They were hungry and tired and had been sleeping in the aisles. But that was the attitude, "How dare these service people come in and want something to eat?" It really floored me.

11

AFTERMATH

What was the impact of the war years on our cities, towns, institutions, the nation, and the people themselves? In these concluding pages a few Americans who were on the home front give their answers.

Carey McWilliams:

It is very difficult to assess the effect of the war on the nation. I have always been about three-quarters pacifist. While I've never been quite able to make the total commitment, I think the war has had some long-term unfortunate effects on American life. I admire those of my friends who were consistently pacifist and who right straight through said, "It's a mistake to fight; violence is violence, and there will be unfortunate circumstances." But I've never been able to convince myself.

At the end of the war we were unquestionably going to be the top military power in the world. And I think this predisposed us to take the position that we were going to police the world, we were going to do this, we were going to do that. And as I see it, the period that extends from 1945, the dropping of the bomb, our withdrawal from Vietnam, Nixon's ouster—that's all tied together as one. I think the mess we're in today is a result of the policies of that period. You say: "What effect did World War II have?" Well, World War II set the stage for the Cold War. You can't separate them.

The Reverend Harold Toliver:

Just like the total community, black and white, everybody was anxious for it to be over. When it finally came to a conclusion, I think it set in motion that "Here we are now. What are we going to do about life as we try to reestablish it in our community?" And the first thing we knew, we blacks found ourselves facing some of the very same problems—prejudice, racism, intolerance—which precipitated the war. Some grew very much discouraged and said, "Well, you see, it wasn't worth it." But the majority of the people, I think, just rededicated themselves to the struggle and said, "This has to go on." If the war did nothing else to me as a minister—or just as an ordinary person—it made me more determined to give what little energy I had to bringing people of the world together. I suppose you might describe me as a populist, a person who believes in the people coming together, all races and types, learning to understand one another and to get along. We have the beginnings of that in the United Nations, with all of its weaknesses and faults.

What the future holds, I don't know. But I think we're nearer today to a world that's gradually coming to its senses than ever before in history. I really believe that.

Melville Grosvenor:

I think that World War II was a great thing for America. It unified us—made a country out of us. Before the war, we were a bunch of vacillating isolationists displaying not much character. But the war and the victory showed us what we could do in the world. Showed us the role we could play. However, it is honest to admit that it did us some harm. The victory caused us to think that we could dominate the world. Ever since the war, in every part of the world, we've been trying to tell individual countries what to do and what not to do, and we still are. I think it's goddamn foolishness, if you don't mind my saying so. This postwar attitude has brought us untold grief. Vietnam is an example. While the war did affect us favorably in our world position, it brought an overconfidence that has caused us a good deal of ultimate sorrow.

Former senator from Vermont, George Aiken:

The impact of the war probably was favorable in a way. As it is now, Japan and Germany are two of our best customers. We did pay a pretty high price, but we learned quite a lot from it. I think we learned that war does not pay and that people who go all out for the defense of our own country won't be as enthusiastic when it comes to helping other countries, even smaller ones.

Marquis Childs:

Before the war it was a much simpler country—a country in which the individual counted for more than he does today. I was thinking of my hometown, Clinton, Iowa, where you still had character. The town, in a way, has lost its character, and I think that is what has happened to America.

I spent about three hours in one of the big industrial plants in Michigan once, and I thought at the time that this was the nearest equivalent to hell that I could ever think of, the smoke, the dirt, noise, and filth, and people doing the same thing all day long. I don't know if we hadn't got into the war whether this would have happened.

Then, of course there is the problem of blacks coming into industry. That is what transformed America. The mechanical cotton picker had already begun to displace them. Of course, they were recruited. They heard word about these big wages. It is one of the greatest migrations in history, really. We have not begun to resolve it or to put it in any order, whatsoever. And it still is at the root of our trouble.

R. W. Danischefsky in Washington:

As a result of the war, the public generally and industry, too, became more aware of the government's influence on our everyday life. It wasn't too long after the war when most big industry began to move offices here. I think today practically all of your larger industries have representatives in Washington because of the influence and the participation by government.

Marquis Childs:

What it did was to start this business of background information given on a confidential basis—and it wasn't just General Marshall and Admiral King; everyone did it. It became a common practice. Later someone invented the phrase *deep backgrounder*. Of course, we had to have it during the war. We all welcomed it. But then, after the war, I think it has been greatly misused and abused.

Congressman Ray Madden (D-Ind.):

A war like that changes a lot of things. One of the most ridiculous things that happened was that it gave the military a lot of power. Hell, if we had not had World War II, we probably would not have had Eisenhower in the White House. There was a period of eight years when the country sank more and more in debt. We had three depressions under Ike because he did not know anything about running a government, but you could not blame him. He got elected because he was made to order for the same money changers that ran the government in the 1920s—the DuPonts, Andy Mellon, and that group.

The war is one of the reasons why we are in such a financial debacle today. I saw where somebody asked the State Department how much we loaned other countries during the World War II period, and I think they said $500 billion. After World War II we appropriated money to go ahead and help reconstruct the nations we helped to destroy. Billions! About three-quarters of our national debt is not from running this country, but it's taking care of the globe, you might say.

Newton Tolman:

It certainly speeded up all kinds of things like going to the moon, outdoing the Russians. I would say that the national impact was to give the technocrats, or whatever you call them—big-business people—the green light to totally pollute the national government.

World War II got government into business and business into government, and we're still there.

Hezekiah Goodwin:

The war brought about changes that started and more or less mushroomed. Higher taxes. The man who would paint your house used to work for seventy-five cents an hour; now he gets six dollars. The same was true of the carpenter, the plumber. Those are changes that, if the war didn't bring about, it certainly made possible. They wouldn't have occurred otherwise. We know the war cost us in permanent inflation. It brought about great social changes which were probably needed, but nevertheless had a hell of an impact on us here. These small farms, the success of them is predicated on cheap labor. There was no denying it; there no longer was any cheap labor.

Jack Altshul:

The war was the dividing line between depression and the prosperity that followed. And what it took to get that was the boys that were killed. It was a stiff price to pay. Up to that time, twenty dollars a week was a manageable salary. Many people would have signed away their souls for a hundred-dollar-a-week job for life. They couldn't see beyond that. I certainly couldn't. Then all of a sudden you get the wartime boom, and just as suddenly a few years later the war is over. Luxuries that only millionaires could have, before the war, suddenly became available to everybody on credit—refrigerators, televisions, dishwashers, washing machines. And I guarantee that if a person had to pay seven hundred dollars for a television set out of his pocket, they wouldn't have sold as many television sets. Multiply that by all the other fancy things they were putting into new homes, and I think people started living above their means.

Richard Lingeman discusses the impact of the war on the nation from the special vantage point of someone who spent five years researching the subject.

I think the war had an obvious economic impact in bringing the country out of the doldrums of the depression by stimulating industry—making a lot of corporations richer and bigger and starting this relationship between military procurement and big corporations called the military-industrial complex. It moved a lot of people around. They migrated to the cities for war jobs, and I guess some went back home after it was over, but there was a lot of permanent migration.

The war was also a significant turning point for women. They were needed so suddenly and to a great extent temporarily, all kinds of jobs were open to women—not only industry, but driving buses, managing baseball teams, police work. Suddenly all the traditional barriers broke down, with blacks and women in better jobs. After the war, of course, it was the old "last hired, first fired" thing, but it must have implanted something, certain expectations or awareness on the part of blacks and women.

It was a period of great moral upheaval. There were, for example, the Allotment Annies—not a lot of them, but there were enough—who married servicemen just to collect allotments, insurance benefits, and whatever. One woman married I don't know how many flyers, about ten, I think. They'd pick flyers because they had the highest mortality rate.

Also, the moral question was raised about servicemen and sex. There was a famous article in which Gene Tunney recommended abstention for soldiers. At the same time there was the idea: Well, to save the nice girls of the town we'd better let them have some prostitutes around, too, so they will not get the nice girls pregnant. Of course, there were the V-girls—teen-age girls who would hang around the bus stops where sailors and soldiers were passing through. They weren't prostitutes, they were the khaki-wackies looking for boys, the excitement of going out with soldiers, acting older than they really were. So the war probably hastened maturity in some of these girls.

The war certainly gave us a sense of our power and involvement in the world, and it gave us a great confidence. I don't think we knew quite what to do with this power. Initially there was idealism and support for the United Nations, which, I suppose, was a concrete embodiment of internationalism. Everybody thought it was going to be a great thing, and there was a lot of talk about world government at the time. But it never worked out, of course.

I think most people have a nostalgia for those days, the time of a good war, a just war. Some guys in the army did have a sense of adventure, going off to faraway places, exotic places. If they could avoid the fighting, there was that excitement, that adventure.

Alison Arnold on the Boston Herald:

I think the war had a great impact on the social scene. It broke down all the social barriers, and now society is sort of a forbidden word. It ironed out all the class distinctions. I don't know what caused it, but I know that when I first went to the [Beacon] Hill, we weren't allowed to use any names in the story that were not in the Social Register. Then, after the war, all that was gone, and we democratized society.

Nelson Poynter:

The GI Bill of Rights, of course, had more to do with thrusting us into a new era than anything else. Millions of people whose parents or grandparents had never dreamed of going to college saw that they could go, and I don't have to tell anyone what a broad effect that has had on so many of the private and public institutions within our society. Essentially I think it made us a far more democratic people, because people could think more nearly in terms of equality. Of course, we never had the sense that is reflected in Britain, where working people would say, "You know, that's not for the likes of me." I think, as a people, we've always been rather confident that maybe if that guy could have it, so could I.

Helen Wilson, University of Michigan:

I think it loosened up the regulations at the university a great deal. When the veterans returned after the war, they were a much older group of students. They tripled the enrollment, and some of the stuffy old professors had problems dealing with the fellows who had been through the war. They were really a very sheltered group of old fuddy-duddies, and the military returnees were more than they could cope with.

I think the war also elevated women. They had to be accepted as replacing men at home. I applied to law school in the spring of 1945, and I think that's why I got in. It probably was the start of the women's movement.

Lois Raymond:

I was working at the University of Chicago right after the war. I remember talking to various faculty people who said the best students they ever had were the GIs. They had been out long enough to really know what they wanted to do.

Elmer Louis Kayser, George Washington University, Washington, D.C.:

The war tended to magnify everything around here. It seemed to magnify our mission, to magnify our commitments, to magnify our ideas and our efforts and the expression of them in tangible development. It was here, for example, that the first announcement was made about atomic fission—at one of those conferences on theoretical physics that used to be held in cooperation with the Carnegie Institution of Washington. The university was given so many more opportunities to expand in wartime Washington. The times were themselves more spacious and once and for all demonstrated, I think, the fact that the university of the future was to be the great urban university, rather than the cow college and cloisters of the past.

Al Sweeney:

Efforts to desegregate Washington didn't gain impetus until after the war. A lot of the fellows came back, and, on top of it, the GI Bill of Rights gave opportunity to a lot of them to go to college, and they became part of the whole movement. Most of the leaders were ex-GIs in the army, ex-military.

Washington at that time had a caste system within the black community. Some of the older families, light-skinned families, wouldn't accept the darker skinned people. That was the end of the black caste system in Washington. The people came from all over the country to work in government. More blacks came into this town from all over, from the South, the Midwest; and the great majority of blacks that came during the war stayed. It was the only place a black could find a white-collar job. It was pretty rare to find a real Washingtonian.

David Soergal, an electrical engineer:

There was more freedom then to explore what you wanted to. The trouble with big technology now is that it's too organized, and that's no good, because technology depends on creativity and innovation; organization frustrates it. During the war there was less trying to guess whether a guy was right or wrong. If the idea was reasonable, that's all. The test was reasonableness, not certainty.

Leonard Williamson, a construction foreman:

The work I was in made good business. It made money for a lot of people working at it, and the company made money too. They were really boom times!

Bryson Rash, with NBC and ABC during the war:

It was the war that really developed electronic journalism. Prior to World War II there weren't many people on the air doing news. The capability of conveying war via electronic media occurred in the Spanish civil war, where for the first time you got broadcasts from battlegrounds, from areas of conflict and capitals that were at war. I think one of the most famous of these early broadcasts was H. V. Kaltenborn reporting on the Spanish war with the sound of guns heard in the background. Then we had the electronic capability of instant communication via shortwave, and that was something new.

Nelson Poynter, St. Petersburg, Florida:

Literally millions of youngsters were brought through Florida in their training for war service, and many of them liked it. They said, "You know, when the war is over, I want to go to Florida." That started the postwar boom, and it's still going on. It affected the whole state of Florida.

Americans Remember the Home Front

Jack Altshul, Long Island, New York:

Levit asked for a change of zoning in the town of Hempstead [Long Island] to permit building houses on smaller lots, and they didn't want to grant it. So *Newsday* went out and packed that meeting with war veterans, because they were the ones who needed the housing. They were coming back, some of them were married, and nobody had a house except their mother-in-law, and they couldn't handle that too long.

Merlo Pusey, Washington, D.C.:

The war really made Washington, for the first time, a world capital. All the top Allied people came here. Then after the war was over, we were the only ones who had any industrial capacity left to go into operation, and we naturally had to carry a lot of things.

It was a more difficult place to live after the war, I think, because the war brought a tremendous influx of people; it got to be a crowded city. And they didn't go home.

Mercedes Fritzching, Washington, D.C.:

When I came back to Washington after the war, it was totally different. First of all, there was a tremendous housing shortage in Washington. And, of course, every family I went to see, my old friends, all had had some relative overseas—some of the children had not come back, some of the husbands had not come back, some of the fathers had not come back. There was a lot of hard feelings against the Germans that I felt very strongly, although there was a lot of curiosity also to know what my experiences had been under the bombs in Berlin.

When their husbands and sons had actually been in the air force and had been bombing Germany, they wanted to know what it was like on the ground. All my old friends were very nice. They accepted me as what I was, not really a German in a sense. I had German parents. Washington was tremendously changed. It had been a peaceful, quiet little hick town, a very moral town. And in '46, when I came back, my goodness! Anything went. It was crowded, you couldn't get apartments anywhere, and oodles of people who had come during the war were still working here in postwar jobs. Girls were living with men very freely—it was just a totally changed town.

Frank Platt, Louisville, Kentucky:

Prior to the war Louisville was living in the past. But the war changed all that. People could no longer have the closed society they had had. There were just too many Yankees and others that moved in there. General Electric opened up a huge industrial park there with somewhere between 16,000 and 20,000 people. And that had quite an impact on a city the size of Louisville, which at that time had a population of perhaps 400 to 500,000. Today Louisville is around 1,000,000. The old order changed, and the war was the catalyst. It was definitely a change for the better. Louisville is in much better financial condition than it was prior to the war. There is big, good industry there, well diversified. Before the war it was primarily tobacco, liquor, and horses.

Esther Dudley, Philadelphia:

Jobs were plentiful in Philadelphia during the war, and money was just flowing to the war workers. It was an arsenal, produced textiles and all sorts of things for the service, and, I think, Philadelphia was the goal of many unskilled Negro families migrating from the South. I think, like any industrial city, that was about it. That was the start of unskilled labor coming up and causing quite a few of our racial problems.

Newton Tolman, Nelson, New Hampshire:

Well, I would say that it was the end of a way of life, an end of a way of thinking, the end of education, and certainly the end of any kind of local autonomous government. I could name you a dozen guys I went to school with—they were working, trying to, selling real estate, or running a tractor, or any number of things; they were just about making it. One was even a magna cum laude graduate of the Yale School of

Forestry. They went into the army and stayed. They became army bureaucrats. I meet them even today. Most of them have died from too much drinking and easy living and one thing or another. But they stayed with it. They became our rich; colonels with retirement pay and everything else.

Industry thrives on war. Look at Vietnam and Korea. The mills in Harrisville, which had been dead for years, ran until last year. But along with that came all these people with new ideas. They came back from the army, these boys with big ideas, and absolutely no knowledge of anything. They took over everything—the schools, everything.

Joseph Skelly, New York City:

I think that during the war years there was a holding back of civilian construction of all kinds, so this produced a certain gap in the normal building of homes. The war also brought about the establishment of rent control, which is still in existence in New York and many other cities and which has had a big effect on the state of city houses and real estate. It's a very moot question; there are two sides to it certainly. But rent control is by no means an unmixed blessing. It's had a lot of unfortunate results. The war brought the United Nations to New York City, and that, I think, had quite an effect on the general international tone of the city.

Don Baldwin, San Francisco:

As far as San Francisco goes, I don't really think the war made that much difference. It's still about the same size that it was then. There are more tall buildings down on Montgomery Street and that area, waiting for the next earthquake. But the nature of the people is pretty much the same, the pace is pretty much the same. There are about 800,000 people now and about 800,000 in 1945.

One thing that did happen—the blacks moved into the areas that the Japanese had lived in. A lot of blacks moved into the areas south of San Francisco down around Hunter's Point, where there had been war housing, which became public housing, and these have become sort of ghetto areas. San Francisco, I think, has accommodated better than most cities, and it's had lots of problems. But I think the war really was a turning point for blacks, because it opened up all of these opportunities. A sharecropper from Mississippi was able to go to San Francisco and build ships for unheard-of money. Kaiser would pay his way up there and find houses for him and put his wife to work driving a streetcar. This was the good life.

I also think the war had a real effect on family relationships. My two sisters went through years with their husbands gone and did a lot of worrying. The women who stayed at home really had a tough time, and some of the marriages never did really pull back together. I do think that the war was a real launching pad for women's liberation, because Kaiser's shipyards were manned by many women. "Rosie the Riveter" was a real thing; women found out that they could do it. They could earn good money, they could drive streetcars—there never was a female streetcar operator in San Francisco until the war. This really was a turning point, and I think for the good.

Robert Wheeler, Great Barrington, Massachusetts:

I think we were far enough away from it not to get too many problems, and like a good farmer, just kept plowing and going ahead. I don't think the war affected Barrington any more than many small towns. It's still a small town. And while I'm in the real estate business, I'd like to see it continue many, many years to come as a small town. I think this country needs more small towns.

Gus Robbins, Hopewell, Virginia:

I think that the war helped develop it [Hopewell]. I really do. We were pretty active in the war effort with our big chemical plants there, and business stayed pretty good after the war. And Camp Lee is still there. It's Fort Lee today—the biggest quartermaster training center in the world. We've got more retired colonels around than you can shake a stick at. You see all the colonels come to the quartermaster a year or two before they retire. They're putting them on the shelf, getting ready to kick them out. They like it in Virginia, so they stay. I'll bet you there must be five hundred of them in what we call the tri-city area—Hopewell, Petersburg, and Colonial Heights.

Americans Remember the Home Front

Ann Hoskins, Salisbury, Connecticut:

One of the war things we did that I thought was great and should have been kept up afterward, was to make a census of everybody in the town of Salisbury. We had a card file noting each person's interests and abilities, which would have been useful if there had been an invasion. It's too bad that it wasn't kept up.

Jerome Thirion, Buffalo, New York:

Buffalo before the war had a basically sound economy. Everybody had a good job. The social levels were pretty well established, and you didn't have a seasonal economic situation. The war, of course, inflated everything. Buffalo had a lot of defense plants, and those who worked in the plants made easy, free money during the war. But after the war it was kind of slow.

Paul Kneeland, Medford, Massachusetts:

In Medford the war didn't mean a thing; Medford just slept right through it, except for the availability or unavailability of certain things, such as tires, gasoline, et cetera.

Rudolph Spitzer, Kenmore, New York:

I think the effect of the war on our town was probably no different than on thousands of similar communities throughout the nation— boom times with cost no object for a couple of years and then a gradual settling down to normalcy. Aside from that, I cannot see much change. The world is in a turmoil, and we still have wars.

Coralee Redmond moved from Beach, North Dakota to Tacoma, Washington, during the war but returned to Beach each summer with her sons.

Beach is a small town, a farming center where lots of wheat was raised. Many farmers in World War II moved into town and left their

380

sons to run the farms as their reason not to be drafted. But the boys and men who lived in town, they all went into the service. We lost some boys who were almost like sons to me—they were my daughters' and sons' ages. We lost our minister too, who we were very fond of. He was a chaplain in the service. The war had its impact in Beach.

The war increased the population in Tacoma, because many people who came out to work in the defense plants stayed. People who were coming out of the service liked the Pacific Northwest and stayed— either here in Tacoma or round about. I would say the town really grew.

PERSONAL IMPACT

Capt. Fred Kirkham:

After the war everything seemed to collapse. The whole economy was based on the shipyard, and jobs became pretty scarce right around the end of the war. People were glad it was over, but they were sorry that the jobs were gone. I was with Philco in Boston by the end of the war, and I transferred to the storage-battery division as a field engineer. I was lucky, because a lot of people just didn't get a job afterward. That area was hit pretty hard—after General Electric and all the big shipyards closed down, it was pretty rough. The war changed my life, and it's hard to figure out for the better or for worse.

Stephen Ailes:

Working in Washington during the war was a real education for me. You know, your attitudes are tremendously affected by your environment, and I'd been practicing law up in Martinsburg [West Virginia] with a Republican lawyer who was quite conservative. Then I came down here, and the legal staff I was working with and the economists were a whole lot of young guys who were far more liberal in their point of view than anybody I'd ever associated with.

Working in the Office of Price Administration was an incredible opportunity. It was my first association with really top-notch economists. I got a look at the whole American business structure and learned a lot about how the government operates, where the levers are, how Congress functions. My God! I wouldn't put the whole country at war just to train someone, but I must say it was an unbelievable experience.

Sid Luckman, Chicago Bears quarterback:

The war, really, to me was one of the most crushing things that could ever happen. You saw your friends go to war, you saw some of them killed, some of them wounded, you also saw one of the finest groups of young men ever assembled in the history of sports—the Chicago Bears of 1940–41—some of the finest men the good Lord has ever put on this earth, so dedicated to each other, so dedicated to George Halas. To see it all dissipated by a horrible catastrophe that was so unnecessary to the world, it was a very disheartening situation.

However, in the final analysis, all of us were very happy to pay the price. Freedom and democracy prevailed, and the world continued being at least a place to be able to live the kind of life you always hoped for and not have to live under dictatorship and fear. So whatever the price was and whatever it cost all of us, it was worth it.

Erwin Hargrove, who was fourteen on V-J Day:

The amazing thing to me is that it had such little effect on me. I wonder if there isn't a generalization you could make here that great public events are only tangential to the lives of ordinary people. I remember seeing a documentary on television about the appeasement during the war years in England. The interviewer asked a working-class woman why people ignored Churchill and if she was conscious of the importance of Hitler and the rise of aggression and so on. And she said, "How was I supposed to know? I was worried about the really important things, like my husband and his job, and the children—that they had enough to eat." I think in many ways a lot of these distant events don't strike people at home as much as you might think. For me it was a kind of frolic. I would be surprised if people of my generation said anything differently, unless they were caught up in it, their parents leaving.

Sally Knox:

The war helped my career. I don't like to think that war is used for that, but it actually did. I might not have gotten such a good job otherwise.

Jack Altshul:

I'd like to think whatever talent I had helped me get ahead at *Newsday,* but there's no question that the war pushed me into the city editorship there. And that was the turning point in my career.

Margaret Oakham:

I made great strides during the war, and it improved my life. If anybody had ever told me that I was going to get into some of the things and do some of the things that I did, I would never have believed it. I wouldn't change any of it.

Necei Degen:

The man that I married had come from the Midwest. He would never have come East had it not been for that great war. Many of the people who came East whom I met changed the complexion and character of my life personally. So it affected my life, from that point on until this day.

Simon Greco:

I think the war separated me more from people. I must admit that I'm basically introverted to begin with. But I think the war gave it an added push. And I believe that's probably why I left New York very quickly and moved to Ridgefield, Connecticut. My whole idea was to get out in the country, where I couldn't see another house. I think the war played a big part in that. Up to that time I didn't have this feeling, this need to isolate myself from the rest of humanity.

Cathleen Schurr, who was on a ship that was torpedoed early in the war:

One thing that I think has happened in every war is that it has given an enormous impetus to women. A lot of women got out from under and stayed out. Many of them did not rush back to the traditional "children, church, and cooking." The opportunities that opened up were enormous. Women realized they could, in fact, do many things—be wives and have families and still work outside the home for money.

How does war experience affect a civilian? I could not walk down the streets of lower Manhattan, where tall buildings were close together and the streets were very narrow, without a sense of those buildings caving in on me. It was years before I could get on any kind of boat. I think tragedy can go beyond losing someone. It can be a permanent scar. People survive in concentration camps. People survive all kinds of horrible experiences. I saw people killed. I was very nearly killed myself. I don't know whether some of the people I was associated with actually were killed or not, which leaves a large, tragic question mark in my life. I have a real sense of physical fear, having watched a ship go down, a large ship, very big and husky and probably in length about the size of one of those downtown buildings.

Heli Swyter:

After the war my husband went back to Shell. But he had to pick up from where he left, as far as salary goes. That was six years before, and the living standards had changed so much. He got the living-standard raises, but he had missed his promotions. He was behind everyone for his age. But we were so glad that we were together again. We had known such a long separation, because, after all, we were married only three years, when we were separated for almost four. So we were strangers, in a way, to each other when he came back. We had evolved each on our own in these very important years. When you evolve together, you don't notice it. It wasn't just that easy all of a sudden. But when you are so much in love, you don't give up. We saw around us old friends, Dutch friends, who were in the same boat. They all behaved differently, a lot of marriages just went all on the rocks. There were all these divorces. It's terrible, and I said something to my husband, more or less jokingly, but there was a fragment of truth in it, "Well, what's the matter with us, how come we are still together?" And he answered with another joke, "Oh, you know why? At least I know what I have—and I don't know what I'm going to get!" That was typical of him. It took a very long time, the readjustment.

Kent Chetlain:

I think it made us more conscious of the world about us. It brought to us the names of far-off geographic places that we would have never been exposed to. For example, I can remember Minsk, Oreal, Smolensk, Kharkov, and places like that. These names became familiar to me for the first time, and the different Pacific islands like Guadalcanal, New Britain.

Joseph Skelly:

The war brought my wife and me together. I think we quite likely wouldn't have gotten married if it hadn't been for the war. It was a very definite result of the war, and I'm glad.

Merlo Pusey:

I suppose it was a great stimulus, because it was a wonderful period in the journalistic field. It stimulated me to get more serious in the book area. I wrote this book, *The Way We Go to War*, and since then I've sort of had the disease which I gather you have. I always say it's a disease; when you get it, you don't get over it. The war stimulated me to do this work and, I guess, contributed a great deal to my knowledge about the country and the government and the world.

Mercedes Fritzching, who was sent back to Germany with her German parents after Pearl Harbor:

I had only two weeks at American University before the war. And of course, when I came back to the United States, I had to earn a living, and so it robbed me of my education. It absolutely split my life in half. In Germany I got a job, because if I hadn't had a war-important job, as I did with the German broadcasting company, using my knowledge of English and Spanish, I would have been called up to serve in the army and man the ack-ack guns of Berlin. The only education I got was the education of life, and I got a big, big dose of that!

Paul Kneeland:

If the war had not come about, I don't think I'd have had the nerve to ask for a job on a Boston newspaper. In late 1941 the *Globe* started hiring war replacements. We all signed releases that we were temporary employees—I was one of twenty-four. Twenty-two of the reporters were told that they were no longer needed at the end of the war. They kept two—a graduate of Harvard University, and me, a high school graduate. Today you couldn't get a job there as an office boy unless you had a master's degree. The war opened up an opportunity that might not have come otherwise.

Joseph Clement:

I don't think the war did anything for my career really. I didn't advance myself; there was nothing I learned there that I could have used for any advantage later on. It was just really a blank four years as far as I was concerned. In fact, I had to start all over again in getting into consumer goods, and at that time you could sell anything you made, so who needed a designer? I finally managed to get back in and became a chief designer for Wurlitzer after the war. I designed jukeboxes, of all things. A far cry from the war, so I felt that any part of my war effort was useless to me personally.

George Garrott:

Looking back on it, it was an exciting time for me. I felt I had bogged down in New York. What I wanted to do was go to Paris and work for the Paris *Herald Tribune* and write novels. But in those days before the war, anybody who had a job held on to it. So when the war came along, it jolted me out of that comfortable chair I had been sitting on in the newsroom of the *New York Times*. I got out of the office and moved around as a live, active reporter, especially after the war, for the USIA. I went on the Truman trip to Wake Island, the secret trip to meet General MacArthur. I got a three-week press trip to Europe and another three-month trip to the Far East. On one trip with Truman I spent eight weeks in Key West, and driving back through Florida, I figured "Gee, this is the part of the country I want to live in." I took leave from USIA and went down to Florida again. After about six weeks of looking around, I walked into the *St. Petersburg Times*. Somebody had just quit that day, and there was an opening, so I went to work the next day.

I have no complaints about the war at all. I didn't have a single war wound. I got a good-conduct medal just for not going AWOL, and I got a sharpshooter's medal for pulling a trigger on a rifle.

Ray Hartman, who lost an older brother:

My father lost heart when my brother was killed. I was too young to take over the restaurant, and he had really counted on my brother to help him out, so he was brokenhearted. He was also a sick man and lived not quite a year longer. After my father died on April 2, 1945, my mother liquidated the business at a tremendous loss. Unfortunately, my father was not the kind of man who believed in insurance, so my mother had to go to work in a factory, and I went to work part time in a wood shop making molds for tools and dies.

Losing a lucrative business delayed my education, because as soon as I graduated from high school, I went to work full time to support a younger sister and my mother. I didn't go back to college for four years. Most of my classmates were twenty-five or twenty-six years old and were going to school on the GI Bill of Rights. In the fifties the fellows that I grew up with were getting drafted into the Korean thing, and that was a bit embarrassing. Everybody thought I was 4-F since I never got drafted. I was exempt because of the Sullivan incident. The Sullivan brothers, five of them, I believe, went down on the same ship during the war, and immediately after that, Congress passed a law that brothers could not be on the same ship or plane. It also provided that the last surviving son of a Gold Star mother could not be drafted or enlist. Now that I'm older, I'm glad I didn't have to, but at the time I was hurt about it, because all my buddies were joining up, and I was keeping the home fires burning.

Don Baldwin:

I think it was good for my life. I got started quicker and was able to do some things that I would not have been able to do if a lot of AP guys hadn't been going out into foreign service to cover the war. It created job openings that I was able to seize on. We were coming out of the depression, and newspaper jobs were very difficult to get. It would have been much harder to get out of Idaho and into big city operations without the war.

John Lacey:

It changed my career completely. From a patent attorney working in private practice, I became a contract employee and was one for thirty years, not with the government, but with Johns Hopkins.

Marquis Childs:

I was under contract with the *St. Louis Post-Dispatch* when Raymond Clapper was killed in February 1944. He was flying off of an aircraft carrier in the Pacific somewhere. The syndicate then asked me to do a column and to take over as many of his clients as I could. That made a terrific change in my life. Joseph Pulitzer was very reluctant to release me—I remember telephone conversations of three or four hours—but finally he did. It dramatically changed my life, and it has never been the same since.

Nelson Poynter, editor of the St. Petersburg (Fla.) Times:

I think the war broadened my life, undoubtedly. I was involved in something on a far bigger scale than anything we would have had here, because this was a relatively small town, a relatively small paper at that time.

Mary Lacey:

It had so many emotional overtones to it that it really is hard to assess. Because I managed to live through it and survive, I guess it made me a stronger person, more aware of things, more appreciative of happiness in my second marriage, never knowing what's going to happen to somebody the next time you turn. It probably did something to sharpen my awareness of human relations. I hope it had some good effect.

Evelyn Keyes:

I was just then changing from a bigot into a liberal. I was out of the South, from Atlanta, a total bigot, and I was slowly learning. Hitler helped me to understand how dangerous bigotry is. I happened to be in my formative years when the war came along, just becoming an adult. Atlanta is a cosmopolitan place, but in those days it certainly was in the backwaters. It was a little bigger than Plains, but not that much. And so it was an extreme to go from that into the big time overnight. It happened very fast, at a time when I was absolutely wild and ready. I went to Hollywood at a time when they were making a lot of pictures; that's not so now. The studios were at their zenith, and pinups were fashionable. There's luck in coming along at the right time.

Anna Mae Lindberg:

I'm definitely a different person now than I was then, but I don't know how much the war had to do with it. We lived from day to day, and, as it turned out, my husband was never called. I was extremely thankful and still am to this day that our family came through it safely. I think the big impact of the war was economic. We had just come out of a depression when Russ and I were married, and soon after, there were rent and price controls and things like that. They brought advantages to those of us who were doing the renting, because rent and prices were controlled and wages climbed. So we were able to save some money, and when the war was over, we had enough money for a down payment on a house. I guess that was a long-range impact of the war, but at the time we didn't count that as a blessing. If we had the choice between the war and the money, there is no question.

David Soergal:

Somehow the war just really didn't touch me the way it touched most people. It was interesting from a technical point of view, which was my background and training. I had exciting projects to work on, met some interesting people, particularly in the radiation laboratory at MIT. I think most of the guys who stayed in the industry did contribute, although obviously it was not as direct as being in combat, but we did contribute. The guys who were permitted to do that had a tremendous advantage after the war in terms of jobs, opportunities, progress.

Jane Malach:

It's probably a terrible thing to say, but when I look back on it, it was a beneficent experience. In spite of the emotional impact, it was a very broadening experience, and I would never have had it otherwise.People were picked up from where they had lived all their lives and plunged into something. They had to adjust.

Edward Stuntz:

I had a very good job during the war and enjoyed it thoroughly, but it wasn't the job I wanted. I wanted to be a combat correspondent and get back into what I had been doing abroad. Then, after the war, I stayed with the Pan American Institute, and I became enchanted again, very much interested in these cooperative services continuing and wrote a book about it, and I supposed you could call that the zenith of my career. The book was called *To Make the People Strong*. I wanted to call it *No Purple Hearts*, because it was a book about the work of doctors, agricultural experts, teachers, engineers with Latin American doctors to elevate the standard of living and the health of these countries. There were people coming back from the bloody fronts with purple hearts and everything. But these men, I figured, were doing a great thing for the war effort, and I wanted to call it *No Purple Hearts*. These programs were devised and kept going to make the people strong, rather than the governments, because I had the theory then, as I have now, that dictatorships can't exist over a strong people. You have to have a weak people to have a strong-man government.

Betty Bryce in Fort Collins, Colorado:

I can tell you one thing the town is not as patriotic as it was. On Memorial Day hardly anybody shows up, not even your veterans' organizations. If you get the color guard out, of course, the kids will always get in with bicycles, but people just don't seem to salute the flag. The young children have no respect at the cemetery when you're holding a service. And this is bad. I don't know—when I look at that flag, to me the red's a little redder, the white's a little whiter, and the stars are a little brighter because of all those boys who gave their lives. And at Arlington Cemetery in Washington, D.C., when I was sitting there one Sunday, I thought, "If all those boys in those graves were to rise up, I wonder what they would think about why they had died, and the way conditions are now, if it was worth it." I just wonder.

INDEX